BOTHE RICHTER TEHERANI

KLAUS-DIETER WEISS

BOTHE RICHTER TEHERANI

BIRKHÄUSER - PUBLISHERS FOR ARCHITECTURE
BASEL · BOSTON · BERLIN

"Hamburg, which is about as German as San Francisco is American, or Maastricht Dutch, is trying to go its own way without being likened to Berlin or Munich. The secret lies in this metropolitan port's dense network, in which the cityscape and responsibility for it are still very much present." Hadi Teherani

The architecture of the future is a symphony of spatial forms, each space a necessary part of the whole. Construction materials, walls, ceilings and floors are but means to achieve a singular purpose: the definition of spatial forms. Form is neither an end in itself nor the result of a design process, but a design tool. Use and form of a building are two different expressions of space as a common basis. In this, the prime focus is on the virtual and the dynamic of architecture, the dissolution of its limitations and conventions, rather than adherence to historic models. Architectural revolutions always occur on a spatial level. Technological achievements may inspire a new spatial concept, but they cannot provoke it. Nothing can truly replace the emotionality of the third dimension: space.

Convincing architecture is sensuality, culture, morality and message translated into form. Architecture communicates a worldview, awakens science to life and is at the same time possessed of a quality that conveys joy. Changing values and innovative technologies are expressed early on in architecture; thus, good architecture illustrates and accompanies the evolution and changes in society. Hence, architecture is by no means styling or a mere aesthetic cloak of function. The decisive architectonic criteria of quality are the space, the volume, the view, the dynamic of layers, intersections, and relationships.

Buildings that create identity call for a clearly defined, attractive architecture with functional advantages, but above all for emotional charisma. In the chaos of sprawling cities, a surprising presence and provocative leap in scale have been the mark of architectural objects as signposts of meaning—not only since the Centre Pompidou in Paris. The social event is the pivot and fulcrum of the city. For centuries, the loss of the urban spectacle has been viewed as punishment for good reason.

Translating entrepreneurial values in an individual, specific and nevertheless long-term and timeless manner, that is an architectural translation, will always prevail over simple signals by means of colours, signage and logos. It is virtually impossible to communicate an entrepreneurial culture that cannot be experienced in a corresponding architecture. Highly qualified and highly motivated employees are dependent on a work culture that unifies the collective with the individual. It is important, however, to avoid misinterpretation of the term "timelessness." Architecture that does not reflect the spirit and circumstances of the time fails to fulfill its cultural task.

The beauty of a building is based on its logic and efficiency, not on *décor* and *Zeitgeist*. Streamlined forms in architecture not only diminish the optics of large forms, they are also more efficient in terms of ecology and construction. Artificial paradises and enchanted sites have been part of the urban culture since the nineteenth century. Today, the plants formerly housed in historic greenhouses thrive high above the ground in the center of office towers. Through the fusion of individual and social spheres, the glassy transparency of an office tower operates on a micro and a macro level. Internally, the visual union of the employees creates a group spirit that secures the success of the company. Externally, the integration with the outside world establishes a higher sense of responsibility, both politically and ecologically.

Our goal is to link the maximum organisational and spatial individuality of the single workstation with a building design that is as specific as it is communicative, without calling the structural order of the city into question. This does not rule out the fact, however, that architectural symbols of otherness and exclusivity are especially committed to social exchange. The city requires creativity, in buildings and in the urban space.

Progressive architecture can build a bridge between the emotionality or poetics of the space and a futurism of new dimensions that creates points of orientation and signals of urban community and social events within the multi-layered and labyrinthine maze of the city, in a world without center where everything is periphery and nothing is middle. Architecture is devoted to the visible. A simple composition, a clear yet surprising idea can easily be perceived in its entirety. Large forms reinvigorate the amorphous urban space.

What matters is to strengthen the centers in order to reestablish the middle. Spectacular urban landmarks that emphasize the utopian dimension of urbanity ensure the legibility of the labyrinth city. The goal here is not the recreation of "history," but the narration of new, fascinating stories with contemporary means. This alone will perpetuate the history of the city. Every helpless imitation, on the other hand, translates into a loss of history. Hamburg's grandiose architectural heritage is not threatened by a modern vis-à-vis but by buildings that want to make us believe that they are just as old as the historic structures.

Architecture is exploration, not decoration. In other words: architecture is something one does. The utilitarian value is complemented by a cultural surplus value that requires a point of view. This realization can only take hold in an iconic fashion through concrete experience. In the day-to-day context, architecture acts as an important impulse for this process. However, as the client function is increasingly broken up into committees, it is becoming ever more difficult to define a clear cultural position.

Architecture should inspire enthusiasm in open-minded, sensitive people. It should provoke urban intricacies and overlapping uses and convey a sense for the challenges of our time. In this manner, architecture can become an orientation tool for both the people and the city. We must focus our attention on cities, on densification models, traffic models, and time budgets, on a more intelligent and complex integration of nature, science, technology and design. Our reality has come perilously close to that of Americans, who are already spending ten years of their lives in the car, because all we are doing is sorting and dividing instead of connecting and layering.

Architects must develop comprehensive solutions, paying equal attention to urban design, ecology, economy, identity and emotion. In the absence of this complexity, planning that is purely based in economics leads to illusory successes that are short-lived indeed. Since architects are not independent artists, they require the complicity of the client to work on the social meaning of architectural forms. The ideal client has a desire to profit from the dynamic evolutionary potential of the building and will therefore expand the task beyond the parameters of pure function and economy.

Clever clients avoid spending too much money. Wise clients know that it is far more dangerous to invest too little. If you pay too much, you lose some of your money. However, if you invest too little, you lose everything because the investment fails to fulfil its long-term purpose. In the best case scenario, architectural quality, the economic interests of the investors and also the emotional yearnings of people should not be mutually exclusive but build upon a common strategic basis.

Regardless of the building task at hand, in the broadest sense it is always a question of liveable space, interior and exterior. Technical form and practical shelter on the inside are not mutually exclusive; on the contrary, they are interdependent on the emotional level. The decisive point in a debate on architectural qualities is the question related to the mediation between the world of architectural objects and the subjective mood it triggers. Architecture is created for people. Architecture mediates scenes, spaces for living, and charisma.

Hadi Teherani

SUPER SYMBOLS WITH EMOTIONAL VALUE

THE ARCHITECTURE OF BOTHE, RICHTER, TEHERANI

A good two hundred years have passed since the famous "Querelle des anciens et des modernes" flared up in the final phase of French absolutism. The principles of architecture that had prevailed since Roman antiquity were shaken to their foundations and the preconditions created for modern aesthetics. In his dispute with Blondel, the "ancient" theoretician of architecture, Perrault, the "modern" architect, questioned the immutability of antique proportions and orders, ascribing them to taste, fashion, and custom. Thenceforth, classical architectural theory was no longer considered an objective norm but an empirical reality, mediated by human reason. The "modern" Perrault introduced a new distinction in his dispute with the "ancient" Blondel: between "positive" values, i.e., values deemed to be timeless—which to him meant firmitas (structural strength) and utilitas (functionalism)—on the one side, and mutable "arbitrary" values, i.e., venustas (beauty), on the other. This distinction triggered a new interest in the character and expressive quality of buildings and was to have far-reaching consequences: now, for the very first time, architecture's symbolic intellectual energy was liberated and its affiliation with art established. The architecture parlante of the French Revolution and the English landscape gardens began to lay emphasis on expressing emotions artistically.

At the end of the twentieth century, a similar querelle suddenly made its appearance. After the triumphal global advance of classical vulgar modernism, a younger generation of architects called into question the immutable rules of construction-industry functionalism, preferring to design a more emotionally charged and visually descriptive architecture, so that the construction and design of the environment were no longer separated from the fine and performing arts.

Ever since they founded their Hamburg office in 1991, the architects Jens Bothe, Kai Richter and Hadi Teherani (BRT) have distinguished themselves with spectacular large forms that display some of the features of a speaking architecture. They designed a police headquarters as an extraordinarily large sheriff's badge, planned a port in the form of a glass cloud-frame, an airship-like airport train station and a lamp factory in the form of a cockpit, not to mention countless space shuttles and "Snow-White's coffins". With such unique designs and landmarks, BRT have created not only narcissistic gems, but also reference points and signposts in the no-man's-land of outskirts and traffic junctions. Instead of lamenting the decline of the city, BRT have placed striking objects in the overdeveloped residual spaces so that these objects create their own environments out of their lack of context. Their work displays a novel monumentality that is not of sheer magnitude but of an exoticism that conjures up out of nothingness new locations of powerful emotional value.

Visually considered, BRT's designs frequently combine the passion for movement of the Futurists at the dawning of modernism with the pop-art techniques of the sixties. Even so, all their buildings are designed in the minimalist spirit of the latest organ-ecological high-tech approach. This, however, has little to do with the latest biomorphic blob architecture, but with reduction, lightness, and transparency. The architects want to enhance the beauty of buildings by designing them in a way that increases their ecological and structural efficiency. The incontestable basic demands of architectural tradition—structural strength and functionalism—are not only fulfilled with great composure, but also ennobled sensuously and aesthetically with contemporary expression and a contemporary feeling for beauty.

Whilst they were still studying in the spirit of classical modernism, the three architects recognized that the unsensuous reductionism of the previous generation of architects would no longer do. This shortcoming could only be remedied, in their view, if a three-dimensional concept created an architecture with a memorable, monumental physiognomy. In the meantime, BRT have become specialists in hopeless residual spaces. They want to respond to the fierce rivalry between the center and the periphery by creating "great scenes for public life and large forms that create identity" (Hadi Teherani). Teherani once described the Centre Pompidou in Paris as a moment of truth: when he saw it for the first time, he became aware "that its astonishing appearance and the provocative, abrupt change in scale are intrinsic to the architectural object as a bearer of meaning among the chaos of urban proliferation."

Since their first success, when, in 1991, they built a huge vibrating showcase with what was then the largest planar glass front in Germany for the car showroom of Car & Driver on the outskirts of Hamburg, the architects have increasingly executed commissions for commercial buildings in dreary areas. In 1997, they began designing the company headquarters in Rellingen for the Hamburg lamp designer Tobias Grau; a critic described this building as a "spring roll with a streamline design." The way the floor, walls and ceilings seem to pass into one another as in a space shuttle makes the building appear to hover just above the earth. The outer skin is borne by 20-meter-high wood-cement binders clad with composite material whose synthetic core is coated in aluminum. The panels are mounted with such accuracy that the entire building resembles

"Solving individual problems isn't a problem.
Good architecture involves taking into account
all the different needs." Hadi Teherani

the precisely cutout bodywork of a motor vehicle. The minimalist spatial program is structured by an inserted concrete slab that provides reinforcement and creates an upper floor. The client and the architects have benefited equally from the great attraction of this corporate design, whilst the convincing forcefulness of the huge building is further heightened by successfully executed architectural details.

BRT were able to make it in conservative Hamburg because their designs represented an innovative counterpoint to the existing gloomy brick buildings that set the tone there. Their office evolved into a kind of streamlined speedboat shooting past the fat brick colossi of Hanseatic mainstream architecture. Hamburg's retired building and planning director, Egbert Kossack, was so impressed by their glass gap-fillers alongside Hamburg's canals and their powerful courtyard buildings (the ABC-Bogen at the Gänsemarkt, for example) that, as early as the mid-nineties, he said of the three newcomers: "They have what it takes to determine the shape of German architecture for the next twenty years."

With remarkable planning foresight, BRT designed an ICE station as a major intersection between different flows of traffic at Rhine-Main Airport, a notorious crisis area for modern high-speed transport. The passengers, who had had to put up with creeping like rats through the underground tunnel at the airport railway station for many years, can now identify and locate from afar the central interface between air and rail traffic. A 700-meter-long Zeppelin – whose gigantic belly contains the transmission gear switching between the different transport speeds, has landed in front of the terminals. BRT also designed a luxury railway station for a wretched-looking residual plot between the expressway and the access bridges. Situated like an island of tranquility in a sea of airport noise, the station, which opened in 1999, handles up to nine million passengers a year.

The interior of the majestic silver hull is constructed like a layer cake. At ground level, the station hall, glazed on all sides, accommodates four tracks. Above, in the belly of the building, is the lounge area and, higher still, the glass-vaulted cockpit-booking hall linked to the airport by a bridge. Like the Dutchman Rem Koolhaas, with his TGV railway station in the northern French town of Lille, the architects have also moved the trains out of the basement level. Furthermore, following the design of Nicholas Grimshaw's Waterloo Station in London, the station in Frankfurt celebrates with its streamlined design the elegance of the ultra-fast express trains. A special feature of BRT's design is the way it avoids the cardinal sin committed at Rhine-Main Airport, where unanticipated spurts of growth led to increasingly haphazard lateral development. For their station extension, the architects included verticals in their design from the very start. The statics of the central floor slab, which rests on telescopic columns and freely spans the station hall at a height of 60 meters, have been computed to support up to 180,000 square meters of future office and commercial space. The platform simultaneously serves as a horizontal fence around the building site: whilst the floors are being stacked on one another, business goes on as usual in the station below.

In Dortmund, they succeeded in creating an image that almost surpassed their other works in sheer forcefulness, although the project is currently stuck in the planning stage. BRT wanted to have a multifunctional hall flown into the amorphous station district; the hall was supposed to float above the tracks like a UFO and transform the railway station into an urban entertainment center. Such a striking symbol—which combined the "walking cities" with the superstructures of British pop architecture from Archigram to Future Systems—obviously also drew considerable criticism. People asserted that the gigantic silver egg would suck all life out of an already weakened city, dealing it a final deathblow. BRT's counter-thesis, namely, that their powerful symbol would be the first thing to lure people back into the center, will remain unconfirmed as long as the UFO remains on the drawing board. Confirmation of this thesis will be furnished more quickly by the Europa-Passage, now under construction in Hamburg.

Such isolationist longings and island fantasies, which often endanger cities when applied to their centers, have become a means of architectural survival in BRT's favored field of operation. In the business wasteland of Hamburg's southern city area they have transformed two forsaken areas into architectural reference points. Next to a six-lane road leading out of the city, they erected a double tower that, like a gigantic hothouse, creates its own microclimate beneath its glass skin. In fact, the "Doppel-XX-Haus" reverses the relationship between exterior and interior. The twelve-story building, which is constructed like a card-house, is penetrated on the inside by large gardens on some floors and, on the exterior, by conservatories that rise the entire height of the building. BRT have thus created inward-facing city squares, so that passersby, looking in through the windows from the outside, can see what they are missing. A small vertical city arises above two X-shaped plans, creating an almost autarchic microcosmos with its passageways, terraces and pedestrian zones, and even restoring the ecological balance for both the building and humans alike. Consistently designed as a low-tech complex, this "Snow-White's" coffin has natural air-conditioning, allowing each office employee to slide open his or her window despite the wall of noise outside. The glass thermal and sound envelope functions as a conservatory during cold periods; in the summer, warm air is extracted thermally from the building. The interior gardens provide an additional flow of fresh air between the sunny and shaded sides of the building. Thanks to this design, the energy costs of the building have been cut by half. The "Berliner Bogen" next door operates on a similar principle, offering not only climatic but also structural advantages. The ten-story building, which is suspended on slender oval steel arches, spans a subterranean water-retention basin, creating a new building on land not considered suitable for development.

The most convincing attempt so far to lend a "non-location" a completely new quality is BRT's new building for the Swiss Re (formerly Bayerisch Rück) insurance giant on the Unterföhring commercial estate in Munich. To compensate the employees for having to move from their idyllic traditional headquarters at the English Garden—which had become too small—the architects came up with a suitable landscape design for their new domicile. Around a group of interlocking glass cubes, they placed a three-story-high steel pergola, which is now overgrown by vines and wisterias that, like a banderole, bind together the individual, multi-member, interlocking pavilions. The effect is a floating, green cloister that flatters the eye in an otherwise dreary environment. The office wings, which spread out like the sails of a windmill, and the access towers are skillfully stacked so that the courtyards and passages can remain free. Despite its high density, the complex, which is lavishly interspersed with places to rest and linger, as well as with cafés and loggias, opens generously to the outside world. The entire ensemble, which seems to float, can be understood as the constructed expression of the flat company hierarchy, and is intended to establish a balance between individuality and group feeling. Above all else, the complex has created a context for any later buildings and, as a new reference point, could soon encourage others to follow in its wake.

In the old post-war *querelle* between the "old" and "new" modernists, which flared up in the United States as early as 1970 and in Europe in 1980, the initial point of contention was the revival of architecture by means of figuration, narration and pictorial quality. The architecture of this counter-movement has meanwhile long since undergone a process of differentiation in the form of neo-geometrical, minimalist and even tectonic approaches, in contrast to the representatives of a sculptural, organic and biomorphic design. It is difficult to pinpoint BRT's precise position in this spectrum because they are also performing a balancing act with their constructed super symbols. They are endeavoring to translate the object fetishism of the classical modernists into the new context aesthetics of a generation of urban-minded planners and thereby to grasp the city again as a community event and social festival.

At this decisive urban level, architecture, as the most public of all arts, has to submit itself to an effective democratic test procedure that determines whether the interplay of the solitary structure and the ensemble is a success. It is the assembly of buildings in the built city that decides the success or failure of each individual building. However, since this process often only permits the pronouncement of valid judgments generations later, architects such as BRT have already achieved a lot in pursuing one of the most profound human ideals in their search for this difficult synthesis, an ideal which reached its full flowering in architecture two hundred years ago: the desire to achieve contemporary feeling for beauty.

Michael Mönninger

01

INDUSTRY

The plight of architecture is more desperate than ever before in our non-recycling urban cultures. Given the widespread alliance between revenue maximization and cultural decline, there is not much hope that the situation can be remedied. Long before industry and commerce were expelled to the garbage dumps of urbanity—a trend attacked in 1965 by Alexander Mitscherlich and Christopher Alexander—the fate of architecture was tacitly sealed and approved, and no appeal of its case was permitted. And all those who profited had their own way of arguing it was for the public good.

Commercial buildings—essential for the tax base but often of dubious architectural and urban-planning value—surround the city like hastily thrown-together trailer communities. Urban culture now only exists in the center (and there, only in monotonous form), where it is arduous to reach, no matter what direction we come from. The hygienic approach to urban planning, conceived in the eighteenth century and proclaimed in the 1943 Charter of Athens, has mutated today into an embarrassingly fragmented way of thinking that has lost track of its original *raison d'être*: the noise and smell of production. As the belt of monofunctional commercial and industrial areas around the city has widened, counter-measures have become increasingly ineffectual. At the same time, the willingness of municipalities to perform their labors of love to secure business taxes has remained unbroken, a practice that has devalued large areas of the city.

With just a few exceptions, Henry Ford's architectural credo dominates the thinking in peripheral profit zones. In 1922—the fifteenth year of production for his famous Model T—the American industrialist implemented an important strategy for sinking production costs: Ford was against erecting prestigious buildings as a symbol of company success, because he regarded the construction costs and interest payments as an unnecessary financial burden on the product. Often the "monument" to the company became nothing more than its cenotaph. America's great industrialist wanted to become famous for his products, not for the buildings in which they were manufactured.

Eight decades later, the most sophisticated computers and cameras are still being manufactured, bought and sold on the city periphery in windowless containers, whose architecture testifies to a monumental lack of ideas. Walter Henn, the Nestor of German industrial architecture, has repeatedly pointed out that architectural added value enhances not only a company's economic success but also employee motivation, and in this way brings in more than its costs. However, only a few developers have taken this simple message to heart. The Tobias Grau building—a think tank and logistics center that hardly offends anyone's sensibilities—could have been built anywhere. It need not have been subjected to the urban planning chaos of an industrial zone, utterly devoid of architectural goals. And it need not have been concealed behind a noise and visibility barrier as if it were a slaughterhouse or a junkyard. However, in the early 1990s the city of Hamburg refused to make any location available *intra muros*. Today, ten years later, one could expect different treatment.

If cities wish to set out for new frontiers and reinvent themselves, they must break free of existing systems through the
creation of central functions and new tasks. Planners must
proceed in a goal-oriented and yet contrasting manner. Not
all parts of the city should be subordinated to the whole in
hierarchical fashion. Large forms *within* the city, not high-rises
above it, can create new tensile relationships within fragmented urban space. These forms are not intended to break
up the desolate, endlessly subdivided city with its areas of
green, but rather to hold it together at a more advanced organizational level. This is one essential aspect of the architecture of BRT, especially when it comes to the central definition
of tasks, the social catalyst of the new millennium.

01.1

A MOBILE ZEITGEIST
CAR & DRIVER SHOWROOM

CAR DEALER'S/REPAIR SHOP/GARAGE
HAMBURG
GROSS FLOOR AREA 9,160 SQ M
BUILT NOV 1990–MAY 1991
BUILDING OF THE YEAR 1991, AIV

Street front up to now

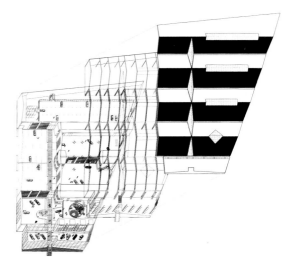

Isometric view of entire complex

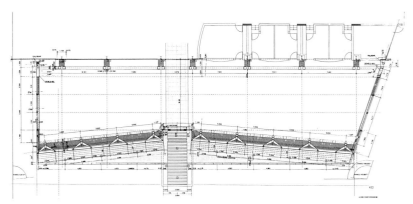

Plan of exhibition room

A MOBILE ZEITGEIST

In violation of sound marketing strategy, the uninspired design of car showrooms has simply been reinterpreted as "accommodating the customer" along the lines of supermarket architecture—even by premium brands. Le Corbusier, himself enamored of car design and aesthetics, may have expected something more of architecture, but who will share these expectations if the object of his desire is itself a gleaming *Gesamtkunstwerk*. With just a few exceptions—including Karl Schwanzer's legendary Four Cylinder Building—sophisticated design and attractive styling have been reserved for the automobile: "The loveliest form of technology" (Alfa Romeo), "The power of creativity" (Citroen), "Those who do their jobs with style" (Porsche). As in red-light districts, what is on display outshines any architectural banality. After all, the first Beetle emerged in a two-car garage, the first Porsche in a sawmill. It's no accident that BRT's first completed project, the remodeling of an old structure on the edge of the city, sets its sights on a mass phenomenon: the gap between product and presentation. With the exception of BMW, automobile execs first developed a taste for corporate identity in the 1980s. At that time, the company poster, logo, and slogan (see above) were conceived as an aphrodisiac for the customer, conveying appealing qualities through typeface and color. An architecture that communicated company goals, reflecting the image of different brands, was first realized in exemplary fashion with the Car & Driver showroom in Hamburg. A pity that the experiment failed despite the architecture, and the electronics store that moved in afterward did not attempt to reinterpret the space for its own purposes.

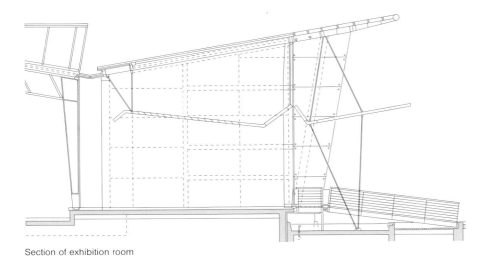

Section of exhibition room

Schematic section

Car & Driver Showroom

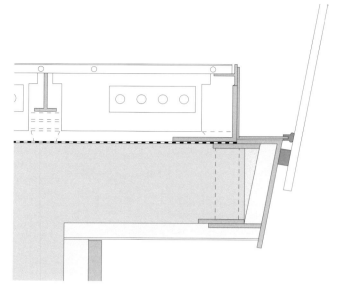

Detail of hinged joint

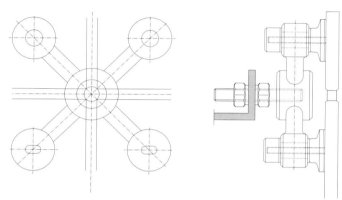

Detail of glass support

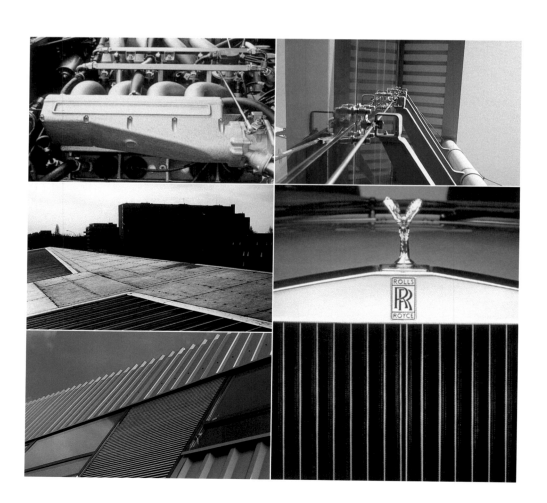

"The design is already there in the plot of land, all we have to do is recognize it." Hadi Teherani

BRAND WORLD

At the end of the 1980s, copywriters for car manufacturers bravely headed into the waters of open competition with the "built" reality of their clients in the search for image glory and style consciousness. Renault chose a Bauhaus villa as the "rose" in its label, Mazda and Lancia dreamt up concepts such as "la belle différence," "pleasure for aesthetes" or even "the art of living." Peugeot's lion roared that it offered "haute couture on the outside, high-tech on the inside," whereas Saab went with the Nordic-socialist understatement of claiming to be "one of the best workplaces in the world." Citroën hired Grace Jones to bare her teeth and growl: "I want luxury. I want power. I want technology. I want everything …" Next to shiny chrome poster walls, where pert girls dig their high heels into car hoods, a wide chasm opens up between product and presentation, between technological progress and urban image, between entrepreneurial success and urban culture. A dichotomy that is hard to understand, given the style consciousness that is inherent to the product, which inspired Le Corbusier to draw comparisons with the Parthenon in 1922. The involuntary and accidental support of solid historic buildings aside, there is only a marginal difference between these buildings and the built image of supermarkets. On the contrary, the American chain "Best" already put its faith in architecture in order to achieve brand success. Little has changed to this day with regard to high-tech representation on site. If the buildings that accompany the car from gas station to bus terminal are highly resistant to being tamed into urban design, do car showrooms, service and repair shops, and finally production sites themselves have to join in the swan song to the city? Should there not be an architectural culture of the automobile, comparable to that of rail and air transportation? Even Daimler-Chrysler continues to do without a pronounced architectural statement. The Mercedes plant in Bremen even went so far as to indulge in the luxury of disfiguring the Borgard Works designed by Rudolf Lodders, the most convincing historic architectural example of German car manufacturing, for its own purposes. On the occasion of the official opening of the plant in 1938, the press was head over heels, vying for superlative ovations to modernity in glass: "The halls seem to consist entirely of glass, light flows in from all sides, only a skeleton of concrete pillars, iron and timber girders supports the glass walls and ceilings." The large glass areas not only allowed light and air to flow into the halls, they also offered a visual perspective from the outside into the interior life of the production hall. Automobile manufacturing techniques and the rhythm of mass production at the conveyor belt were reflected in the glass walls. Lodders adopted the production technology

and transformed it into an aesthetic *leitmotif*. The inspiration for the "glass factory" was real, although it would not be translated into concrete form until 2001, the year of terror, by VW in Dresden.

In the summer of 2000, Daimler-Chrysler opened Mercedes World in Berlin, the world's largest automobile showroom. Anyone assuming that the luxury car manufacturer would finally make its long-overdue *entrée* into architecture was sorely disappointed. No doubt the glass palace on Berlin's Salzufer, a stone's throw from the Strasse des 17. Juni, is an impressive and massive hall with a length of 160 meters. Despite impressive statistics such as 1.2 million visitors per year, over 5,000 new cars sold, and a total turnover of over a quarter billion euro, the building is by no stretch of the imagination architecture that helps to shape the city. Mercedes has learned from Nike and now adds mystique to its products between climbing roses and water fountains on spiralling theme islands, but architecture as a message of the brand and symbol of its values is still seen as dispensable. The result is a leisure park with restaurant, 300 cars, 40 sales associates, Formula One simulator, and traffic kindergarten—complete with a driver's license on Daimler-Chrysler electronic cars. The multi-story car canyon behind a 25-meter-high glass facade integrated into the streetscape of Paris, which Laprade and Bazin staged in their "Maison de Vente Marbeuf" for Citroen in 1929, has been forgotten. The architectural and urban design blunder in Berlin, with a price tag of 40 million euro, is to be repeated in Munich, Hamburg, Cologne, Milan, and London because of the tremendous revenues it has generated. The traditional network of car dealerships spread out across a market is increasingly unimportant for manufacturers. Simply cancelling orders with all dealers has become standard practice in order to implement restructuring measures. According to the new sales strategy, customers test the emotional experiential space of the makes in question in central "car cities" or "brand worlds" and order on the Internet by selecting specific car configurations. Ultimately, automobile architecture will become irrelevant across the board. The revolutionary outpost in Hamburg for the supposedly innovative marketing thesis in the car trade, the "most opulent car showroom in the world" according to Rolls Royce, has thus fulfilled its task, even if it no longer exists in its original role as the flagship house for the luxury makes Bentley, Aston Martin, Lagonda, and Rolls Royce.

The idea of rediscovering and finding a new translation for the tectonic, spatial ideas of automobile brands originates on a four-lane highway that runs eastbound out of Hamburg—precisely the type of road

that is popularly occupied by a cluster of car dealerships. Despite these conditions, the stretch on Friedrich-Ebert-Damm with a run-down gas station, neighboring allotments, and a 1970s high-rise was not thought of very highly. In contrast to current car boutiques and showroom "biotopes" with space for exhibitions, seminars, and events in prime downtown locations, often hidden away in nondescript office buildings as in the case of Daimler-Chrysler on Berlin's Potsdamer Platz, commercial districts with a certain suburban charm were perfectly appropriate according to the old dictum for purchases on the scale of single-family homes. The point of departure for the design was a multi-aisled, open industrial hall of nearly 8,000 square meters from the 1970s, which already required renovating by the end of the 1980s due to the simplicity of its construction and which was equipped with a new roof of aluminum sheeting installed on a shallow angle.

ENFILADE

The client, whose goal was to make the most aristocratic cars in the world even more luxurious and to gather historic models with an impressive worth of millions into an unofficial automobile museum for Hamburg, decided to go with a transparent structure that aesthetically dominates the immediate surroundings while at the same time responding to Hamburg as a maritime site. Above all, he put his faith in young architects, who still had to establish their name. The architects proposed a 100-meter-long gap that would run through the aluminum saddle roofs and function as spine and orientation axis, as a light corridor in the roof and an internal street through all the institutions of the building, in order to complete this royal-baroque enfilade on the street elevation with a head building that signals the spatial and automotive claim to the public from the outside. To passers-by, the message conveyed by the building—kept entirely in steel and glass in synch with the language of the automobile and maintaining its high quality across the entire building depth through stock-rooms, offices, warehouses and workshops—is unequivocal and convincing: the product offered here is exclusive and of the highest standard. At the gas-station site, the glass showroom, with its glazed facade inclined by a gentle 10 degrees to avoid mirror effects in the background, even features an ennobling phalanx of columns. The glazing of the showroom was realized as a suspended planar facade on fixed girders. Each 15-millimeter-thick standard pane, with maximum dimensions of 2.5 meters by 1.4 meters, is attached to angle brackets at four fastening points. The girders, which resemble a boomerang, are welded to the 29-cen-

timeter-thick steel masts at intervals of 1.4 meters and linked with ties that absorb the weight of the panes. The external screw caps are set flush into the glass by means of laser technology, maintaining the evenness of the facade even at the fastening points. The icons of luxury parade 80 centimeters above street level on a wooden ship's deck as if they were housed on a sailboat with glass sails and masts angled in the wind. In front of the glass wing, whose numerous structural details and overall shape interpret the company logos of the featured luxury models, a 2-meter-wide pool sets the appropriate tone and water-effects playing across the glass facade. The access into the building in the form of a wooden jack ladder brings visitors straight into the axis of the enfilade and the staged spectacle of the automobile beneath a theater-red, lightning-shaped baldachin—an opening act that is continued in rhombic light openings in the roof and via a visitor terrace in black granite. To the left and right of the path, open halls of varying dimensions and uses with inserted two-story white villas modelled on the Hamburg modern follow the rhythm of the old structure, with the only difference that the window profiles are undoubtedly far more shallow in these models than in the originals. The old street structure was rendered in matt grey and completed with white plaster surfaces and glass block fields or strips of glass near the columns. No post-modernism here, rather a kind of constructivism that is as emotional as it is economic. The costs according to DIN 277 came to 1,000 EUR/m^2.

There is no clash between the original building and the new elements. The staged scenario runs from the island with a tree at the center of the office zone via the work benches designed by the architects to the steel bar in such a smooth and logical manner as if the stage set had been designed from scratch instead of making use of a fund of existing props. Anyone with a taste for extravagance can even request the custom addition of a refrigerator faced in exotic wood. Not for nothing did one of the advertising slogans of Car & Driver read: "If you want more than a car…"

EMOTION AND IMAGE FOLLOW FORM
TOBIAS GRAU BUILDING

OFFICES/WAREHOUSE/FACTORY
RELLINGEN
GROSS FLOOR AREA 4,160 SQ M
BUILT APRIL 1997–APRIL 1998, JULY 2000–JULY 2001
BDA SCHLESWIG-HOLSTEIN ARCHITEKTURPREIS 1999

"An architect has to have the courage to be innovative, try out new ideas and be a prophet. Timid architects see the limits, not the opportunities that lie in going beyond them." Hadi Teherani

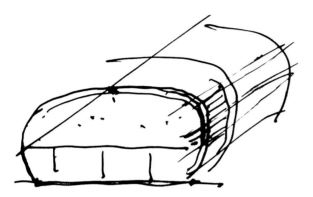

Design sketch

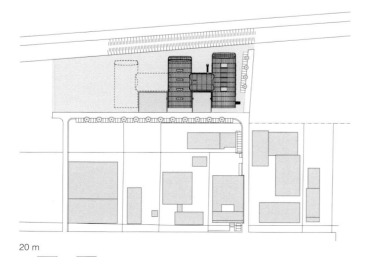

20 m

EMOTION AND IMAGE FOLLOW FORM

It is not the construction but the automotive industry that appears to have a monopoly on the term "formal expression." Independent of functional considerations and technical particularities that are understood by only a few, "formal expression," as it appears in the media, is presented as an important argument to buy, constituting a discrete qualitative feature. Only if a car's form "speaks" does it define brand image; and only then does it say: "The front and back of the car, through their design, express youthful appeal and charm" (Mercedes). A BMW, on the other hand, is sold as a piece of "high tech, high emotion" sporting equipment. In architecture, the quality of form is neither conveyed nor discussed. There is no sensibility for it, in contrast to the automobile. And yet, even in the field of architecture, emotion and image are defined via form—which becomes evident once advertisers seek an architectural framework on an equal footing with the car in order to stress mobile elegance and formal expression. Or, the other way round (as in the case of Audi), once they realize they have been stuck with banal architecture. Despite all the euphoria for the terms "UFO" and "spaceship" in current architectural debate, Tobias Grau's silver space station, located in the industrial area of Rellingen and now appearing in duplicate, remains the only real example of spaceship-like design in Germany (at least according to the client). It draws inspiration from the concept of art as design science developed by Buckminster Fuller and Jean Prouvé. In historical terms, Fuller's Dymaxion Dwelling Machine is arguably architecture's most significant attempt to solve the problem of industrial design. By simple structural means—and via the World Wide Web—the Tobias Grau spaceship on the periphery of Hamburg, as a major industrial building, launches the inner emotionality of the "house" into the outer orbit of a "spatial object." At the same time, it is a striking representation of the company.

"Simple ideas are easy to get across: we take a concrete table, build over it with glued wooden frames and wrap it in sheet metal." Hadi Teherani

CARCHITECTURE

The Natwest Media Center on Lord's Cricket Grounds has become something of a cult object. Designed in 1999 by the English architecture group Future Systems, it is the first double-shelled building to be made entirely of aluminum. Like the ribs and rafters used in plane and ship construction, the 100-ton semi-monocoque structure is formed by rows of welded-together I-section ribs and sheet metal strips with a maximum size of 4.5 meters by 20 meters. The giant pod, which was in fact constructed in a boatyard, has an outer metal skin ranging in thickness from 6 to 20 millimeters. The resulting shape, with its double curves, is far more dramatic than a simple cube. In addition, the shell structure eliminates the need for exterior cladding and interior pillars. The oversize "viewfinder," which stands on two 15-meter-high cement towers, does not even make use of an expansion joint; on the outside, it has merely been painted like the hull of a ship. It has only one shortcoming: the price. Costs rose from 2.3 million to 5.8 million pounds, in part because no air-conditioning system was initially planned. The panoramic windows (behind which 120 journalists sit in four rows) have a 25-degree tilt, and they can only be opened slightly, making it difficult to ventilate the space.

"The very least one could expect of sculpture is that it moves," Salvador Dalí once said while standing in front of one of Alexander Calder's first "Mobiles." In the mid-1960s, the revolutionaries from Archigram sought to escape this dictate with architectural mobiles that one could fly away on like airships: "We couldn't resist the idea of 'Instant City' hovering in from nowhere, landing and then gathering up its skirt and disappearing at the end of events." In 1992, Claude Vasconi conducted the last mobile experiment of this kind before a crowd of 1,200 people on a stage in Weimar that resembled a medieval traveling theater. His half organic, half galactic aluminum capsule, which stood on telescopic legs and was accessible via airport gangways, resembled a spider about to skitter away. The 1999 project in the capital of culture was never realized due to estimated construction costs of 12.5 million euro—which were to be raised by private investors.

The aerodynamic space station, which appears to have taken a second-row seat only by accident (and only temporarily), also toys with such themes as technology, machinery, dynamics, and mobility. The spaceship image is consistent right down to the contrasting archaic gangway that, in line with flight control regulations, appears to have been moved up to the cabin door by ground personnel. Even so, the silver idea accelerator, with a dark-blue solar drive in the glass tailpiece, remains motionless. A disappointment? After all, seventy years ago, Angelo Invernizzi pulled off the engineering feat of a revolving house, which he constructed in shiny aluminum: the Casa Girasole in Marcellise near Verona. This building demonstrates the surprisingly long history of architectural "inventions." The rotating eco-house by the Freiburg architect Rolf Disch, however, is nothing more than an oversized gimmick.

Naturally, the crosssection of BRT's hovercraft is not an innovation in the sense of patent law. "Innovation," writes the art historian Boris Groys, "does not involve uncovering an element previously concealed, but rather reassessing something that we are familiar with." The history of transforming vertical glass cylinders into large horizontal forms goes back to "Mega Bridge," developed by Raimund Abraham in 1965. As early as 1931, though, Jakov Cernichov adopted this motif for his chemical plant. In 1972, Coop Himmelblau unveiled the project "Frischzelle" (Live Cell), a vertical, bioclimatic park/recreational facility in the form of a rooftop glass survival tank. In 1968, there were plans to expand the historical building of the Düsseldorf Kunstakademie (Academy of Art) using two translucent cylinders 15 meters in diameter and 120 meters long. Twenty years later, Toyo Ito designed an end structure for the Yatsushiro Historical Museum that was related typographically and had a freely designed cross section. In 1990, one year prior to the founding of BRT, William Alsop used the dynamic motif several times: for the British EXPO pavilion in Seville, the Hamburg ferry terminal, the local government headquarters in Marseille, and the Cardiff Bay visitor center. Only the last two designs were realized in their original form. The single-level steel structure in Cardiff, which has an elliptic crosssection and stands above the ground, features abstract-decorative, organically shaped lighting openings in the outer skin, which is made of plywood and a weatherproof fabric covering. These counteract its high-tech image. So much for the typological background.

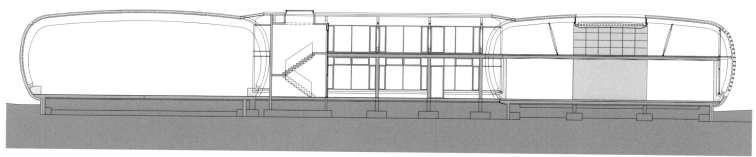

Cross section

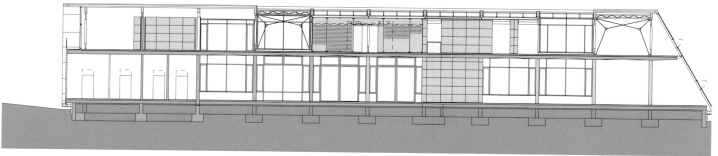

Longitudinal section

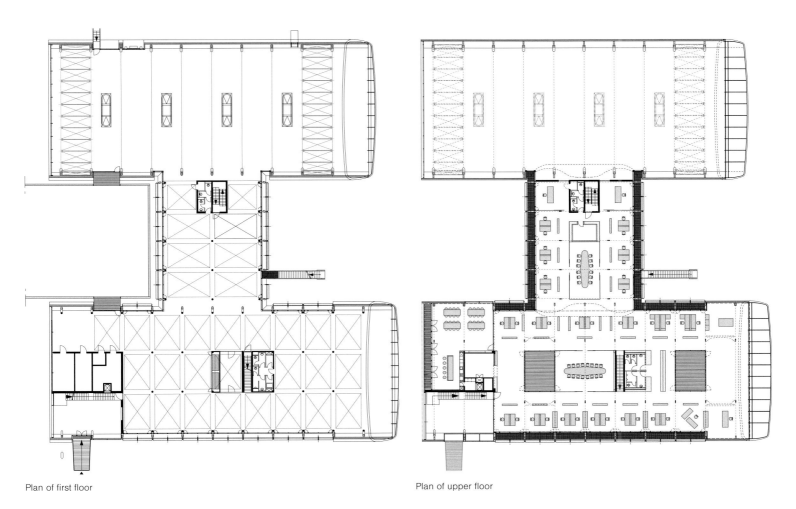

Plan of first floor

Plan of upper floor

ONE FORM

The building designed by BRT is based on similar concepts, also viewing the building as passageway, location as path, roof as main floor, and single shape as a quantum leap to new dimensions. However, there are many differences, including its emphasis on economy and ecology. As a lamp designer's headquarters, the two-story spacecraft unites very diverse functional areas: the upper floor accommodates a lobby, the development department (with a showroom for dealers), and the cafeteria. The ground floor houses the shipping department, a final assembly unit and a warehouse. More offices are located in the linking section, and there is additional warehouse space in the second tube. The first tube, 58 meters long and 24 meters wide, is divided into three sections and contains two atriums not visible from the outside. When it was expanded, its typology necessitated opening the structure on its longitudinal sides. This was done without adversely affecting the persuasive power of its formal design or interfering with the "flight safety" of a body that appears to be hovering just above the ground. In spite of the visible camber of the "floor panel," the cross section remains a stabile architectural motif, thanks to its southern facade and the fascinating aesthetics of subdivided space. The ship is "stabile," as Hans Arp would say, not "mobile" in Marcel Duchamp's sense.

The architects did not intend to parody or fetishize 1970s Pop Art, whose naive enthusiasm for technology and the moon landing were always shaky. Even the machine aesthetic of the 1983 dental lab by Shin Takamatsu—imitating a locomotive—would be an anachronism. After all, who would want to interpret this building as a lamp in postmodernist fashion? Such an association—though effective for corporate identity—could only be triggered by the concept of the single form as implemented in the lobby lighting. No, the well-rehearsed spatial magicians from BRT were seeking a consistent, independent, functional and, above all, moving design for an industrial building that is part factory, think tank, and showroom. The flying object in Rellingen has broken free of the sphere of imagination. Rub your eyes all you want—Le Corbusier's vision from 1922 has become reality: "If a structure is to be given the full glory of its form in the light of day, with its outer skin adapted to user-related requirements, the elements that suggest and create form must assert themselves in the structuring of the outer skin." Nowhere is this demand more clearly fulfilled than here. Generally, the successful self-definition and self-portrayal of a firm via architecture must be in proportion to cost (though Foster's Hong Kong and Shanghai Bank and the examples mentioned at the beginning are exceptions). However, the cost—which is primarily planning-related—will be seen in a new light if the client realizes what slips through his fingers with a building that does not make a strong architectural statement. The Tobias Grau building, which was the subject of a private competition, is proof of this. Construction costs were roughly the same as those of a high-quality office building. In structural terms, it consists of a reinforcing concrete table with an underside in the form of a groin arch with a 10-centimeter camber. Laminated wood rafters, supported by oak pin-end columns, form the skeleton and bear the trapezoidal sheet metal elements of the roof and facade. There is a second layer consisting of Alucobond panels, screwed on as in plane construction. They have the precise look of a car body. The dark-blue solar

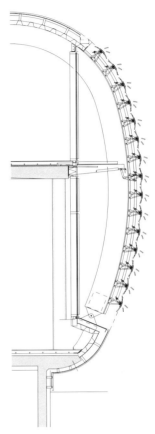

Facade section

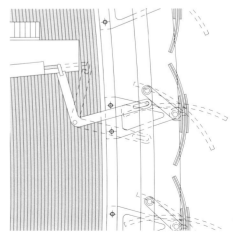

Detail of glass louvers

facades, frameless and transparent, cover an area of 54 (and 180) square meters and have been incorporated into the building as structural glazing. They are an essential feature of the design and have also been used in the rear of the kitchen and cafeteria. The 2.5-meter-long, motorized side ribs—an independent development that initially seemed doomed to fail—offer protection from the sun and were necessary not only for formal reasons but also due to the lack of air-conditioning. At first, glass ribs were designed with holographic-optic elements, but these were not lightweight or long enough. An adequate lighting and structural solution was only found when the elements were printed on the underside and arched so that they could be installed without any substructure. The ecological energy concept is supplemented by concrete core conditioning and a cogeneration power unit.

Thus, a very homogenous, object-based architecture has come into being that, liberated from all banal details (rain gutters, connections to the base, etc.) broadens the debate on architecture. The simple composition, with its clear but breathtaking idea, can be quickly grasped as a whole and stays in mind. This was a trick mastered by the Russian constructivists and even used by Hans Poelzig, the dramatic non-conformist and sculptor of modernism. His most important credo: though technology leads to formlessness, architecture possesses the domain of the visible world. Thus architects must avoid all ambiguity and neutrality.

Only architects know what fine-tuned planning and detail work is necessary for this meta-language of super signs—a language spoken by such luminaries as Rem Koolhaas (Zeebrugge Ferry Terminal, 1989) and Ben van Berkel (Yokohama International Port Terminal, 1995). "Simplicity is always the most difficult thing, for it does not forgive any mistakes." Such streamlined architecture cannot be grasped in all its complexity at a single glance.

The urban-planning conception of sculpture is inevitably inimical to context insofar as sculpture's real place is on stage, not in the back row. Even if a third parallel tube is added, this building will free itself from the desolate surroundings by brute force. Such force is necessary given the fact that it is located in an industrial area that has been demoted to a non-place, hidden behind a visibility barrier like a junkyard or slaughterhouse. In Rellingen this game of concealment is so exaggerated that a regulation was passed that any structure rising above the ghetto wall had to be red and have a 45-degree slope. As can be expected, BRT fulfilled this requirement with its "cockpit" without ruining the chosen design. If required, the architects were also prepared to make the upper strip of the cockpit windows red—though as protection from the sun, not in an act of submission to a curious regulation. Legislators in nearby Hamburg now regret that the building is not located within the city walls—although the client looked in vain for an inner-city location for three long years.

SURREALIST GALLERY

Besides its outer shape, the spaceship has another surprise in store for visitors, one that is hard to convey via photos and plans. When visitors enter the high-tech form—which has drawn international attention despite its remote location—the architecture unexpectedly offers them the practical security of everyday life. In other words, despite its aluminum skin—as smooth as a plane's wing—a very specific spatial atmosphere has evolved. In a wonderful way, this sensitive large form cordially embraces one like an oh-so-creative artists' garret. People can think and invent here even though it is not old architecture. For once, conventional methods were *not* used to foster creativity. Method 1: Gleaming modernity, deep-frozen and far removed from everyday life, promises and makes possible a viable future, though without the pleasures of normality. Method 2: Imagining the future requires a secure basis in the past, if not in an old building, then at least in a randomly manufactured cocktail of styles. The most astonishing thing: it is precisely the uniformity of the large form that engenders specific interior spaces. The curved outer walls give rise to spatial dynamics that Friedrich Kiesler skillfully used in 1942

"A building whose mobility simultaneously symbolizes independence from place and creates place." Kai Richter

Tobias Grau Building

for the "surrealist" gallery in Peggy Guggenheim's New York exhibition "Art of the Century." The arching roof creates changing ceiling heights. The middle area with atriums, which illuminate the ground level via glass floors, differs from the edge of the tube where the workstations are located. And these differ not only in terms of views or orientation, but also in their relation to the middle area and the arching roof. The spaceship operates with a rhythmic change of space and materials. The front sections differ in shape and slope. What looks so uniform from the outside is not at all predictable within.

Thus, this minor building assignment—designing a lamp factory in an industrial area—has evolved into a critique of stylistic faintheartedness, a critique of the developed surroundings and a fundamental critique of urban planning. It offers its affront on the city's periphery, where it is much too classy for its neighbors and for that reason has been equipped—at least optically—with the mobility of a flying object.

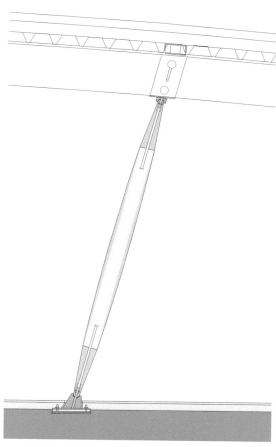

Detail of wooden support

01.3

MACHINE SYMBOLISM
SH:Z PRINTING CENTER

PRINTING CENTER/OFFICE BUILDING
RENDSBURG-BÜDELSDORF
GROSS FLOOR AREA 12,500 SQ M
BUILT DEC 1999–AUG 2001

MACHINE SYMBOLISM

In 1922, Henry Ford stated his business goal of becoming famous for his products alone, not for his factories—and yet this wish was to elude him. The Ford factories designed by Albert Kahn marked the dawn of a new architecture. Even so, in his 1927 essay, "Das Ornament der Masse" (The Mass Ornament), Siegfried Kracauer voiced criticism, explaining that the logic of the capitalistic system did not represent reason itself, but rather a dimmed understanding of the world that held no place for the human being. According to Kracauer, even if production processes remained "hidden in the public sphere," the workplace had a major impact on the workers' lives and everyday experiences.

It follows that the decisive factor is not only state-of-the-art technology in the form of mammoth printing presses and sorting machinery, but also the workers' mood and a company's image—in other words: a striking architectural presence that, like a convincing speech "rouses the emotions" (Aristotle). Conceived as black boxes on the edge of the highway, industrial buildings at best constitute a neutral backdrop to the company name. In the case of the Printing Center in Büdelsdorf, the client realized in the nick of time that the "how" was just as important as the "what." Behind the redesigned reception building, which BRT later redesigned the structural frame of the plant was already under construction before the contract was awarded, and yet its appearance was thoroughly reevaluated in a competition. The Taylor System, which Kracauer criticized for equating the Tiller girls' legs with factory hands, had to be overcome aesthetically. The architects have captured the image of a rotary printer in a building that calls to mind spinning strips of paper. This provides the machinery with an architectural script—breaking all the rules, in retrospect.

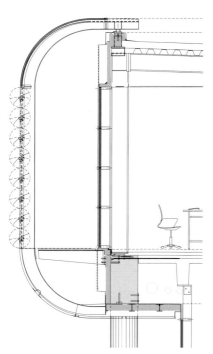

Facade section, administration

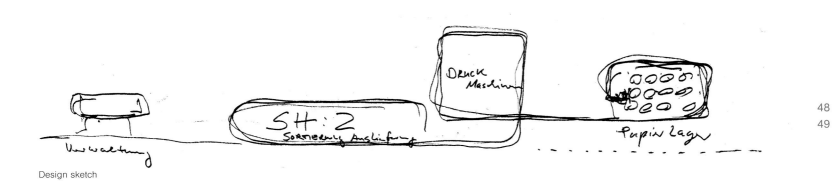

Design sketch

10 m

sh:z Printing Center

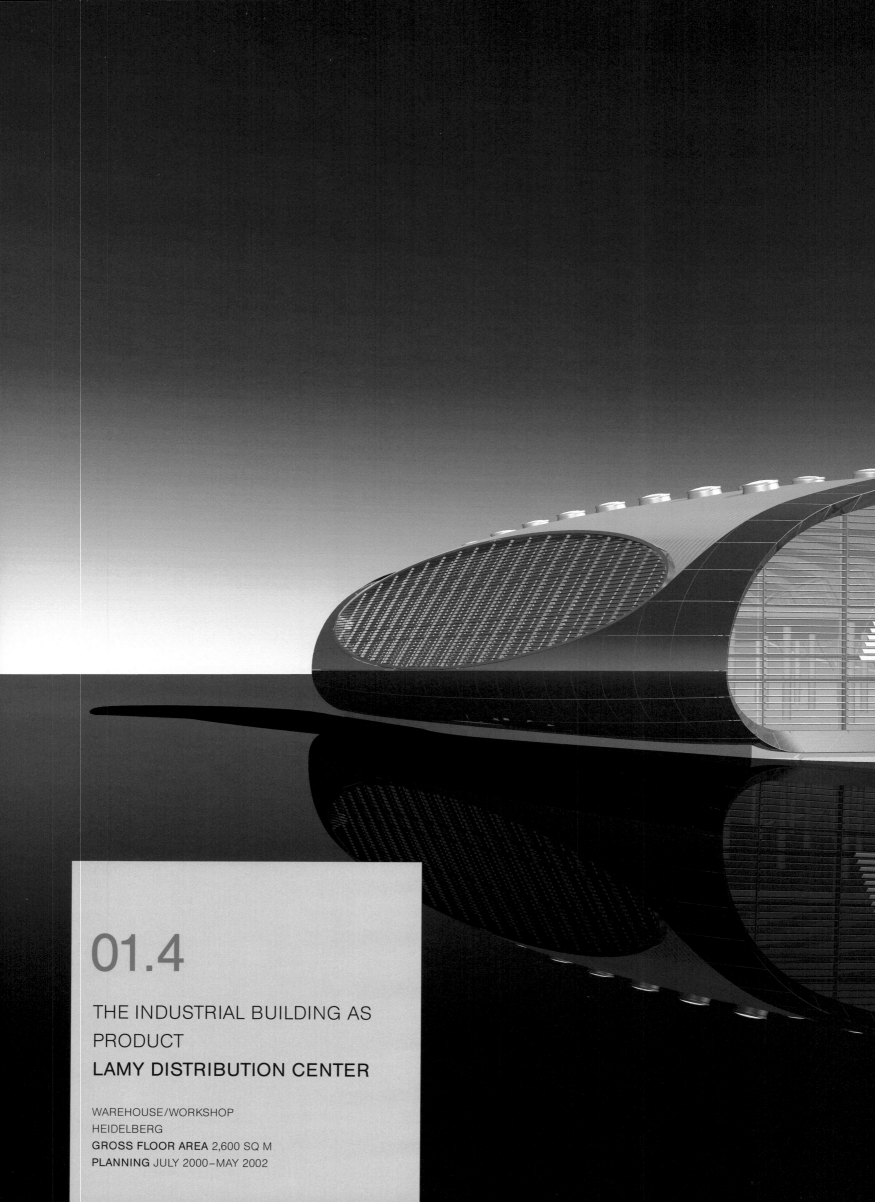

01.4

THE INDUSTRIAL BUILDING AS PRODUCT
LAMY DISTRIBUTION CENTER

WAREHOUSE/WORKSHOP
HEIDELBERG
GROSS FLOOR AREA 2,600 SQ M
PLANNING JULY 2000–MAY 2002

"Freedom in architektural design is, among other things, not having to get involved with the taste of the masses." Kai Richter

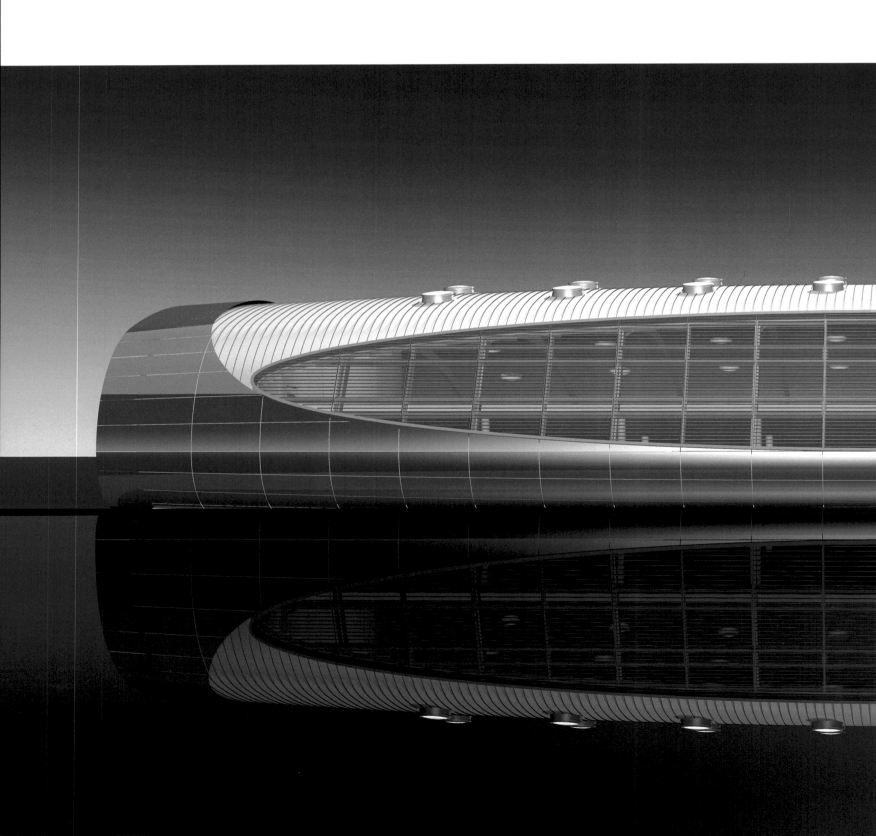

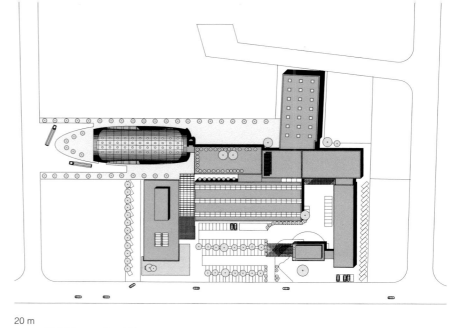

20 m

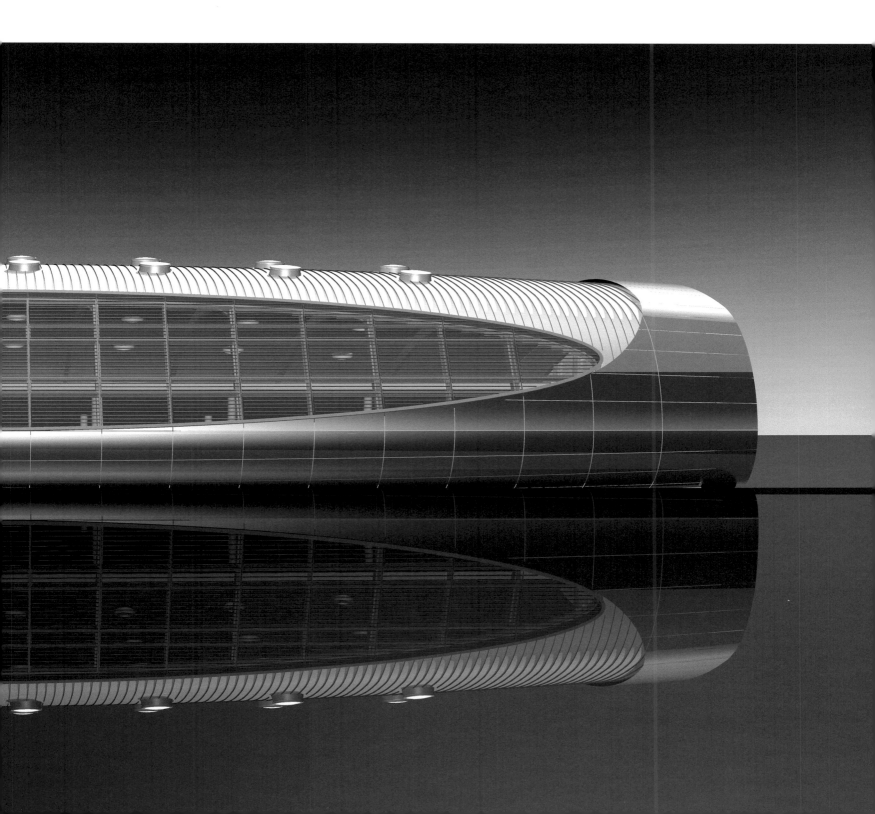

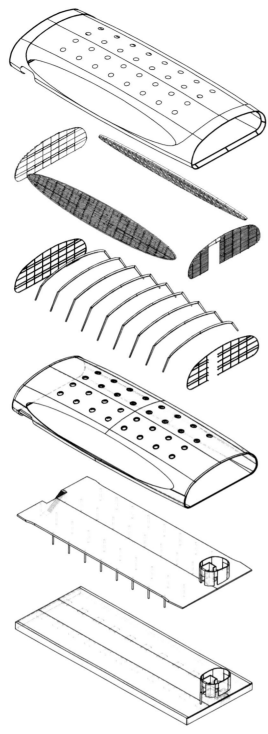

Construction scheme

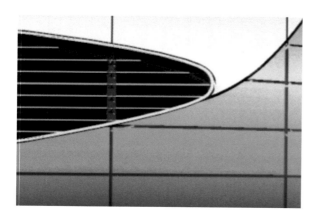

THE INDUSTRIAL BUILDING AS PRODUCT

The formal style of modernism has made a significant contribution to the leveling of typological idiosyncrasy. The reduction of all architectural forms to primary geometric bodies has ultimately led to a neutral container architecture. With the greatly decimated range of building types, it has become increasingly difficult for architecture and its target groups to communicate. The meaning and function of a building are rarely conveyed. Added to this is an uncertainty about the future that set in with the new millennium. The confusion of structures, the blurring of edges, the dissolution of building solidity, the loosening of its connection with the ground, the orchestration of movement with materials seemingly foreign to architecture, the impression of incompleteness and vagueness, and the mystical indecisiveness about goals (primeval hut? space station?)—all of this has apparently been discredited. Should architecture, in the historical present, tell the story of a world that is standing still? Indeed, architecture as a sign system has the task of disseminating ideas and messages in society. If an industrial building is to be more than the shell of a mechanical, functional process, companies must market themselves through communicative architecture. These goals were already being implemented when the *Werkbund* was established; even if back then they were not paraphrased with the buzzwords "corporate identity" and "corporate design."

A successful example of how the latent analogy between a company's product and its architecture can be exploited is Stirling's 1972 Olivetti School in Haslemere. As for the Lamy building, surely no one will interpret its sides as "handles." Nonetheless the design works with forms typical of Lamy.

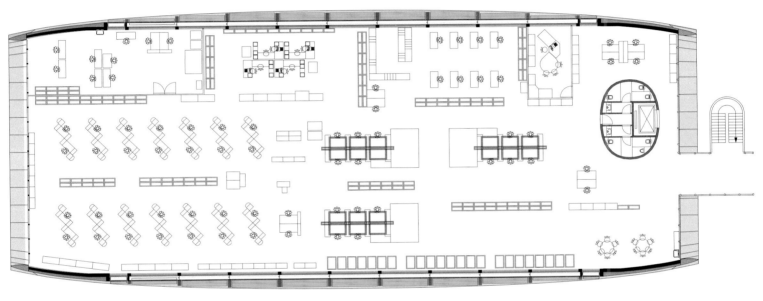

Plan of upper floor

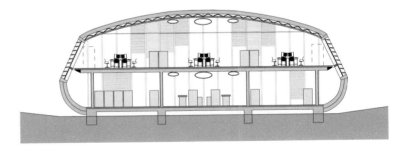

Cross section

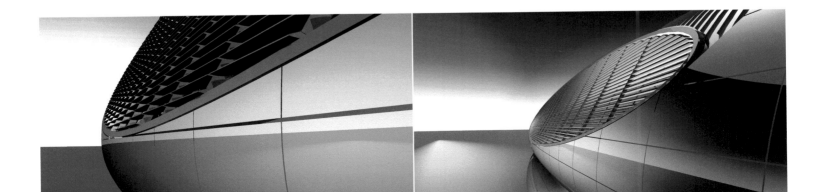

Lamy Distribution Center

01.5

PROJECTING COMPANY HISTORY
INTO THE FUTURE
PALM PAPER-MILL

ADMINISTRATION OFFICE BUILDING
AALEN-NEUKOCHEN
GROSS FLOOR AREA 1,883 SQ M
BUILT MARCH 2001–JULY 2002
COMPETITION 2000, 1ST PLACE

PROJECTING COMPANY HISTORY INTO THE FUTURE

By bringing the world's largest 200-meter-long paper mill into service in Wörth—built entirely of stainless steel with a production width of 10 meter—the firm, which has been operated by the same family for four generations (since 1872), was faced with having to expand its administration headquarters in Aalen. The annual production of 700 employees at three locations is roughly 540,000 tons of graphic paper and 820,000 tons of corrugated cardboard and raw paper. The manufacturing process operates within a closed water cycle and utilizes 100 percent recycled fibres. The expansion symbolizes the production of the company by means of a filigree, cantilevered roof, the gentle curvature of which suggests the floating lightness of paper. The steel load-bearing structure was pre-assembled and installed on site on a minimum number of columns. As calculated, the curvature of the roof shell, visible on the inside, resulted as if on its own accord. The structure and volume of the neighboring administration building from the 1970s was doubled by the simple expedient of adding a glazed gallery for the reception area. Both building (components) present a unique character; they are, however, connected by a common water area as an expression of an essential element in the production process. The third element of this corporate identity comes to life in a sculpture composed of millstones in the center of the artificial lake—testimony of the historic use of ground rags and old clothes as a manufacturing basis. Even the stainless steel railings and the functional containers in the shape of dynamically deformed rolls of paper, which are scattered around the central atrium, can be interpreted as symbols of paper manufacture. However the image is chiefly defined by the airy breadth and transparency of the new building, inspired in part by the company owner's view of the ABC-Bogen in Hamburg.

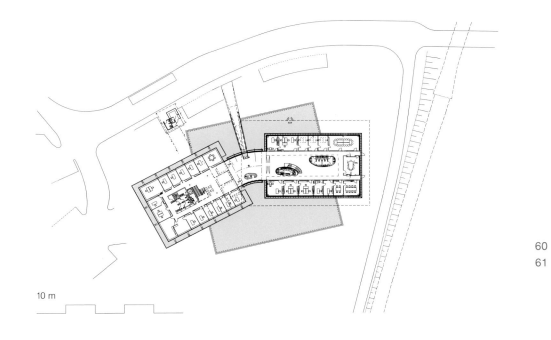

10 m

Palm Paper-Mill

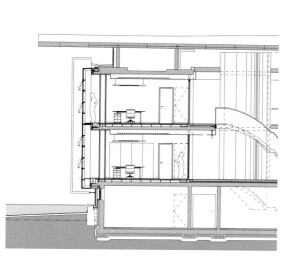

Section of office area

Palm Paper-Mill

"We judge the quality
of a design not least by
a building's economic
efficiency." Jens Bothe

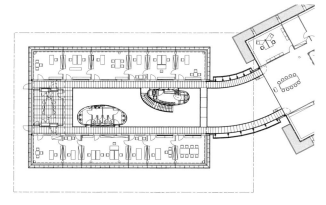

Plan of upper floor

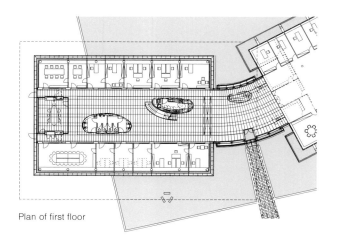

Plan of first floor

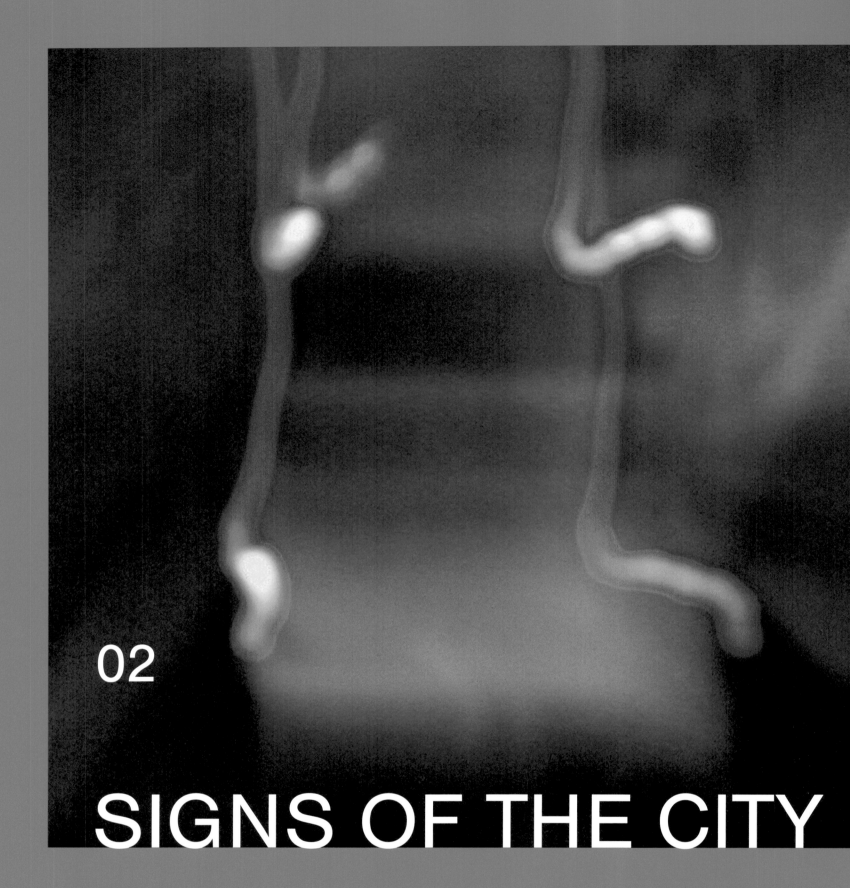

02

SIGNS OF THE CITY

Around 20.3 million people lived in eastern Germany and Berlin in 1950; today there are more than three million fewer. The decrease in population and aging are making the fears of a stagnating society even more concrete—a "society in the rigidity of endurance." Economic recession and ecological catastrophes intensify the aversion to social and cultural change. In many cases, public life is retreating into the private sphere; debate and dynamism are avoided there as well. Even Berlin, which ten years ago boldly overestimated itself by hoping to house six million people and surpass Paris and London as a European metropolis, now stakes its claim as a metropolis only on the courage lacking in Hamburg, Munich and Frankfurt to vie with it for the honors. In this competition, the city on the water has the best prerequisites: the highest skyscraper in Europe, planned within the Hafen-City development, would be a clear challenge—even to London. Germany's experimenting with how great and national it wants to be has not yet been concluded. Nowhere else can a country be found with over 80 million inhabitants, but whose largest city has a population of just 3.5 million.

Kurt Tucholsky's admonition of the 1920s—that if Berlin believed it was the core and heart of the country, it would excessively overestimate itself—has lost none of its explosive power. The city is not lacking the palace—an empty, reconstructed facade serving as another replica of the 1930s—but rather the discourse, the vision (oriented toward the future!), especially, architecturally. It is not enough to unify the disadvantages of the large American city with those of the German provinces—once again, Tucholsky. Unflinchingly nostalgic, the city of the joy of defeat is not capable of propulsion under its own steam, and remains dependent on enduring transfer subsidies. In no other German city is the average income so low, no western German economic center is, measured in terms of its proportion of foreigners, so feebly international. In the place of the international concerns driven out by the Berlin construction laws came Polish migrant workers; in the place of global players, the fortune hunters of the bazaar economy. The shopping center at Potsdamer Platz looks just like the one in Pirmasens; the reconstruction of the once famous Café Kranzler could just as well be a café in the Salzgitter train station.

Even Marc-Antoine Laugier, the first critic of the planning of Paris in the eighteenth century, advocated both order and confusion: "It needs squares, intersections, streets. It needs regularity, parallels and opposites, coincidences which bring variation into the picture, great order in the details, confusion, violence and tumult in the whole." Paris created its epoch-making points of order within Haussmann's revolutionary system with "Grands Projets"—both historical and up-to-date. Architecture thus challenges societal passivity and its resistance to change. The city always has a utopian dimension, because it opposes the natural order. The location of the city is Utopia; the essential role of architecture is to assume a position that is both distanced and emancipated from the present. The new sobriety cultivated in Berlin, the provocation of the everyday, is confronted by the new awakening of city-planning taking place in Manhattan since the dotcom crash and "9/11," a new mood of "thinking big" in spite of all isolationist endeavors. Above and beyond economic efficiency, societal spaces, innovative milieus and intellectual atmospheres are what determine urbanity.

For the European city, the issue is not standardized uniformity based on the roof heights of the late nineteenth century, a forest of skyscrapers run wild, the decision for New York's midtown eighty years ago or today, but rather to tolerate, to create, and to combat disorder simultaneously in a playful understanding of city planning. If more than half of the world's population already lives in labyrinthine cities, the image-ability and place legibility of the city, in Kevin Lynch's sense, become even more important. The triumph of the visibility of the city over its invisibility becomes a prerequisite for a functioning community. In view of new functional hybrids that relate urbanity to the building, the legibility of the city is being recreated not only by height records and the construction tasks of society as a whole. The daily rush of tourists in the Empire State Building exceeds the number of office employees by 100 percent. The more clearly a building, a network of streets or a traffic structure stands out from the urban ground as an urban figure, the greater the resulting place legibility. In this value system of signs, the 417-meter-high World Trade Center, attacked for its symbolism, is on the same level as the only 87-meter-high Flatiron Building, whose striking shape sparked a hundred years of competition in skyscraper construction.

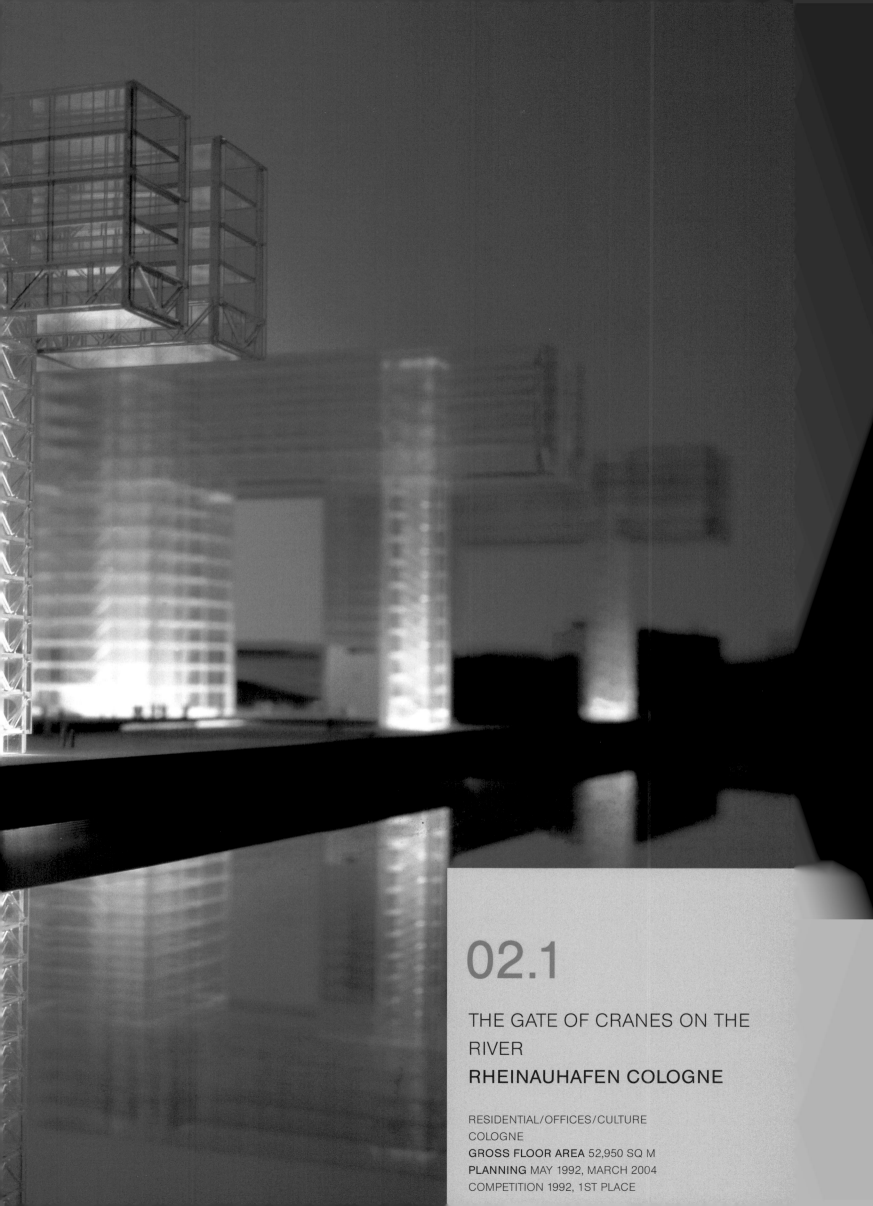

02.1

THE GATE OF CRANES ON THE RIVER
RHEINAUHAFEN COLOGNE

RESIDENTIAL/OFFICES/CULTURE
COLOGNE
GROSS FLOOR AREA 52,950 SQ M
PLANNING MAY 1992, MARCH 2004
COMPETITION 1992, 1ST PLACE

El Lissitzky, Cloud Hanger for Moscow, 1924/25

THE GATE OF CRANES ON THE RIVER

Were the Ruhr region and the banks of the Rhine to combine into a polycentric Rhine Ruhr City area, there is no doubt that Cologne would be its predestinated center. The city is architecturally still quite far from such a future. However, while miles of its land are located directly on the Rhine, Cologne still does not have a bustling waterfront that integrates the urban power of water—a significant feature in defining metropolitan attractiveness—or architecturally exploits the phenomenon of being a "city on the water." Visionary consolidations and the interweavings of the city fabric grow neither on petty nostalgia nor on the reconstruction of the harbor area along the lines of Josef Stübben's medieval conception in 1898. This design was not only damaged heavily in the war, but worst of all, was severed in two by the Severin Bridge constructed in 1959. According to Freud, dreams never occupy themselves with petty details. That the architectural history of a dynamic city cannot be exhausted in monotony and mediocrity is documented these days by the 170-meter-long storage building of the Agrippina Wharf. Known as the "Siebengebirge" (Seven Mountains), the building was constructed in 1910 completely of ferro-concrete. Such historical building substance, especially, lives on the architecturally documented jump into the present, while any unjustified attempt at familiarity devalues historical authenticity to a synthetic mass to be disposed of at will. After years of opposition and repeated competitions, deserted quay systems are finally to be reactivated—something attempted all over the world, and long on the itinerary in Hamburg and even Berlin—to recharge and consolidate the urban atmosphere in Cologne. In keeping with the original idea, the design is reminiscent of the existing cranes, which were integrated into the urban environs and actually used in the pre-industrial complex of the city's history.

10 m

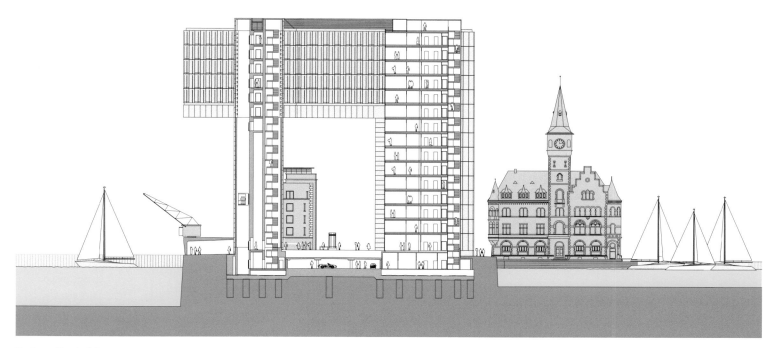

Section, office building

Rheinauhafen Cologne

Historical Rheinauhafen

CATHEDRAL CITY

Ireland, formerly Europe's poorhouse, whose historic boom has occurred thanks to computer technology, is currently undergoing the most rapid transformation it has ever experienced in the docklands of Dublin. The Dublin Docklands Development Authority, founded in 1997, has set itself an ambitious program for the 520 hectare site, whose population is projected to rise by nearly 150 percent by the year 2012: "We will develop the Dublin Docklands into a world-class city quarter paragon of sustainable inner city regeneration—one in which the whole community enjoys the highest standards of access to education, employment, housing, and social amenity and which delivers a major contribution to the social and economic prosperity of Dublin and the whole of Ireland."[1] The construction of a 60-meter-high docklands tower at the end of the Britain Quay was ratified in August 2003, upon the initiative, among others, of the pop group U2, who are going to benefit from having a spectacular recording studio. Five hundred international architecture teams participated in the competition. If one were to compare Dublin's euphoric embrace of progress with that of Cologne, the Irish design would have to first go through a decade of debate and argument, undergo expensive questioning through additional competitions only to be realized after all against all expectations once the euphoria had faded. And even then it would be at the mercy of market forces without any official backing. The future of Cologne's Rheinauhafen has been debated since 1969. According to a council decision from 1976, the historic "port- and shipyards at Cologne," a distinctly homogeneous district that had served primarily for grain shipping and lost its significance after World War II, was to be reinvented as a "leisure and recreation complex." This does not mean, however, that the endless discussions have come to an end after thirty years. What is happening in Cologne has little to do with formulating a better vision for architecture and urban planning; instead, this is but the most recent incarnation of a conservative and small-minded medievalism. Thus the most popular argument against an architecturally distinctive formula for progress in urban development is the need to protect Cologne Cathedral from structures that compete with it in height—an argument that became mute as long ago as 1980 when a television tower, 109 meters higher than the cathedral, obscured be best view of the landmark from the river perspective.

What is overlooked in this argument is that the 157-meter-high cathedral, completed in 1880, ignored a traditional height scale of the medieval city: the tower of the medieval town hall, which had long been the tallest structure and a dominant symbol of pride of the burghers of Cologne. Consequently the debate on high-rise aspirations in Cologne began with this town hall tower. To begin with, the tower was to be extended in height; later on the design for a twelve-story high-rise by Fritz Schumacher sparked a national outrage. Even the then lord mayor Konrad Adenauer, known for his visionary approach to urban planning and architecture and dedicated to modernizing the image of the city through the inclusion of high-rises, succeeded only in obtaining permission in principle but was forced ultimately to yield to the criticism of the Prussian state ministry of this intervention in Cologne's city panorama. The hint of metropolis, which had begun to emerge in Cologne at the time of the "Pressa," the international press fair in 1928 as well as previously on the occasion of the Werkbund Exhibition in 1914, did not, unfortunately, translate into a lasting motif. It was this very goal, however, with which Adenauer had courted Fritz Schumacher to accept the post of deputy director for urban architecture and planning (1920–1923). Strong urban design had been a lost cause in Cologne for centuries—ever since the expulsion of Cologne's archbishop in 1288. Until the French occupation in 1794, the city belonged to itself, to the citizens, a self-contained entity. This heritage seems too difficult to shake even today. With the end of the Hanseatic era and the economic stagnation that followed, the development of the city became increasingly provincial and petit bourgeois. Even industrialization and reconstruction were largely executed within the maze of the medieval plan in the core. In 1991, Klaus Novy remarked that Cologne could hardly boast a building or an architect from the foundation period of any supra-regional significance.[2] It is all the more disappointing, therefore, that the waterfront theme—which has inspired revolutionary renewal in so many other cities—has thus far failed to mobilize a new architectural departure. Aside from the excitement about the three glass cloud hangers there is no architectural goal whatsoever. Anyone who adheres to the volumes defined in the development plan and the relics from the harbor era, is given free reign. The terse New York-style motto for urban planning reads: "We deal in building lots; the client has the right to seek out his own architect."[3] Urban development as capitalistic roulette, individual interventions as pseudo debate on architecture.

Populist restrictions cannot provide a basis for excellence in architectural quality: one need only look at the pale contributions of even prominent architects in the cathedral city. The "Cologne Tower" in the Media-Park, originally designed by Jean Nouvel, was politely kept to a lesser height than the cathedral (by 9 meters), but was robbed of any remnant of elegance when the floor area was increased for economic

Rheinauhafen 1938

reasons and the project realized in an expanded partnership. And to crown it all—corrupting a successful competition design after the fact, a fate that had already befallen Nouvel's Cologne publishing house—the glass facade of the high-rise was ornamented with nebulous historic city scenes instead of the type originally intended by Nouvel: an odd attempt at obscuring the presence of a high-rise immediately after its completion. The consequence is a reversal of fortunes, where shattered hopes serve as renewed ammunition for the arguments of high-rise opponents. It would be far more useful and clever to argue for architectural quality on the basis of concern for the appearance and image of the city. This would, however, require an ability to engage in a debate based on factual knowledge and clear goals. The highly visible landmark of change on the waterfront was a thorn in the eyes of conservative complainants in partic- ular, who seem to have forgotten their great model Adenauer. The online site dedicated to the architecture of Cologne, which has been laboriously trying to inspire a debate and is supported by eleven partners including the city of the Cologne, has thus far failed to come up with any viable counter argument.[4] According to the Rheinauhafen initiative, the historic silhouette that has grown in the shadow of the cathedral and towers in the old town is in danger of being distorted through "the utopian urban devel- opment," once again a "sellout of the city panorama." In 1999, the Green Party seized the opportunity to mark the height of the planned high-rises with balloons as a visible illustration for the population of the effect, deemed so devastating for the urban image. In a daring argument, the alternative party's banners proclaimed the looming loss of quality of life in Colognes' Südstadt as well as the loss of an unobstructed view of the Rhine. Even though, at 58 meters, the height of the barely 30-meter-wide "crane houses" stayed below the limit that defined Cologne in the 1920s as the "high-rise metropolis of Europe." At that time, Cologne beat its arch rival Düsseldorf, home to the 56-meter-high Wilhelm-Marx-House (1921–1924) by Wilhelm Kreis, Germany's first high-rise, with the 65- meter-high Hansa high-rise by Jacob Koerfer (1924/25), Europe's tallest "skyscraper" that stood uncontested for four years. To this day, Cologne is virtually unbeaten in the discipline of the residential high-rise. For decades, the Colonia high-rise, completed in 1973 and rising to height of 138 meters, was second only to the slightly taller Tour Blanche, erected in Paris at the same time. The thesis that urban planning and architecture play a central role for human happiness and well being, especially when they stand as symbols of new beginnings and progress, available to every Dubliner in elaborate Internet presentations, would only inspire dis- belief, shoulder shrugging, and preservation arguments in Cologne. Only the head of the economic department is frustrated that unlike Munich,

Frankfurt, Hamburg, and Berlin, Cologne has not joined the ranks of Ger- many's prime office locations. The appeal issued by the most prominent architecture critics and architects of the 1920s to evaluate high-rise designs with a view to the "future image of the city" has sunk into oblivion. Siegfried Kracauer's caution against "towering monsters that owe their very existence to the unbridled will to power of predatory enterprises," issued in 1921 with Manhattan in mind, had such a profound influence in Germany that permits for expensive height-additions are handed out in Berlin today to rectify the urban image: permission has been granted, for example, for a height increase from eleven to fifteen stories in the Kant triangle.

RHINE PANORAMA

The conceptual urban planning competition for the Rhein- auhafen (1992) called for a new image for the 2-kilometer-long peninsula, located in part in front of the southern old town and in part in front of the Kölner Neustadt. The disused port area was to be reactivated through a mixed use of residential, commercial, and cultural facilities, thus bringing the city closer to the river. Two first prizes representing fundamentally dif- ferent urban goals illustrated the perplexity of the city even then: "The [proposal] by the architecture studio Linster from Trier [is] moderately urban, remaining true to the structure of the quarter and the port. The other by BRT has an image-forming silhouette and represents an attempt to transform the symbolism of the former port atmosphere."[5] After several reviews, an expert opinion and yet another urban competition in 1999 (1st prize: Bernhard Winking, Hamburg), succinctness and marketability prompted a decision in favor of BRT's "stirrup" buildings reminiscent of Constructivism. Even conservative council members were suddenly hail- ing it as "a great success and a trailblazing project for the new century." The utilization of the port area had, in the meantime, been increased from 100,000 to a total of 230,000 square meters gross story area; the original idea of giving equal weight to cultural, residential, and commercial uses had given way to reserving forty percent of the entire development for business, service industries, retail, and restaurants. And the sixteen-story cloud hangers, each with an effective floor area of 15,000 square meters, are no longer designed to rise from the water but from dry land. Estimates predict that the entire building project, involving thirty different fields of construction, will cost as much as 600 million euro, including a 1.5-kilo- meter-long underground garage with 2,400 public parking spots. Nearly 5,000 people will live and work in the Rheinauhafen. If it were up to the

Historical warehouse "Siebengebirge"

mayor, the district would be renamed "Europaport" in order to keep up with the race among big cities. Since the building plan has come into final and binding effect in the summer of 2002, the latest hitch has been a complaint on the part of investors deploring a lack of prominent political backing for the spectacular project. Devising a marketing strategy for 80,000 square meters commercial floor area is no easy task in today's climate. Unfortunately, the cathedral city was slow in picking up on the idea of "Cologne's new calling card with top notch European architecture." As long ago as July 1990, which marked the centennial of the artist's birth, the *Frankfurter Allgemeine Zeitung* had suggested that El Lissitzky's cloud hanger should be realized and completed for EXPO Hanover.[6] "Once built, the 60-meter-high office tower with horizontal booms would undoubtedly have become one of the most exciting monuments to modern architecture," wrote Werner Oechslin in the catalogue to an exhibition at the ETH in Zurich, the first to fully explore the story behind the spectacular project. The cover of Adolf Behne's *Der moderne Zweckbau* was appropriately illustrated with a bird's-eye view of the cloud hanger. Friedrich Kiesler (1925), Maurice Braillard (1931), Kenzo Tange (1960), and Stephan Braunfels are known to have created comparable designs. Since 1988, the Munich architect Peter Stürzebecher has campaigned repeatedly for the realization of an aesthetic steel and glass adaptation of the cloud hanger—as a motif of the Berlin-Moscow axis in Berlin and as part of the Grands Projets in Paris—all to no avail. The project seemed to be irrevocably banished to the sphere of utopia.

CLOUD HANGER

The dream of the cloud hanger was at the very core of El Lissitzky's exploration of architecture.[7] After his appointment as director of the architecture faculty at the WChUTEMAS art academy in Moscow, the Russian constructivist traveled to Berlin in 1921 where he met the artistic avant-garde and, through introductions by Theo van Doesburg, also the leading Dutch architects and artists of the time. He already had a connection to Hanover from having had his first solo exhibition for the Kestner Society. When he was diagnosed with a serious case of tuberculosis, the architect who had been trained at the College of Technology in Darmstadt but had always dreamt of becoming a painter, moved to Switzerland in 1924; there, he met Hans Schmidt, Emil Roth and Mart Stam. The design for the cloud hanger emerged in the same year in Minusio near Locarno during a creative phase that was extraordinarily productive despite extremely difficult personal circumstances. Emil Roth drafted the con-

struction plan in steel, which had a major impact on the design—including the wide projection for structural reasons. Mart Stam contributed his own design variations on the cloud hanger theme. Christoph Bürkle identifies the triggers for the design, the ground for which had already been prepared by Lissitzky's work on the "Proun" idea (Proun = "For the New Art", Penguin Dictionary of Architecture), especially Proun 88 (circa 1923), as being the artist's new personal contacts with architects, an emerging building boom in the USSR, as well as the artist's attempt to establish his own position vis-à-vis various artistic theories. El Lissitzky insisted upon the following conditions for his reduced semantic urban symbol: flowing traffic as an immediate reference point (Roth had cautioned against setting the baseline of the building 50 meters above ground for no obvious reason); the clear separation of vertical and horizontal lines of movement on the building; asymmetrically alternating elevations; instant perception of the dynamic symbol even when traveling by at great speed. To Lissitzky, whose programmatic declaration even in 1920 was "The city is our goal," the cloud hanger design addressed urban planning first and foremost. On a plan of Moscow, he envisioned eight cloud hangers as super symbols of supremacy or city gates in a concentric arrangement at the location of today's inner city ring, each at intersections or squares, with the horizontal principal element oriented directly toward the center or rather the Kremlin. Contrary to Le Corbusier's schematic universal urban vision, which preserved only the symbolism of the city gate in his *Ville contemporaine* (1922) while suspending all other traditions in accordance with the academic concept of the "city in the void," Lissitzky sought contrast without diminishing the old city, albeit without the direct adaptation of historic styles that has become so popular today. "The city consists of dying old parts and growing, living new ones. We aim to deepen this contrast."[8] The cloud hanger project and the realization of the three "crane houses" that are not linked by horizontal booms are fundamentally in agreement with regard to this motif of structuring and defining urban space, of creating a symbol of orientation and identification and also providing functional areas—a motif that is especially important in Cologne. On the other hand, there are no formal analogies whatsoever. Preservation proponents never tire of emphasizing the importance of the historic cranes on the Rheinauhafen, calling for the preservation of as many cranes of differing types as possible.[9] The architectural reference to this port technology is thus a decisive basis for the symbolism employed here. However, it would be a postmodern fallacy to assume that the mere suggestion of a historic formula with emotional connotations could revive the longed-for significance of architecture. In El Lissitzky's eyes the American skyscraper eclecticism that was first evident in the result of the com-

Plan of 13th–15th floors

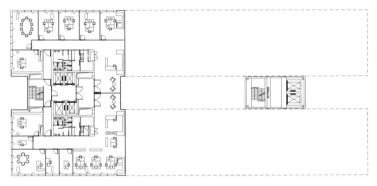

Plan of 2nd floor

petition for the Chicago Tribune Tower, represented a fatal retrograde development in architecture even then. In this regard, Russian Constructivism was far ahead of its time. With its daring cantilevers and recesses, the high-rise for the Supreme Council of the Soviet, designed by N. A. Ladowski in 1922, appears almost like a precursor to Behnisch's Nord/LB headquarters in Hanover.

RIVERPORT

The current shape of Cologne's Rheinauhafen is the result of older port structures created between 1892 and 1898 on the basis of plans drafted by the urban planning authority under Josef Stübben and a competition held specifically for the architectural details to be realized in this area, all of which was complemented by buildings erected in 1909 and 1922. The competition called for "facades in the medieval style," although towers, oriels, and gables were to "correspond with the inner organism of the buildings" in contrast to Hamburg's old warehouse district. In the words of the city, the ambitious design stipulations were entirely appropriate for "what has been Germany's most important city panorama since the Middle Ages and also in the present day." Preservation authorities see the value of the surviving historic elements including several dominant gantry or portal cranes and semiportal cranes, as well as two cranes dating back to the turn of the last century, in the unique character of the port that is a product of its exposed urban position and the unique design challenges resulting from it.[10] Cologne's wealth was very much founded in the city's exclusive right to launch and trade in goods, which only expired in 1832. All goods that were transported on the Rhine, regardless of the direction in which they were being shipped, had to be offered for sale in Cologne for three days. Rhine shipping, which became significant only from the twelfth century onward, made use of the natural shoreline in front of the city wall for anchorage and loading. Pictorial documents of harbor fortifications with public warehouses, cranes, and shipyards, especially on the later Rheinau Island, exist from the early fifteenth century. The steamships used from 1820 onward and the railroad, which was launched as a private enterprise, intensified the movement of goods and the port activity. The structural improvements required to meet these demands were focused on the Rheinau Island, known as the "Werthchen" (perhaps "small wharf"), which had served as a shipyard in the Middle Ages but had become a central, park-like recreation area by the nineteenth century. The southern tip of the island was only linked to the mainland in the middle of the nineteenth century in order to create

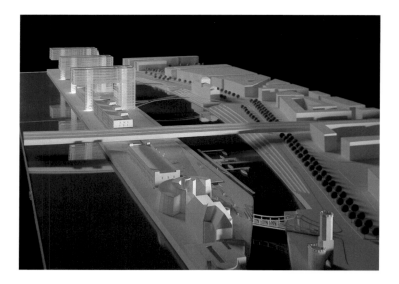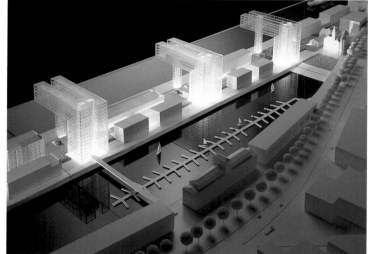

a defined harbor basin with solid quay walls. When the new development was approved for this area under Joseph Stübben, the originally crescent-shaped island, which stretched to a maximum width of 40 meters at the center, was expanded to a width of 75 meters along its entire length. Although the buildings in the Rheinauhafen were severely damaged in World War II, the extent of destruction was still less by comparison to the inner city. The construction of the Severins Bridge (1956–1959) was a serious intervention into the port area because it interrupted the visual link between the warehouses. The contemporary commentary of the *Deutsche Bauzeitung* provides an excellent insight into the difference of the city's current planning strategy, still clumsily preoccupied with preserving its "face." When the harbor buildings were erected in the nineteenth century, the city believed that "shipping [companies] should not be granted the liberty of creating their sheds according to their own taste or lack of taste, but that all structures are created for the city and then made available to private hands in exchange for a lease. As a result, the new harbor has an unusual, uniform, and at the same time architecturally pleasing aspect."[11] It remains to be seen whether this claim can be preserved beyond the three crane buildings. The modernistic chocolate museum, which occupies the northern tip of the port area since 1993, framing and penetrating the neo-gothic building of the former customs house, does not give rise to too much hope. As other port conversions have shown, not least of all Düsseldorf's Mediaport, which is devoid of life at night, the principle of *laisser-faire* is no more than a utopian tool if positive surprises are the hoped-for outcome. Here is a reference to the future that is highly unusual for urban planning in Cologne. Now, however, the leadership of the city is looking to the future: "The crane houses are to stand as a signal that will demonstrate the confidence of our city in the twenty-first century."[12] A tall order for architects in Germany.

The uproar will only abate once the inner city is expanded by 2 kilometers of riverside promenade and spectacular maisonette apartments on airy residential streets in the northern Kranhaus district. Perhaps then, the question why the "high-rises" are so low will finally arise. Thirty-five kilometers of Rhine cut through the riverside city in whose modern ports 10 million tons of goods are still being handled today. An architectural reference point of Cologne's downtown to the water was long overdue.

Notes

1   See: www.dublindocklands.ie and www.reflectingcity.com

2   Klaus Novy, Arno Mersmann, Bodo Hombach (eds): *Reformführer NRW. Soziale Bewegungen, Sozialreform und ihre Bauten*, Cologne/Weimar/Vienna 1991, pp. 411 ff.

3   Ortwin Gönner, Gesellschaft für Stadtentwicklung mbH »modernes köln«, after: Köln rückt näher an den Rhein (25.06.2001), www.koelnarchitektur.de

4   ibid.

5   ibid.

6   P. W.: El Lissitzkys Wolkenbügel für Hannover?, *Frankfurter Allgemeine Zeitung* July 23rd, 1990, p. 24

7   See: J. Christoph Bürkle: *El Lissitzky. Der Traum vom Wolkenbügel*, Zurich 1991

8   El Lissitzky: *Proun und Wolkenbügel*, Dresden 1977, p. 82/83, after: J. Christoph Bürkle: *El Lissitzky. Der Traum vom Wolkenbügel*, Zurich 1991; p. 42

9   Ulrich Krings: Bedeutung und denkmalgerechte Erhaltung des Rheinauhafens in Köln, in: Kulturbehörde/Denkmalschutzamt der Freien und Hansestadt Hamburg (ed.): *Industriekultur und Arbeitswelt an der Wasserkante. Zum Umgang mit Zeugnissen der Hafen- und Schiffahrtsgeschichte* (Arbeitshefte zur Denkmalpflege in Hamburg Nr. 11), Hamburg 1992, p. 134

10   See: Axel Föhl: Watching the River Flow…, in: Kulturbehörde/Denkmalschutzamt der Freien und Hansestadt Hamburg (Hrsg.): *Altstadt – City – Denkmalort, Jahrestagung der Vereinigung der Landesdenkmalpfleger in der Bundesrepublik Deutschland 1995* (Arbeitshefte zur Denkmalpflege in Hamburg Nr. 16), Hamburg 1996, pp. 93 ff.

11   *Deutsche Bauzeitung db* 32/1898, p. 270, after: Ulrich Krings: *Bedeutung und denkmalgerechte Erhaltung des Rheinauhafens in Köln*, op. cit., p. 133

12   Szenenwechsel in Köln, *Frankfurter Allgemeine Sonntagszeitung*, June 9th, 2002

"The architectural imprint on voids opens up undreamt–of angels and views. The resulting spaces are unlike anything one could have anticipated." Hadi Teherani

Rheinauhafen Cologne

02.2

INTEGRATED SKYSCRAPER ENSEMBLE
TANGO TOWER DÜSSELDORF

OFFICES / HOTEL
DÜSSELDORF
GROSS FLOOR AREA 42,310 SQ M
PLANNING MAY 2000

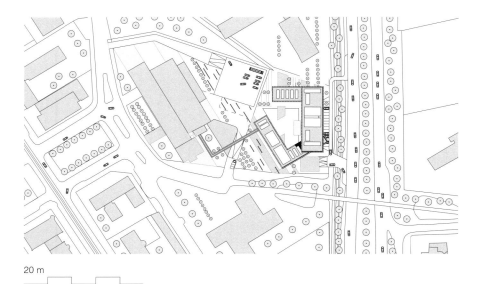

20 m

INTEGRATED SKYSCRAPER ENSEMBLE

If you believe Jean Baudrillard, the David Bowie of philosophy, then the Twin Towers of the World Trade Center, as "the perfect embodiment of a definitive order," carried the fate of their destruction in themselves: "monstrous" towers, whose cloned doubleness and symmetry evoked a longing for the restoration of asymmetry and singularity. According to this philosophy, every power becomes an accomplice to its own destruction, because every expansion of power gives rise to opposition. Without the temporal reference to September 11, 2001, the Tango Tower project appears to anticipate this thesis. At a height of 112 meters, it is definitely a skyscraper, but the effect of the building hinge and the lower components meeting it at a right angle is to create a largely closed triangular courtyard ensemble. The complex structure is composed of many parts, broken and twisted, and presents a different appearance on each side. As such, it strives to escape from the typology of the tower with all the city-planning means at its disposal, primarily deriving its composition from the structure of the city at the road that leads to the expressway and the airport north of the old city center, and away from the preferred sight lines. Decisive is that the Tango Tower, in wise foresight, does not pay tribute to American writer Gertrude Stein's observation that skyscrapers are all "without mystery and complexity…, smooth and straight and slender and hard and white and high."[1] This group of buildings composed with a view to city spaces may indeed attract attention, but not through the American tendency to impress with pretentiousness or through the narcissistic pose of postmodern "look-at-me-buildings."

Notes

1   Gertrude Stein, after: Michael Jaye, Anne C. Watts (eds): *Literature and the Urban Experience*, New Brunswick (NJ) 1981, p. 88

Tango Tower Düsseldorf

"Architecture is entitled to be stunning, but not disturbing." Hadi Teherani

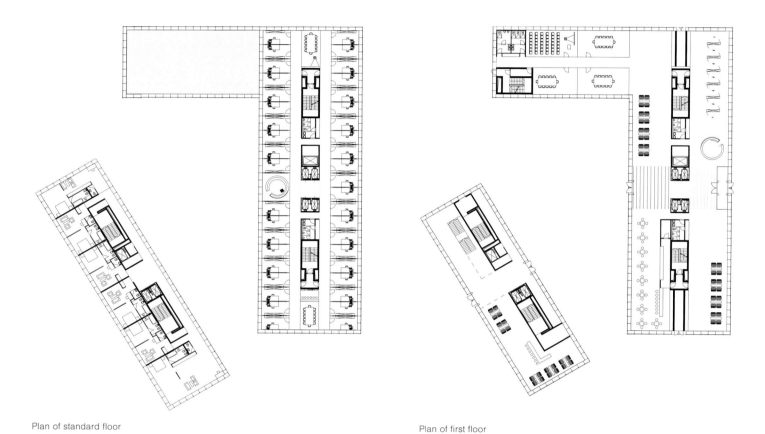

Plan of standard floor   Plan of first floor

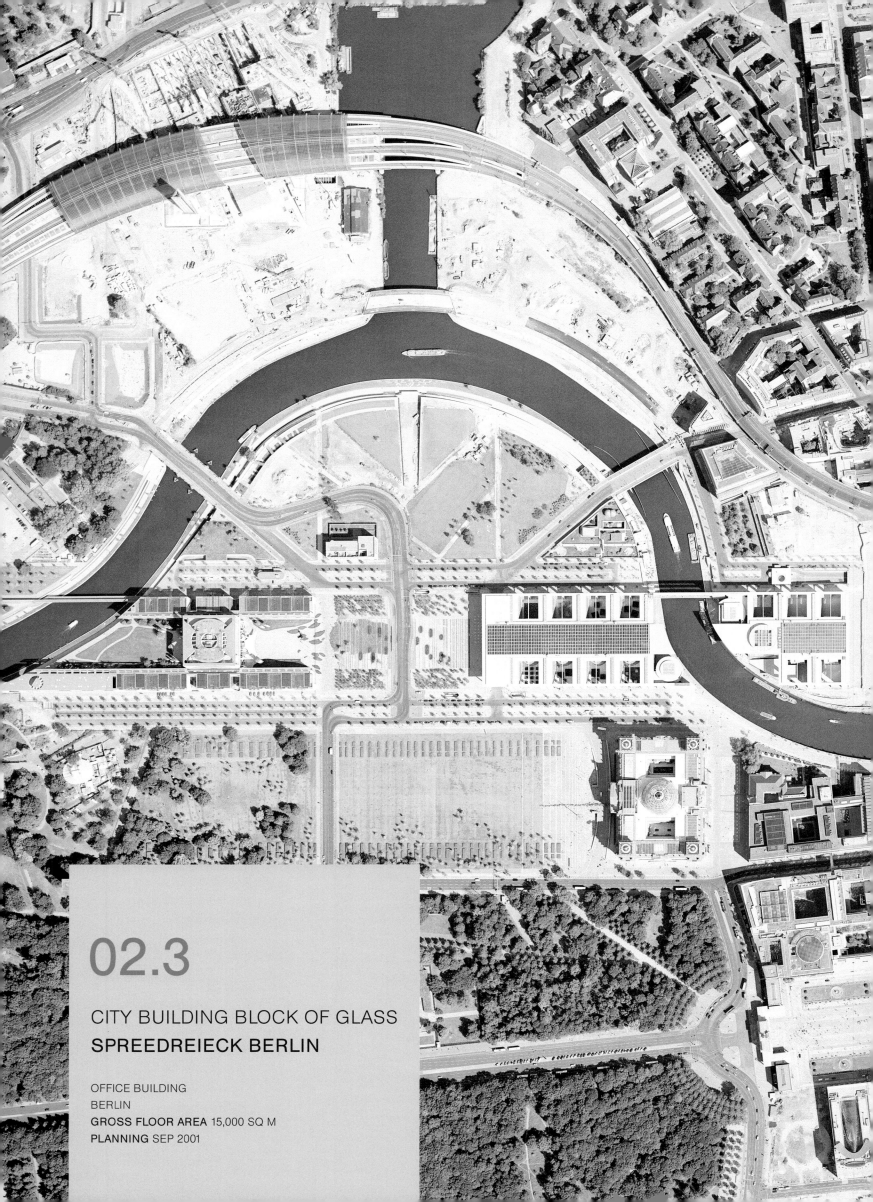

02.3

CITY BUILDING BLOCK OF GLASS
SPREEDREIECK BERLIN

OFFICE BUILDING
BERLIN
GROSS FLOOR AREA 15,000 SQ M
PLANNING SEP 2001

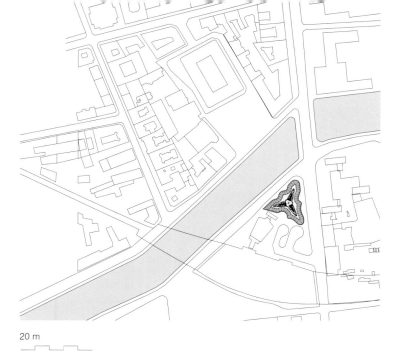

20 m

Mies van der Rohe, Project for a Glass Tower,
Berlin Friedrichstraße, 1921/22

CITY BUILDING BLOCK OF GLASS

The search for "architectural focal points in the boring and restless sea of houses that is Berlin" did not begin until 1920. In 1921, the year of the historical competition for designs for the Spreedreieck (Spree Triangle), Le Corbusier made great fun—justifiably—of the ungainly German plans for tower construction in the journal *L'Esprit Nouveau*. Almost without exception, it was the conservative designs that won prizes. In any case, the contract had long since been awarded; among the winners was the creator of Le Corbusier's malicious gloating. Nothing was built, however. The most consequential entry was a project called "Beehive," which was submitted by the 35-year-old Mies van der Rohe. Radically programmatic in nature, the design broke loose of the specifications of the competition and was not even mentioned in the publication issued by the competition. Mies van der Rohe based the central idea of the building on poet Paul Scheerbart's enthusiasm for glass, declaring "raw brickwork" to be the primeval form of a new metropolitan aesthetic, as Karl Scheffler had described nine years previously. This form of construction was true to van der Rohe's motto: "Skyscrapers show bold, constructive thought only while they are under construction; with the masonry of the facades this impression is thoroughly destroyed." As irreverent of the standards as it was conciliatory in its reflections, the heroic monolith was both a solitary object and a fitted city building block. Far beyond its time in terms of construction and technology, and in its intended lightness and transparency, the building can only now be fully appreciated, which, in view of van der Rohe's dictum, "Architecture is the will of time fixed in space; only today can be formed," makes its experimental setup significantly more justified than the dream of reconstructing the Berlin City Palace. The modified ground plan, divisible into multiple parts, incorporates van der Rohe's subsequent design of 1922, and organizes its development in accordance with valid construction regulations.

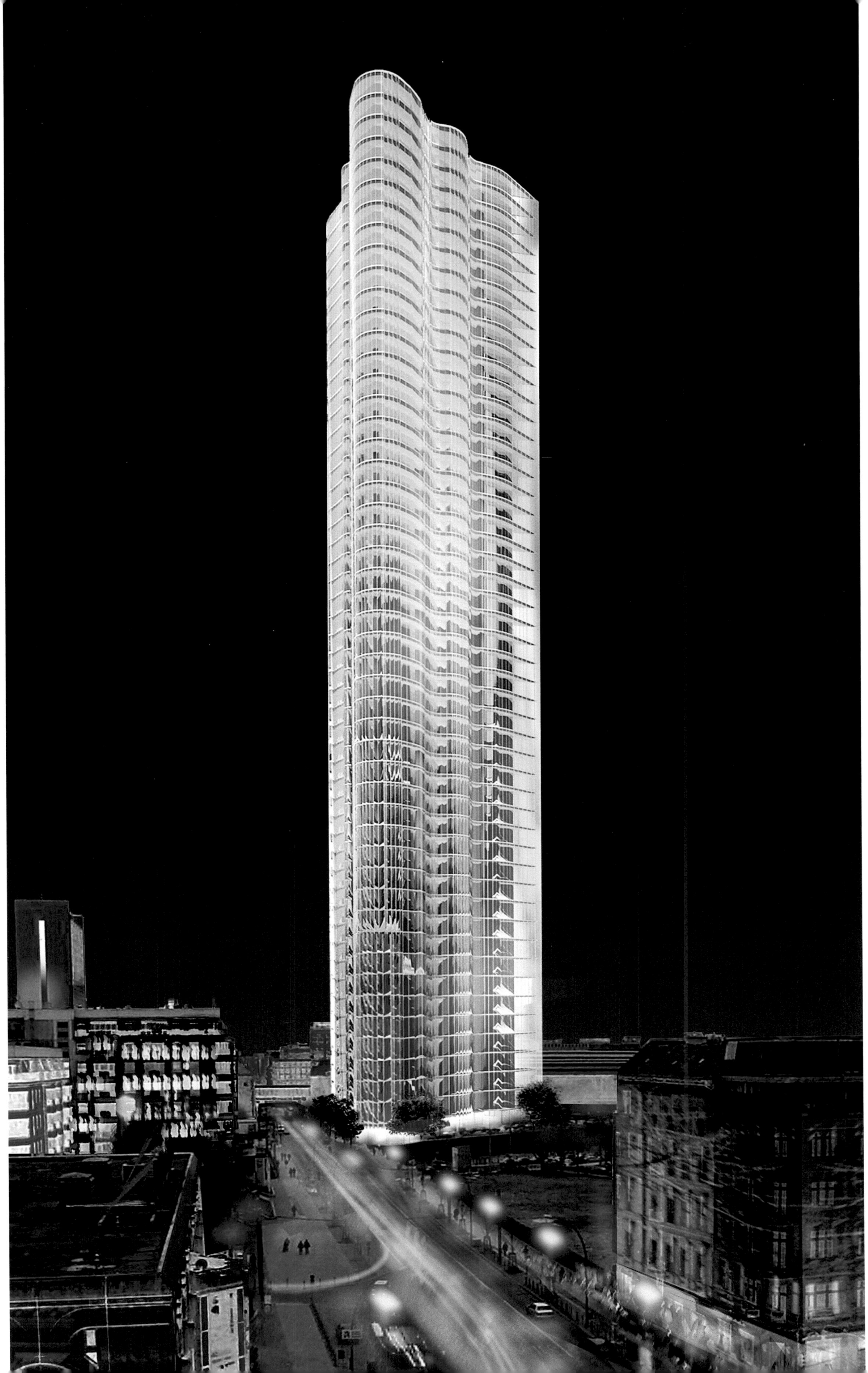

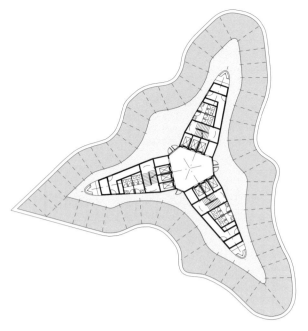

Plan showing office cubicles version

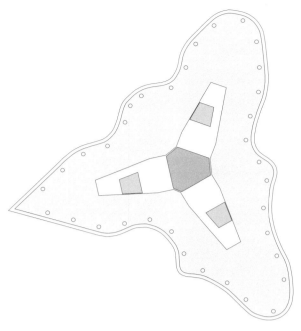

Plan showing open-plan office version

"Better to trigger a discussion than drown in the silence of mediocrity." Hadi Teherani

02.4

THE ECSTASY OF SPACE IN THE WATER
LIGHTHOUSE HAMBURG

OFFICES/RETAIL/HOTEL
HAMBURG
GROSS FLOOR AREA 104,000 SQ M
PLANNING FEB 2002

THE ECSTASY OF SPACE IN THE WATER

A dormant, complacent beauty one hundred years ago, the glowing image of the Hanseatic city of Hamburg is endangered today by a lack of dynamics and a mood of fundamental change. According to the new Hamburg Senate: "Hamburg must have the ambition to become a city of two million, and to link this with the will to occupy national and international top positions in science, culture and architecture." The Senate has grand aspirations for the city and considers it a challenge to strive for comparison with such international metropolises as Barcelona, Toronto, and Sydney. In fact, this claim is hardly far-fetched: in Europe, only central London is economically stronger than Hamburg. Among the great visions to unite the city are: the expansion of the Hafen-City and the business area at the harbor; the enlargement of the inner city on the Elbe side by an area of 100 hectares of land and 50 hectares of water; and the gradual integration of the entire region with branched-off waterways in the south of the city. The waterside, rising from a swamp to an urban skyline, is the greatest emotional amplifier of a specific Hamburg feeling, an ecstasy of space that is captured time and again on film, but whose visionary character is still missing in architectural form as a companion to the Köhlbrand Bridge. The "Flying Dutchman," the fastest train in the world, linked Hamburg with the capital as early as 1932. Designed in the shape of a drop of water, the project complements the streamlined shape of the famous express train locomotive. With the 288-meter-high lighthouse—unique in its dimensions in all of Europe, and complete with a concert hall set in the Elbe River—Hamburg would testify to a city-planning claim which, in contrast to the dictated creative wasteland of Berlin, has long since been realized in numerous spectacular elements of the city. The skyscrapers, necessary for an ecological city density even after "9/11," make the charm and the risk of the city more visible than any other form of construction. Their zooming between the larger perspective (toward the North Sea) and minute detail, between world standards and individual responsibility, is essential.

"Today, Hamburg does not possess a single landmark that does justice to its modernity, élan vital and international significance."

Jens Bothe

Hamburg: high points

200 m

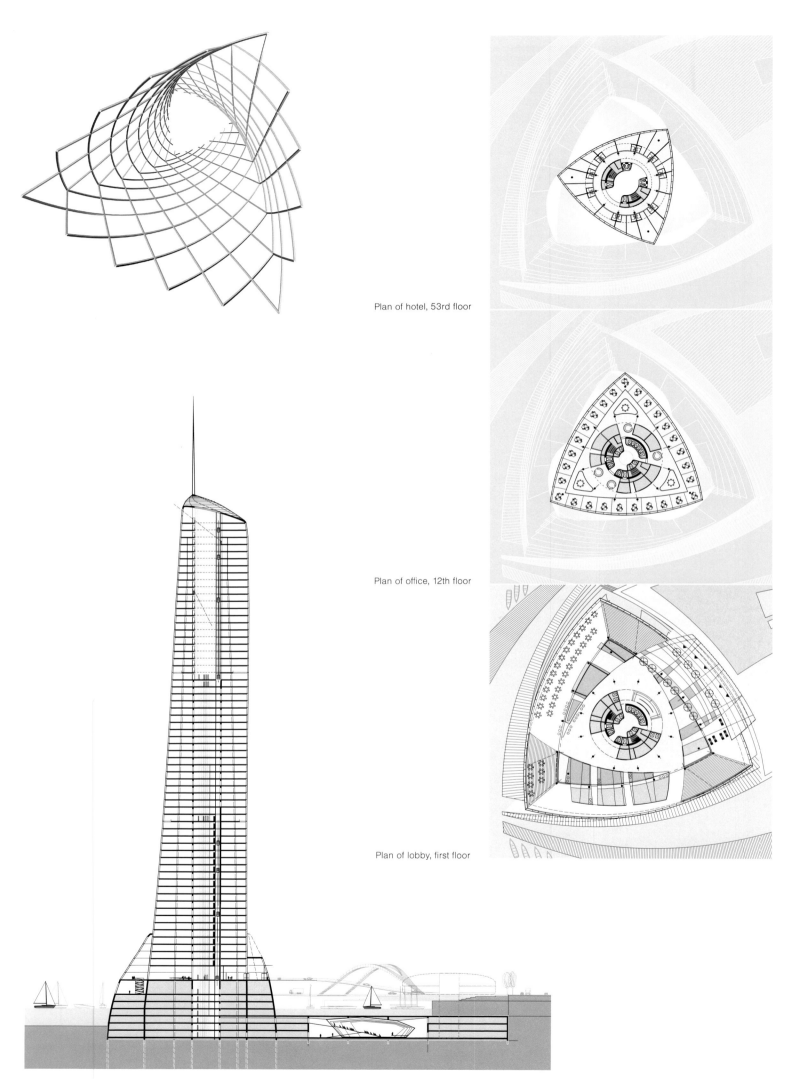

Plan of hotel, 53rd floor

Plan of office, 12th floor

Plan of lobby, first floor

Vertical section

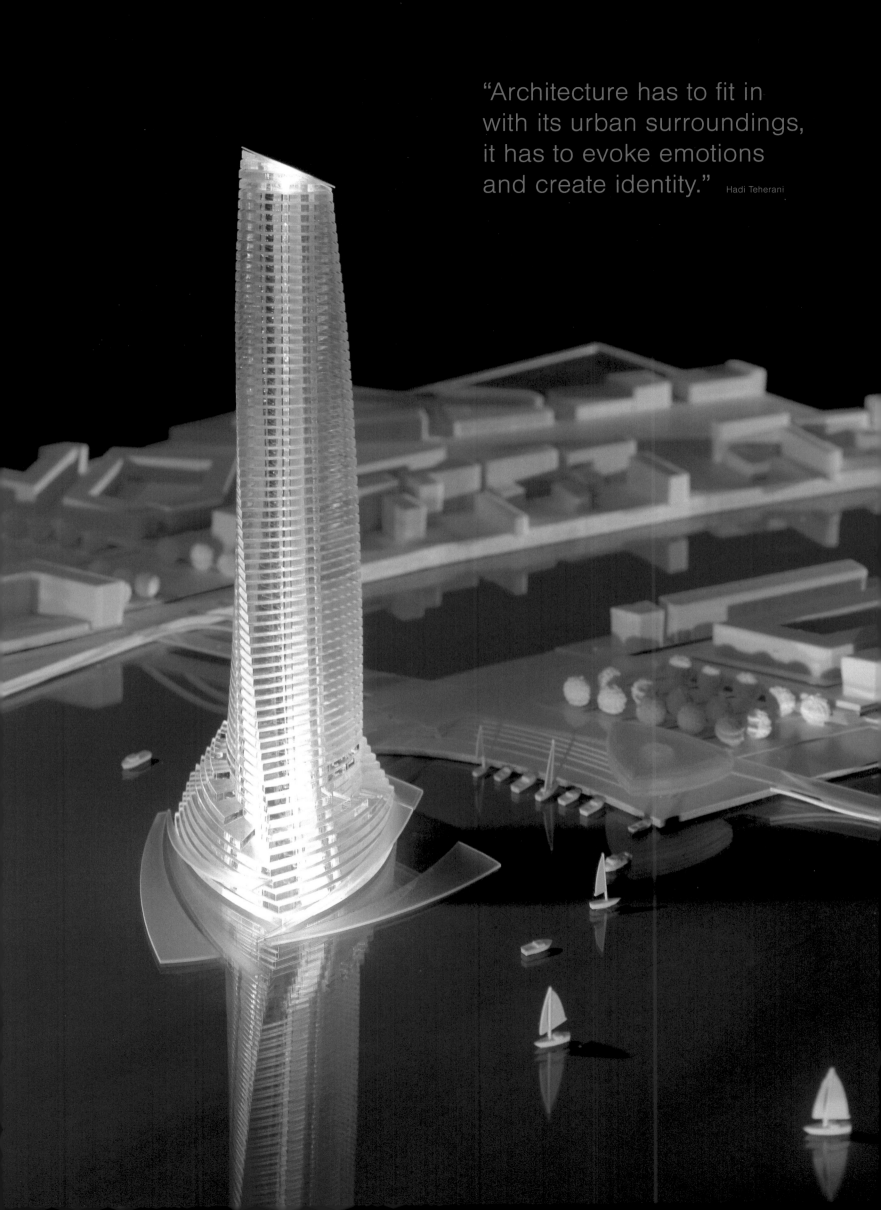

"Architecture has to fit in with its urban surroundings, it has to evoke emotions and create identity." Hadi Teherani

"The task is not to recreate 'history', but to tell a new, fascinating story with contemporary means." Hadi Teherani

Lighthouse Hamburg

02.5

DANCING TOWERS
HIGHRISE REEPERBAHN 1

OFFICES/HOTEL
HAMBURG
GROSS FLOOR AREA 35,000 SQ M
PLANNING JUNE 2003
COMPETITION 2003, 1ST PRICE

DANCING TOWERS

"Reeperbahn" is a German word dating back to the era of large ships under sail, referring to the long corridors along which "Reepe," the German word for the ropes and cordage used on sailboats, were laid out and stretched. Since 1626, they were located in this 400-meter-long area between the streets now named Reeperbahn, Hamburger Berg, Simon-von-Utrecht-Straße, and Kleine Seilerstraße—across from Spielbudenplatz at the foot of the new symbolic landmark that occupies the line where the inner city and the historically grown suburb of St Pauli meet. Ever since ships stopped unloading their holds directly at the landing bridges as they did 150 years ago, Hamburg's poorest district has been changing from a red light district into a residential and business district. Today, the Reeperbahn is no longer a strip frequented only by streetwalkers, bar keepers, and clubbers, as well as being remembered for the Beatles gig at the Star-Club in 1962; it is also home to countless computer and Internet firms, among others AOL's German and European headquarters. The conversion planned for the Spielbudenplatz (1795), where junk shops, buskers, market stalls, animal tamers, and artistes of all kinds provided thrills and entertainment at the city gates in the nineteenth century, will finally banish the *tristesse* that is the legacy of the 1950s and 1960s. Occupying the site of the legendary Mojo-Club, the new angled high-rises herald the prelude to this change, the urban and architectural renewal of this area, still today Hamburg's notoriously "crooked" district. Amidst the Hanseatic elegance, on the one hand, and the ordinariness of the surroundings on the other, the structure seems like a stone of contention in glass, ensuring that the entertainment district will retain a unique character. Architecturally, too, the goal is to prevent the red light district from deteriorating into a grimy cesspit. Unfortunately, today the idiosyncrasy of an individual building is no longer associated with the specific context that inspired it in the first place. The same idea is therefore already aimlessly underfoot in Frankfurt's rigid banking district.

"Like all human creation, architecture can be sustainable in the long term on a holistic basis." Kai Richter

Section of office area

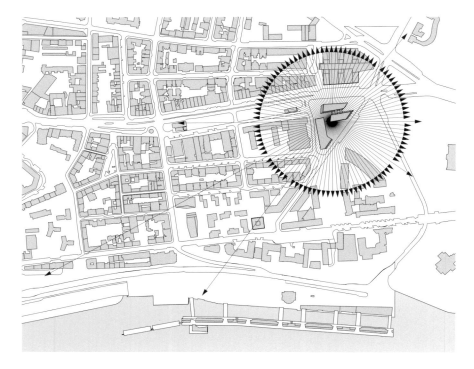

Visual axes

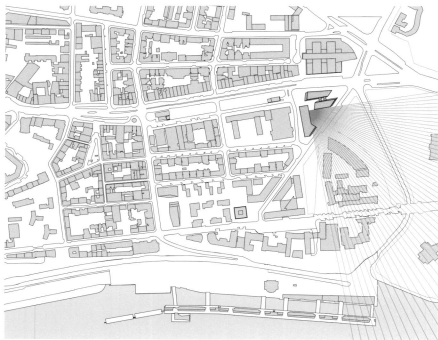

Relationship to green areas

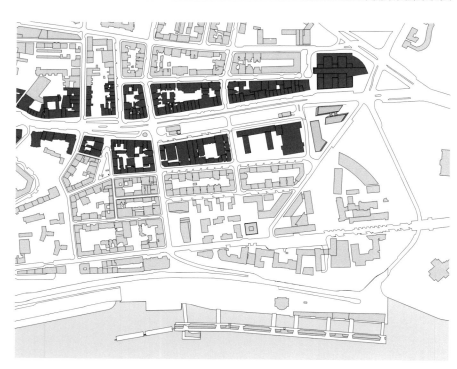

Spatial boundaries

Plan of first floor

5 m

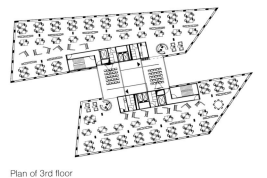

Plan of 3rd floor

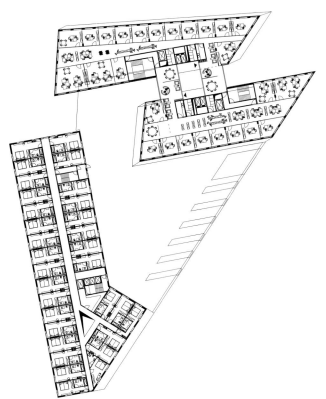

Plan of hotel, 8th floor, office, 7th floor

Highrise Reeperbahn 1

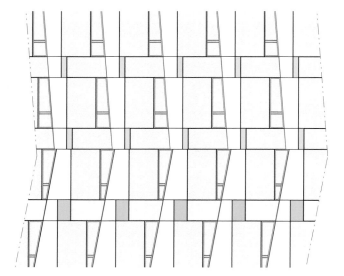

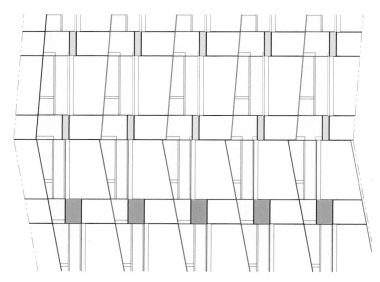

Facade detail of office block, north/west

Facade detail of office block, south/east

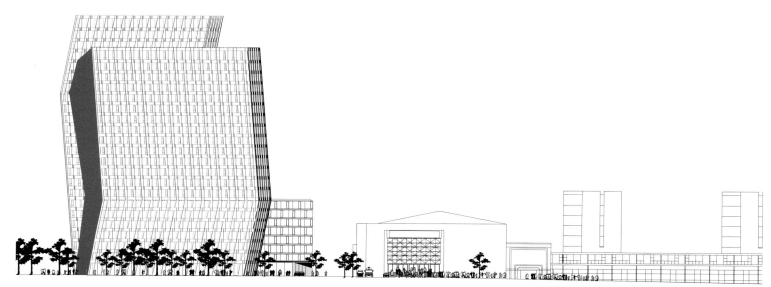

North elevation, Reeperbahn

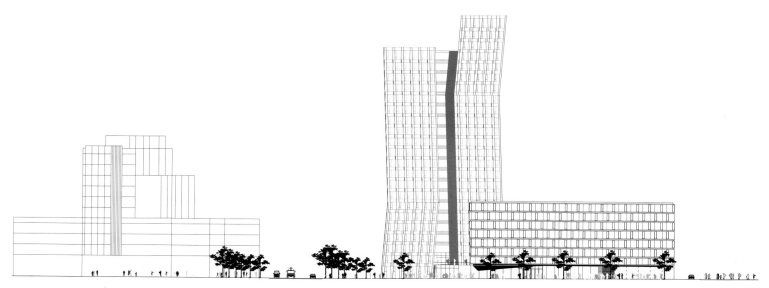

West elevation, Spielbudenplatz

Caught in a Babylonian confusion between traditionalists and proponents of the age of Retro-Pop, the Gen- and the Cyber-generation in architecture and urban design, architecture is not only subscribing to the multiplicity of anything goes, but has also largely lost its attractiveness. "Retro-design wherever you look and everywhere the yearning for times when walls were massive and hitting the gas still helped… One either escapes helter-skelter into nostalgic *décor*, wallows in sensitive eco-aesthetics—or accepts the deliberate confusion and takes the insanity of illusory truths and fiction to the extreme."[1] The beauty of a building is based on logic and efficiency, not on *décor* and *Zeitgeist*. Streamlined forms in architecture not only optically reduce large forms; they also increase their ecological and structural efficiency. These relationships have been evident in the railcars for over seven decades—coinciding with the invention of the term "science fiction" in 1929. Examples are the "railplane"[2] car, which William B. Stout designed for Pullman in 1932 or the "Flying Hamburg," developed in 1931 and used on the Hamburg to Berlin route two years later. Contemporary automobiles of the time were the "Dymaxion Car" by Buckminster Fuller from 1933, followed one year later by Chrysler's "Airflow" and Volkswagen's "Beetle." The legendary Citroen DS 19 came only twenty years later.

STREAMLINED FORM

Even in the early 1920s, calculations had already demonstrated definite energy savings through streamlined bodywork. As the example of Walter Gropius's attempts at automobile design demonstrates, architects had great trouble making the leap from the structural, quasi-analytical load-bearing structures to the elemental-additive design concepts that were derived from them. In 1930, Gropius designed two different versions of an Adler limousine. Differing only in length, the aesthetic of the International Style based on an orthogonal spatial economy already appeared as an outdated ideal of form in these models. The conditions for creating a harmony between external form and the logic of technical functions, which Gropius had specifically identified as a premise for his design, had become more complex prior to the knowledge of aerodynamic efficiency than the Bauhaus master was willing to acknowledge. "If one looks at bodywork, what strikes the eye is its determinedly right-angled character with an additive allocation of engine block and interior—a formal repertoire, in other words, that is taken right out of the pages of a preliminary Bauhaus course. And this was very much the intention; during a lecture in 1933, Gropius stressed that automobile and house were subject to 'the

same laws of form' as all three-dimensional objects. One could say that his Adler limousine, albeit a luxury product, is an apartment for the existential minimum. In this, however, Gropius adhered to an elemental aesthetic of architecture instead of a technical logic of function, contrary to his ambition."[3]

In the wake of a cult of objectivity and constructivism, the beginning of the 1930s saw a return to the body, "a body that appears sleek and fit in the case of a human body and fast and efficient in the case of machines. What is noticeable is the fascination at that time with the sleekness of bodies, with the union of all individual elements into the fluid continuum of integrated large forms. This begs the question whether this design mode does not at the same time generate specific images of socialization."[4] Circa 1930, Le Corbusier, unlike Gropius, made the transition from orthogonal systems to plastic-dynamic bodies. He had designed a car in 1928, published only in 1935 as "voiture maximum," which was based on a completely different approach to Gropius's historic-classical automobile design and which may have inspired the prototype for the Citroën 2CV developed in 1939, although no link has been proven to this day. In his book *Aircraft*[5] published in 1935, Le Corbusier employed images of airplane details to illustrate that his interest lay in a smooth and irresistible body, in the expressive quality of the streamlined form as an aesthetic principle. Parabolic arches, as for the Palace of the Soviet in Moscow (1931) and freely swinging large bodies as for Plan Obus in Algiers (1931), coincided with Le Corbusier's many studies of nudes in his "carnets." One can even discover traces of an analogy with the proportional analysis of a portrait of a woman on the lower level of the Villa Savoye in his anthropomorphisms in ground plans. The airplane not only served as a tangible model for a new plasticity in architecture, it also opened up the possibility of controlling architectural events within the larger urban planning context from the air.

In contrast to renewed efforts on the part of the railways, electric cars and experimental vehicles, aside form a few unviable exceptions, are the only determined examples today of drawing upon the knowledge gained on aerodynamics—and this despite the ubiquitous complaints about gasoline prices. Since the 1980s, architecture and urban design has focused on the material and facade of the building, on isolated fragments of the urban space. Are these the only answers to global issues and changes? Could a leap in scale in both thought and planning not lead to new strategies that help to overcome the architectural as well as the urban fragmentation? Does not the greatest appeal of shopping centers amidst green meadows lie in the fact that the individual can escape the age of the mass-culture and dissolution in the anonymity of the city, in an imaginary world in which reality can no longer be experienced? As in nineteenth-century panoramas, in which the exploding city of the industrial revolution became an island of retreat, worlds closed within themselves in a public space that was expanding in all directions, the seductive appeal of "imagineering" and "theming" in the shopping worlds in front of the city obviously lies in their synthetic screens and boundaries—albeit with the considerable downside of having to leave the city with all its conveniences and complexity behind.

SCIENCE IN FICTION

Flying saucers and UFOs became an everyday topic in the 1950s after the US pilot Kenneth Arnold had claimed on October 27, 1947, of having observed nine such unknown flying objects above Washington. Four months later, RCA records released a fitting hit song: "You better pray to the Lord when you see those flying saucers / It may be the coming of judgment day." In the time that followed, 600 similar observations were registered on average per year, and the US Air Force had an annual budget of 60,000 dollars for reconnaissance. Now the UFO seems to have finally landed: on the tracks for regional and long-distance trains right in the center of Dortmund. Stuttgart would be only too happy to be able to realize a similarly effective railway station, in terms of both urban planning and transportation logistics, without having to spend 2.5 billion euro for a subterranean track, that is, for a reduction in travel time of five minutes.[6] Since 1976, Hanover has been struggling to make its retail strip beneath the railway station, which links several urban districts, more functional—all to no avail. The excitement in Dortmund was nevertheless great, amidst romantic or neutral but always supposedly identity-forming buildings in stone. The unfamiliar architectural approach has a polarizing effect and it is through this that a visionary concept becomes noticeable in the first place. The same is true for the model of a pyramid-shaped apartment tower, accommodating parking garages, a subway station, and a fitness center in its belly, which was featured as an argument in the fight against urban sprawl at the architecture biennial in Venice in 2000. In architecture today there is hardly anything that talks and acts in a contemporary voice more current than the Neo-Wilhelminian retro-design in Berlin.

According to a *Newsweek* survey from 1996, a staggering number of 48 percent of Americans believed in UFOs and 40 percent believed in supernatural forces. Twenty years earlier, the citizens of Lake City (Pennsylvania/USA) built a landing stage for alien space ships in all sincerity—on the occasion of the bicentennial celebrations of the United States. Not to mention the UFO craze in advertising and the media during the 1950s, an era when even the Michelin man was seen as an extraterrestrial space traveller, magazine covers as well as paper plates were graced with images of cigar-shaped rockets and space ships, and when not a few roof tops sent a message of "Welcome Flying Saucers" in giant letters into the sky. Since the railway station project in Dortmund, every distinctive large form that has not been divided into fragments and goes beyond the convention of building runs the risk of being seen as a UFO. This applies equally to Jean Nouvel's Culture and Conference Center in Lucerne, whose deeply cantilevered roof "seems to float above the city like a space ship out of 'Independence Day',"[7] as to Herzog & de Meuron's new football stadium in Munich. "Even while the visitor approaches the amorphous-gigantic object, beyond all sense of scale, via the 'streamlines' of the enormous landscape bridge, even before he (as in the film 'Encounters of the Third Kind') disappears in the blazing light opening of the UFO hovering above the ground, he becomes part of a unique experience."[8] Even Zaha Hadid's polymorphous Science Center in Wolfsburg fluctuates symbolically between "ice floe" and "space ship."[9] And naturally the post-Piranesian labyrinth of consumption, which Daniel Libeskind is planning above the highway near Berne, is also interpreted as a "space ship." Dortmund, where the collaborating inner city is to be improved through a triumphal procession of architectural variety in the sense of machines of illusion unfit for flying such as the CentrO Oberhausen or Warner Brother's Movie World in Los Angeles, is the only place where talk of the future has died down.[10] There, beyond the architectural *Gesamtkunstwerk*, leisure architecture is reduced to the built experiential part of a show, a common phenomenon on the periphery without any impact on the regional identity: "Pure prosit modernism"[11] as *Spiegel* magazine noted in reference to Stuttgart. If, in the distant future, the high-speed Metrorapid train should start in Dortmund, a stylistic collision between vehicular and urban architecture would be unavoidable.

In the face of the competition on the periphery, the inner city needs new attractive sites where society can be active. The advantages of urban theme parks on the periphery are thus worthwhile re-importing into the city center.[12] "Urban development since the end of World War II has shown that trade is not dependent on the city, but city is very much [dependent] on trade. (…) From halls to arcades to department store, be it a mall or a bazaar, these forms can today all claim to being building blocks of urbanity to equal measure."[13]

EXCLUSIVITY

The competition between cities and regions, which is spreading throughout Europe, is vying above all for attention given to people, themes, buildings, and, of course, products. Attention is the dominant currency at the dawn of the twenty-first century and exclusive forms are at the center of interest in architecture. The significance of external appearance and internal organization in architecture makes it easier to identify the location and use of a building. "A broad public is willing today to grant far-reaching powers to the designers of projects, which endow [place] with meaning."[14] In the competition for visitors and tourists, a new Europe of competing cities and regions is emerging. "Attention is the most irresistible of all drugs. Cashing in on it beats all other sources of income. This is why glory outstrips power and why wealth pales when compared to prominence."[15] In all this, the image of the UFO becomes a cipher, which—more than any other spatial image—indicates artificial urban focal points in such a memorable fashion as both distinctive and visionary. A superordinate architectural identity can only evolve through a formal smoothing out of complex programs and contents. Jean Nouvel's work is a case in point: the exclusive object-like quality of the Culture and Conference Center in Lucerne resulting from the massive roof; the bodywork for the opera house in Tokyo; the barred Kaaba of the cultural center at St. Herblain. "All of theses concepts explore an exclusive theme of veiling or, rather, sectioning, in which heterogeneous spatial forms are combined into an identity-giving large form through the literal corset."[16] The only time Nouvel decided to forego this meta-motif was in the competition for Dortmund's railway station—and he failed. In the mid-1970s and right up to the current "Grands Projets," the Centre Pompidou in Paris was a prominent trigger for the architectural object as a modern vehicle of meaning, when it became a tourist sensation despite its unusual presentation and provocative scale in the guise of a "culture refinery." Even then, this museum made use of design tools that can be linked to the seduction strategies employed in shopping centers. Why should architecture wish to conceal its social context? Beginning with the spark that was triggered by the Centre Pompidou, museums have long since changed from sites of collections and preservation to "experiential spaces," sites of encounter and entertainment—without any noticeable loss in meaning.

"It is naïve to believe that popular culture is merely entertainment. The public does want to be educated—just not in the sense of the old culture of erudite education."[17]

SUPERCONDUCTORS

In the chaos of rampantly expanding cities, a leap in scale, a super sign is the only means of introducing order. The architect cannot change the urban planning conditions; all that he has at his disposal is provocation or the symbolism of a meta-language, provided it is appropriate for a central function. The "built superconductor" (Rem Koolhaas) is a historically proven trick: all one has to do is to cite Hans Poelzig as a source of the large form or, going further into the past, the prophet of the age of the masses, Alexis de Tocqueville, who wrote on democracy in America in 1840: "In democratic nations, individuals are very weak; conversely, the state that represents them all and holds them in its hands, is very strong. Nowhere do citizens appear smaller than among a democratic people. Nowhere does the nation itself appear greater and does the mind more easily cast it in a violent image. In democratic societies, the imagination of people shrivels when they think of themselves; it expands immeasurably, when they think of the state. The result is that the same people, who live humbly cheek by jowl in small apartments, strive for the huge scale when public monuments are concerned. (…) Thus democracy not only spurs people on to create a multitude of trivial works; it also spurs them on to erect a small number of very large buildings."[18] Contrary to the naive assumption that a society, which strives for equality, must become ossified by uniformity, it seems to have a limitless need for difference so that the equality may not appear as an obvious suppression of individuality and freedom. The unexpected, according to Alexis de Tocqueville, as an aesthetic value per se.

For Hans Poelzig, the nonconformist and sculptural architect of the modern, who could be somewhat melodramatic at times, building always remained the emotional achievement of an artist with three-dimensional imagination. Poelzig rejected the purism of the radical modern and insisted on his artistic freedom. The conversion of the former Schumann circus into the Große Schauspielhaus for three thousand or even five thousand was an intentional signal, a *Gesamtkunstwerk* for the mass age. Poelzig did not take with keeping large volumes smaller; he wanted them large. And every time he chose undivided, uniformly shaped fabrics covered in the identical skin. It was a modern that did not want to reveal everything at once. It showed different faces and reacted differently to differing situations. The architect was entirely indifferent to the architectural viewpoints of opposing parties. In this respect, the fear of the large form is unfounded. In Germany there is simply a lack of courage for it. The Roman people, Cicero said in his speech "Pro Murena," despise private luxury but love public expressions of pomp. The opposite is true for Germans: they love private comfort and disdain public representation. Christina Weisse, the Federal Minister of Culture, rightly bemoans, "how uncreative and non-visionary this society has become." The writer Peter Schneider argues in a similar fashion: "Germany, it would seem, has become a corporation for the purpose of avoiding risk and pain. Life here is viewed as an event for the abolition of surprises and the unforesee-able."[19] The consequence: ossification, discouragement, and despon-dency, a "cold" culture according to a category defined by Claude Lévi-Strauss. "'Hot' societies act in exactly the opposite way: they embrace what is new, find their equilibrium in constant change, do not look back upon imaginary origins, but forward to (as yet) undiscovered visions; they do not seek a lasting Here and Now, but its constant mobilization and transgression."[20] In 1927, Poelzig planned a perfectly circular spa palace for Berlin, with a diameter of at least 160 meters. And one year later he built the administration building for IG Farben with a total length of 250 meters. Luigi Snozzi's urban edge in Maastricht, "agreeably presumptu-ous" in the words of the Frankfurter Rundschau, measures 300 meters, while the new ferry terminal in Yokohama by Foreign Office Architects is 420 meters long. In Barcelona, Herzog & de Meuron's contribution for the World Culture Forum 2004 floats as a triangle with 160-meter-long sides above an Arabian bazaar and a wedding chapel. Large forms convey grandeur and communicate a political message. Scale alone is not criti-cal; what matters is the quality of the architectural and organisational translation. How much longer will innovative counter movements con-tinue to fail because of depressive urban design that reveals its self-pity in the images of yesterday?

Klaus-Dieter Weiss

Notes

1   Niklas Maak: Fremder in der Nacht. Technik, Design und Architektur verwandeln das Reale in Fiktion, *Süddeutsche Zeitung* September 25/26th, 1999, p. 17

2   Claude Lichtenstein, Franz Engler (eds): *Stromlinienform*, Zurich/Baden 1993, p. 21

3   Christoph Asendorf: *Super Constellation – Flugzeug und Raumrevolution. Die Wirkung der Luftfahrt auf Kunst und Kultur der Moderne*, Vienna/New York 1997, p. 84

4   Christoph Asendorf: *Super Constellation – Flugzeug und Raumrevolution. Die Wirkung der Luftfahrt auf Kunst und Kultur der Moderne*, Vienna/New York 1997, p. 91

5   Le Corbusier: *Aircraft. »L'avion accuse…«* (London/New York 1935), New York 1988

6   Walter Hönscheidt: Fünf Milliarden Mark für fünf Minuten Zeitgewinn, *Frankfurter Allgemeine Zeitung*, 20.6.2000, p. 7

7   Niklas Maak, *Frankfurter Allgemeine Zeitung* 5.1. 2002, p. 41

8   *Baumeister* 1/2002, p. 7

9   *BauNetz*-Meldung 25.3.2002

10   *Baumeister* 12/2001, p. 10

11   *Der Spiegel* 48/1996, pp. 194 ff.

12   Dieter Hoffmann-Axthelm: Der Weg zu einer neuen Stadt, *Arch+* 114–115, December 1992, pp. 114–116

13   Michael Mönninger: Tauschen und konsumieren, in: Romana Schneider, Winfried Nerdinger, Wilfried Wang (eds): *Architektur im 20. Jahrhundert. Deutschland*, Munich 2000, p. 201

14   André Bideau: Ereignis, Atmosphäre, Architektur, *Werk, Bauen + Wohnen* 6/2000, p. 26

15   Georg Franck: *Ökonomie der Aufmerksamkeit*, Munich 1998, p. 10

16   André Bideau: Ereignis, Atmosphäre, Architektur, *Werk, Bauen + Wohnen* 6/2000, p. 28

17   Georg Franck: *Ökonomie der Aufmerksamkeit*, Munich 1998, p. 169

18   Alexis de Tocqueville: *Über die Demokratie in Amerika*, vol.2 (1840), Zurich 1987, pp. 80/81

19   Peter Schneider: Der deutsche Gulliver, *Der Spiegel* 16.9.2002 (38/2002), p. 193

20   Hartmut Böhme: Über Geschwindigkeit und Wiederholung im Cyberspace: das Alte im Neuen, in: Götz-Lothar Darsow (ed.): *Metamorphosen des Gedächtnisses*, Stuttgart/Bad Cannstadt 1999, p. 23–43

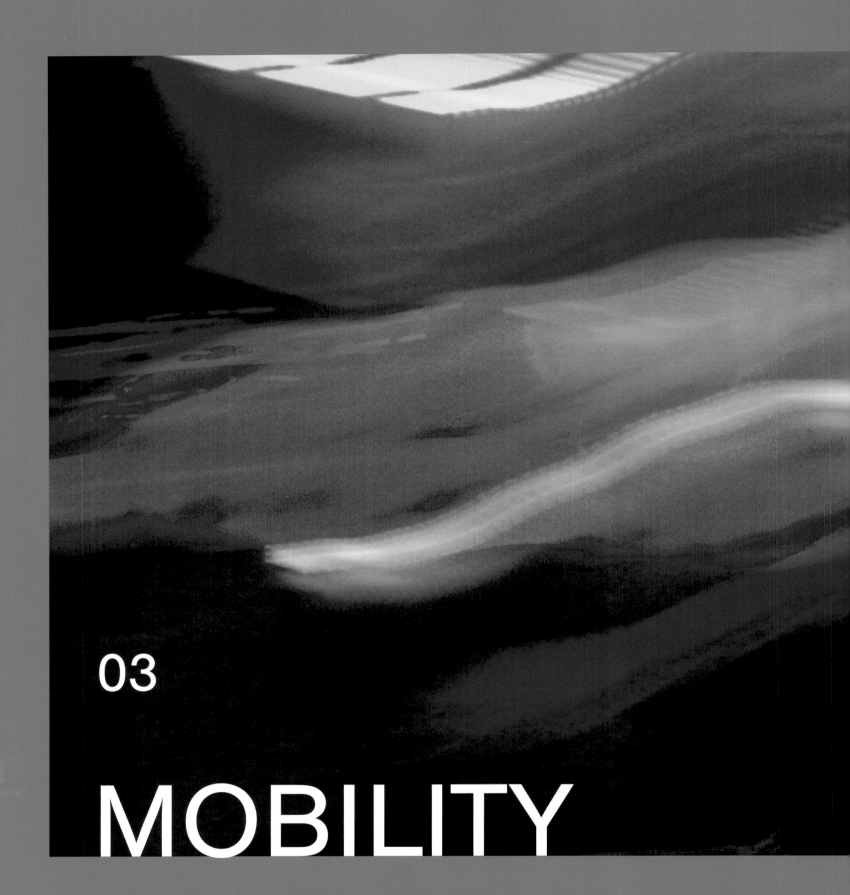

03

MOBILITY

The last time the finiteness of resources entered the public discourse was during the oil crises of the 1970s. Then, atomic power and research on fusion reactors were believed to be the gleam of hope on the horizon. Free power for everyone in unlimited quantities, extracted from the hydrogen of the world's oceans, was considered a scientifically sound vision of the future. In the meantime, and for good reason, many power plants have been shut down, and in some of the worst ones, much oil has been burned. But no realistic alternative to fossil fuels has been found yet. All of the other apocalyptic scenarios of humanity—collision with an asteroid or Al-Qaeda, climatic catastrophe or war—are "maybes." But the fact that our fossil energy resources are limited is inescapable—even though 65 percent of all humans on this planet have never used a telephone, let alone a car. "Automobilization" has led to an urban design that overflows even further into the cities' surrounding environs, and which are politically compelled through benefits for reducing population density and payments for building new one-family houses. Everyday destinations like schools, workplaces, shops, swimming pools and cinemas are so distant from each other that not even the city works without a car. Yet, the systemic question of what transportation infrastructure makes sense has never been posed. The decisive flaw in the cloth of urban networking has resulted from countless minor missteps, as if a matter of course. By now this process appears to be irreversible. Anyone without a car to spend ten years of his life in (like the average American) has to take the bus. We must challenge this forced mobility and destabilize the mystique of the car as freedom gained. The first phase of the development of mobility, lasting until 1968, was characterized by the car taking over the railroad as the most important means of travel. In the second phase, lasting until 1990, the airplane continued to gain importance—bus traffic decreased, the share of car traffic stagnated. In the third phase, since 1990, even the car is losing its share to the airplane. Distant destinations—which cannot be reached with terrestrially bound means of transport—are increasingly popular. In 2001, 140 million passengers boarded airplanes in Germany—despite September 11. The exotic, the other, the novel is becoming even more attractive—with all of its attendant positive social consequences, but also its negative ecological costs, as well. In today's society, there has been a value shift away from labor, toward leisure. As the physical strains decrease, the mental strains increase. Against the backdrop of automation, alienation, isolation, the loss of authenticity and inadequate potential for challenges, satisfaction with the workplace and with one's place of residence diminish. Mobility turns out to be not only a function of cultural curiosity, but also a means of escape. The multi-option society opens up constantly shifting worlds of consumption and interests, which are linked to new demands for mobility. Traveling—a cultural practice that liberates new designs of meaning—is emerging as the dominant leisure activity and influences the traveler's life-world. In the course of the "touristification" of life-worlds, the contents of these worlds are becoming increasingly interchangeable. Elements of the entertainment and adventure culture can be installed everywhere artificially, all the way to the veritable desert fort of the United Arab Emirates at the EXPO 2000 in Hanover—with real desert sand delivered by jet.

If mobility inevitably must be defined as a necessity—the capability and the need for living beings to change their location in order to acquire the resources of life, not just food, but also curiosity—then the first chance of organizing mobility intelligently, and in an ecologically justifiable manner, can be found in the efficiency of intermodal traffic nodes and networked transport systems. A second potential is found in the urbanized networking and overlapping of "elective places," "obligatory places" and "shelters," all the way to the generation of multifunctional transit points. The third potential lies in the mass-less movement, which was first realized on October 10, 1969—the mobilization of information into computer networks. Exploiting these potentials could help realize the slogan to "double your time," so that even train stations in Madrid, Vienna, Frankfurt and Dortmund could become more than just train stations.

03.1

HYBRID TRAFFIC JUNCTION
TRAIN STATION FRANKFURT
AIRPORT

LONG-DISTANCE TRAIN STATION
FRANKFURT/MAIN
GROSS FLOOR AREA 38,155 SQ M
BUILT NOV 1996–MAY 1999
COMPETITION 1996, 2ND PLACE;
RENAULT TRAFFIC DESIGN AWARD 2003

HYBRID TRAFFIC JUNCTION

With its nine million passengers, this "train station" is atypical in many ways, not only because of its glass facades and air locks. First of all, rail transport often approaches airports underground, which only reinforces the trend to build megaports like confusing rabbit warrens. Secondly, the 690-meter-long pivot and hub for networking national rail and air traffic takes advantage of its above-ground location to attain a rare significance in rail station construction—even despite its competition with a number of other local systems of transport including, not only the airport, but the busiest interchange of the German Autobahn, under which the rails branch off into a tunnel system. This "surfboard" in the breakers of automotive traffic—from which airplanes could take off except for the six-story office and hotel superstructure—does without the classic station quarter and functions as a foundation for a variety of uses in the upper stories. Thus, those phenomena accompanying train station activity are eliminated, which defenders of the traditional train station hold to be indispensable in the sense of urbanity: "red-light districts, accommodations of all kinds and colors, a robust restaurant sector, marginal groups, the socially disadvantageous, the demimonde, deviant behavior, isolation..." (Dieter Hoffmann-Axthelm). The station at the "Intermodal Traffic Port Frankfurt" concentrates, both functionally and formally, on its transport system, particularly on the ecological objective of avoiding uneconomical short domestic flights (20,000 flights per year), in order to make possible another 50 percent expansion of capacity to up to 80 million passengers yearly. For rail passengers to and from Stuttgart, Cologne and Düsseldorf, the connection guaranteed a rapid transfer to connecting flights, including luggage in just 45 minutes.

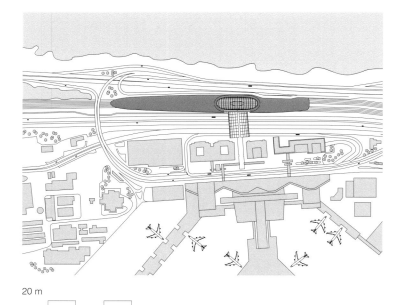

20 m

Train Station, Frankfurt Airport

SURFBOARD

The evolution that began in Dayton/Ohio in 1904 at a country road section between meadows has culminated in environments today that differ so drastically as to be almost unrecognizable. The scale of Frankfurt airport is almost comparable to the size of Frankfurt's downtown. Given the higher degree of complexity and a more rapid transformation by comparison to the latter, however, the identity-shaping grand form, the dream of creating a stage for aviation in heroic halls and the architectural link to the region come close to being utopian. Travelling across continents from Frankfurt to Shanghai, passengers encounter terminals designed by the same hand, instead of memorable, distinctive architectural visions. As with hospitals and railway stations, the topic "Gateway to the World" seems to defy architecture. The task appears to be so confusing in nature, safe only in the hands of a few experts, that the prevailing opinion among all participants is that an organizational task of such complexity must simply do without architecture. "We aren't builders of cosy little homes. Shanghai airport might just as well lie outside of Stuttgart, as far as I'm concerned. What matters is that we decrease building costs without detracting from the architecture."[1] Counter arguments by Eero Saarinen, Norman Foster, Renzo Piano, Kisho Kurokawa, Rafael Moneo or Santiago Calatrava go unheard in Frankfurt. Over the course of three, and half decades, the cleverly devised, yet aesthetically uninspired mega projects, which could still "embody" Frankfurt's megaport despite its modular structure, have culminated in a sprawling labyrinth of shells with a total building length of 4.5 kilometers, all cast from a single mould. "A mega monster, with giant jets clinging to its claws, in which passengers are transported through a maze of bridges, footbridges, and claustrophobic elevator cabins or groping their way through parking caves in whose dark jaws a car can only be located with the help of the parking ticket, thus securing the blessed escape via downward spiralling tubes. Stereotypical building fabrics and utilitarian containers fill the gaps between multi-story traffic corridors, orientation grids and smaller access networks, and form deep gorges from whose crevices indefinable odors and sounds emanate. The airport as a symbol of nearly limitless access to distant locations is thus divorced from the immediate cultural and regional context, achieving complete detachment from the territory that surrounds it."[2]

Despite its multifunctional character—between railway station and bank, mall and multiplex, casino and chapel—intended to serve as an "alternate city," this airport by no means fulfills the function of the medieval market place. It is a daily focal point only for the tireless population of jetsetters; but what it lacks, above all, is architectural interest and focus with regard to the urban model. Instead, travellers are ruled by a regime of pictograms. Are airports the blind spots of architecture?

For a brief moment in the history of German airports, the reality of the confusing and unsightly conglomeration of buildings seemed to be lifted off its hinges. Not because of Frankfurt's "Gateway to the World," but, of all things, because of its anchored Intercity terminal. Unlike the airport railway terminals in Munich or Cologne-Wahn, this terminal is not a subterranean "fox-den," but a 700-meter-long structure boldly inserted between the four ribbons of highway on the northern edge of the airfield and linked to the nomadic territory, a nondescript area devoid of architecture beyond the city walls of the airport linked via an ellipsoid, glass pedestrian tunnel that leads directly to Terminal I. The 80-meter-wide and 200-meter-long connecting structure created by the competition winner (architects: Braun & Schlockermann and Köhler/Menzel + Moosbrugger) is designed to ensure a comfortable check-in process. In future, luggage will no longer be required for flight transfers. "Although other competition participants had also envisioned rail travel arrivals and departures on the ground floor, check-in and flight transfers on the first floor, BRT covered the entire tracks with a bomb-proof, concrete 'ironing board,' on top of which buildings of up to nine storeys high can provide earthquake-proof accommodation for all auxiliary uses."[3] The client was convinced, but decided to open the so-called Airrail-Center for development above the relay function and base plate: judging from the plans known thus far, the center is unlikely to fulfil the aesthetic promise of the overall design proposed by BRT. Despite this "horizontal site fence"—the distinctive 34,000-square-meter-large and, counting the hollow spaces, 5-meter-thick foundation platform above the traffic—Frankfurt airport remains true to its long practice of doing without form, image, and character. Foregoing the added value of architectural character in the case of this zeppelin lit from within is simply beyond comprehension given a construction cost of more than 600 million Euro and a construction period of over three years. The reality above the railway station will unfortunately fall far short of the client's hope: "It will be the most distinctive building and the new architectural symbol of Frankfurt airport." At the sister buildings at Frankfurt's airport, the architecture freaks, which had been anticipated for the Airrail-Center, have failed to show thus far. Even IVG Immobilien AG, a client investor, was compelled to concede: "In the past years, this city has experienced rapid, at times even rampant, growth. It seems more like a

Train Station, Frankfurt Airport

"When the train pulls into the station, the passengers are supposed to feel as if they are coming to rest beneath a jumbo jet. Telescope-like columns create the impression that the building really could take off."

Hadi Teherani

Train Station, Frankfurt Airport

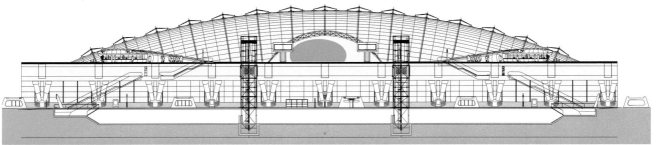

Longitudinal section of station hall, platform

Train Station, Frankfurt Airport

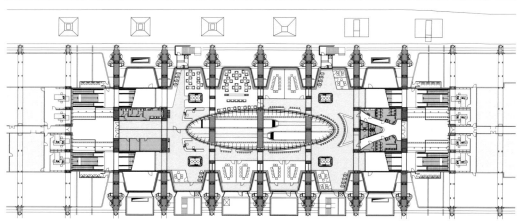

Plan of lounge (structure)

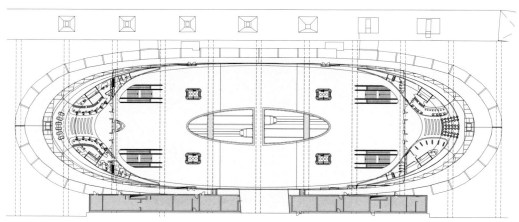

Plan of station hall

Cross section

conglomerate of many, often carelessly designed individual buildings than an architectural organism."[5]

Changing architects took its toll on the client in as much as Helmut W. Joos's planning in Frankfurt failed to architecturally or even functionally incorporate the temporary glass dome integrated into the "surfboard" into the railway terminal above the tracks. The technical problems this triggered with regard to fire protection have, in the meantime, delayed the project to such a degree that the crisis for the hotel operator of the nine-story building, which is decisive for the structure, now threatens the entire project.[6] The French group "Le Méridien," which operates 126 hotels worldwide, had planned to use roughly one third of the gross floor area (185,619 square meters), that is 117,000 square meters rental area for a five-star hotel with 680 rooms, a business center, as well as conference and sports facilities. April 28, 2006 had been agreed upon as the opening date. Their competitor Accor had previously planned to create 850 rooms in the three- and five-star category. According to the latest planning stage, the 660-meter-long and 47-m-high block edge development on the roof of the ICE railway station, on which construction was originally slated to begin in 2000, a 30-meter-high and equally wide atrium dominating the structure was to be surrounded by an additional 73,000 square meters office space, 3,500 square meters for retail and restaurants as well as 943 parking spots on the lower levels—just in time for the soccer World Cup in 2006. Up to 6,000 people, one tenth of the current airport personnel, are to be employed there. A shopping center, which was originally part of the plan, was abandoned in order to avoid unfavorable competition in the region. A medical care center and a 4,000-square meter-large diagnostic center with direct airport link for private patients were also dropped from the plan. Whether the more than 600-meter-long atrium—a distance that corresponds to the "Frankfurter Zeil" in the city—can come alive as an urban element without these magnets that are so important for the overall design, is questionable. In the meantime, the surfboard amidst the breakers of passing traffic seems to transport emptiness rather than content above the rail traffic.

GLASS DOME

The 145-meter-long and 14-meter-wide glass dome with its skin of scales composed of plane rectangular panels above the busy railway terminal, which cost 7.5 million euro, was to be disassembled for the planned expansion and reused elsewhere. Frankfurt Zoo had expressed interest, as did a nearby museum of Celtic history and the city of Dort-

mund. The roughly 40 by 10 meter large elliptical opening, through which daylight floods into the fully glazed railway station which was opened in May of 1999, was to be continued across all levels and eventually become an integrated component of the interior as a full-height atrium. Since the railway corporation assumed rightly that the construction of the upper levels would only be completed some years hence, the glass construction was intended to serve as an architectural building completion and not as a stopgap measure. The corporation had also secured some 5 million Euro from investors as compensation for the disassembly of the dome. When the architects of the Airrail-Center were unable to provide the necessary fire protection between the station and its superstructure without the glass dome, and conversely, the railroad corporation was no longer willing to do without the generous, bright hall in the shape of an airport cockpit for its showcase ICE terminal, an odd architectural compromise solution was found. The dome, which thus far houses a restaurant and the railroad service center, will be truncated by several metres on both sides and equipped with fireproof doors. Restaurant and service center will be moved to the Airrail-Center. And to crown it all, the dome—which no longer fulfills a function as a result of these changes—now divides the verdant boulevard into two parts, creates an entirely nonsensical opening of the streamlined fabric on the exterior, and reduces the gross floor area by as much as 9,000 square meters.[7] This readiness to form a compromise does not do justice to the sweeping line of the bodywork design, realized by BRT and demonstrated for the entire fabric, the first German railway station of distinction equal to modern airport terminals. On the contrary, in losing the public appeal so necessary for its success, the building loses more than it might ultimately gain through clever cost-benefit analyses, no matter how cleverly calculated, that have nothing to do with architecture or through savings in mechanical ventilation. No doubt, Peter Zumthor's thermal baths in Vals or Frank O. Gehry's museum in Bilbao could have been built at lower cost. But they would not have been successful. Or, as W. Joos put it in an interview: "One has to constantly check whether a modification would turn the entire original concept upside down. Then you have to have the courage to tell the client: it's better to drop this plan altogether and begin anew."[8]

INTERMODALITY

In 1998, Lufthansa and the German Railway agreed to link their routes. A faster, more comfortable and environmentally friendly way of travelling thanks to seamless travel between bus, rail, and air requires a

sophisticated level of smooth connections. Comfort and time are uppermost in the passenger's set of priorities. The duration of a combined rail and air trip cannot be noticeably longer than an air-only trip with stopovers and changes between flights. The only viable alternative to flights on short routes is to travel by high-speed train. To this end, the ICE-route Frankfurt airport–Stuttgart central station was created in 2001, followed by the "Airrail-Service" between Frankfurt and Cologne in 2003. The interregional railway station in the "Airrail-Terminal" points the way to the future for "Frankfurt's Intermodal Transportation Port." The seamless luggage logistics at this rail terminal is unique in the world.

Lufthansa passengers checkin their luggage at Cologne train station and only collect it once they have reached the destination airport. Conversely, the boarding pass issued in Los Angeles is also valid for the train from Frankfurt to Stuttgart. As many as 280 Airrail passengers are already using this service on the Cologne–Frankfurt route every day. Düsseldorf will be the next railway station to be linked to Frankfurt airport. Nevertheless, experts maintain that only four to 5 percent of flights at Frankfurt are suitable for alternative travel by train. Given the importance of an integrated transportation system for Europe's economy, the EU is already striving to create intermodal transportation services for cross-border freight traffic. Otherwise, the monomodality of freight transportation on roads will increase the overall traffic volume by 50 percent by the year 2010.

On July 25, 2002, more than three decades after first declaring its intention to construct a high-speed route between Cologne and Frankfurt, the Federal Railway inaugurated one of the largest infrastructure projects in German rail traffic with the new route that cost 6 billion euro. In October 1969, the newly elected SPD chancellor Willy Brandt had identified the project as one of the goals of his government. The 177-kilometer-long mountainous route through Siebengebirge, Westerwald, and Taunus with inclines of up to 40 percent and a tunnel and bridge ratio of 25 percent is one of the busiest links in Europe. Frankfurt, the city with Germany's most imposing skyline and the oldest half-timbered houses, with the highest debts and the largest banks, with the most generous urban forest and the highest traffic volume, attracts 15 million visitors per year. With over 100,000 passengers per day, the Rhein-Main airport is the busiest airport on the European continent. Germany's prime railway triangle lies directly beneath the Frankfurter Kreuz, Germany's busiest highway interchange, in some areas with a clearance of only 7 meters. Following Frankfurt's model, the railway has committed to the strategy of creating links to German airports in order to replace domestic air travel as far as possible and to operate as a feeder service for European and intercontinental flights. For routes where the journey takes up to three hours by rail, air travel was already transferred to rail at the beginning of the 1990s. By connecting with the high-speed rail network, the catchment area of Frankfurt airport in a radius of 200 kilometers and a potential 35 million inhabitants will be reachable within one hour. Regional rail traffic will continue to operate out of the existing tunnel station. Up to 34,000 train passengers per day are to be handled by the airport station alone. That amounts to 9 to 10 million people, who will not only travel, but also avail themselves of the services offered by hotels, business and conference facilities, restaurants, park and shopping areas—all available just 18 meters above the tracks at Frankfurt.

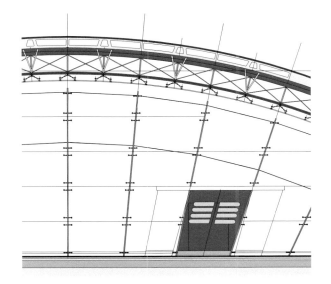

Section of glass wall

Glass wall elevation

DENSIFICATION

According to Ben van Berkel the evolution of airport architecture should be defined by deep planning, densification, and overlapping functions. It would seem that with its satellite-like complexity and autonomy, Frankfurt's Airrail-Center has already taken the lead in this movement. The bridge structure at the integrated airport/railway station with two island platforms, four tracks and a clear view of the sky cost 225 million Euro. In the third-generation ICE, the view of the sky corresponds to the view through the cockpit window en route—at a maximum speed of 300 kilometers per hour. The railway seeks to create a profile of being equal to air travel as a means of transportation through its DB-lounge inside the massive core of the new structure, placed in an elevated position between platform and glass dome, and affording a view of ICE trains pulling in and out of the station. With an inventory of 6,100 railway stations, which are 90 years old on average, the leeway for architectural expression in German rail travel is naturally limited. However, the new image of the railway service will only come into its own if the generous form and high-tech character of the voluminous air terminal above the station is preserved. The foundation platforms, which forms the roof, rests on 43 steel trussed frames with 86 diagonal, V-shaped telescope supports in three sections at 15 meter intervals. Each support is calibrated to absorb a load of 7,500 tons. A total of 13,000 tons of steel and 32,000 tons of concrete were used in the construction. Visually, however, the result is not a cumbersome bridge structure, but a seamless metallic object that spans the tracks in a light and free manner. Rather than carrying the structure, the supports seem to anchor it, to keep it from taking off into the sky—like a zeppelin just before the lines are cast off. The inclined glass skin, matched to the angle of the supports, which provides a comfortable indoor climate in summer and winter with the help of air locks at the entrance portals and an unobstructed view of the outside, appears more like a glass curtain blowing in the breeze than a hermetically sealed facade. The railway station itself—an oddly antiquated term in this context—becomes a means of transport fantasy: spaceship, steamship, hovercraft, … not just a "railway station."

In 1996, the year the airport railway terminal was designed, the architects commented on the topic on the occasion of renovating and expanding the historic central railway in Hanover in the accompanying report to the successful competition design that was, however, only partially realized: "As an interface of several traffic systems and the corresponding number of users, railway stations play an essential economic role. The central railway station is once again a gate to the city and a focal point of public life. The legend of the railway station is alive and well, not only as a technical facility but as a cultural and social urban component."[9] Hanover, too, let a great opportunity slip by when it truncated such a grandiose concept.

Notes

1   Roland Stimpel: Transparenz ist entscheidend (interview with Helmut W. Joos),
    Plan – Das Immobilien Journal von IVG 1/2002, pp. 11–12

2   Anett-Maud Joppien, Jörg Joppien: Der Flughafen. Eine Momentaufnahme von
    Geschwindigkeit, in: Martin Wentz (ed.): Region (Die Zukunft des Städtischen-
    Frankfurter Beiträge, vol. 5), Frankfurt/Main/New York 1994, pp. 43–52

3   Werner Jacob: Die Spinne im Zentrum des Verkehrsnetzes, Der Tagesspiegel
    July, 14th 1999

4   Gerd Ruepp, cit. after: Ernst D. Ampolli: Ein Bau hebt ab, Plan – Das Immobilien
    Journal von IVG 2/2002, p. 13

5   Ernst D. Ampolli: Ein Bau hebt ab, Plan – Das Immobilien Journal von IVG 2/2002,
    p. 13

6   Bau des Airrail Center gefährdet, Frankfurter Allgemeine Zeitung 11.8.2003

7   Wolfgang Schubert: Die Glaskuppel bleibt am Frankfurter Flughafen, Frankfurter
    Rundschau 14.8.2001

8   Roland Stimpel: Transparenz ist entscheidend (interview with Helmut W. Joos),
    Plan – Das Immobilien Journal von IVG 1/2002, p. 12

9   Bothe Richter Teherani: Erläuterungsbericht Hauptbahnhof Hannover,
    January 1996

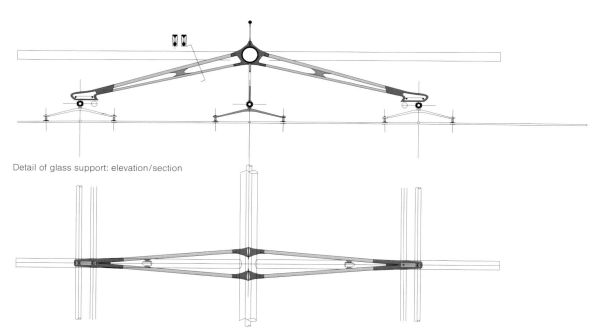

Detail of glass support: elevation/section

Detail of glass support: view from below

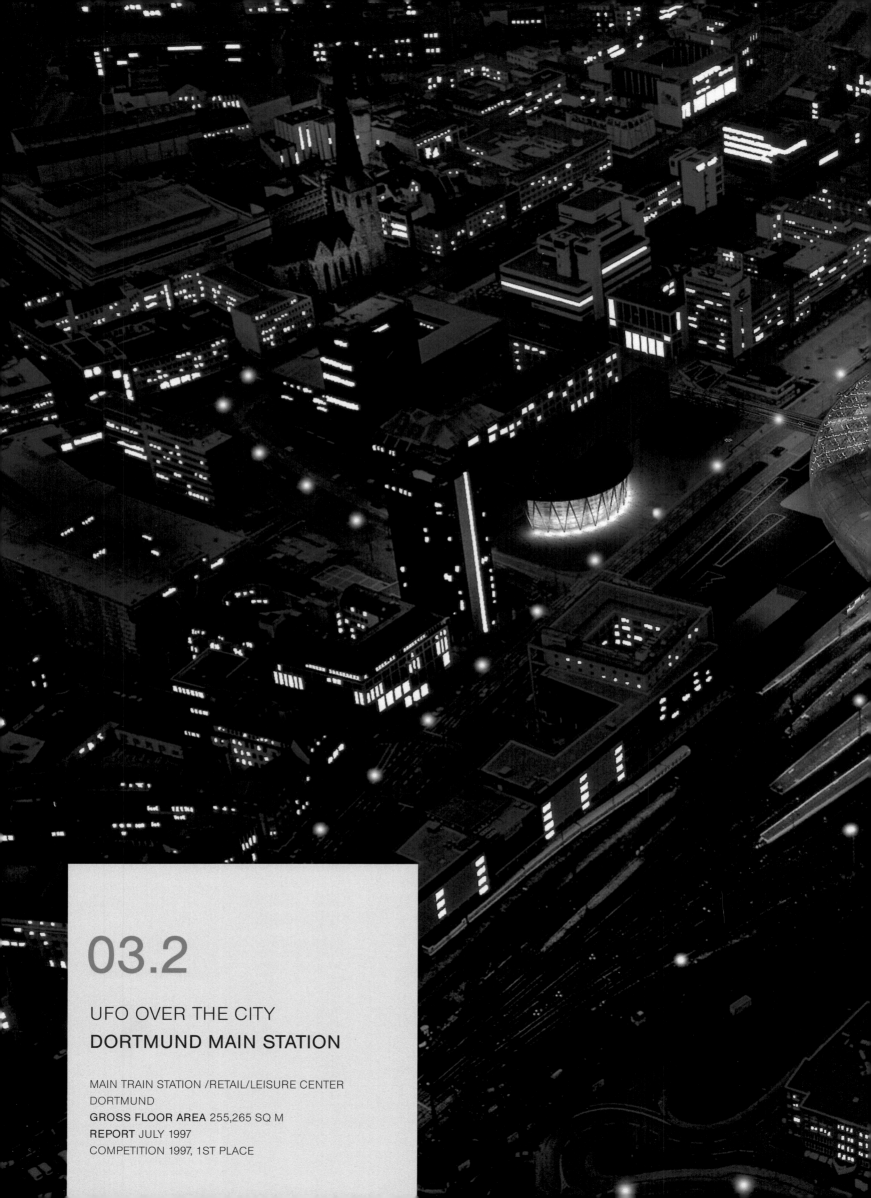

03.2

UFO OVER THE CITY
DORTMUND MAIN STATION

MAIN TRAIN STATION /RETAIL/LEISURE CENTER
DORTMUND
GROSS FLOOR AREA 255,265 SQ M
REPORT JULY 1997
COMPETITION 1997, 1ST PLACE

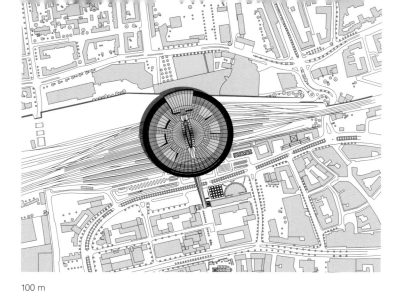

100 m

UFO OVER THE CITY

Parallel to the construction of the Chancellory in Berlin is an "aircraft carrier against a life of feeling frustrated with history and politics" (Michael Mönninger). The communal location and functional hybrid of the "UFO" at the eastern gateway to the Ruhr territory formulates an enthusiastic focus for the future-oriented renovation of a region that became the heartland of Europe as a consequence of German unity and the European common market. From the outset, the political fragmentation of this metropolitan region—which has yet to be recognized on any map—and the competition among its approximately fifty local administrations, presented an uncalculated risk of failure. With relatively modest dimensions compared to those of other transport projects, the winning entry triumphed over such competitors as Jean Nouvel and Helmut Jahn. In the orbital, streamlined shape of the eight-story "UFO," construction components were standardized and integrated to the greatest degree possible, creating an overarching formal mantle while demarcating the structure from the organized disorderliness of the city, and thus presenting a broad surface for attack: by city planners, who subordinate business and traffic to the museum-like, monofunctional city; by politicians, to whom consolidation and overlaying are unfamiliar as means of regulating the centering and medium of urban grandeur. At the same time, the expenses of American cities to revitalize their downtown areas by constructing vital oases for social encounters rose to at least 4 to 5 billion dollars in the last ten years. The main train station in the center of the city can and must achieve more than is expected of it today. With its revitalization into a functional hybrid, the development of the city is executing an about-face: back to the central city.

Plan of level 3

Dortmund Main Station

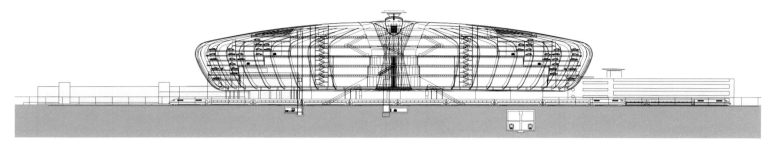

Section east-west

CENTERING

Ernst Bloch regarded utopia as an indispensable dimension of urban planning and urban design. The railway station in Dortmund, a project from 1997 reminiscent of a UFO, was nevertheless misunderstood as a neo-futuristic hoax, as a techno toy world. Unjustly so, we realize today, when we look at the provincial clichés of the type "medieval age with high-rise" that characterized subsequent planning initiatives in Dortmund and at current international urban markers such as the futuristic art museum zeppelin by Peter Cook and Colin Fournier in Graz. It is true that the UFO—the most popular metaphor among architecture critics—is neither new nor revolutionary as a building form. Unlike the traditional Chinese palace form, which Albert Speer planned to employ for the central railway station at Beijing, however, it does have the symbolic force and eloquence of a streamlined dome that marks the ambition of an evolutionary projection of architectural history: forward from the past, and backward into the future.

The image of the city is characterized by industrialization, war damage, and economic downfall. Until the mid-nineteenth century, Dortmund was a walled city with small half-timbered houses and a maze of narrow lanes. The inauguration of the railway line between Cologne and Minden in 1847 was a catalyst for the city's development as a center of the coal and steel industries. As a national traffic hub, Dortmund became the most important industrial site in the rapidly developing Ruhr area. Until 1913, 20 percent of the steel production and 23 percent of the coal production in the Ruhr came from Dortmund. Nevertheless, the advantages of the location gradually shifted along the Rhine to Essen, Düsseldorf, and Duisburg. After the ravages of World War II—one hundred bombing raids since the fall of 1944—all that was left of the historic inner city was the ring road. It is remarkable that the largest, free-span hall in Germany, the Westfalenhalle (1949–1952) with a seating capacity of 20,000, could be created under these conditions. Here was an architectural departure whose influence radiated far beyond the city boundaries that was hardly ever mentioned in the numerous debates on the UFO. Above all, however, the historical background illustrates the city's yearning for grandeur, stature, and a clearly defined city center. Projections, which see the current Ruhr population of 5.4 million, already down from the peak of 6.2 million in 1962, drop by a further million over the next ten to fifteen years are justified. During the sensitive stage of a region's economic decline, it is especially important to gather all the forces of the city to enhance distinctive features through selected interventions in the urban design with a view to creating a sustainable regional strategy that also incorporates ecological criteria: by integrating work, leisure, consumption, culture, traffic, and housing right in the city center.

After the misguided strategy, begun in 1947, of creating a "representative design for the city center"[1] by loosening and restructuring or rather after the deliberate shift from a traditional to a "nondescript and mute" city (Rem Koolhaas), the UFO represented an attempt in Dortmund to create a collective spatial experience within the park city with the help of a city-forming crystallizing core: a site of social polarizations, a mix between Noah's arc, shopping mall, railway station, and temporary gated community. The symbol of utopia as an island, an anchor in the loneliness of a city that is merely "many cities"—more than the largest ferries wheel in the world could ever achieve as a new landmark for Berlin. The complex spatial program oscillating between pragmatism and vision, between industrial and urban landscape, fills a building fabric with a clear and memorable form that can gladly do without staging a cabaret or borrowing from historic styles. The transparent foyer strengthens the promise of something grandiose. A moon-sized people's hall of the kind that was also included in the proposals for New York's new World Trade Center, albeit without a rail link. The fact that the UFO leisure object embodies the urban community through technological machinery that is akin to the Centre Pompidou in Paris is only surprising at first glance. The symbolic use of industry and technology is part of the traditional orientation of the Ruhr region. With the UFO, the symbolic power of industry was reinterpreted into fresh, media-friendly images to provide the region with a new visibility and identity. Symbolic and aesthetic re-interpretation is a proven means of redefining economically challenging situations—a tool that is fundamentally characterized by its affinity with the visionary. In the end, the idea of progress of the modern was based on the assumption that architecture would reconcile humans with themselves provided it was sufficiently advanced in terms of technology. Even Zaha Hadid's "latent utopias," presented in Graz in 2002, failed to go beyond this idea. How else could the necessary signal effect of the "city center" be realized, especially when floating above railway tracks, than by creating distance to an urban reality that seems more provincial than metropolitan? The rhythm of the industrialized world has given way to unfettered confusion— the best breading ground for traditional motifs, not for experiments. The outrage was correspondingly great.

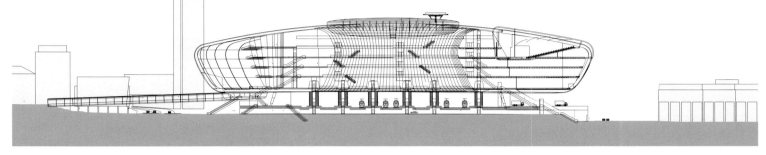

Section north-south

MAGIC BULLET

One drives through the Ruhr and thinks of Los Angeles. The citadels in the latter include the Music Center, the Getty complex and the new cathedral by Rafael Moneo.

Dortmund is the largest city of the Ruhr region—a sheer endless industrial "conglomerate city" with almost 5.5 million inhabitants. During the heyday prior to restructuring, identity and urban image in the region were always realized through monumental solitary buildings and gigantic structures: massive town halls, churches, department stores, winding and water towers, gasometers, administrative headquarters, and industrial halls, with the cathedrals of coal and steel, of railroad and shipping. In 1914, Alfred Fischer erected a domed hall (height, 24.5 meters; diameter 41 meters) that is comparable to the Centennial Hall in Breslau, the most significant multipurpose building of the Kaiser era, solely for the steam engines of the Alte Emscher pump station. In Dortmund, the now exhausted "heart chamber of social democracy" (Herbert Wehner), there is no political support today for this characteristic *leitmotif* of the Ruhr region—the spontaneous, polycentric evaluation of the urban image—because the destruction of the urban plan and of valuable existing structures that was authorized in 1947 has left planners with a bad conscience and moved them to embrace romanticism in a place where contrast and tension, generosity and orientation, distance and alternatives are indispensable. Is the triumphant progress of smallness and fussiness a reaction to the centralism of National Socialism? The charm of the region has always been a function of its unique, almost grotesque complexity: the cow next to the blast furnace; the pub next to the hall; the forest next to the water tower. Dortmund should reinvent itself with dynamic architecture, not continue in a linear fashion with red brick walls and iron gray window frames. Contrary to its European neighbors, however, Germany has lost much architectural courage. Sweden and Denmark, on the other hand, are not only embellishing their new Øresund link with gigantic solitary buildings but with a newly founded city. In Germany, Bilbao is not seen as an example of how an aesthetic attraction can operate as a powerful economic argument, but as an abhorrence, an architectural aphrodisiac that rapidly loses its potency.[2] Even the professional debate among experts skims merely the surface; popular prejudices that are effective with the public at large are only rarely questioned. Cities where a spirit of departure and "AUF-RUHR" (lit. "revolt," public slogan in the Ruhr region proclaiming the need for structural change) would be required, are condemned to a standstill. "There are no more functioning city centers—

unless they are newly created. If old city centers are to avoid being pushed to the margins of this evolution, they must revise their visions on their own initiative and learn from shopping centers. In other words, cities must learn to design a simulacrum of themselves in the form of an abstract and cleaned-up ideal of urbanity in order to avoid disappearing as sites."[3] Finding a new magic bullet for prosperity is no easy task. Without reference to the character of the site and without new forms of entertainment, leisure, and tourism, it seems virtually impossible. The Ruhr, which is the geographic heart of Europe, is largely unknown. "This is largely due to the lack of urbanity, architectural highlights, and entertainment value as well as to the fact that the public spaces between Lippe and Ruhr are not very attractive urban backdrops for face-to-face encounters and weekend tourists."[4] Chaotic, not exactly beautiful, but lively, Dortmund will only succeed as a leading center of micro-technology and logistics if a modern match is found for the blast furnaces of the abandoned Phoenix-West steelworks or the superannuated Westfalenhalle. A manmade lake for swimming in place of the industrial area Phoenix-East will not provide a sufficient basis.

With the exception of Frankfurt's combined airport/railway station and Berlin's central railway station, neither of which exude the hoped-for euphoria in their completed forms, the symbolic and ritual function of a national railway—still trying to catch up with the *transrapid* and its own future and the prestige of dominant urban terminals, that was beginning to emerge in Dortmund in the mid-nineteenth century—seems to have become meaningless. "The railway terminal with its conspicuous station buildings and crowds … In Dortmund's railway station, which has an exquisite spacious principal structure, there is always a mighty crush of people and goods …, in short: a small railway city."[5] Is the Ruhr region not being deprived of its identity for the second time, of its "sensory theater of life?"[6] When Heinz Rühmann's parents ran the railway station restaurant in Wanne-Eickel, passengers could still travel from Wanne-Eickel to Milan without changing trains.[7]

CITY OBJECT

What is the image of a UFO above streamlined track vehicles based on? Do real and virtual words combine in the digital age into a vision of a "trans-architecture," a "cyber-real" or "bio-electronic" architecture, as Florian Rötzer assumed in 1996? "The future belongs to man-nature-machine-environments—and, globalism notwithstanding, it draws

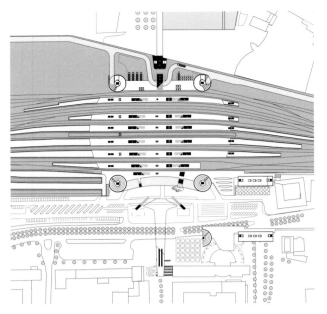

Plan of platform level

"A city that doesn't change doesn't deserve to be called a city. In addition to harmony, cities also need events that distinguish them, that inspire enthusiasm and demonstrate that they are alive." Jens Bothe

Dortmund Main Station

new boundaries that will become more impenetrable than ever before. Monads, unique specimens of small communities, spaceships, are the living environments [of the future], regardless of where they may be. [...] People are returning to the caves in which they sought shelter once upon a time, equipping them in a manner that means they never have to leave."[8] Perhaps this is why all we see is a copy of the technology euphoria of the 1950s and 1960s, when the Independent Group and Archigram developed futuristic-organic buildings in order to liberate science fiction from its ghetto of triviality and make use of it, provocatively, for social analysis and against aesthetic standards.[9] In 1964, the Canadian communication guru Marshall McLuhan, author of *The medium is the message* (1967), went so far as to define the end of the era of circular buildings as having occurred when people became settled and began to specialize in terms of work division and organization. "The rectangular room or the rectangular house speak the language of the settled specialist, while the round hut or the igloo represents proof of the undivided nomadic lifestyle of the hunter and gatherer society."[10] We can no longer refer to this image today, even though the theme of mobility is inseparable from the railway station. But "innovation," according to art historian Boris Groys, "does not consist in the emergence of something that was hidden, but in the fact that the value of that which has always been seen and known is redefined."[11] The arena, as a symbol of a place of congregation, and the synergistic performance of wide-span building skins are models of far greater clarity. At the 7th Biennial of Architecture in Venice, the theme of science fiction re-emerged at the turn of the millenium, albeit with a different terminology and on a bio-technological basis. There was talk of "computer-assisted liquefaction of architecture," of "space capsules" and "space stations," of "organic architecture sculptures," "futuristic formalism," "bulging cyber fantasy," "curvaceous bio-design," and "mutated reptile skins," as if the future of humankind lay in the extraterrestrial dreams of yesterday. "Everything that seeks to be seen as progressive at this Biennial is cloaked in soft, dissolved forms."[12] In the Italian pavilion, the stylistic diversity of today's architecture was represented by the giant model of a space station, which announced a better world against a backdrop of the celestial music.[13]

Perhaps the form is based on theoretical marginalia such as resistance to form and friction, or rather—and this is more important for stationary structures—on the ideal relationship between the built space and the necessary envelope surface? For a round, cylindrical or even spherical building fabric offers the smallest surface by comparison to other forms in plan. Heat radiation and facade construction are thereby minimized—in the sense of ecological building for economic not emotional reasons. Even this marginalia was given new recognition at the Biennial of Architecture when Greg Lynn, one of the superstars of the current American scene, posed the question: "We buy drop-shaped, ergonomically perfect running shoes, drive cars that are built around the body and live in angular boxes—why?"[14]

UTOPIA

Perhaps, the question is social and communication contents rather than form? The public focal point in the form of a "living bridge" that links urban districts, that merges communication, commerce, and trade into a single unit? A type that was explored as a theme in an exhibition mounted in 1996 at the Centre Pompidou in Paris and the Royal Academy in London. For the market square becomes more and more important as the urban sprawl in our residential and commercial suburbs increases. The idea of the city based on markets and an exchange of goods is still ideologically and critically suspected of being a degenerate form of urbanity. But the origin of urban settlement has always been linked to trade opportunities and trade rights. Did not Walter Benjamin rightly remark that the *flaneur's* goal is the market? In this sense, the fear that "gatherings may soon come to mean only one thing: group consumerism" is unjustified.[15] It was always thus. Even in 1838, Russian station planners demonstrated at the end of the line of their first railroad from Saint Petersburg to Pavlosk that a real railway station is more than a stop along the line. The station was dance hall, restaurant, casino, traffic hub, and trading place all in one.

Surely one of the issues is also the ability to change the rooms within their distinctive skin. The architectural answer to the growing mobility can only be that buildings are designed for multifunctional and flexible use, allowing for and provoking organizational opportunities for change and growth. Mixed use and function have always been the essential prerequisites for the development of a dynamic and animated region. Especially for inner cities, which, as far as development areas are concerned, have the greatest lack in building lots, the only chance of preserving the downtown as a living space of interaction and of making growth possible despite central open space lies in the spatial overlapping of different functions. Only hybrid structures are capable of adapting in a multifunctional manner to changing requirements—building on the prototypes by Adler and Sullivan, the Schiller Building in Chicago (1892) with retail stores, theaters, clubs, and vast office spaces.

When culture is no longer a place of critical distance but the arena in which reality is played out, then neither art nor architecture can furnish the answer to such questions; they can only articulate the questions. "Without trade, a city loses its public character; without commerce, there is no urban culture. (...) Greek stoa market halls, Roman porticoed shopping streets or medieval market squares were inseparable from the political gathering sites—agora, forum, and town square."[16] "Spaces for gatherings such as the Cloth Hall at Cracow, the basilica in Vicenza or the Palazzo della Ragione in Padua, for a long time the largest hall structure in the world, mark the city centers to this day."[17] During the Empire, fair halls and sports palaces such as the one in Berlin became gathering places without political definition and for all strata of society. For a long time, the Westfalenhalle in Dortmund was the largest gathering place in the Federal Republic. However, the clarity of a precise city center in connection with this function is still lacking in Dortmund. Yet an urban culture for all can only develop in the casual setting of a central market square and/or traffic hub, not in decentralized cultural institutions. To which degree the boundaries between politics, culture, and consumption can be shifted should be demonstrated through experiments, not prejudices. In the architectural debate, this goal is reflected in attempts at unifying urban space and object into a dynamic whole and exploring the character of the space. The unavoidable, albeit predictable consequence of this strategy is that, as sites of a non-elitist urban culture, the traditional public space as well as the space which cultural institutions can claim for their own use no longer belong to a clearly defined and controlled territory. "What we observe is a cultural, political, and economic entanglement/disentanglement in each relevant field, whenever politicians promote the developers' leisure projects in the fabric of the city today as they did urban repair in the eighties."[18]

LIVING BRIDGES

The bridge, which creates a focal point for all urban districts and does so, moreover, without occupying a building lot, follows a typology that was very common in Europe from the thirteenth to the fourteenth century. As a link between two parts of a city, "living" bridges became the center of public life, indispensable and integral components of the urban organism. Their location at the most important trade routes transformed the bridges, which had mutated into central "squares," into popular sites of trade. Markets were held on bridges since the Middle Ages. Even churches, chapels, and mills found their distinctive locations at bridges. "Triumphal bridges" became the stage for public festivities. Today, the vision goes beyond a Ponte Vecchio in Florence or a Pulteney Bridge in Bath; the historical evolution reached its conclusion in 1778. After Le Corbusier's bridge cities for Algiers and Rio de Janeiro, a bridge with housing above train tracks by Ebenezer Howard, a skyscraper bridge across San Francisco Bay, and a twenty-part bridge city for one million people in Manhattan (1950), plans for projects of this kind have been launched for Boston, Dubai, Rome, and London in recent times. Frank Lloyd Wright realized the modern precursor for these projects with the Marin County Community Center on a bridge in California.

The functional variety in the plans for these projects is astonishing. Geoffrey Jellicoe's bridge plans in London included apartment buildings, a shopping center, a skating rink, sculpture gardens, parks, and cafés. The competition launched by the social housing society the Peabody Trust in 1998 called for a school, a hospital, a museum, and an open-air arena for concerts and theater performances in addition to housing. Yet another competition, the "Thames Water Habitable Bridge Competition," went even further by stipulating that the bridge must become an attraction for people, enriching the entire city. Dortmund was therefore by no means alone in facing the decision for a living bridge. By contrast to mega-cities with millions of inhabitants, this city benefits from the advantages of how manageable medium-sized agglomerations can be without having to forego the ever more rapid passage of tourists, passengers, goods, and information in the age of mobility and integrated communication.

DENSIFICATION

Perhaps, however, urban densification is more a question of making use of the blind spots of a city, of utilizing unused or neglected spaces as a pressure valve and of transforming transitional spaces into primary spaces in the sense of urbanity and city. For urban life will continue to concentrate within the densified environment even as suburbanization progresses with the help of computer networks. The appeal of consumer markets and shopping centers on the periphery profits from a lack in the inner cities and banks on the so-called "Nevada effect" (Rem Koolhaas). "Nevada was forced to make itself artificially interesting due to the lack of cultural and natural attractions, making everything that was forbidden elsewhere permissible here—unregulated gambling, instant weddings, and firearms. The conventional shopping centers in the commercial districts on the urban periphery also survive by discarding nearly all social constraints imposed on customers in the cities—from dress codes to pricing to parking restrictions."[19] Every reversal of this development must therefore take the conditions at the periphery, which are based on authentic needs, into consideration. "To create long-term appeal for their customers, the mall operators of today offer more than mountains of goods; they offer what is an inherent part of the character of every true city: public space, room to roam and the eroticism of the social sphere."[20]

Dortmund's new central railway station, which was such a point of contention among opponents and proponents alike because of its urban, architectural, and commercial complexity and concentration, has existed for a long time in its communicative, mercantile, and social densification—as the consequence of a social change. Not in Dortmund, but in Utrecht, for example. One of the largest indoor shopping centers in Europe is directly connected to the most important national and international railroad junction in the Netherlands. Honk Kong is another example: the "Hong Kong Coliseum" beneath a 95-meter free-span, square roof, built in 1983, is one of the most recognizable landmarks of the city. These examples are not about science fiction for a distant future; on the contrary, they are founded in a historic typology, whose origins reach back millennia with a view to the market and public gathering function.

The galactic railway station seems to float above the tracks like a nomad's tent. Less a building than a traffic element and symbol that breathes new life into the lost, a spatial concept of the city in the modern era by virtue of a railway station that has been functionally and formally enhanced to become the nucleus of the city visualizes the functions of the rail network in the sense of Habermas, much like "the city gates once constituted concrete links to surrounding villages and to the next city."[21] Does the archaic form of a space ship awaken a primeval image or anticipate a future archaic? The combination of familiar modern technology with archaic form is reminiscent of Buckminster Fuller's geodesic domes and their retro-utopian quality. A railway station caught between archaic and modern polarities, a counterpart, amidst an unusual post-industrial archaic, to all that is artificial and indecisive in the city of today, which looks more to the decorative past than to a visionary future. Square and cube are unknown in nature, while circle and sphere are understood through analogies in nature. Square and cube mean order, unity, and clarity. As un-natural constructs, they break with the traditional image of representation, with mimesis in the more specific sense. Cubic reality as in Schinkel's Bauakademie in Berlin, amplified in the architect's favorite rendering into a pure cube through the reflection in the waters of the Spree, has always been perceived as offensive, unnatural, and revolutionary.

The block was associated with being grounded until Le Corbusier overthrew this basic assumption by creating a floating configuration in the shape of a modern structure on pilotis at the Villa Savoye in Poissy—no more than "a landed space ship [which] is at home everywhere and nowhere" in the eyes of conservative observers like Hans Sedlmayr. What is wrong with this image for a traffic hub as a gateway to the Ruhr region? Alternative spatial images submitted to the competition were a cube with a footbridge and a bridge with linear slabs parallel to the tracks; one compromise solution proposed an exploded cube with a broad winged roof in the direction of the tracks. The common factor in all three alternatives is that they expand the superstructure development in order to complete the image of the city in as traditional a manner as possible, despite the unavoidable leap in scale, while accommodating a railway station without any architectural definition quasi as an afterthought. This contradicts the complexity of the task as well as the ambition to center and order the overgrown chaos of the city through a single central function, creating meaning through topography that points beyond the chaos theory of fractal cluster growth. The most recent attempt of meeting the dilemma in a city that cannot decide between the vocabulary of the medieval and the high-rise turned out to be entirely futile. Architecturally, the greatest social challenge of the present time remains unanswered – "the mess [caught] between the turbo-capitalistic redefinition of public space and the interests of the urban society"[22]—ideally right in the middle of the city.

Notes

1   Thomas Schilp: Zeit-Räume. Aus der Geschichte einer Stadt, exhibition catalogue and documentation on the history of Dortmund presented in the new town hall, Dortmund 1989, p. 184

2   Gerd Kähler: Warnung vor einer Architektur des Spektakels. Sie nutzt sich rasch ab und dient nur den Interessen der Stadtvermarkter, Die Zeit, 48/2002

3   Susanne Hauser: Städte ohne Orte, Centrum. Jahrbuch Architektur und Stadt 2000–2001, (yearbook), Basel/Boston/Berlin 2000, p. 81/82

4   Klaus R. Kunzmann: Wie heißt der Pott auf englisch?, Frankfurter Allgemeine Zeitung, February 12, 2002, p. 47

5   Levin Schückin: Eine Eisenbahnfahrt von Minden nach Köln, (Leipzig 1856) Minden 1987, p. 118/119

6   Roland Günter: Im Tal der Könige. Ein Reisebuch zu Emscher, Rhein und Rhur, Essen 1994, p. 12

7   Note: Heinz Rühmann (1902–1994), popular German film and stage actor who embodied the 'little man' whose honesty and moral integrity always win out in the end.

8   Florian Rötzer: Vom Bauen im Raum, Telepolis, December 9, 1996

9   Florian Zeyfang: Die Entdeckung der Ästhetik der Massen, Telepolis, March 21, 2000

10 Marshall McLuhan: Understanding Media: The Extensions of Man (1964), German ed. Basel/Boston/Berlin 1995, p. 94

11 Boris Groys: Über das Neue. Versuch einer Kulturökonomie, Munich 1992, p. 14

12 Michael Mönninger: Die Suche nach der verlorenen Stadtharmonie, Berliner Zeitung, June 19, 2000

13 Roman Hollenstein: Sehnsucht nach Utopia, Neue Zürcher Zeitung, June 20, 2000

14 Niklas Maak: Bauen für den Menschenpark, Süddeutsche Zeitung, June 20, 2000, p. 17

15 Winfried Nerdinger: Sich versammeln. Architektur und öffentliches Leben, in: Romana Schneider, Winfried Nerdinger, Wilfried Wang (ed.): Architektur im 20. Jahrhundert, Deutschland, Munich 2000, p. 270

16 Michael Mönninger: Tauschen und konsumieren, in: Romana Schneider, Winfried Nerdinger, Wilfried Wang (ed.): Architektur im 20. Jahrhundert, Deutschland, Munich 2000, p. 197

17 Winfried Nerdinger op. cit., p. 265

18 André Bideau: Ereignis, Atmosphäre, Architektur, Werk, Bauen + Wohnen 6/2000, p. 28

19 Michael Mönninger op. cit., p. 199

20 Michael Mönninger op. cit., p. 200

21 Jürgen Habermas: Moderne und postmoderne Architektur, in: Die neue Unübersichtlichkeit. Kleine politische Schriften V, Frankfurt 1985, pp. 24ff

22 Niklas Maak: Mut zur Brücke, Süddeutsche Zeitung, January 20, 2001, p. 13

Dortmund Main Station

03.3

CITY GATES WITH RAIL
CONNECTION
CHAMARTIN TRAIN STATION

TRAIN STATION/RETAIL/LEISURE CENTER
MADRID
GROSS FLOOR AREA 275,000 SQ M
PLANNING MAY 1998

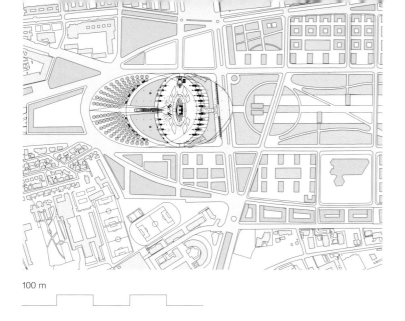

100 m

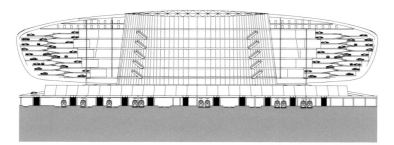

Cross section

CITY GATES WITH RAIL CONNECTION

Train traffic in Spain takes place predominantly in Madrid. With around 200 million passengers per year, it serves far more travelers than both Barcelona and Bilbao. Travelers on the long-distance routes, both national and international, amount to only approximately five percent of the total number of passengers in the capital, the majority of whom use local public transport. The corresponding disproportion between the users of long-distance and regional trains versus the total number of passengers of local trains (360 million) amounts to approximately ten percent. In 1992, as a way of maintaining Madrid's importance as a transport center, the historical train station Atocha, in the city center, was restored and expanded by adding a station for high-speed trains. The Chamartin station is located in the far north of the city, the point of entry for all connections from France and Germany. With its 1980s-style utilitarian structure, Chamartin station does not possess the allure of Atocha station. The municipal master plan, designed by Ricardo Bofill, creates an elliptical plateau, which uses the three-story structure of the old building as its foundation. The inner life of the UFO—with its train station, hotel, and shopping and entertainment areas—is grouped around a central atrium extending through all levels, which ensures natural light and ventilation, and creates an open and communicative space. The new design of the station thus routes the public to both the tracks below and to the shops above. A glass hall placed on the lower level—an ellipse perpendicular to the building—takes on the function of the station hall. The large, elliptical shape of the glass hall is surrounded by skyscrapers and, with its panoramic vista of Madrid, emphasizes the northern entrance into the city. Neither modular nor decentralized structures can impart a comparable message.

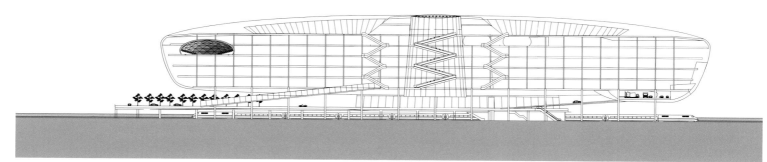

Longitudinal section

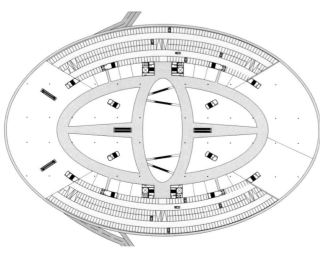

Plan of level 2

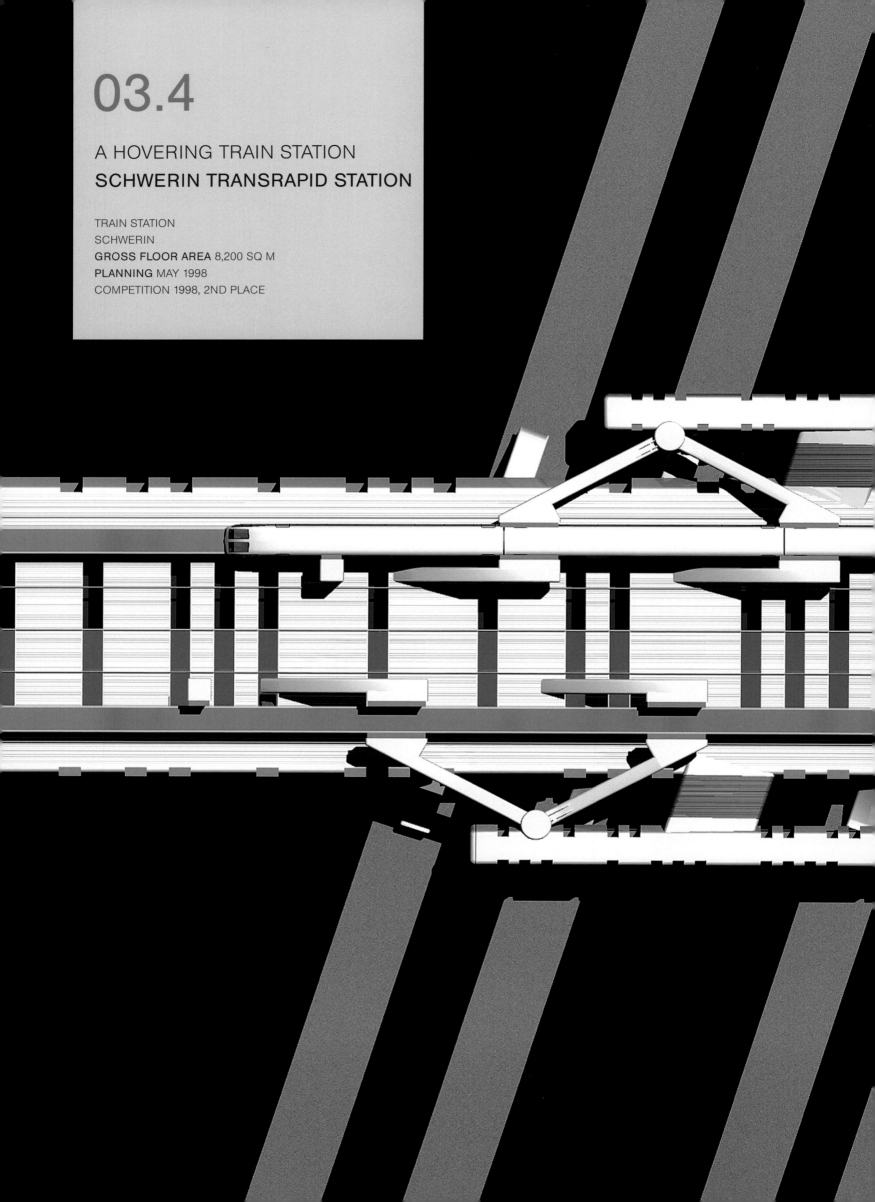

A HOVERING TRAIN STATION
SCHWERIN TRANSRAPID STATION

TRAIN STATION
SCHWERIN
GROSS FLOOR AREA 8,200 SQ M
PLANNING MAY 1998
COMPETITION 1998, 2ND PLACE

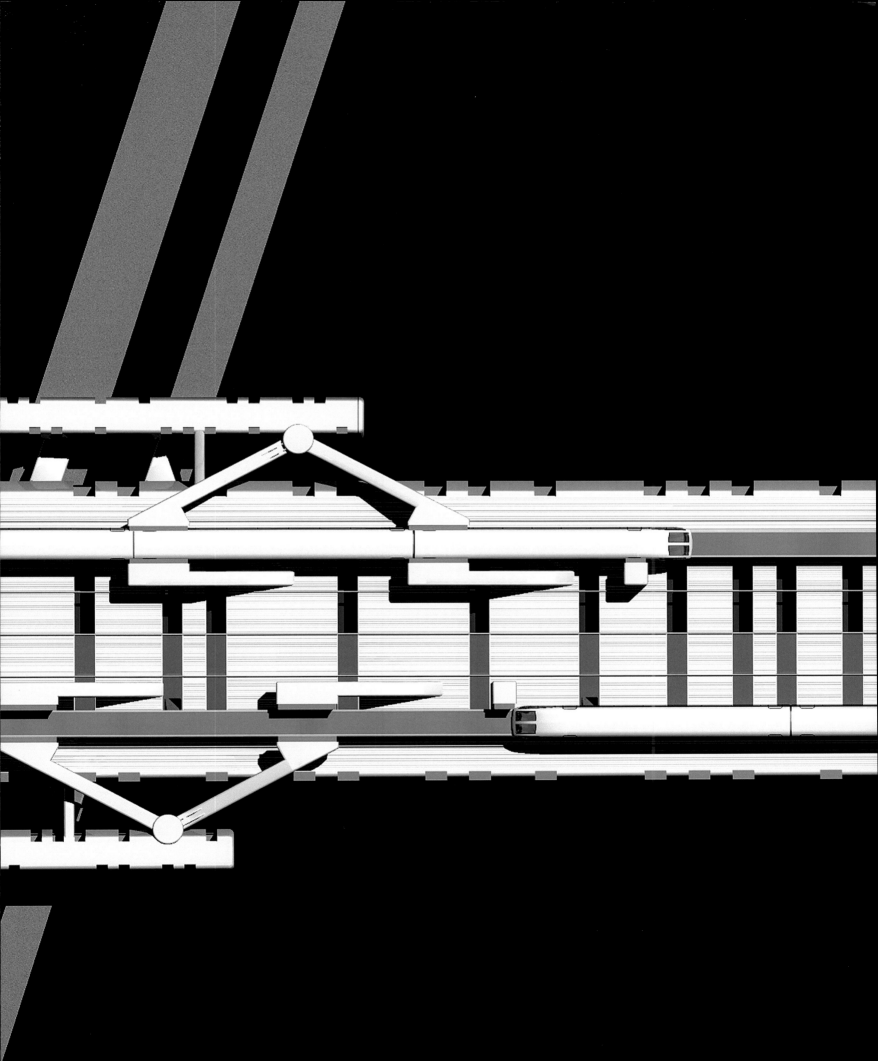

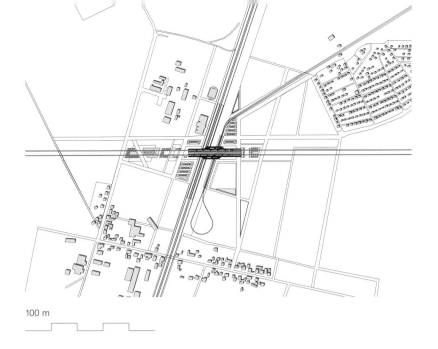

100 m

A HOVERING TRAIN STATION

For the eight architectural teams invited, the task of the competition for construction along the planned, but since rejected, Transrapid connection from Hamburg to Berlin was to design four train stations at a construction cost totaling 51 million euro: at the Hamburg Main Station in Hamburg-Moorfleet, in Schwerin, in Berlin at Spandau Station, and at Lehrter Station. Depending on local conditions, the typology of the stations alternated between subterranean and elevated, or, in the case of the Hamburg station, was left open. The terminus was located in a narrow tunnel below Lehrter Station. In Moorfleet, the station was elevated above the open landscape to make room for park-and-ride spaces below. In Schwerin, the high-speed train was to be routed above the railroad tracks so that the Transrapid station could function simultaneously as a hall and a router for the perpendicular ICE section—typologically, the most interesting case. The travel time between Hamburg and Berlin would have amounted to less than one hour. Another advantage of the system is that the Transrapid can handle gradients much more easily than any track-bound system, eliminating the need for tunnel and bridge constructions, and thus allowing significant savings. The architectural emphasis of the project was to reflect both the costly and intelligent technology developed in a wind tunnel, and to expand the Transrapid system elements through specific, significant halts. In order to stage the "flight object" of the Transrapid, platforms and station halls were thus abandoned for exact docking points on gangways and waiting tubes.

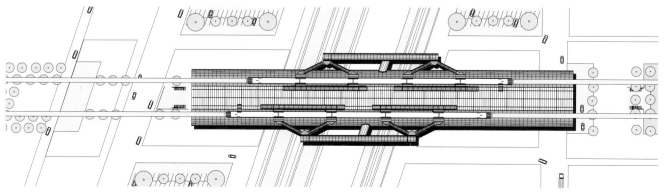

Road access

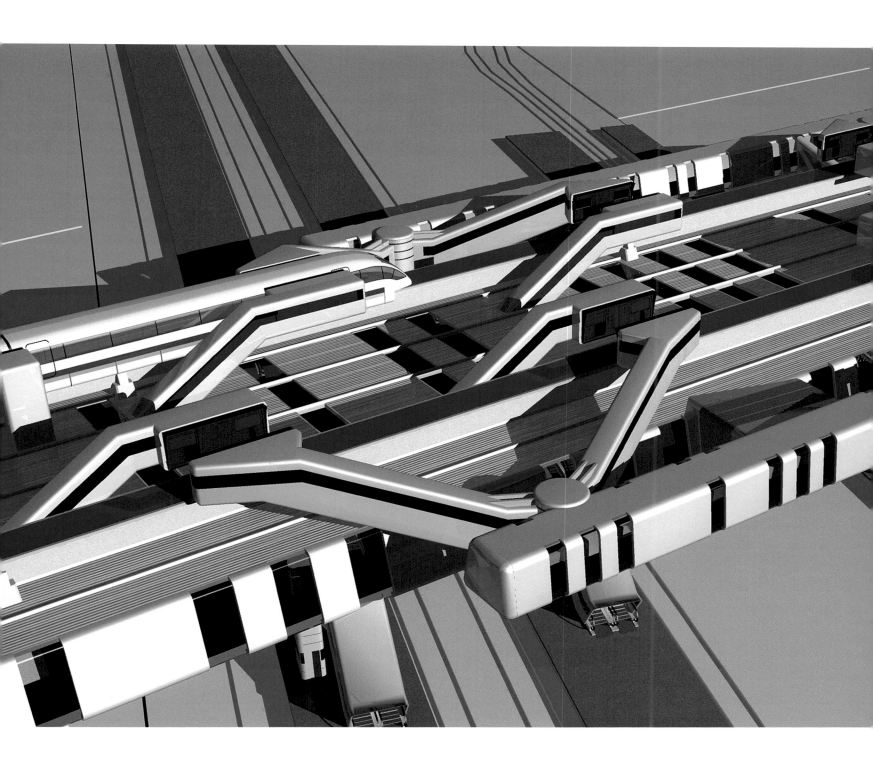

Schwerin Transrapid Station

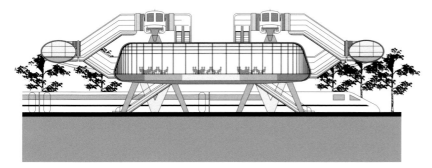

Elevation

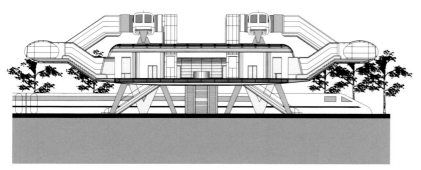

Cross section

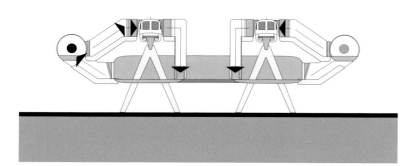

Schematic section

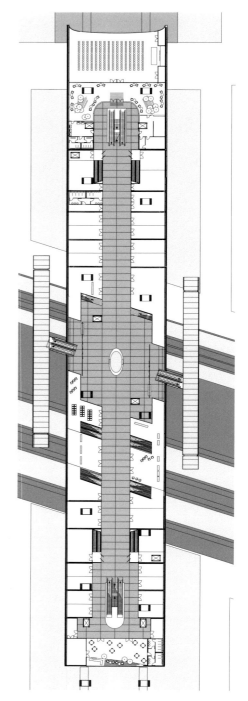

Plan of station hall

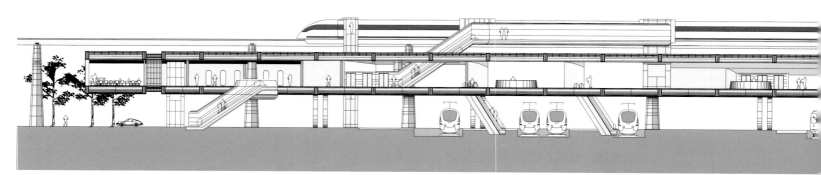

Longitudinal section

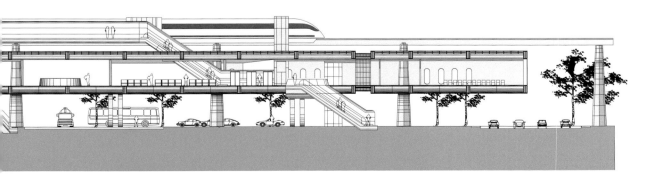

Schwerin Transrapid Station

03.5

RECONSTRUCTING LOCATIONS
PRATERSTERN VIENNA

TRAIN STATION/OFFICE BUILDING
ROOFING FOR THE VIENNA NORTH TRAIN STATION
VIENNA
GROSS FLOOR AREA 20,000 SQ M
PLANNING SEP 1998

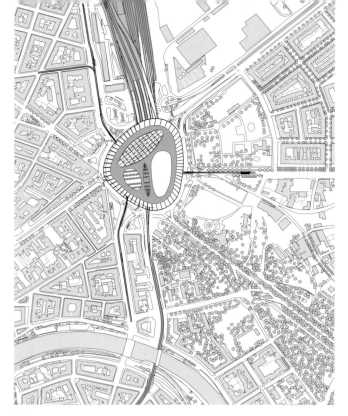

100 m

RECONSTRUCTING LOCATIONS: PRATERSTERN

The push to innovate the Viennese Prater, hard-pressed by competing projects outside the city, is based on a capital bankruptcy. The neighboring fairground of the first Vienna World Fair of 1837 proved to be too large, too uninteresting and too expensive. The city bought the 40-hectare property and is planning a mixed utilization including entertainment (Cirque du Soleil), gastronomy and shopping. Thus, the Praterstern (Prater Star), a traffic node and an entrance to the Prater located in the shadow of the Vienna giant wheel, has been integrated into the project to renovate the North Train Station. This project will mutate the space from a non-location glorifying the automobile to an island of entertainment. Part of an overarching plan to utilize open spaces within the city limits, all of the train stations in Vienna and their adjacent city squares are to be transformed into representative sites. The abstract ubiquity of the modern city, the disintegration of its concrete locations and arenas, are thus confronted by an attempt to sate our hunger for metaphors of location, and to heroically reconcile the spheres of the world of consumption and culture once again. As even Charles Baudelaire's leisurely excursions through the passages of the nineteenth century made apparent: The fetish is the good that inspires loitering and demands a new aesthetic consciousness. The urban cultures of the nineteenth and twentieth centuries were marked by the culturally enriched locations of consumption and their space-time regime. If malls and shopping centers—Rem Koolhaas' urban theater without an admission charge—represent the last bastion of the public, the disappearance of collectivity and participation is not to be feared until realization of the electronic mall.

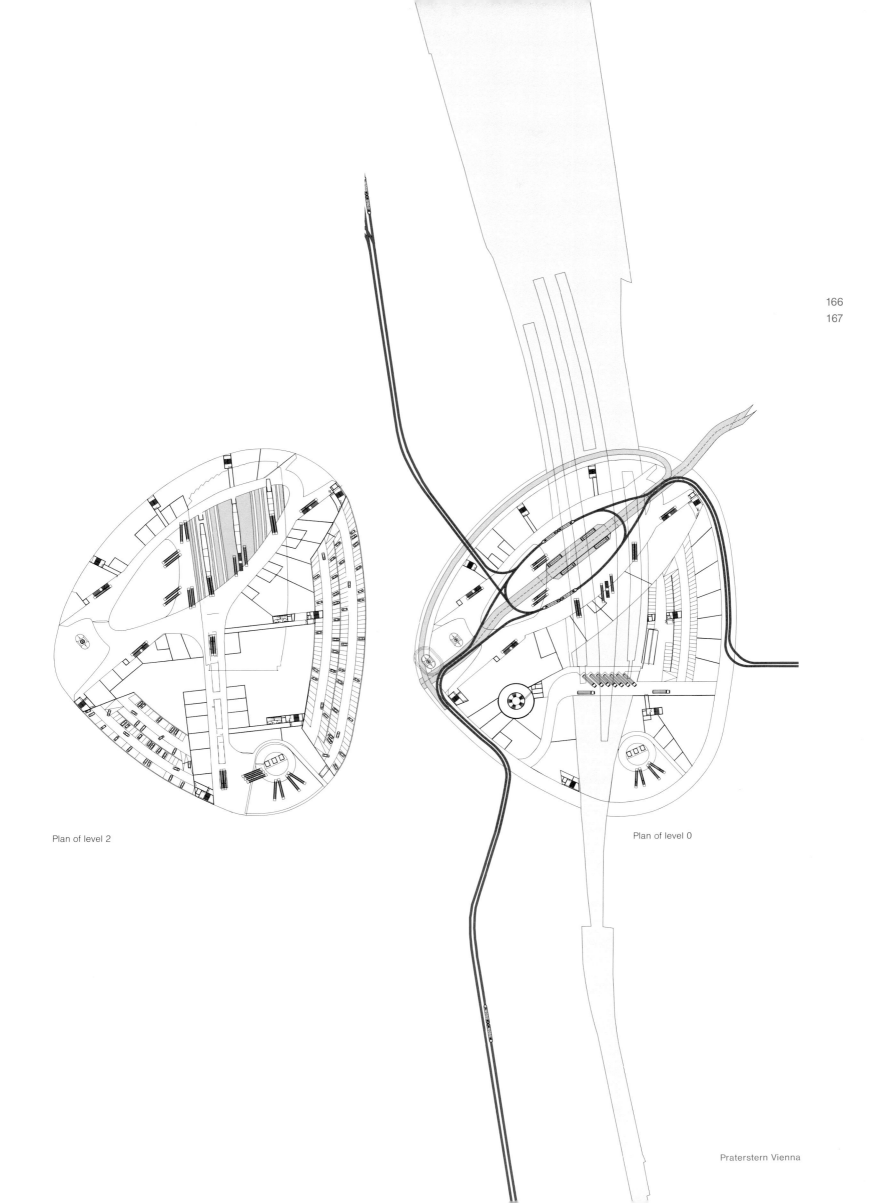

Plan of level 2

Plan of level 0

Praterstern Vienna

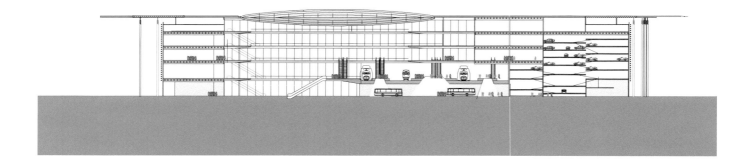

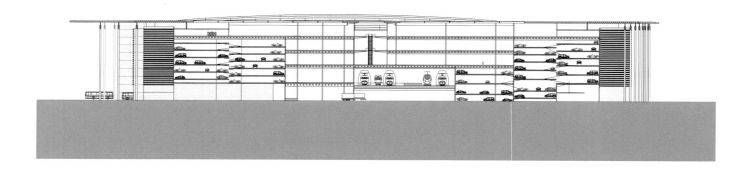

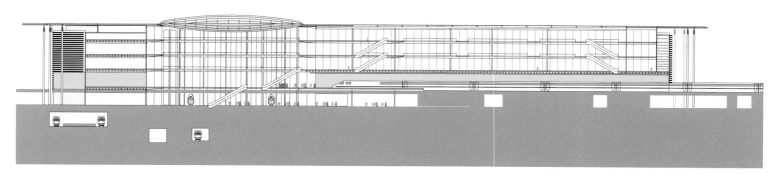

Sections

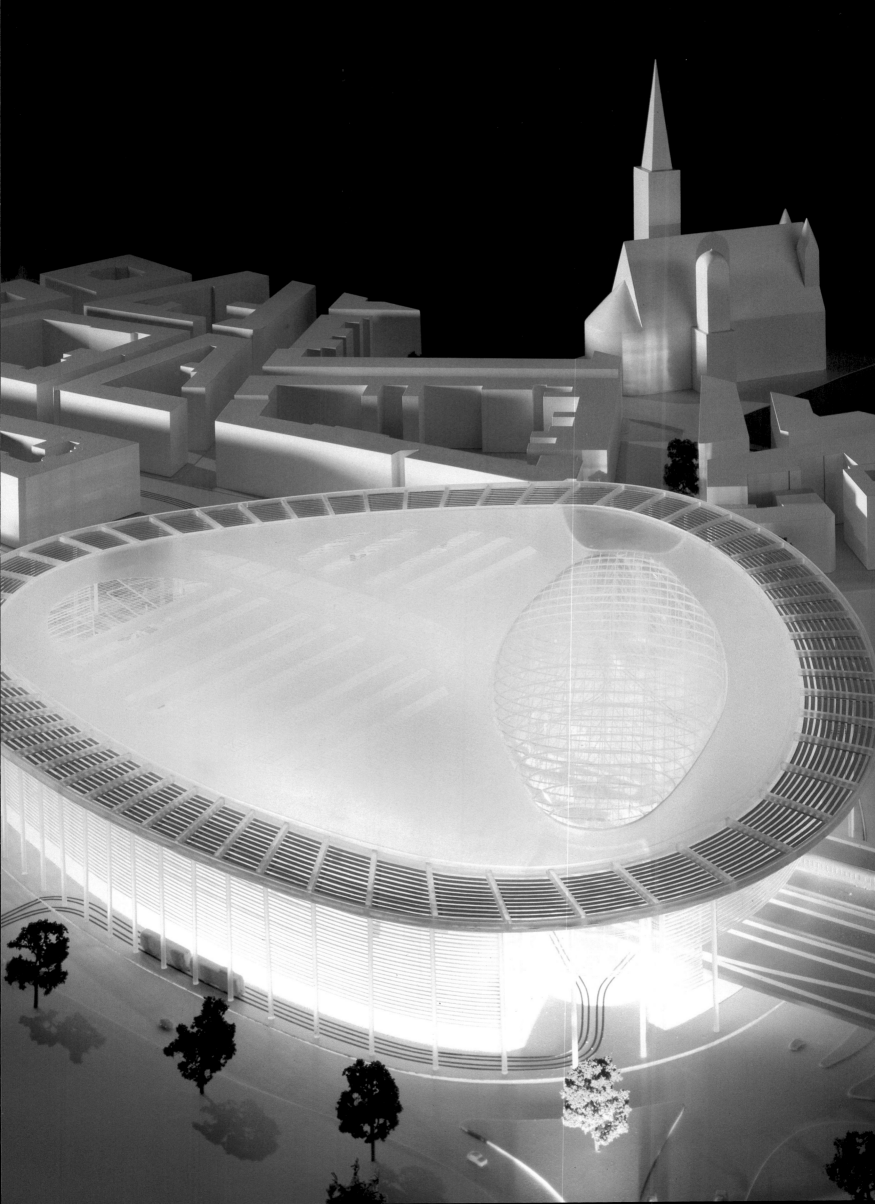

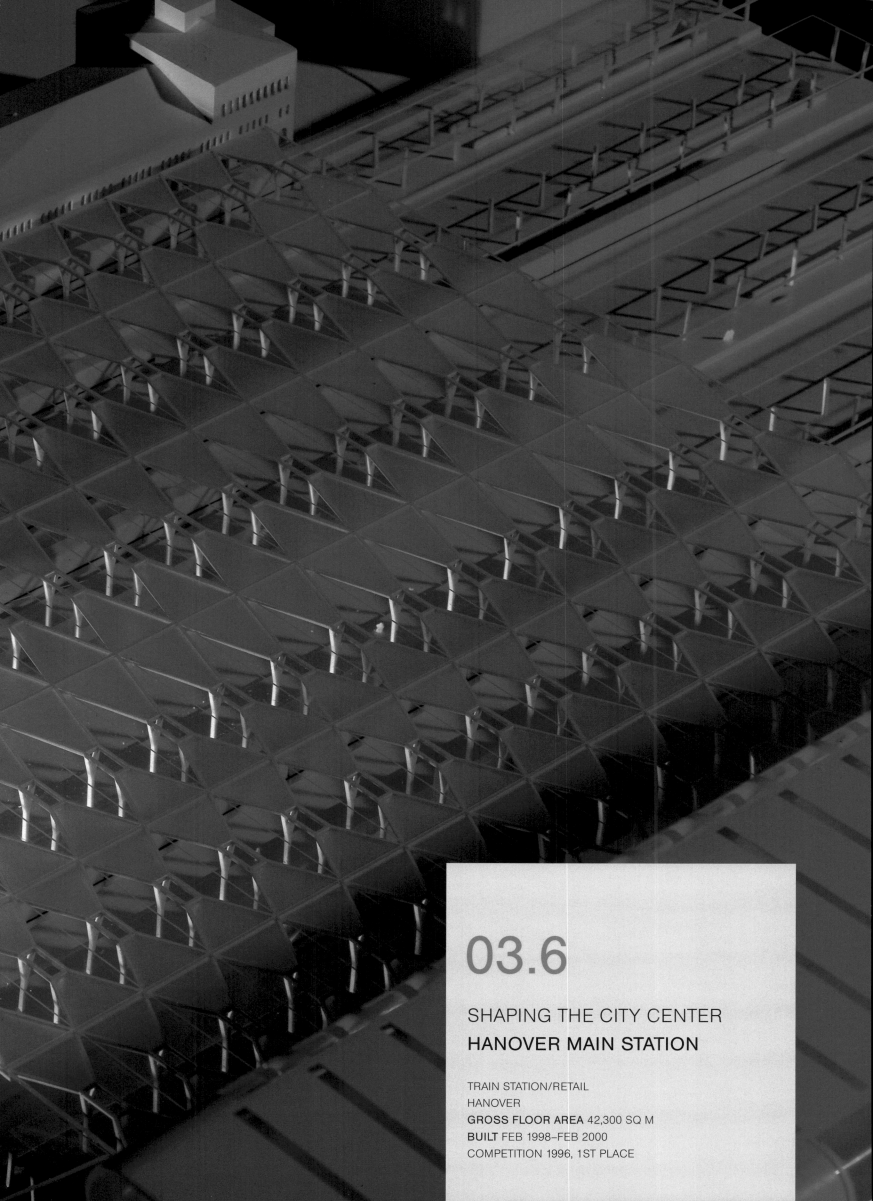

03.6

SHAPING THE CITY CENTER
HANOVER MAIN STATION

TRAIN STATION/RETAIL
HANOVER
GROSS FLOOR AREA 42,300 SQ M
BUILT FEB 1998–FEB 2000
COMPETITION 1996, 1ST PLACE

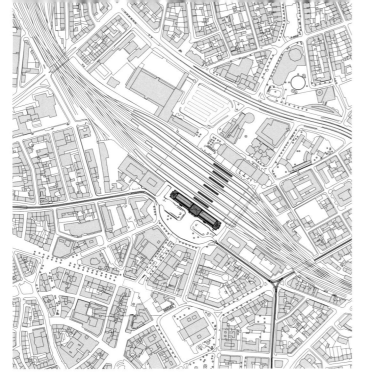

100 m

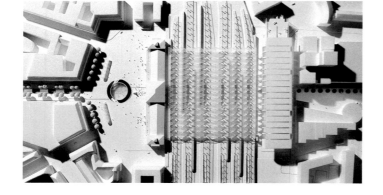

SHAPING THE CITY CENTER

In Hanover, the monumental square in front of the railway station (1845) is regarded as Georg L. F. Laves's most significant contribution to urban planning, opening—as it does—a spatial sequence to Georgsplatz that fundamentally characterizes the image of the city. The first building (Ferdinand Schwarz, 1847), one of the few transit railway stations in Germany at the time, had already been contested for twenty years when work began of raising the tracks up to a height of 4.3 meter along a 8-kilometer-stretch in order to replace existing railway crossings with 22 underpasses. However, the successor building by Hubert Stier, heavily damaged in World War II but used to this day, was not accessible from the rear (Raschplatz) and stood in the way of a pedestrian link to "Ernst-August-Stadt" and the city center. This shortcoming was only overcome by the link realized by Hanns Adrian and Detlef Draser in 1976: bordered by retail stores on the underground level, the pedestrian zone starts out above ground at the Kröpcke in the city center, passes beneath the railroad tracks, and crosses the sunken Raschplatz before reaching the Oststadt, a densely populated nineteenth-century residential district. Ever since the terminal was damaged in the war, the platforms have simply been sheltered with the help of separate roof coverings. The most recent plans emerging from a successful competition proposal envisioned a new, continuous roof above the tracks, an enclosure of the parking garage on Raschplatz incorporating a feature that would attract the public and a generous glass dome on the square in front of the station to light the dim pedestrian zone. The railroad management reduced their plans to conversion and commercialization despite EXPO 2000, and discarded these focal points of the original design. The reduced conversion has nevertheless achieved a far greater degree of order and transparency.

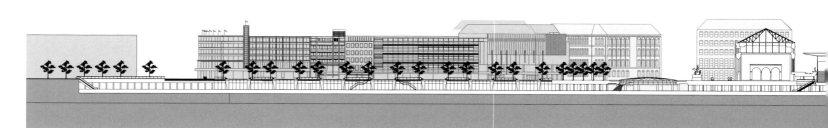

Longitudinal section of bridge

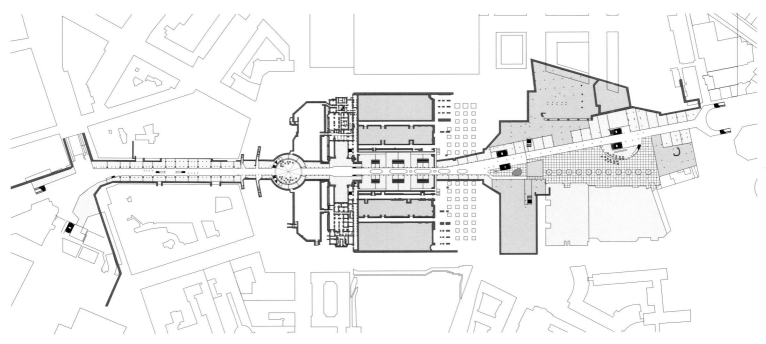

Plan Passerelle, level –1

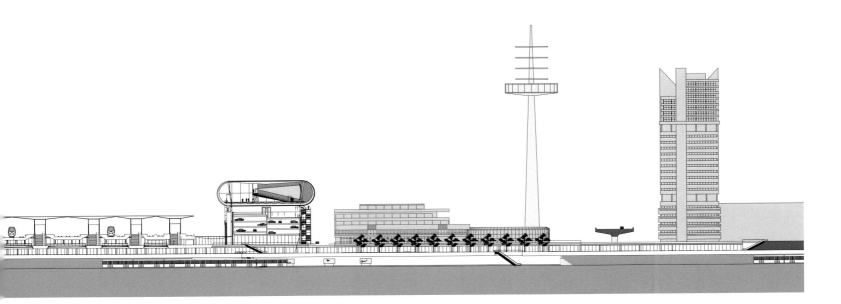

Hanover Main Station

Hanover Main Station

"A design derives its power of conviction from analysis and synthesis." Kai Richter

Hanover Main Station

04

LIVING SPACE

Every dream of a living space begins with a combination of yearning for private happiness and the idea of bequeathing a fairytale villa on a lake—not with an apartment in the city. The consequences for the city are dire because it loses inhabitants over the long term. With regard to innovation in housing construction, the consequences are equally dramatic when demand is focused entirely on finding interim solutions. The beautiful illusion of country living covers up many hidden problems, however, even in the ideal scenario of the villa on the lake—apart from the fact that the reality in small, prefabricated mass homes on small lots far from the city is quite different than the unfailingly optimistic calculations of running costs would have one believe. Today, housing no longer takes the needs of urbanity, integration and self-determination into account. The boom in books on tape began with traffic jams on US highways, because commuters no longer read in the comfort of their own backyard: all they are able to do is to listen in the car. Nevertheless, none of the stressed single-family homeowners and daily commuters is willing to include the time factor in the overall balance sheet of their residential location. There's no time, even for this.

Living in linear order in the so-called countryside turns out to be isolation on plots without spatial qualities or urban context. In practice, a modest distance of two times three meters between detached homes translates into an inhospitable and labor intensive annoyance rather than into a space where individuality can thrive. Acoustic buffers and independence from one's neighbors are far more effectively achieved through technical means in the form of built sound protection.

When the immediate vicinity is neither seen nor heard, the urban apartment in the integrated built environment can be much more luxurious than the country home in a small independent house, provided both alternatives offer identical, home-like living qualities. This applies to the interiors and to the transitional space to the exterior: a small garden, a winter garden or a (roof-) patio. Unfortunately, apartments that meet this requirement in multi-story buildings are still the exception. And even then, usually only when architects build for their own use. The seemingly free decision to opt for home ownership outside of the city is thus in fact a decision against the insufficient living spaces provided in the city, and not against the city itself as a place to live.

Despite shrinkages and restructuring plans in Germany's hardest hit regions, housing demands in conurbations such as Munich or Hamburg continue unabated. Under the motto "Metropolis Hamburg—Growing City," Hamburg has even gone so far as to aim for considerable population growth, from 1.7 million inhabitants thus far to 2 million. Hamburg in particular is therefore in need of housing options that go far beyond mere accommodation, the makeshift of the apartment. On the other hand, the expulsion of residential neighborhoods with a rural appearance from the limited urban area of the city-state is equally counterproductive in the long term. Hamburg's greatest appeal lies in its new waterfront, the Hafen-City. With an average living area of 35.6 square meters per inhabitant, the city occupies the last but one position in a comparison of all states in the Federal Republic. Young people are the driving force behind the gains Hamburg is making with a new influx of people; they are open to new ideas and ownership options in the housing industry, which have little in common with traditional settlements behind picket fences on the periphery apart from living on two storys and freedom with regard to internal divisions or layout.

Living together in the city offers irreplaceable advantages provided the multiplicity of urban life is played out within reach of one's front door. City cannot be replaced by suburb, periphery or country retreats. Conversely, the quality of independent living in the country can easily be surpassed in a privately owned apartment in the city with the appropriate architectural and technical means. The fascination of historic cities lies in their spatial complexity that has by no means grown without human involvement, but was professionally planned. Far from losing out, the individual elements of these urban structures gain through their urban integration. The modern revolutionary Le Corbusier, of all people, who would have liked to raze the old city to the ground, applied this motif to the vertical plan seventy years ago, thus multiplying, at least in theory, the possibilities of realizing single-family homes in the city through properties in multi-story dwellings—in the form of a substructure beneath a highway along the seaside at Algiers.

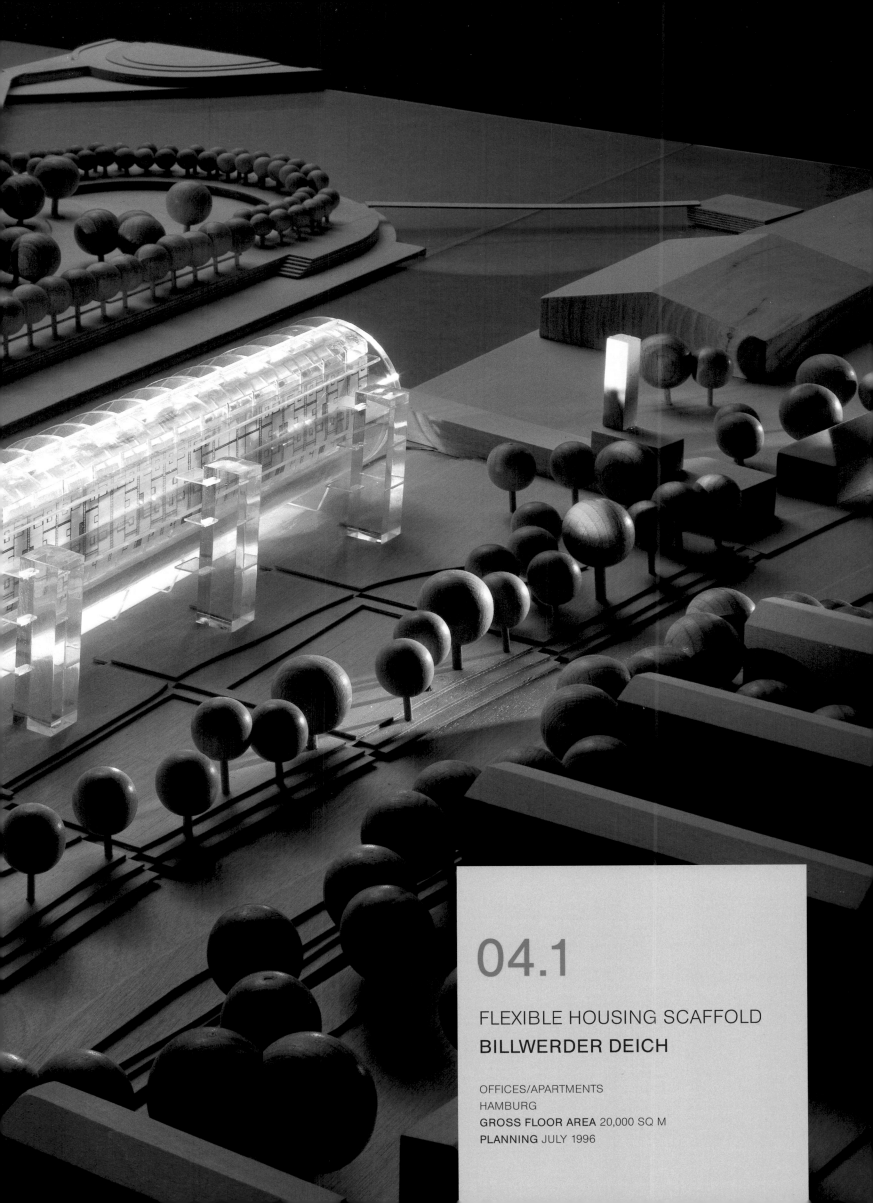

04.1

FLEXIBLE HOUSING SCAFFOLD
BILLWERDER DEICH

OFFICES/APARTMENTS
HAMBURG
GROSS FLOOR AREA 20,000 SQ M
PLANNING JULY 1996

FLEXIBLE HOUSING SCAFFOLD

Ideal highway connections right at the Elbe bridges, Europe's second largest port, the Elbe River and an abundance of nature feature prominently in the advertising material of the high-rise hotel that is a familiar landmark to everyone travelling by car from a southerly direction toward downtown Hamburg. From here, it is but two subway stops to the city's main railway station. And yet this location in Rothenburgsort on the Entenwerder Elbpark is still undiscovered as a residential district, offering converted factory lofts, for example, that would fetch astronomical prices in other urban districts. On the far shore of the Norderelbe, in the industrial area known as "auf der Veddel," the Norddeutsche Affinerie produces copper with a work force of two thousand. The Kleine Grasbrook district on the other side of the bridge across the Elbe is a hub of activity driven by an overseas shipping center, a container terminal and fruit wholesalers, warehouses, and cold-storage depots. A heating power station and incineration plant add to the mix of this industrial inferno. By comparison to the neighboring port districts of Kleine Grasbrook, Veddel, and Billbrook, Rothenburgsort with its high-rises and red clinker buildings is still densely populated. Further east, grazing horses and historic residential homes paint a surprisingly idyllic scene, before the scale changes yet again in the housing scheme of Mümmelmannsberg. In 1996, four new high-rises were planned for the site, the business center at the Elbe bridges, which had already been approved in part. The new lofts behind arcades—an unusual concept for this location— were designed to meet the demand for low-cost space and flexibility with regard to scale, finishing standards, and use (living/ working). While not unusual in its industrial stetting, the large, 220-meter-long structure composed of reinforced concrete frames raised on pilotis to accommodate fluctuating water levels creates its own urban framework on a micro and macro level, benefiting from the proximity to water and the surrounding green space.

20 m

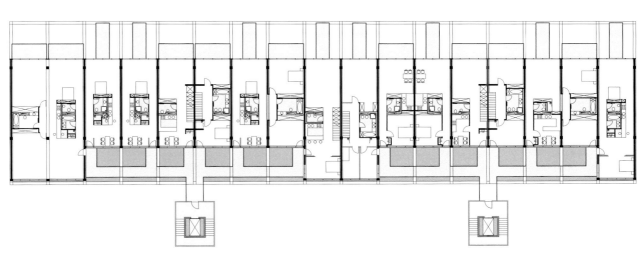

Plan of residential area, 4th floor

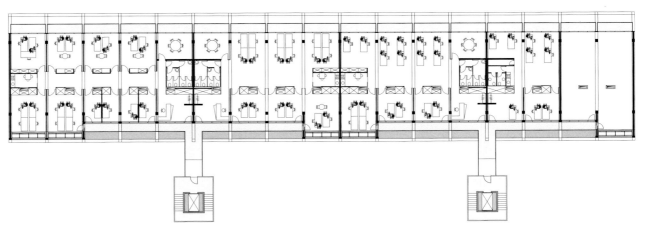

Plan of office, 2nd floor

"Attempts to combine habitation and work in one and the same building are all too often thwarted by the bureaucratic will to impose regulations." Kai Richter

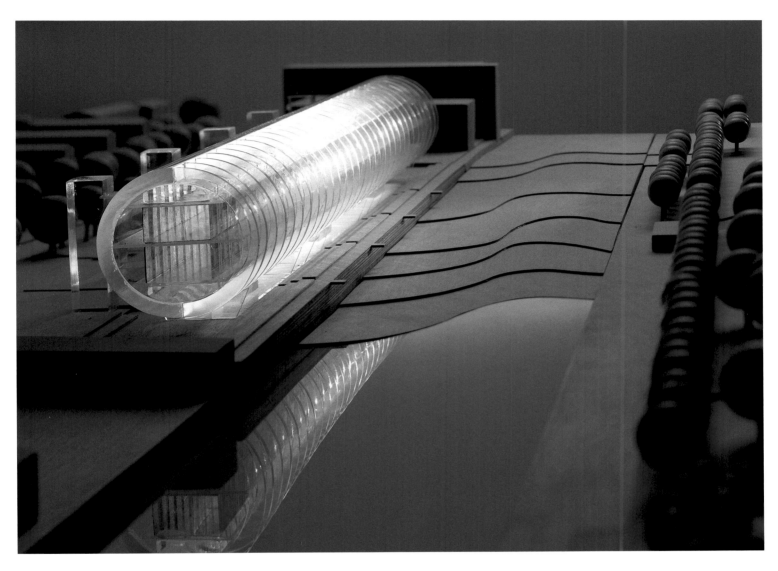

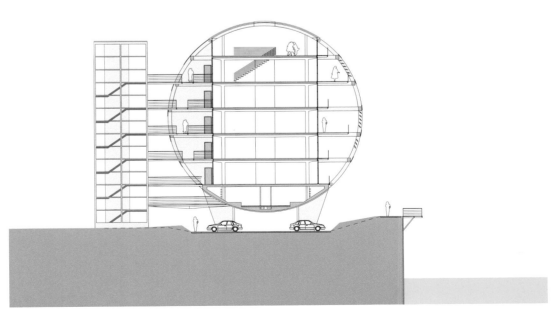

Cross section

04.2

ROUNDED MODERNITY
VILLA, AHRENSBURG

RESIDENTIAL BUILDING
AHRENSBURG
GROSS FLOOR AREA 969 SQ M
BUILT MAY 1996–JULY 1998

ROUNDED MODERNITY

The house in Ahrensburg—an eighteenth-century residential manor founded by a Hamburg merchant some 20 kilometers outside of the city—strikes the eye not because it is provocative and keeps the observer at bay, but because it disregards the convention of aesthetic triviality. It is a manifest expression of architecture, although few elements come into full effect in the streetscape. What is notable is less the change in materials than the intransigence of the rigorously aesthetic line. "The long road from material through function to creative work," Mies van der Rohe remarked, still has "only one goal: to create order that will guide us out of the desperate chaos of our time." Here, however, order does not resort to the mask of anonymity suppressing uniqueness. Property remains an expression of personal freedom, creating a visible anchor and accountability by its very presence. Humus, as Martin Heidegger noted, is related to humanity. Experts in architecture often fail to look beyond the level of a classic-frigid modernity without making allowances for the complexity that accompanied the movement at the time. This impoverished approach leaves ample room for play for charlatans and toxic nostalgia. Few countries can have invested more private and public funds in nondescript housing bliss based on home savings and building center templates than the country that seeks to hide simple-mindedness behind a facade of pomposity. Flat roof, white facade, oriel windows, picture window, two-story focus of the home are derivatives without being copies. The house fits into the landscape without surrendering any of its obstinacy and individuality. One has to circle it on the outside and experience it on the inside: nothing in this house is predictable at first sight. Recesses and glass curves toy with the observer. Differentiated "oriels" and "attics" will be difficult to find.

10 m

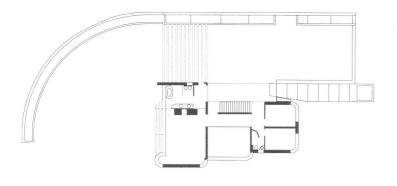

Plan of upper floor

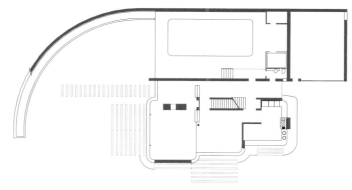

Plan of first floor

Villa, Ahrensburg

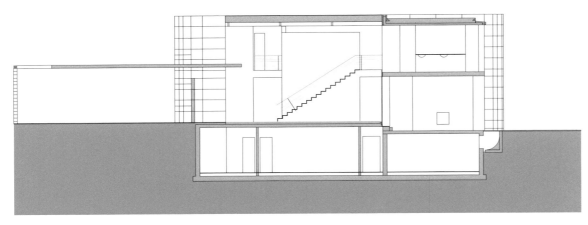

Longitudinal section

Villa, Ahrensburg

"A designer can never be too well informed or too versatile. He must be quick, receptive, and alert. He needs a strong personality, but one shouldn't underestimate such qualities as having a likeable character or being charming." Hadi Teherani

MODERN VILLA ON THE ALSTER
**APARTMENT BUILDING
FÄHRHAUSSTRASSE**

RESIDENTIAL BUILDING
HAMBURG
GROSS FLOOR AREA 2,349 SQ M
BUILT JULY 1997–JUNE 1998

MODERN VILLA ON THE ALSTER

Like the districts of Harvestehude, Rotherbaum, and Winterhude on the outer Alster, the former estate of Uhlenhorst, after which this district is named, grew into an upscale residential neighborhood with villas and city homes. The estate, which included a guesthouse used by the city treasury for a century, had occupied the shore on the Alster between the Feenteich and the Langer Zug tributary up until Hamburg's expansion into a French fortification in 1813. An old structure that could not be converted functionally or spatially into a multi-family dwelling had to make way for the apartment building on these historically significant estate grounds. Uhlenhorst became a suburb in 1871 and was incorporated into the city in 1894. The treasury retained an excellent location when it moved into the guesthouse on the Schöne Aussicht (beautiful vista) shoreline road in 1965. As a result of heavy war damages, the urban image is today largely dominated by modern buildings that have been more or less successfully integrated into the existing historic fabric of Classicist, Neo-Renaissance, and Art Nouveau buildings with a Baroque flair. Away from the shore, the townhouses become more modest, multi-story dwellings more numerous, and further east, residential buildings are intermingled with commercial structures. Given its clever scale and articulation, attic and hidden garden levels, and a facade veiled by adjustable fields of wooden louvers, the new building succeeds in making the transition between grand manor and painfully nondescript apartment house. On the northwest garden elevation, and in particular in the maisonette units on the lower level, the building takes full advantage of the beauty of its deep shoreline lot with large picture windows and sheltered private outdoor spaces. Here, too, however the image of a stylistically ordered, symmetrical villa in the spirit of Palladio is preserved—albeit in a modern style.

20 m

Apartment Building Fährhausstrasse

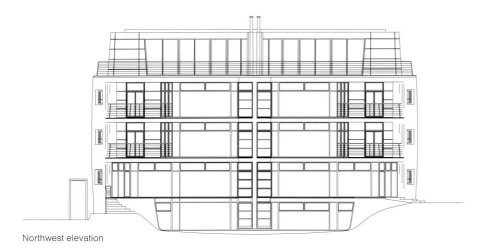

Northwest elevation

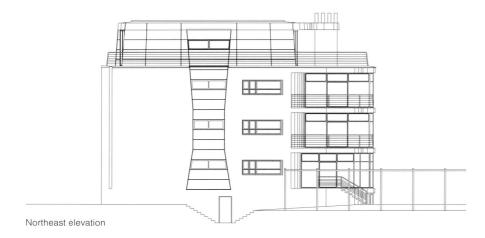

Northeast elevation

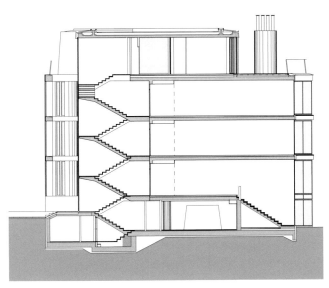

Cross section

Longitudinal section

Apartment Building Fährhausstrasse

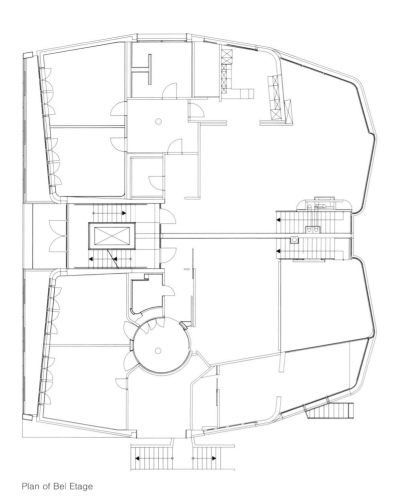

Plan of Bel Etage

"I've always been fascinated by the Bauhaus's idea of creating in one style." Hadi Teherani

04.4

MEANDERING BLOCK OF VILLAS
**APARTMENT BUILDING
MAINZER LANDSTRASSE**

RESIDENTIAL BUILDING
FRANKFURT/MAIN
GROSS FLOOR AREA 3,800 SQ M
BUILT JUNE 2001–MARCH 2003

10 m

MEANDERING BLOCK OF VILLAS

On an extremely small lot, immediately adjacent to the multi-part office complex Carré Mainzer Landstraße, this housing block is the first example where the typology of "home[4]" has been translated into a formal vocabulary on the garden side in the meandering facade design, which reflects the broad spectrum of flexible housing components on the inside. Different materials, facade details, and types of outdoor spaces—from front gardens at the ground level, winter gardens or loggias on the intermediate floors, to roof patios—open up a broad spectrum of possibilities for subsequent projects, room for play to respond to the character of a site and the desires of the inhabitants. For the first time in the genealogy of the house-within-a-house as an identifiable union of individual homes on one floor, function is just as important as architectural aesthetics, all innovation aside. It is unlikely, therefore, that the external image would represent unorthodox forms of multi-story housing. This approach follows in the aesthetic footsteps of Darbourne & Darke or Ralph Erskine, not the parodies of self-realization of the 1970s or post-modernism. After all, Friedensreich Hundertwasser's goal, which is comparable in some ways, consisted in delineating the individual housing unit on the facade—if only in colour. The fact that Le Corbusier was willing to allow Moorish styles cheek by jowl with Louis XVI and Italian Renaissance in his vertical garden city is simply proof of his utter confidence in the utopia of his plan. The interiors of "home4" will provide a greater degree of freedom, even by comparison to Le Corbusier's model from 1922. As simple as this contemporary model may appear at first glance, the project overcomes the challenges of the house-within-a-house, which were deemed insurmountable, with impressive rigor and a harmonious balance of individual criteria.

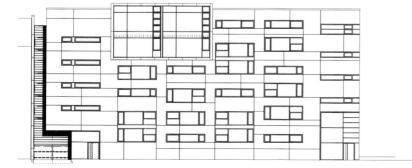

North elevation

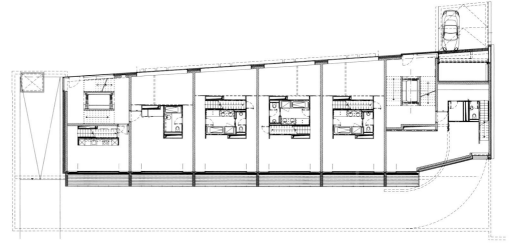

Plan of 3rd floor

Plan of first floor

Apartment Building Mainzer Landstrasse

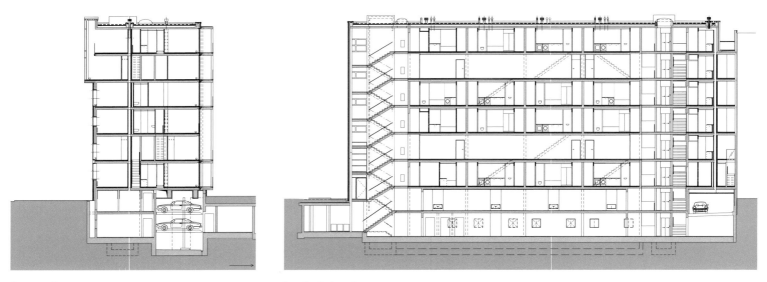

Cross section

Longitudinal section

04.5

URBAN DENSIFICATION
LOFTS FALKENRIED

OFFICES/APARTMENTS
HAMBURG
GROSS FLOOR AREA 7,284 SQ M
BUILT DEC 2001–MARCH 2003
COMPETITION 2000, 1ST PLACE

URBAN DENSIFICATION

The former workshops for public transportation in Eppendorf covering an area of 50,000 square meters is being transformed from streetcar depot into a new urban quarter for some 1,700 inhabitants. Horse-drawn trolleys were still being built here a century ago, and in the years before World War I streetcars and buses were shipped to destinations worldwide. In 1999, the industrial success story came to an end. Aside from office and commercial spaces, the focus for old and new buildings alike is now on apartments and townhouses. Hamburg would like to increase its population, to augment urban density. The common practice of excluding single-family homes from the limited metropolitan area is not a realistic solution. Even at this location there are three-story "townhouses" where the usable floor space on the inside easily surpasses the private outdoor space. Le Corbusier's 70-year-old dream for Algiers was far more rigorous. Then as now the vision consists in creating urban living spaces in multi-story dwellings that provide habitation comparable to being in a single-family home. "home⁴," a project that seeks to implement this goal in the development planned for the docklands, also incorporates the important fourth dimension of habitation: time gain versus the time loss inherent to urban sprawl. The conversion and height increase of the 100-meter-long factory building (1928) in Falkenried are a first step toward translating this concept within the rigorous framework of an old building. The guidelines create a formal vision for an apartment building with two faces, an important phase for Hamburg in making the shift from housing construction to integrated urban building block. Living in the futuristic addition, in airy two-level units, is a quick cure for the American nightmare of spending ten years of one's life commuting by car.

Lofts Falkenried

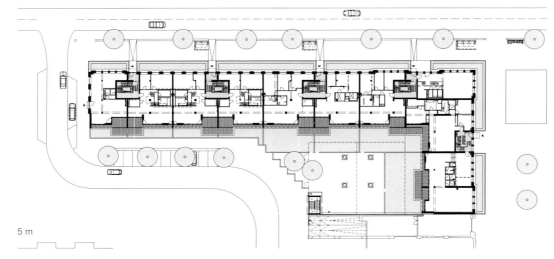

5 m

Plan of first floor

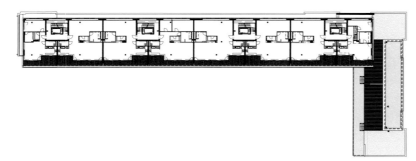

Plan of 4th floor

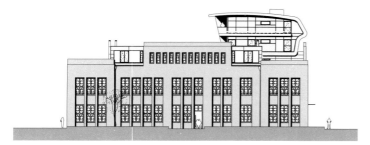

Southeast elevation

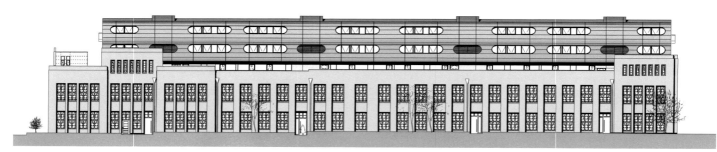

Northeast elevation

Southwest elevation

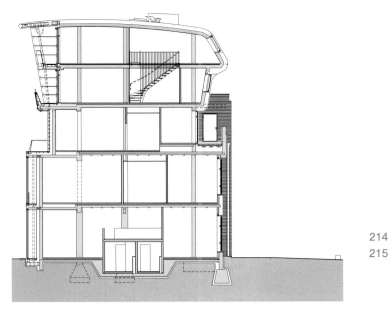

Cross section

"In our architectural concepts, efficiency in form invariably leads to a comprehensive economic solution." Jens Bothe

Lofts Falkenried

04.6

ARTIFICIAL CRYSTAL ROCK

VILLA, MOSCOW

RESIDENTIAL BUILDING
MOSCOW
GROSS FLOOR AREA 1,400 SQ M
PLANNING FEB 2002

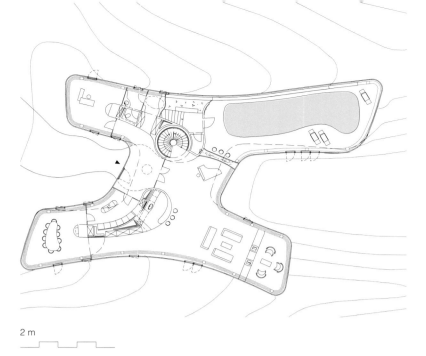

2 m

Plan of first floor

ARTIFICIAL CRYSTAL ROCK

Some of the most famous housing structures of the classic modern are simple glass cubes that expose an interior to an exterior space with a continuous, structural glass box serving as the only separating component. Nature and architecture are visually integrated, albeit formally separated: unfettered growth and landscape versus order and shelter—a roof and a void. Today, computer-synthesized, breathing biomorphism leads the way in the search for new aesthetics, new materials, and technological advances, but also for leaps in architectural philosophy, if realization can be successfully achieved. The idea is not one of spatial integration of nature but of incorporating the dynamic forms of nature or other domains in order to breathe new formal life into architecture from the outside. Reality, however, is stubborn: while sculptured natural forms may add drama to the formal appearance of architecture, they have little impact on its relationship with the exterior or indeed the interior space. The question of new architecture is spatial not formal. Answers were found as far back as the beginning of the modern, when Mies van der Rohe employed glass models in 1919 to experiment with reflections, creating prismatic and polygonal divisions for his spectacular Berlin high-rise projects. Given the limited technological opportunities of the time, the rational approach of modernism prevailed in the years that followed. At the villa in Moscow, a glittering veil of glass is also stretched in a predominantly monotonous rhythm over freeform, exposed concrete floors, which do not reveal their structural bond. The three-dimensional puzzle between interior and exterior nevertheless opens up a spatial relationship with nature, which biomorphism alone cannot achieve under the guise of pure will to form.

Plan of upper floor

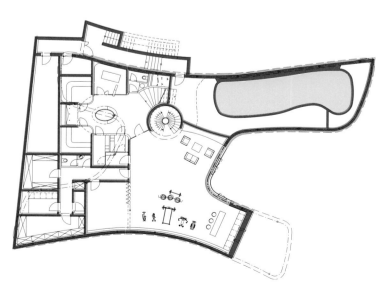

Plan of basement floor

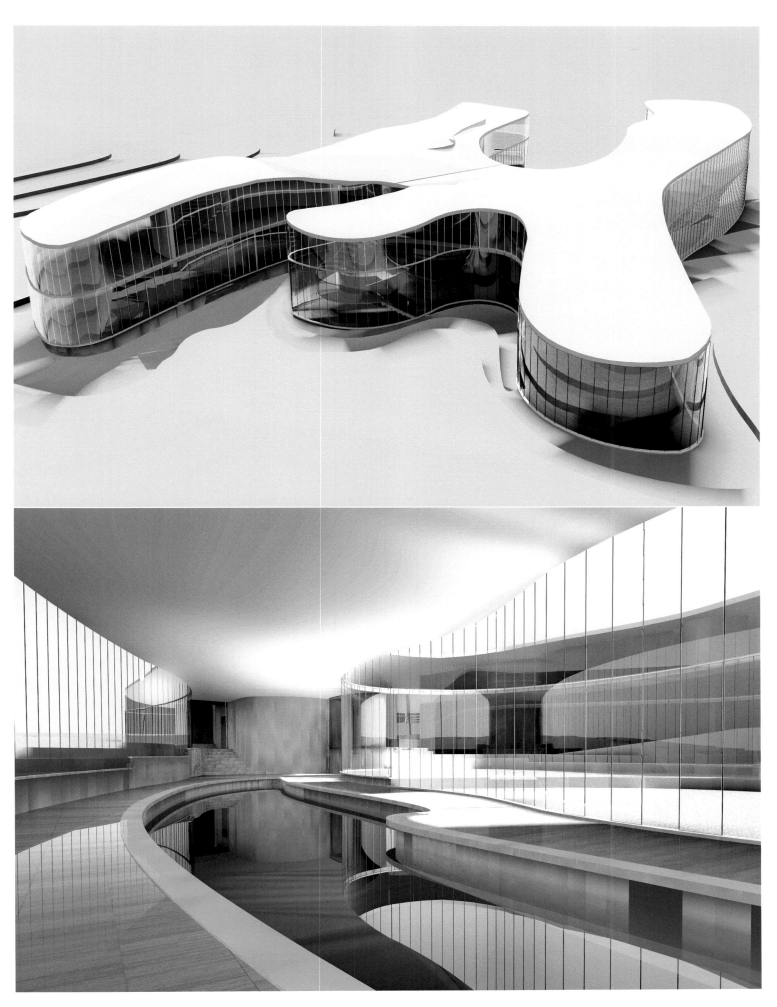

Villa, Moscow

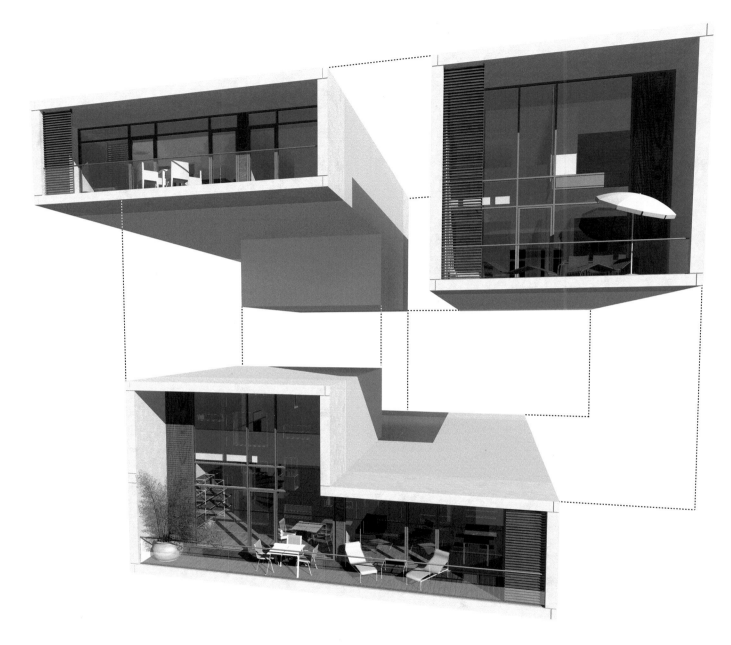

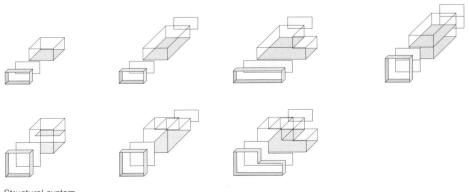

Structural system

Le Corbusier, Vertical Garden City, 1931

deficiencies of one-dimensional living have to be overcome through countless car trips by the homeowner, a countermeasure that his highly questionable both ecologically and economically. The only alternative is to tolerate a complete absence of any cultural or social life. The ability to choose freely among several options, on the other hand, is a quality that differentiates life in high-density housing in the city from the supposedly countrified lifestyle in the periphery. The evil specter of the apartment or "social housing," however, banished all opportunities for insight into these dynamics. Ulrich Conrads, editor-in-chief of the journal *Bauwelt* for many years, unmasked the comparison of apartment versus house as false and exposed the majority of single-family homes as being mere "social houses" when compared to social housing—an apposite synonym that, unfortunately, failed to take hold. The motto of "Society through Density" or "Urbanity through Density" was full of negative connotations when set against the garden city idea of the turn of the last century. And yet there was nothing wrong with it. What *was* universally wrong, however, was the architectural inference—on both sides of the city walls. And worst of all was the slogan: "As many single-family homes as possible, as few apartments as absolutely necessary." For the apartment homes for Algiers, Le Corbusier's revolutionary idea, which he described in uncharacteristically terse language in *La ville radieuse* in 1935, had long been forgotten by then. "Here are 'artificial sites', vertical garden cities. (...) The architectural aspect is stunning! The most absolute diversity, within unity. Every architect will build his villa as he likes; what does it matter to the whole if a Moorish-style villa flanks another in Louis XVI or in Italian Renaissance?"[4]

INTEGRATION

It is almost alarming how the arguments put forth in expert circles around the globe converged in the 1960s without having the slightest impact on the practice of urban planning, a few exceptions aside. The practical solution which the Russian-born Chermayeff, successor to Laszlo Moholy-Nagy at the Institute of Design in Chicago, and the Viennese Christopher Alexander, both trained in England, proposed in 1963, was dense carpet development composed of deep, single-story buildings set around garden courtyards with a network of narrow, labyrinthine pedestrian paths.[5] For the United States, this was a revolutionary, area-efficient approach in the spirit of Roland Rainer, albeit not a constructive, long-term urban strategy by comparison to the far more complex model of the European city. As Lewis Mumford stated, the city is justifiably regarded as "the most precious invention of civilization, second

only to language in its role as a mediator of culture."[6] It is the quintessential repository of history. Nevertheless, the last fifty years have been marked by the unfettered sprawl of subdivisions, all driven by the untouchable decree of home ownership. We have forgotten that the urban experience begins on the doorstep of one's private home, fundamentally influencing daily life with shopping and leisure, the route to school and office, culture and communication: depending on the aesthetic stimuli and the free choice between entering into contact or keeping a distance, this influence is experienced as positive or negative. In their individual districts, large cities should strive to emulate small towns and create a unique space as a focal point, a "small, comfortably everyday public sphere, albeit one that has nothing in common with the pre-industrial village green," as Hans-Paul Bahrdt put it in 1968.[7] Modern apartments in this varied ensemble of functions and forms should not only declare their modernity through advanced technology, but above all by providing their residents with opportunities for cultural growth in the immediate vicinity. Seen from this perspective, the size of a largely autonomous urban quarter is defined by the distance one can comfortably cross on foot: ten minutes, that is, ten thousand residents.

"A city is more than the sum of its inhabitants. It has the power to generate a surplus of amenity, which is one reason why people like to live in communities rather than in isolation," wrote Gordon Cullen, the Camillo Sitte of the sixties. "One building standing alone in the countryside is experienced as a work of architecture, but bring half a dozen buildings together and an art other than architecture is made possible. Several things begin to happen in the group which would be impossible for the isolated building. We may walk through and past the buildings, and as a corner is turned an unsuspected building is suddenly revealed. We may be surprised, even astonished (a reaction generated by the composition of the group and not by the individual building). (...) In fact there is an *art of relationship* just as there is an art of architecture. Its purpose is to take all the elements that go to create the environment: buildings, trees, nature, water, traffic (...), and to weave them together in such a way that drama is released. For a city is a dramatic event in the environment."[8] In this passage, Cullen formulated the decisively more complex antithesis to Le Corbusier's image of the "masterful, correct, and magnificent play of masses brought together in light."[9]

In his housing experiment "Habitat" at EXPO 67 in Montreal, Moshe Safdie demonstrated that the ideal housing form of the future should be sought in a combination of single-family housing and apart-

Caricature of multi-story villa, ca. 1920

ment. The spectacular, strongly articulated macrostructure of 158 housing units, linked by an elaborate network of bridges and constructed from prefabricated, industrial concrete boxes, which are assembled like Lego building blocks into a honeycombed open housing pyramid, inspired countless utopian projects, but few concrete realizations. The British architects and landscape designers John Darbourne and Geoffrey Darke, on whose work no major publication exists to this day with the exception of a small exhibition catalogue, had already designed a more realistic concept in 1961 with the Lillington Gardens project, a residential complex in London that responds to the city and its spatial requirements, the first building phase of which was completed in 1968. Only in this case, in contrast to Le Corbusier's epochal proposal, the individual housing unit was barely legible from the outside due to a complicated arrangement of living levels that served the purpose of providing ground-level access to all units, while nevertheless achieving a building height of up to five stories with the help of traffic bridges between the upper duplex apartment units.

INDIVIDUALITY

A review of innovation in multi-story housing, undertaken in 1987, was thus doomed to reach a negative conclusion: residents are all too ready to interpret the failure of urban housing construction as their own failure to achieve the path toward the ultimate salvation and happiness of their own home—for financial reasons. Any rapprochement between dream and reality in high-density housing is seen as utopian, there is no demand for it and, hence, no supply in keeping with the mechanisms that drive a free-market economy. However, the crude strategy of catering to the building savings plan holder's favorite choice would be tantamount to confusing a preference born from necessity with a well-founded choice between true alternatives. For the public makes a simple choice with regard to accommodation. The less advantageous the stacked goods in mass housing are, the more appealing is the lure of habitation on one's own initiative.[10] According to the liberalism of the Scottish national economist Adam Smith, the free actions of individuals driven by the pursuit of personal advantage are the foundation of all natural and social laws. However, in the context of urban planning the factual renunciation of planning and supervision failed to satisfy the optimistic thesis of an equilibrium based on the fulfillment of all individual interests. With the loss of control over the building ground, the public sector also lost all regulatory influence on the real estate market. Thus the history of ideas and initia-

tives always fell behind the history of trends and facts. While the room to maneuver in the interest of personal decisions was certainly limited in the old bourgeois city, there was freedom for individual architectural expression within a prescribed pattern that was accepted as given. Today, the question of how the ill-advised subjects who were to be the masters of the city, live, or rather how they wish to live, remains unanswered. There is a lack of architectural and urbanistic alternatives, with which the individual could correct his illusions and expand his vision.

In his search for social imagination in urbanity and community, Sigfried Giedion referred in 1956 to Le Corbusier's *Unité d'Habitation* in Marseille, completed four years previously, as stunning proof that housing would in future no longer have to be restricted to "individual housing cells arranged in stacks or rows."[11] The basic idea of expanding the concept of housing, then and now, consists in creating brighter living environments in the high-rise—with the help of two-story spaces even at the expense of living area. Already in his villa blocks from 1922, an individual unit of which was exhibited in Paris in 1925, Le Corbusier designed apartment living in a house-like manner on two floors, exponentially increasing the possibilities for privacy and space in the apartment type. In Marseille, each two-story maisonette (or duplex apartment) was, as Giedion stressed, oriented toward two sides: "To the east, the view embraces an arena of limestone mountains in the distance, as they are seen everywhere in Provence. To the west, the view offers the blue expanse of the Mediterranean in the distance and the tranquil aspect of green tree tops nearby, punctuated by red tiled rooftops." The principal shortcoming of this model was the fact that the urban spatial integration of housing with the immediate vicinity had been abandoned in favor of separating functions in the spirit of the Charter of Athens, which was operative at the time. Yet Le Corbusier's housing model would have been ideally suited to the modular requirements of a modern building industry.

The housing reform, successful both architecturally and in terms of interior space, which Le Corbusier propagated in the context of preserving the qualities of an open and flexible floor plan, and which had already been expressed in the anonymous architectural style of the American single-family house even prior to Frank Lloyd Wright, failed to become the standard in the competition for the private detached home—not even with regard to the internal spatial qualities. Whereas the single-family house could claim to be "unique," even in cases where it satisfied only the lowest common denominator of design in the form of vulgar functionalism on a lot of one's own, mass housing on the urban periphery

The "housing-over" principle

was hit especially hard by the architectonic simplifications of the 1950s, '60s and '70s—further exacerbating the chasm between individual and community, between villa resident and the "average barrack-dwelling Central European" (Roland Rainer). In 1961, the sociologist Hans-Paul Bahrdt had issued an urgent warning against this erroneous development: "The thoughtless identification of home ownership with low-rise building, on the one hand, and rental accommodation and multi-story buildings, on the other, is fatal."[12]

MOBILITY

The ultimate dream home, the detached single-family house, quickly turns into a nightmare when one analyzes the time schedule of its inhabitants: according to statistics gathered by the relevant federal ministry in Germany, every driver spends 96 minutes on the road on average per day, covering an average distance of 44 kilometers (driving to work and schools 21 %, shopping 19 %, errands including "dropping off and picking up" 21 %, leisure 31 %). The average time spent is therefore 11.2 hours per week, or more than 24 days per year. Based on time calculations employed by labor unions, this translates into almost seventeen 35-hour weeks. From a purely economic perspective, the work time required to finance private transportation has to be added as well, especially since every household has an average of 1.1 cars (0.8 in 1989), that is, since over 28 percent of all households run more than one car. According to the ADAC (German automobile association) the total cost of driving a VW Golf, model 1.9 TDI, 44km/day or 16,000 km/year, runs to more than 5,000 euro per year. And this does not even take the ecological and overall economic costs into account. The quickest remedy to the purely economic misery of urban sprawl today are commuter ride programs, which aim for a greater number of passengers per car (1.04 for business commuters). On the other hand, this model of everyday group travel is hardly compatible with the dreamed-of individuality associated with living in a single-family house. In Germany, we may soon see similarly dramatic time losses as those experienced by American commuters. Reversing this trend, both politically and in terms of urban planning, is becoming ever more difficult.

APARTMENT = HOUSE X CITY

But even this thesis is nothing new, as a prominent example illustrates. In the United States, Victor Gruen, born in Vienna in 1903, is widely regarded as the father of the shopping mall and—later on—of the urban pedestrian zone. His plea for a humane-ecological approach to urban planning, released in 1975, is therefore also rooted in his own mistakes: "The tragicomic aspect of the worship of mobility is that the era of the highest point in the civilization of humankind began when man settled down, when he abandoned his nomadic life and his occupation of hunting and gathering and turned to cultivation, crafts, commerce, and trade. (…) The settled way of life gave rise to the virtues of *civitas* or to that which we call civilization thanks to law, art, and science. The only remarkable thing is that after some 10,000 years of practicing a settled way of life, humankind has returned to a nomadic lifestyle. (…) As a result we expend so much time and energy for our vagabond existence that we have very few means and possibilities at our disposal for the provision of our houses and apartments, our neighborhoods and cities."[13] Thirty years ago, Roland Rainer, the prominent champion of high-density, low-rise building, was also fascinated by the alternative and more urban idea of single-family homes in condominiums: "In view of the desolate banality of most rental apartments erected today by various developers, on the one hand, (…) and of the well-documented rapid change in family dynamics, lifestyles, and living standards, on the other hand, the idea of being able to buy or rent a floor, where one could create living spaces with adjacent patios and so on, to one's own specifications and connect them to cables of all kinds, thus gaining an individual home, a single-family house in the air, so to speak, without land use, access costs, or garden 'work,' has tremendous appeal."[14] Le Corbusier created his stunning sketch of this dream seventy years ago as part of his urban planning study for Algiers. In the impressive *Gesamtkunstwerk*, which caused quite a stir at the time, it is above all this small drawing, which became one of the architect's most published works. This was only after 1961, however, when the Dutchman Nicolaas John Habraken found inspiration in it for his book SUPPORTS: *an alternative to mass housing*—albeit without any specific reference to the ideological link between the two works. The English edition was published in 1972, the German edition much later, in 2000.[15] Habraken caused a sensation with his book, even though it did not contain a single illustration, not even a reproduction of Le Corbusier's sketch. On a purely theoretical level, Habraken pleaded in favor of maintaining the medieval, individual structural principle of the bourgeois home in housing development, even in the big city, according to

The "highrise of homes" principle

the old principle which Le Corbusier had pursued since 1922: "Each unit is in truth a two-story house, a villa with a hanging garden, regardless of the height at which it is located. It [the garden] consists of a six-meter-high loggia. The house resembles a giant sponge that sucks in air: the house breathes." [16] In 1970, Le Corbusier's famous sketch had been published in the Netherlands on an enormously large scale of nearly one meter in length, together with a contribution on participation in housing construction. Although sections and plans have survived, neither Le Corbusier's sketch nor Habraken's book were aimed at concrete realization: their impact lay chiefly in the suggestive effect they had.

Attempts at stacking the status symbol of the villa while preserving its antiquated image must be seen as pure utopia. One illusory draft, which the American group of architects S.I.T.E. adopted in 1981 from a then more than seventy-year-old illustration in Life magazine to inspire enthusiasm for a revised edition under the title "Highrise of Homes" in Manhattan, at the site, no less, of New York's Museum of Modern Art, has failed to contribute any built projects to this day. The airspace above the double roof of the homes offers no advantage whatsoever, it does not reveal the sky but only an inescapably banal view of the underside of the ceiling. Both drawings, which should be rated rather as caricatures,—dating from 1909 and 1981, respectively—simply prove how deeply the image of the villa is rooted in pure status value beyond any form of practical utility. The idea is so startling, however, that one need hardly wonder that it has met with so little success. The only project of this kind realized thus far by Erik Friberger in Göteborg failed to draw any attention: a total of no less than eighteen single-family homes were realized as early as 1960 on vertically stacked concrete foundations. [17] The goals, which are as valid as ever, have led to a building in Göteborg that delivers the antithesis to the theoretically logical chain of argumentation. Given the banality of a parking garage structure with awkwardly placed single-family homes, almost like mass housing in type, architecture is increasingly diminished to the level of technical administration of individual interests.

It would make more sense to combine the modular building blocks, which Moshe Safdie had already used like Lego bricks to multiply the spatial options available to the residents, with an individual facade section in the overall elevation of the building. Identification by color alone—as in Le Corbusier's loggias fronting his Unité d'Habitation—is too little, however. Only a structured city is a recognizable city. This task is made easier by the fact that the demand for individual appearance and the necessity of outdoor space as a garden experience on each level

overlap in the exterior view of the condominium. Each unit is indispensably reliant on immediate contact with nature, that is, on an encounter with biological processes. As the Swiss architect Otti Gmür illustrated in 1977, the space required to meet this fundamental need is minute: "But earth, water, and air must be available to us for this purpose. For the experiences and observations must be made on one's own initiative; in a piece of nature that is more than an attempt to decorate a sterile environment." [18]

INTRICACY

When Gordon Cullen introduced the concept of intricacy in his book Townscape, he coined the definitive term for the future of urban housing in general. [19] Neither Le Corbusier's plans for Algiers, nor Moshe Safdie's model project Habitat achieved this intricacy, and the utopian images of a "Highrise of Homes" by the American team S.I.T.E. even less so. Within the genealogy of the high-rise of homes, the distinctive feature of the "home[4]" model lies in the complexity and individuality of the meandering facade image, which reflects the broad spectrum of the different one—or multi-story housing units with flexible internal divisions. At the same time, the labyrinthine motif of this three-dimensional housing puzzle, conceived to be realized at standard market prices, indicates the goal—in contrast to Le Corbusier's visions—of harmonizing the scale with the framework of the existing city. The drafts available thus far present only model solutions. The "home[4]" concept does not aim to revolutionize the urban space, but to close and complete it. In contrast to all utopian housing hills, funnel, or sprawling cities, this concept demands unambiguous, space-forming geometries. The only prerequisite for the variety is that the individual puzzle pieces must combine into a geometric shape without gaps. The new presence of the "bourgeois home" in the city, which amounts to a renewed shift from "country dweller" to "city dweller," will no doubt have a profound and complex impact on the quality of the city. Once the time savings of this type of housing in attractive urban settings by comparison to living completely outside of the urban context are recognized, the migratory balance in attractive cities can develop all the more quickly in a positive direction. The future of living in the city might thus finally gain a new dynamic energy and quality. No step toward a revival of the diversity of the city would be more daring than abandoning the endless repetition of housing, and reversing the trend of exiling the citizen from urban traditions. In 1964, Jacob Berend Bakema posed the thought-provoking question: "If our cities were to be buried in ash as

home⁴ TEHERANI

Pompeii was in ancient times, what would an archaeologist think upon discovering the endless repetition of identical housing units beneath the ash? Would he recognize it as the expression of a living democracy or of a slave state?"[20] The urban citizens of the twentieth century were adept at describing in great detail how to positively influence the progress of urban living and of the city. But it is up to the urban dwellers of the twenty-first century to translate the idea into reality.

Notes

1   Gerhard Boeddinghaus (ed.): "Gesellschaft durch Dichte. Kritische Initiativen zu einem neuen Leitbild für Planung und Städtebau 1963/1964" (Bauwelt Fundamente 107), Braunschweig/Wiesbaden 1995, pp. 42ff.

2   Hans-Paul Bahrdt: *Die moderne Großstadt. Soziologische Überlegungen zum Städtebau*, Reinbek 1961, p. 116

3   Roland Rainer: Für eine lebensgerechtere Stadt, Vienna/Munich 1974 (1968), p. 18

4   Le Corbusier: *The Radiant City*, (New York: The Orian Press, 1967), translated by Eleanor Levieux (Parts II, VI0, p. 42; cf. Arnulf Lüchinger: *2-Komponenten-Bauweise*, Den Haag 2000, p. 19)

5   Serge Chermayeff, Christopher Alexander: *Community and Privacy. Toward a New Architecture of Humanism*. (New York: Anchor Books, Doubleday, 1963), p. 62

6   Lewis Mumford: Die Stadt. Geschichte und Ausblick (1961), after Alexander Mitscherlich: Drei Aspekte der Stadtriesen: Wachstum, Planung, Chaos, in: Uwe Schultz (Hrsg.): *Umwelt aus Beton oder Unsere unmenschlichen Städte*, Reinbek 1971, p. 132

7   Hans-Paul Bahrdt: *Humaner Städtebau* (1968), Hamburg 1971, p. 118

8   Gordon Cullen: *The Concise Townscape*. (London: The Architectural Press, 1961) pp. 7/8

9   Le Corbusier, Towards a New Architecture, translated by John Rodker, in: Essentiel Le Corbusier L´Esprit Noveau Articles (Oxford: Architectual Press, 1998), pp. 29, 131

10 Klaus-Dieter Weiss: Grenzenloses Wohnen: zwischen Wohnung, Haus und Stadt, in: Fischer, Fromm, Gruber, Kähler, Weiß: *Abschied von der Postmoderne* (Bauwelt Fundamente 64), Braunschweig 1987, pp. 103/106

11 Sigfried Giedion, Space, Time and Architecture, Harvard 2003, 5th edition

12 Hans-Paul Bahrdt: op. cit., p. 116

13 Victor Gruen: *Die lebenswerte Stadt*, Munich 1975, p. 33

14 Roland Rainer: Für eine lebensgerechtere Stadt (1974, p. 50), cited in: Gerd Albers, Alexander Papageorgiou-Venetas: *Stadtplanung. Entwicklungslinien 1945–1980* (vol. 2), Tübingen 1984, p. 483

15 Nicolaas John Habraken: *SUPPORTS: an alternative to mass housing.* Translated from the Dutch by B. Vlakenburg Ariba, (London: The Architectural Press, 1972), p. 55. cf.: Arnulf Lüchinger: *2-Komponenten-Bauweise/Die Träger und die Menschen,* The Hague 2000

16 Le Corbusier, after: Sigfried Giedion: *Architektur und Gemeinschaft. Tagebuch einer Entwicklung*, Hamburg 1956, p. 103

17 Klaus-Dieter Weiss: Highrise in Göteborg. Etagengrundstücke, *deutsche bauzeitung* 8/1990, cf.: Wilfried Dechau (ed.): *...in die Jahre gekommen. Wohnungsbauten von gestern heute gesehen*, Stuttgart 1996, pp. 62ff.

18 Otti Gmür: Stadt als Heimat (1977, p. 91), cited in: Gerd Albers, Alexander Papageorgiou-Venetas: *Stadtplanung. Entwicklungslinien 1945–1980* (vol. 2), Tübingen 1984, p. 485

19 Gordon Cullen: op. cit., p. 64

20 Jacob Berend Bakema: Identität und Intimität der Großstadt, *Bauen + Wohnen* 1/1964, cited in: Josef Lehmbrock, Wend Fischer: *Profitopolis oder: Der Mensch braucht eine andere Stadt* (Exhibition catalog, Die Neue Sammlung, Munich, November 29, 1971 to February 13, 1972), Munich 1971, plate 4 (no page)

04.8

URBAN BRIDGE-BUILDING
LIVING BRIDGE HAMBURG

BRIDGE, APARTMENTS, RETAIL
HAMBURG
GROSS FLOOR AREA 200,300 SQ M
PLANNING JAN 2004

200 m

Access

URBAN BRIDGE-BUILDING

Hamburg, one of the least densified cities in the world, is discovering its waterfronts. The potential in the area between the estuary and the inlets seems inexhaustible, for Hamburg's most desirable districts south of the Elbe between the suburbs, the Stadtpark, and the City-Süd can easily be doubled. Wilhelmsburg covers an area that makes it the largest urban district as well as Europe's largest river island, to which Napoleon crossed in 1814 via a 4-kilometer-long wooden bridge. Once the link to the new bridge is completed, the island will lie in the heart of the city. Hamburg's waterfront, 40 percent of which is still occupied by docklands today including areas as close to downtown as Ottensen, offers the best conditions for kilometers of attractive and distinctive waterfront locations. Only 2.7 percent of the city's residents currently inhabit what amounts to 4.6 percent of the metropolitan area. Even without hosting the Olympics in 2012, Hamburg aims to capitalize on the spirit of renewal for its former hinterland and increase its appeal by taking the leap across the Elbe, an ambition that is further aided by the International Garden Exhibition and an International Building Exhibition scheduled for 2013. According to Adolf Max Vogt, the chief advantage of waterfront cities is that water provides space and breathing room for critical introspection and analysis. Bridging the Elbe by developing inner city qualities that will erase the division of the city into two parts on either side of the harbour—the status quo for over a century—changes the Hanseatic image of the city in a dramatic fashion. While the view of Hamburg's skyline remains undiminished, the opportunity for development on this scale in the heart of the city is without compare. The proposed 700-meter-long, multi-story bridge complex across the Norderelbe combines the necessary traffic function with a green park zone and affordable living space on lots that have been literally plucked out of the air.

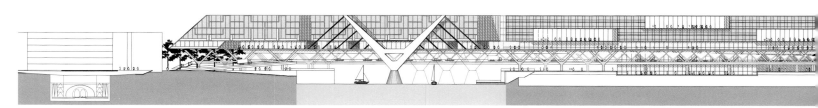

Southwest elevation

"We are always seeking something new – in forms, materials, or uses." Jens Bothe

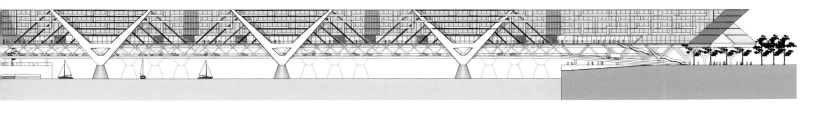

Living Bridge Hamburg

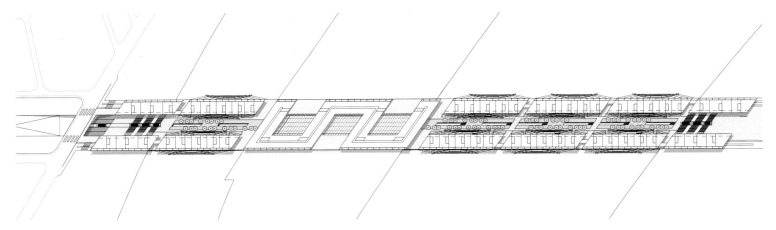

Plan of 2nd to 5th floor

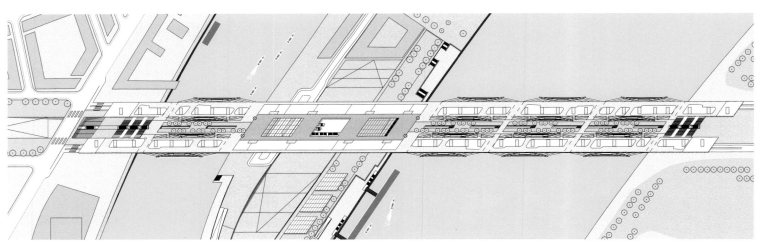

Plan of first floor

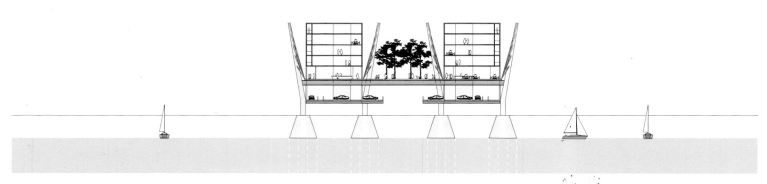

Schematic cross section, above Elbe river

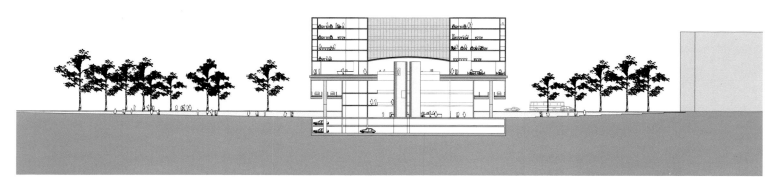

Schematic cross section, peninsula

05

LEISURE TIME

The share of working hours over the course of a lifetime has been halved in the last century; in the past thirty years, the number of working hours per year has dropped by 30 percent while productivity has increased fourfold. In 1850, employees in Germany worked an average of 82 hours per week; at the turn of the century, 60 hours; in 1960, only 45 hours; currently, the average is about 35 hours. Naturally, these statistics do not take into account the more leisurely tempo of work or the higher degree of self-determination in labor these days, nor the self-exploitation and unrealistic demands individuals place on themselves within today's self-determined labor processes. In 1999, the entire volume of paid labor totaled 47.4 billion hours, amounting to an average yearly workload of 1,481 hours per employee—including part-timers. If each of these individuals had performed 250 fewer hours of paid labor (around seven weeks), Germany would currently have full employment, mathematically speaking.

Thanks to a new awareness of ecological issues and the environment—which has resulted in a decrease in usage of conventional energy sources and an increase in recycling—the glorification of growing production by big businesses has been largely obstructed. Whether the service industry can maintain the dream of a constantly rising GNP and the long-term centrality of paid work remains doubtful. The tasks of invention, planning, communication, advising, teaching, entertainment, care, comforting, assisting, accompanying cannot be automated. So, if our level of prosperity can be maintained in the foreseeable future with just 1,000 hours of paid work, what should we do with 7,760 hours of free time per year that we will gain? A culture society à la Bertold Brecht will not emerge on its own: "Someday when there is time / We will ponder the thoughts of all thinkers of all times / examine the pictures of all the masters / laugh at all jokers / flatter all women / and teach all men." Nevertheless, the early Marxist utopia that calls for a dissolution of the division of labor will recede into the wings of our consciousness and a "three-time society" will emerge, which features a new kind of full-time employment in three areas: conventional paid work in the system of social division of labor to ensure prosperity, public welfare work to supplement the bureaucratic social state, and independent and repair work to limit the division of labor's excessive emphasis on productivity and the increasingly fragmentary nature of our conditions of life.

Forty years ago, Hannah Arendt predicted that the labor society would run out of work determined by others. In the expansion of self-determined activity, the rehabilitation of leisure, and contemplation and play based on the life models of antiquity and the Middle Ages, lie the utopian potentials of this epoch—linked with the chance to reduce to a reasonable level the consumption of resources and the burden on the environment in a sustainable kind of economy. The prerequisite for this is that each individual avoid the compulsion to raise consumption and make the wealth of time an integral component of his or her personal model of prosperity—without placing excessive demands on flexibility, mobility and profitability. For this to be possible, the sphere of private and civil relations in society must also be protected from the totalitarian grip of the culture and entertainment industry. For "where there are dreams," according to the Trend Office in Hamburg, "there are also markets. And in the future, markets will hinge on one great vision: to optimize the body so that the individual can shape his or her own life. Those who deal in goods and provide services today, will offer the goods of fate tomorrow: better health, happier relationships, more security, requited love."

The ability of contemporary leisure profiteers to influence their clientele is illustrated best in the success story of the enterprise platform "Autostadt" (Car City) in Wolfsburg. According to a company press release dated September 16, 2002, this brand-name amusement park is second only to the Europa-Park in Rust as the "leisure establishment with the second highest number of visitors in Germany": 5 million visitors in 27 months, which is more than 5,000 per day. Moreover, "95 percent of the visitors perceive of "Autostadt" as a harmonious place, [while] 92 percent are there primarily to relax." In contrast to profit-oriented marketing culture and the philosophy of consumption, the cultivation of free time requires that we refrain from completely marketing ourselves, and demand areas of life that are independent of consumption and derive value from their own existence.

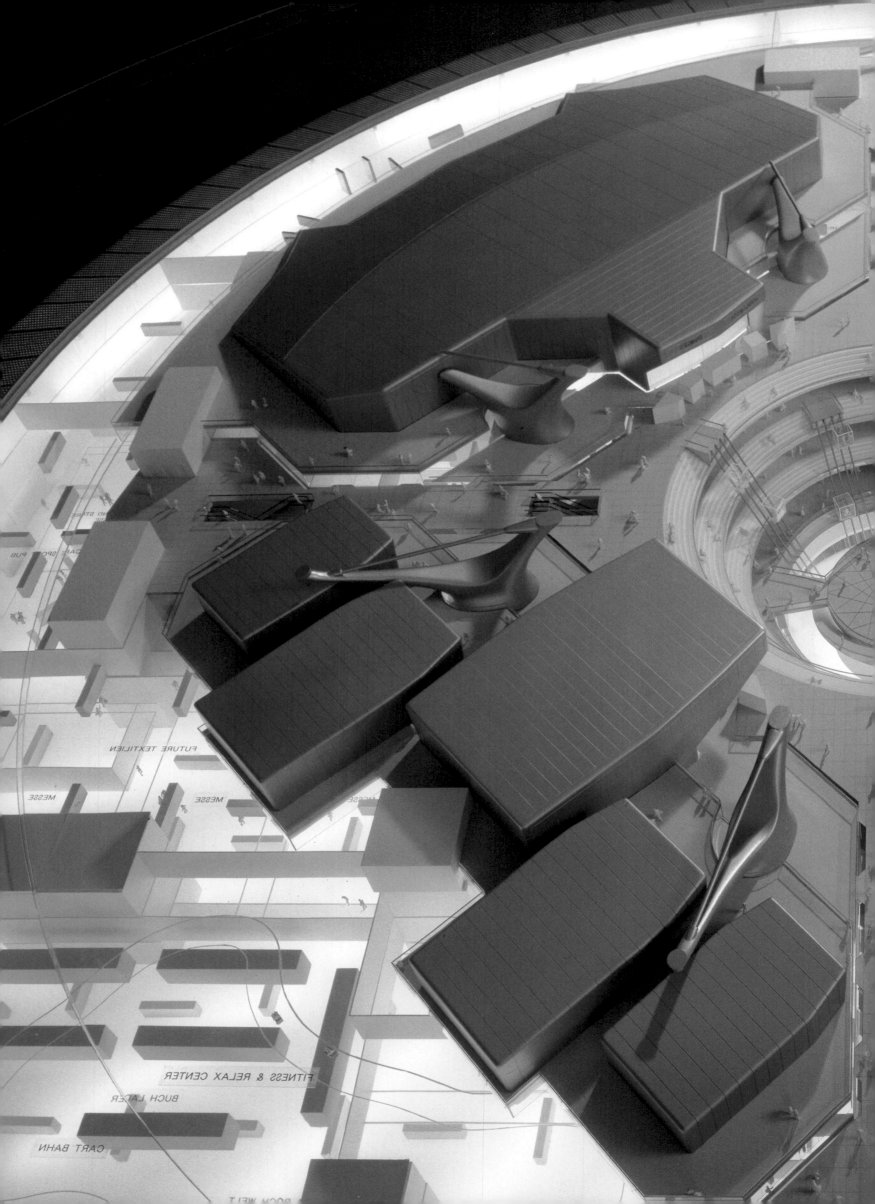

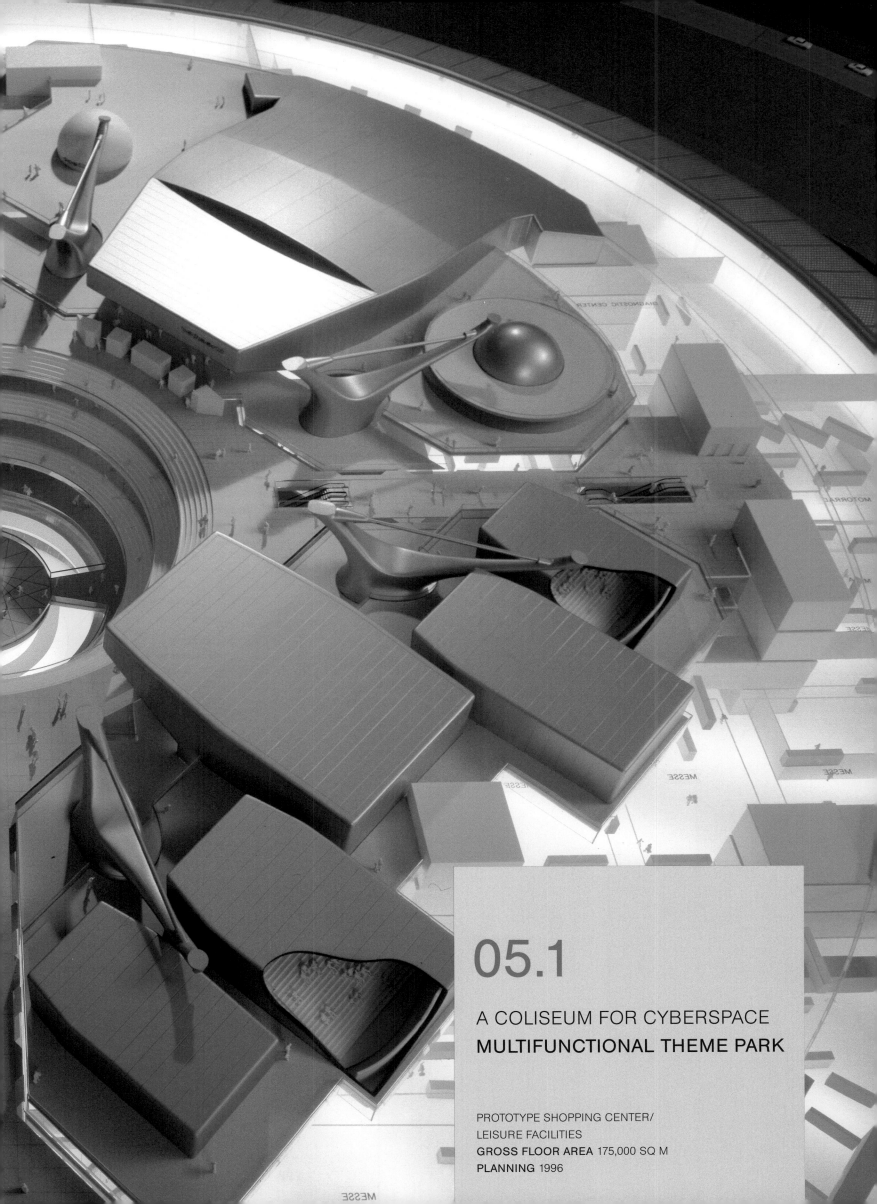

05.1

A COLISEUM FOR CYBERSPACE
MULTIFUNCTIONAL THEME PARK

PROTOTYPE SHOPPING CENTER/
LEISURE FACILITIES
GROSS FLOOR AREA 175,000 SQ M
PLANNING 1996

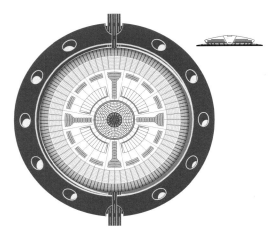

Top view

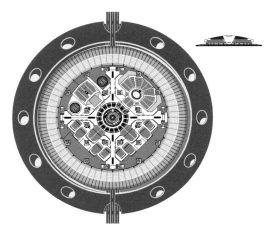

Level 4

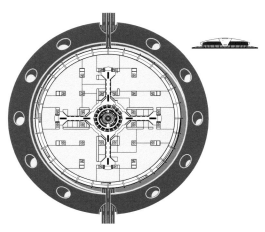

Levels 1–3

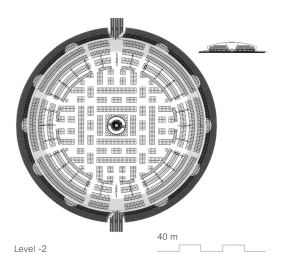

40 m

Level -2

A COLISEUM FOR CYBERSPACE

This attempt to organize the periphery by concentrating all of those functions fleeing the city into an "unlimited free-time object" (UFO) sunk into the landscape is unprecedented. The coliseum erected on the Champ de Mars for the fourth World Fair in 1867 was also a place of spectacles for the masses and for fairs. With a length of 494 meters and a width of 384 meters, the oval exhibition hall with a palm garden in the center, edged with restaurants and cafés, was actually significantly more expansive than the "mere" 280 meters of the minimalist UFO above the structure of the bulwark—with a similar surface area. Unlike the 150,000 square meters of surface area in the historical coliseum of Paris, the UFO offers 135,000 square meters of rentable space. But the concentric arrangement of seven galleries—an attempt to visualize the entire world in a compact form—was typologically nothing more than a series of added-on market halls rather than a flexibly usable structure, spatially and aesthetically conceived as a whole. An example of this latter typology was Fuller's dome pavilion for the USA at the Montreal EXPO one hundred years later—which became the main point of attack for contemporary critics. Its significance is that it has become nearly impossible to bundle and overlap the individual interests that have been at the forefront of economic development since this last attempt in 1867. The advantages are convincing, however: the protection of the landscape from fragmented commercial settlements, the focusing of architecture on leisure and community, integrated logistics and parking (7,400 spaces), economic and ecological optimization (solar energy), and the potential to convert use into a purely industrial or office location. The spatial emphasis is the glass-covered coliseum extending over four stories and containing 1,000 seats. Accessible directly from this core—or by means of glass elevators traveling through diagonal shafts—are malls, cinemas, restaurants, specialty shops and fairs as well as a planetarium, fitness center, musical theater, variety show, disco, and go-cart track.

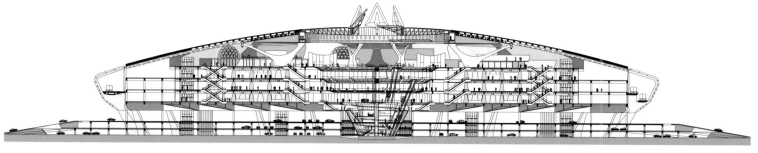

Longitudinal section

Detail of roof construction

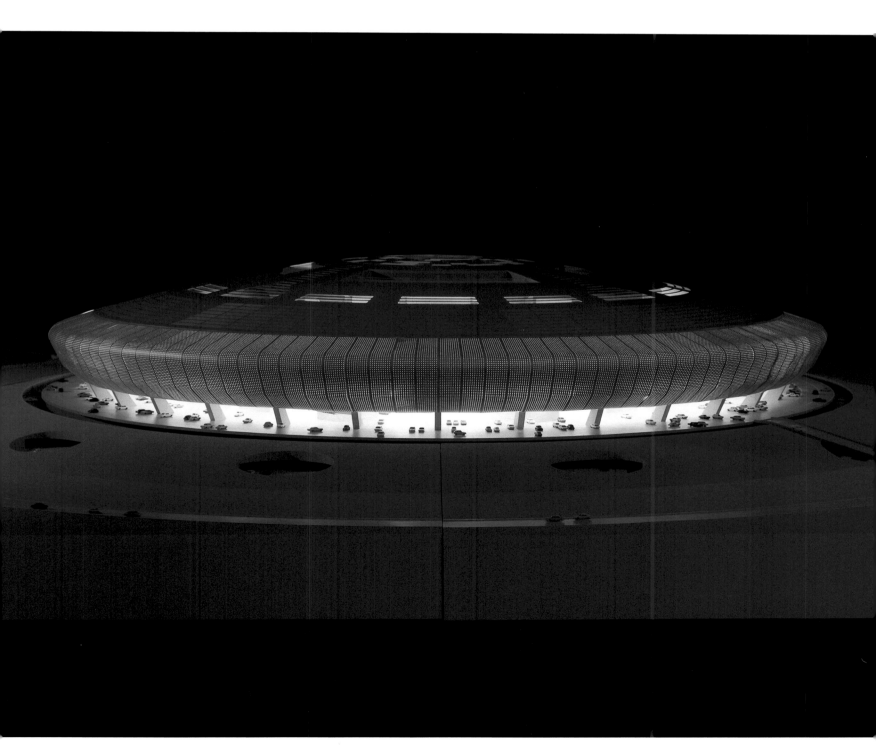

Multifunctional Theme Park

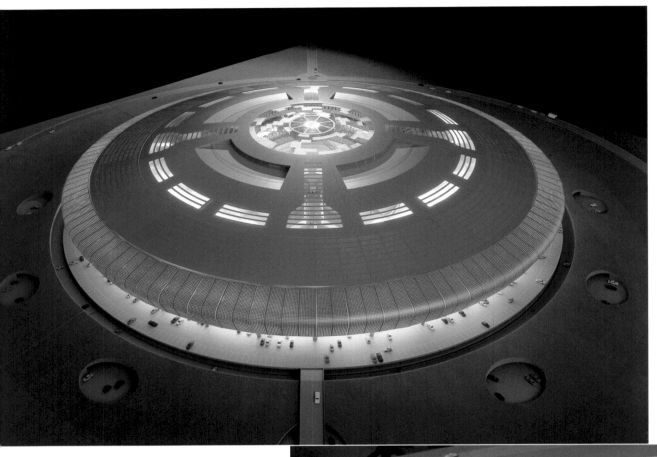

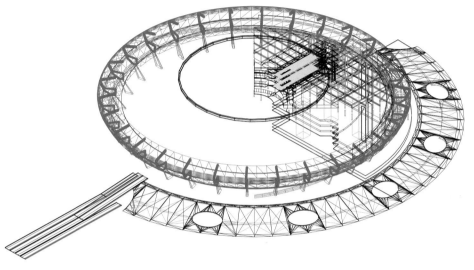

05.2

PEACE FORUM

**GLASS PAVILION NIKOLAI
CHURCH HAMBURG**

PRAYER-, CONCERT-, AND EXHIBITION ROOM
HAMBURG
GROSS FLOOR AREA 360 SQ M
PLANNING OCT 1997
COMPETITION 1997, 1ST PLACE

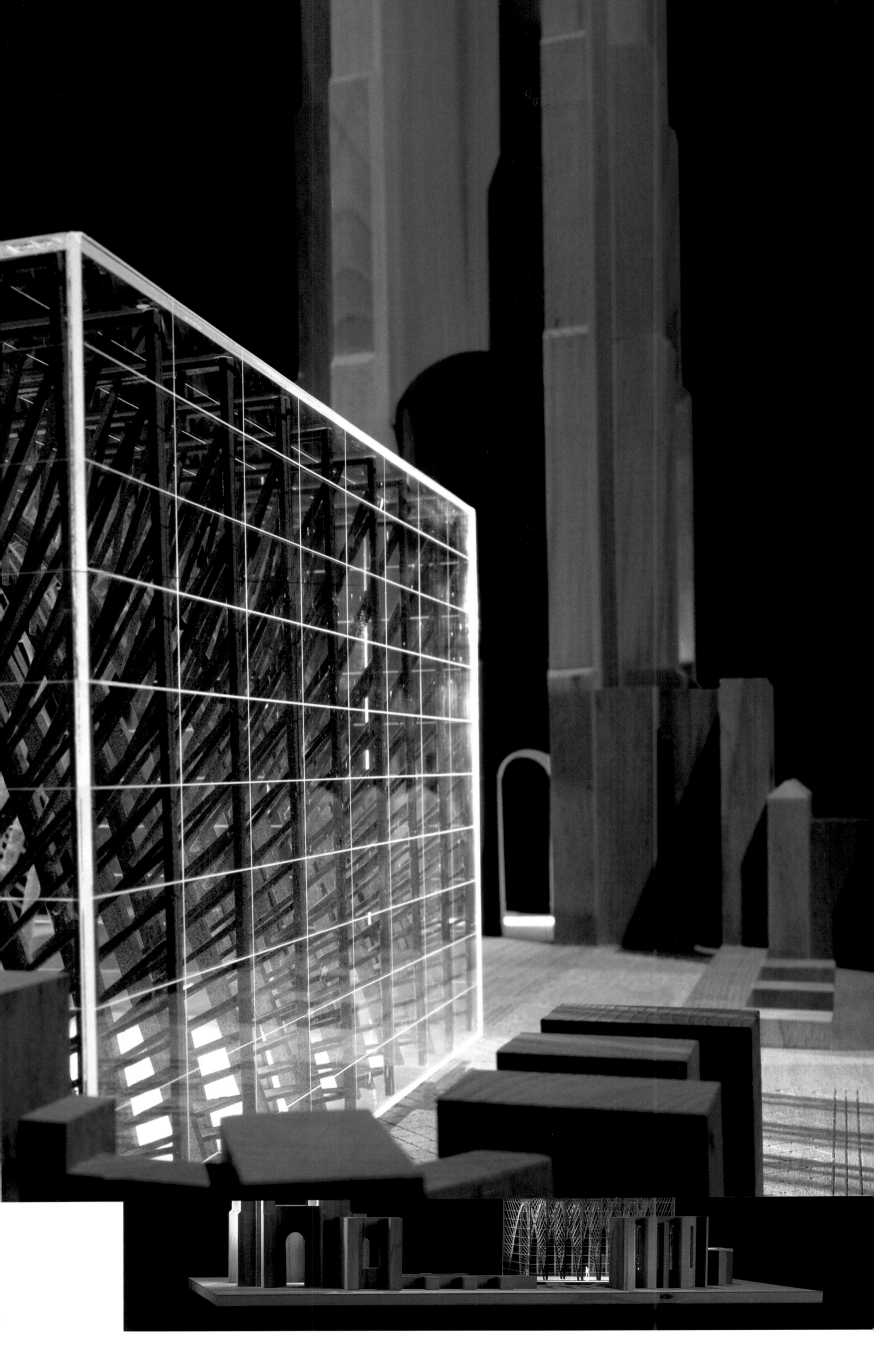

Glass Pavilion Nikolai Church Hamburg

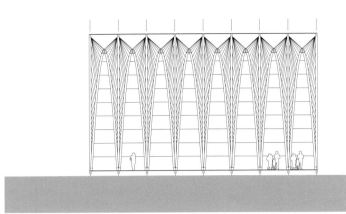

Longitudinal section

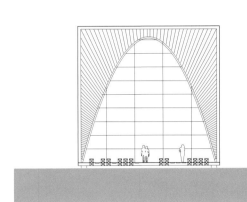

Cross section

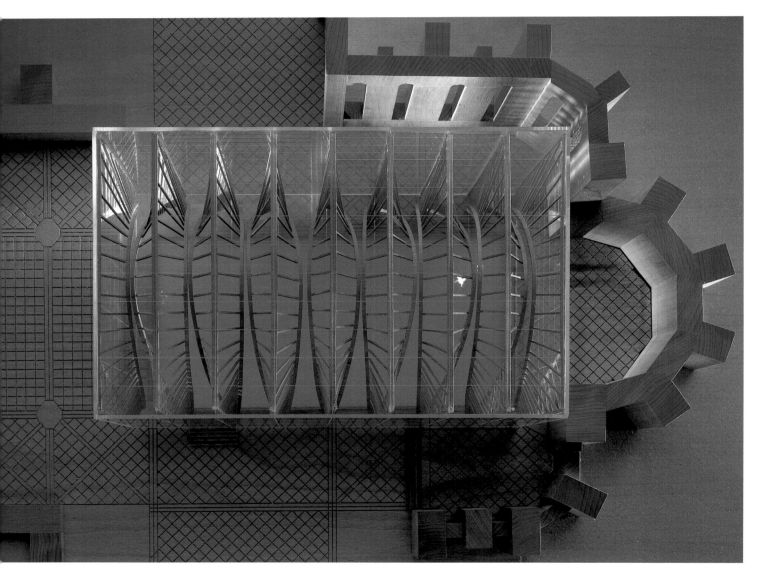

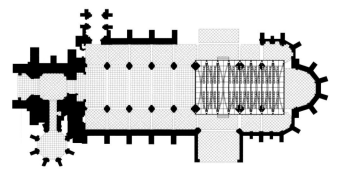

Plan

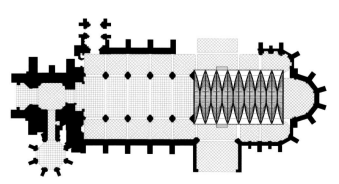

Top view

Glass Pavilion Nikolai Church Hamburg

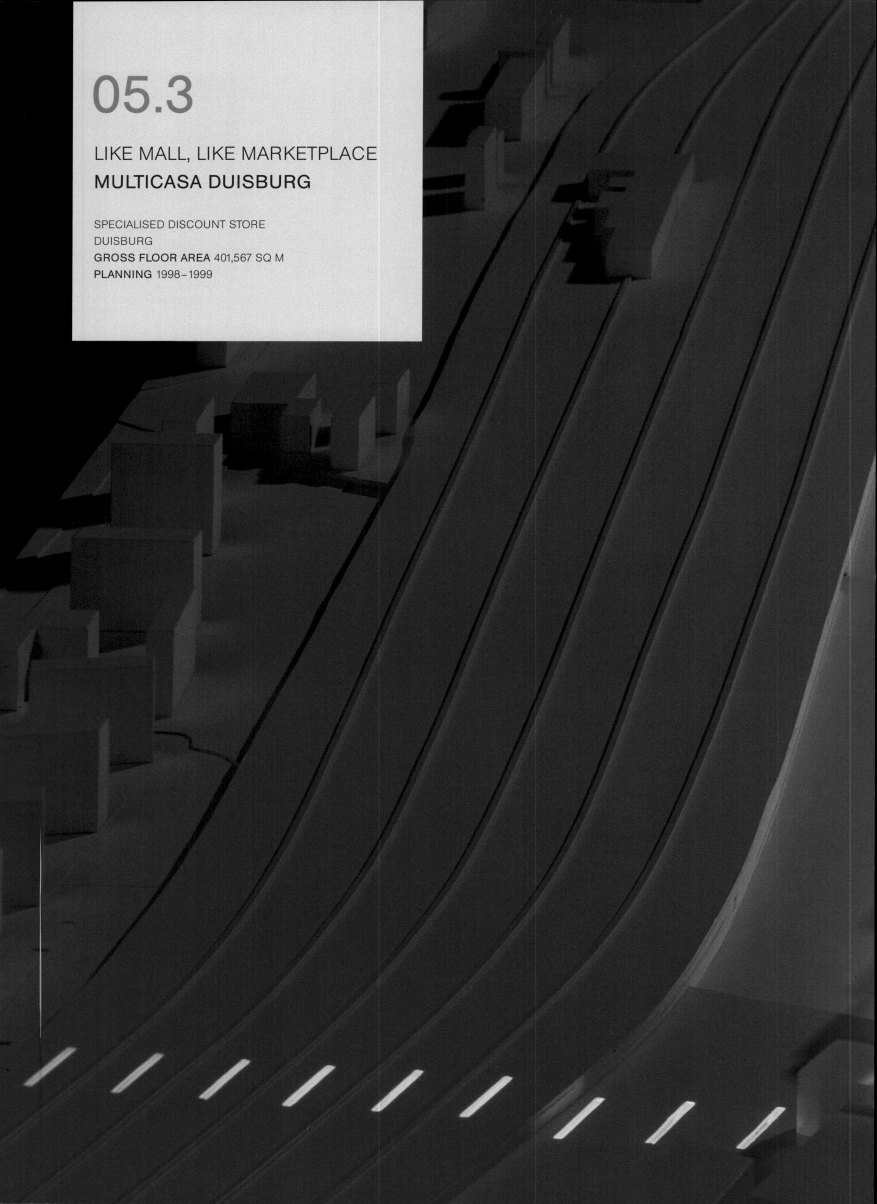

05.3

LIKE MALL, LIKE MARKETPLACE
MULTICASA DUISBURG

SPECIALISED DISCOUNT STORE
DUISBURG
GROSS FLOOR AREA 401,567 SQ M
PLANNING 1998–1999

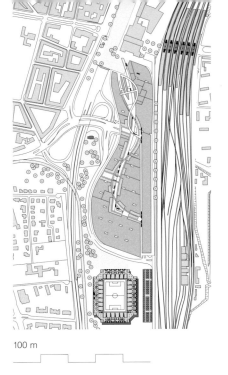

100 m

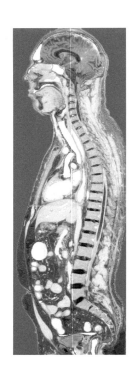

LIKE MALL, LIKE MARKETPLACE

The modern city and its urban society—which are characterized by growing isolation and cultural insecurity—lack places of self-understanding. "Culture is nothing other than a forum for society to talk with itself, in which the questions of just society are considered" (Michael Naumann). Since a community based on spatial proximity has given way to a network of relationships established in the workplace, at leisure, or while shopping, specific places for public exchange and achieving general consensus are lacking. One of the main causes is the aversion to everything large that took hold of all areas of life in post-war Germany. Even in the allocation of cultural infrastructure, many suspect the state of exhibitionism or—in the case of private financing—the compulsion to consume and the elimination of the public, closing the vicious circle. The most important objective of the Grands Travaux in Paris was to facilitate access to the knowledge of both the past and the present for as many people as possible. Creating theaters, think tanks or centers of documentation encourages debate about public aesthetics. Added to this is the attraction of spectacular buildings emerging from the competition of metropolises among each other, which can be traced back to a time even before the medieval cathedrals. Against this backdrop, the functionally stratified Multi-casa project was an attempt to architecturally surmount the political chances of the large space of the mall, as a way of installing it not at the periphery, but within the city itself—in a compound with sports, culture, and a train station. After its failure, we are still waiting for an architectural answer to the great social challenge of the present: how to bridge the gap between the new, turbo-capitalist definition of public space and the interests of urban society.

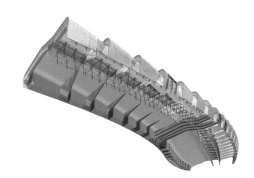

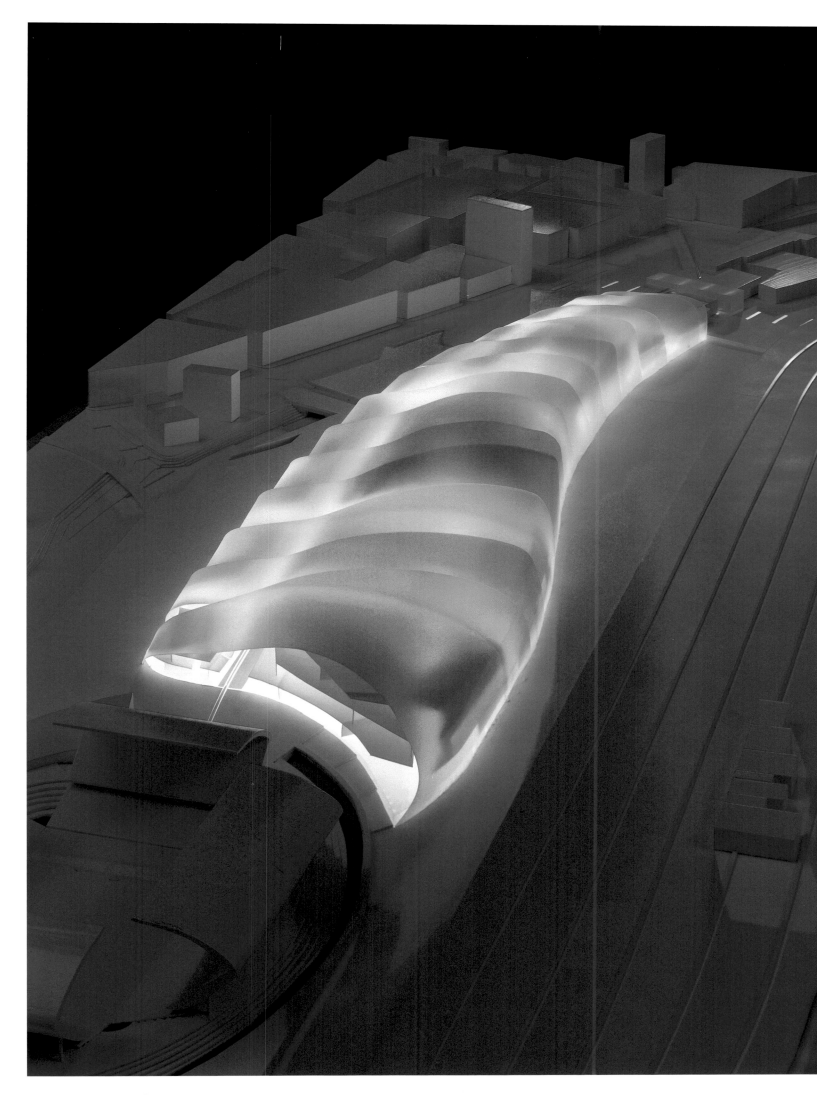

Multicasa Duisburg

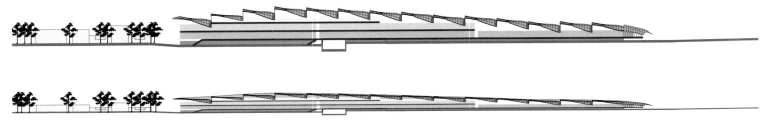

Schematic sections

CHAOS

The shopping center, the mall, and the mega mall are stations in an extremely long development that is often ignored in current discourse. Likewise, the special situation of the Ruhr region, both at present and historically, must be taken into account. For even when the first mining industries went under due to the exhaustion of coal in the southern Ruhr region, the planning strategy for fallow industries consisted in subsequently furnishing the agglomerations, which were not urban and tended to be given over rather unsystematically to the mining companies, with sizable anchor points for leisure and cultural activities.

The classic objective of urban planning has always been to impart to the chaos of the city both methods and structure, legible guides for orientation, and identity at the same time. This position is reflected in the ancient Egyptian hieroglyph for "city": a ring with a diagonal cross inside it. The symbol represents a circular urban ground plan with the mass of buildings divided into four quarters by two streets intersecting at right angles at their midpoints. Historically, building a city had nothing to do with the random accumulation of houses; rather it involved a conscious marking out and settlement. The naïve security of the center was relativized by the discovery of distance. Nowadays we think of cities merely as centers of fiscally prescribed agony. Even economically healthy cities such as Munich have gone bankrupt overnight. Berlin, long rivaled by Hamburg as the top tourist destination among German cities, has recently begun frantically searching for advice as to what deeper significance its reactivated status as capital might have. The recommendations it has gotten, even from prominent figures, have been meager, unrealistic under the circumstances, or simply rather odd, such as proposals for a "Capital City Committee" or Volker Hassemer's idea for a "Content Operations Commissioner." The chance to make Berlin the architectural "capital of European Modernism" or a "laboratory of the New," as Edzard Reuter envisioned, was missed long ago. The city's antique facades and nineteenth-century neighborhood planning hardly make such a prospect likely. But it is primarily the city's lack of financial capital, rather than symbolic capital, that has led newspapers to outbid each other in painting the situation as black as possible—despite the fact that at least since the Renaissance, history has often enough been the history of cities rather than nations. "The conclusion is foregone: the time of cities has come to an end, and we now are living in the terminal phase of an infirmity. […] Only an unstructured urban sprawl, neither city nor country, remains to us —a shadow cast by the vanished metropolis into the future."[1]

City planning features like outplacement and oasis development have been characteristic of the Ruhr region for the past century, a traditional part of its dynamic development. Leisure centers and excursion destinations were being built in the Ruhr as early as a hundred years ago. Fifty years later, enormous supplies of consumer goods and temples of culture grew on the same ground, following the B1/A40 highway. This region along the Emscher River unfortunately is not characterized by picturesque locales and strong town identities. Cities there tend to be settlements that have grown in conjunction with coal mining and steel factories, a battlefield for the military-strategic exploitation of the earth, as Roland Kirbach, a *Die Zeit* correspondent who lives in Essen, has put it. Pits and slag heaps follow on steel and chemical factories, junkyards on warehouses. Tangled railroad lines, highways, and Autobahn arteries cut across the landscape. In their midst, dusty gray housing complexes jut out. These cities do not have centers, and none of them has ever really taken on a form of its own. "Urban planning never happened here."[2] Small wonder, then, that people long for counterexamples, or that a city like Duisburg should make an attempt to break out of the vicious circle, both in a manageable amount of time and at a justifiable cost. Karl Ganser rightly points out that "the settlement area of industrial society can no longer be rebuilt from the ground up. The only alternative is to create form out of chaos, to work selectively on worthwhile assets that are already part of the jumble of habitation," and that "city centers will lose a good part of their retail trade function. This will migrate, increasingly and without anyone being able to do much about it, to enclosed shopping centers at specialized locations in the agglomeration. Nevertheless, the historic city centers will not founder as a result. The adoption of new functions is always possible: more living spaces, more culture and leisure activities, more theater, and even more backdrops from the distant past."[3]

GENEALOGY

Like the Athenian Agora, with its countless shops and market stands, the Forum was the main shopping center in ancient Rome. Following the architectural upgrading of the city's core, however, only gold- and silversmiths remained there. New shopping centers near the Tiber catered to specific, everyday needs. The Forum Boarium, for instance, handled livestock, the Forum Holitorium, fruits and vegetables. The high streets were lined with shops. Taverns, restaurants, and fast food bars substituted for the kitchens lacking in many homes and were places for socializing—as well as for gambling and political scheming. The

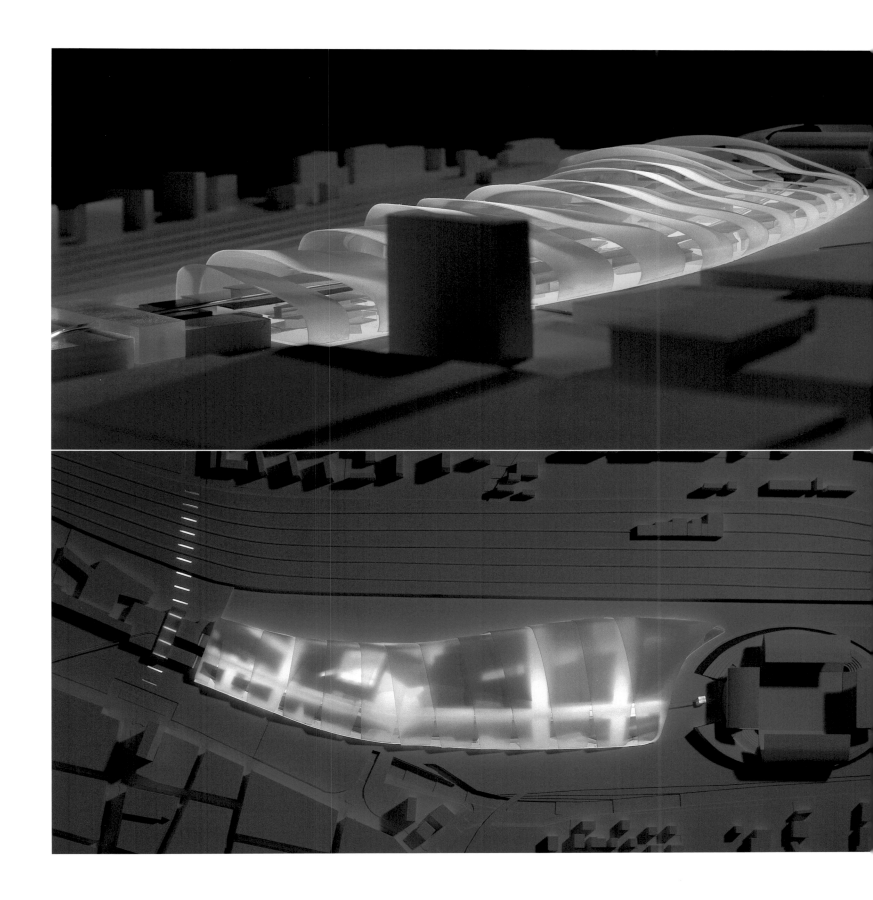

Multicasa Duisburg

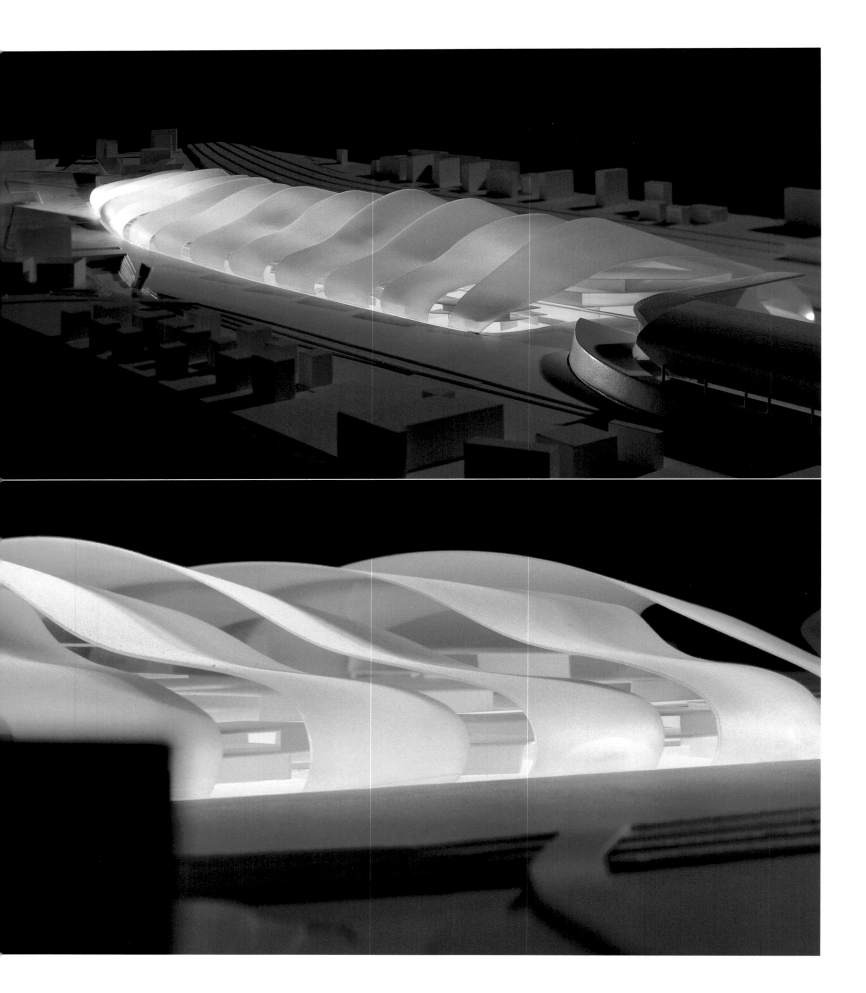

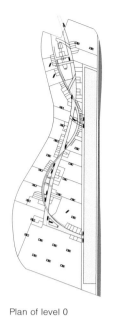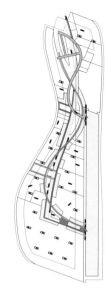

Plan of level -1   Plan of level 0   Plan of level 1

considerable variety of products, ranging from produce to clothing and fabrics to dishware, jewelry, and books, forced the shopkeepers to extend their displays out onto the sidewalks. Many of them set up stalls between the columns of the arcades. The whole city turned into an enormous shopping center despite repeated attempts by authorities to free the streets from incursions by shopkeepers and drive the barbers, barkeeps, butchers, and cooks back behind the thresholds of their establishments. At the beginning of the second century A.D., the five-story Trajan Markets northeast of the Forum housed more than one hundred fifty shops on four shopping levels and a vaulted central hall with twenty-four taverns and pubs.

The question asked by Peter Neitzke in his anthology *Boulevard Ecke Dschungel* (Boulevard Corner Jungle) – "Doesn't a city become less attractive when it is tailored to the needs of a market society?"[4] – would have been incomprehensible to a denizen of antiquity. A city untethered from its commercial origins was unthinkable. The omnipresence of window displays and the enormous warehouses in Paris of the 1850s no doubt heightened the frenzy of consumption described by Émile Zola in his 1883 novel *The Ladies' Paradise*[5]. It no doubt brought to a circensian climax the "mechanism of devouring women" in an era of World Fairs and Expositions that was "throwing itself into the arms of pleasure." But it certainly did not invent it. With his description of the strategies and "secret seducers" fostering sales and turnover, Zola antici-pated the ABCs of modern consumer society. A building the size of a city block reminds him of "an endless sea of glass and zinc shimmering in the sun […] Beyond it extends Paris, but a Paris that has shrunk, half-devoured by the monster […] to the left two hatchmarks for Notre-Dame, to the right a circumflex accent for Les Invalides, in the background the Pantheon, ashamed and lost, tinier than a pea."

With consumption and leisure being combined in a proportion of 1:2 in the urban entertainment center, the speed and dimensions of the development of trade would seem today to have undergone another dramatic transformation. In fact, however, this proportion was hardly different in the past. The Grand Bazaar in Istanbul took up almost 19 hectares. In London in 1855, Joseph Paxton and William Mosely each designed, independently of each other, a glassed-in shopping arcade situated over underground train lines. They were apparently influenced by the 1200-meter-long gallery along the Seine exhibited at the World's Fair in Paris. The Paxton Arcade was to have a full length of 16 kilometers and, like the original transept of the Crystal Palace, was to be 33 meters high and 22 meters wide. Hector Horeau's 1866 plan to cover Paris's boulevards with glass was a similarly herculean project. The "city under glass," which social-utopian Charles Fourier had already called for at the beginning of the nineteenth century, was inspired by the encounter with "nature under glass," and by a dreamy utopian vision of an artificial envi-ronment in an artificial landscape as the ideal site of a new society. Like the arcade, the winter garden was both an object of curiosity and a pub-lic promenade, a meeting place in the center of the city. The *Jardin d'hiver*, which was erected on the Champs Elysées in 1847 as the first public winter garden in Paris, had a glass dome 100 meters long, 40 meters wide, and 20 meters high that could hold up to 8,000 people. The public was drawn in magically by the tropical flora, concerts, an art gallery, a café, billiard tables, and vendors. Like the Arcades, this com-mercially quite successful building was financed by private building investors.

It is impossible to determine who the record-breaker for size and profits is today. Until now, Mall of America was considered the largest mall in the world. Its position, so long as the Arab Emirates have not pushed their way into the lead, is threatened by, of all countries, Indone-sia, whose population is almost 90 percent Muslim, that is to say, by an Islamic competitor. Taman Anggrek, the most spectacular shopping mall in Jakarta and supposedly the largest in the world, houses over five hun-dred shops, three international department stores, thirteen parking garages, and along with all the other usual accessories and as if to spite the heat, a waterfall and an ice-skating rink. Most impressive, however, are the eight massive apartment buildings that loom over this seven-story paradise of consumption and leisure. This bourgeois urbanity is concen-trated at specific points scattered around the entire city. But such a retreat of the middle class, the polarization of the city into purely commercial areas and impoverished neighborhoods, was already prevalent in the middle of the nineteenth century, Manchester in 1850 for instance. Begin-ning in the eighteenth century, the bourgeois public sphere was the exclusive purchase of private persons in salons, clubs, and coffeehouses. As the sociologist Werner Sewing has illustrated, this public sphere avoided the uncertain terrain of urban space.

"The people who can pay for it all have increasingly become the consumers, a manipulated part of this performance. They willingly waive their right to the public sphere, to debate, and to discourse in the worlds of art. Or can anyone imagine the revolution being declared today in a shopping mall, the way it was declared in 1789 in a coffeehouse?

But who on earth wants a revolution? And for those who cannot pay for it all… But who cares about them? They get left on the doorstep anyway."[6] Gert Kähler does an effective hatchet job here on the "shopping center as major event," with all of its "private sheriffs," by contrast with a public, democratic, and completely unregulated Paris coffeehouse at the time of the Revolution. In a similar vein, in a *Frankfurter Rundschau* article on Rem Kohlhaas's *The Harvard Design School Guide to Shopping*, Ulf Jonak laments the "global, epidemic transformation of public space into shimmering shopping districts and shopping malls: city centers have been taken over by corporations and investment firms. […] Their captives amble between display wall and checkout counter as if they were hypnotized. The display window as peepshow has displaced the window that looks out onto the distance, which has never been for sale. Consumption has replaced nature. Shopping as activity, as constant action. Anyone who stops moving for even a moment cannot help but whip out his or her wallet, discreetly but for that all the more insistently, exhorted to consume. The fascination with the glamour of surfaces paralyzes communication. The shopping mall has thus ousted the park and the city square as spaces for free discourse." A society of mature, emancipated citizens, hypnotized, tormented, and devoured by the dinosaur of consumption? Then why does retail trade currently find itself in straits more dire than ever before? The consumption-oriented city and market culture not only have the future, the public sphere, nature, the church, the train station, the museum, and free discourse on their consciences. By depriving public spaces of drinking water, by shutting down public toilets and removing park benches, the commercial universe of the city imposes a kind of entry fee and excludes those who reject or challenge consumption from the city's public space, which according to Peter Neitzke is controlled by state-run and private security institutions like a prison.

URBAN DISCOURSES

The novel *The Cave*[7] by Portuguese Nobel Prize winning novelist José Saramago, which was written before the World Trade Center disaster, provides an even more oppressive, literary metaphor of the modern capitalist world under the sign of globalization and virtualization. Despite all imaginable achievements of progress, neither this combined cathedral of consumption and habitation machine, nor any number of artificial worlds far surpassing Disney's imagination, can succeed in commanding the support of an elderly potter who has been damned out of work by the high sales of cheap plastic dishware in the local shopping

paradise. He and his followers reject the privilege of belonging to that world and seek out instead a future in the unknown. Saramago leaves his protagonists' future, like that of the city, open. The moral watchdogs, however, have already buried it in hypocritical arguments and little white lies. There is good reason to consider these alarm signals exaggerated. They are grievances that operate on the unspoken assumption that everything was better in the past. The public falls victim to carefully worked-out strategies and gets lost in the confusion of substance and representation. Architectural and spatial quality unfortunately gets left out of the discussion. The city is and always was identical with commerce. Even the organizational forms of the modern museum are anchored in the structures of the trade fair and the world exposition. Without trade, a city loses its public character. Without commerce there can be no urban culture at all. The Greek stoa (market halls), Roman portici (shopping streets), and medieval marketplaces were inseparable from political meeting points like the Agora, the Forum, or the town hall square. These commercial features have not been forgotten, nor have all the successful conspiracies by which Mammon has been outwitted and the accompanying architecture made a civic responsibility—to the advantage of both the architecture and the city itself. The markets and market halls vibrating with communicative energy, the elegant streets filled with *flâneurs*, the shopping arcades and the multicultural inventory of the department stores, at least the old, apparently unprofitable, chaste ones. According to the 1922 work *Luxury and Capitalism* by the historian Werner Sombart, the growth of cities is always based on the accumulation of forces of consumption: "the expansion of cities thus results from the concentration of consumption in urban centers." Cities devoted exclusively to trade or production, on the other hand, never expand to dimensions larger than those of a mid-size town.

The history of the modern shopping center as of the amusement park begins no later than the end of the eighteenth century with the Galeries de Bois installed in the Palais Royale in Paris in 1785, and with the English Village begun in 1776 in Hohenheim near Stuttgart. In contrast to the courtly pastoral games organized by Marie Antoinette in Versaille, up to two thousand farmers and laborers and their families were involved in the merry-making in Hohenheim. Le Grand Tivoli, one of Paris's jardins-spectacles, which the aristocratic amusement institutions made accessible, for a price, to all citizens in the wake of the Revolution, was opened in 1795. A hundred years later saw the establishment of "Venice in Vienna" alongside the Volksprater, which had been erected in 1873. This was the immediate forerunner to Disney World, which opened in California only in 1955. The concepts of "Americanization" or "Disney-

> "The simple solution often turns out to be economically, ecologically, functionally and aesthetically unbeatable. But it has to be very well-founded." Hadi Teherani

fication," which are meant apparently to answer the question of who to blame, simply do not hold water: architects like the Austrian Viktor Gruen and the German Ferdinand Kramer, who were in the USA, played a large part in the development of the modern shopping mall and of product display. And are not the ideals of Bauhaus more discernible in the ascetic presentation of most posh brands than in any building project?

PUBLIC SPHERE

The concept of the urban public sphere is currently undergoing its greatest pedagogical ideologization yet. No one is much disturbed, for example, when in Potsdam the rich and beautiful people in charge of the city try to prevent access to the lakefront by the general public or that parks there are subject to an "improvement of visitor quality" by security guards. This kind of thinking, which is suspicious of facts, prefers to call into question the public status of the city, the train station, or the shopping mall—criticism that has no negative effects until a central building project of the city is stigmatized as a result and ends up having its architecture be negotiated under the counter. At the same time, the café of the Palais Royale, where on Sunday, July 12th, 1789, the storming of the Bastille was called for, is considered public—despite the fact that the royal Swiss Guard was installed there as security personnel in order to keep out "soldiers, house servants, persons in caps or jackets, students, pickpockets, beggars, dogs, and laborers," as a contemporary, Albert Babeau, has described. Why is that then considered public space? Perhaps because the Café de Foy was under surveillance by spies from the Paris police, for which the entire area was officially off-limits? The place where Camille Desmoulins called for the storming of the Bastille was actually much more a commercial shopping and entertainment center; in terms of property and house rules, it was about as public as are comparable profit-oriented institutions today. The building complex, which was designed by Viktor Louis for Philippe Egalité, was modeled after St. Mark's in Venice but was enclosed following the construction of the Galeries de Bois in 1785. Despite its expressly speculative objective, it became, according to Heinrich Heine, a "gathering place for all the restless heads" of Paris. Many of the city's sixty thousand citizens, primarily unemployed lawyers, doctors, artists, and writers, weary of the unpleasant streets, preferred to meet in the coffee garden of the Palais Royale, surrounded as it was by countless luxury boutiques, bookshops, painting galleries, coffeehouses, casinos, clubs, betting offices, brothels, the Théâtre Français, little café-theaters, a wax figure museum, the temporary stock exchange, and apartments. A cup of coffee at the time of the Revolution cost three sous (coins), a pound of bread four to eight sous. An industrial laborer at the time earned twenty-five to forty sous. These pleasures were not cheap even then, although the times were hardly good. In order to quench his miserliness, Philippe Egalité, the Duke of Chartres, decided to provide only luxury goods and exclusive diversions, and even published a magazine for his urban entertainment center, the Almanach du Palais Royale. The extremely high rents led to numerous bankruptcies; and prices there were at least twice as high as elsewhere in Paris, which led to the Galeries de Bois, the prototype of the Paris Arcades, being dubbed Camp des Tartares. Yet this piece of prime real estate, a mix of fairground and masked ball, of temple of industry and the Arabian Nights, remained unscathed by its reputation. Heinrich von Kleist nevertheless was horrified by the hedonism of the Palais Royale, where, as he described it in an 1801 letter, "one can meet all of Paris, with all its cruelties and so-called pleasures. There is no sensual craving that cannot be satisfied here to the point of revulsion, no virtue that is not mocked here with impudence, no infamy that is not committed here according to strict principles."

Despite all our technological advances, we are still searching in vain for grand open spaces of public life on common ground, for markers of the European city's social identity. Social nerve centers on the order of Paris's *Jardin d'hiver* remain missing in urban centers today. And the biggest troublemakers of all for cities are the megamalls and amusement parks, not least because of their size. The chaos of the cities needs nothing so much as large structures that are architecturally convincing and functionally attractive. The ideologically fraught critique of consumption has led to the stigmatization of an essential feature of the city and of urban architecture. Architects are doing their best to fulfill once and for all one of the most important urban construction tasks. The 1:2 cocktail of consumption and leisure can be mixed architecturally far more intelligently than it is in the banal urban entertainment centers of the small towns and suburbs. Multicasa already proved this in its planning stages. Functioning historical examples of private building speculation could provide considerable inspiration if typological development processes were to play any role at all in the training of architects. The practically systematic architectural failures of German consumer and leisure centers, the most recent example being the crash-landing of Bremen's Space Park, is the fault not so much of rash investors as of the politicians, city planners, architects, and engineers who follow them without any imagination of their own. With the original form of the Multicasa project, the city of Duisburg has passed up a great opportunity. This can be gauged by considering how often this naturally lit large construction has been taken up by other architects—by Lars Spuybroek/NOX, for example, for the Pop Musik Center in Nancy.[8]

Notes

1 Peter Michalzik, "Das Ende der Stadt. Eine kleine Chronik der rasanten Zerstörung urbanen Lebens (The end of the city. A brief history of the rapid destruction of urban life)," *Frankfurter Rundschau* (7. August 2003).

2 Roland Kirbach, "Grüne Neue Welt (Green new world)," *Merian* (Ruhrgebiet) (October 1993), p. 68.

3 Karl Ganser, "Zum Stand der Dinge… (On the state of things…)," *in Wandel ohne Wachstum? Stadt-Bau-Kultur im 21. Jahrhundert. Venice Biennale Catalog 1996*, ed. Kunibert Wachten (Braunschweig & Wiesbaden, 1996), pp. 17 and 23.

4 Elisabeth Blum, Peter Neitzke, eds., *Boulevard Ecke Dschungel. Stadtprotokolle* (Boulevard corner jungle. Urban documents) (Hamburg, 2002), p. 101.

5 Émile Zola, *The Ladies' Paradise* (Au bonheur des dames, 1883). (The passages here are translated from the 1958 German edition *Paradies der Damen* cited in the original essay.—Trans.)

6 Gert Kähler, "Reisen bildet? Vom Freizeitpark zur neuen Stadt (Travel is educational? From the amusement park to the new city)," in: *Die Inszenierung der Freiheit. Die künstliche Welt der Freizeitparks und Ferienparadiese*, ed. Max Stemshorn (Ulm, 2000), pp. 53–54.

7 José Saramago, *The Cave* (*A Caverna*, 2000) (New York, 2002).

8 See Zaha Hadid and Patrik Schumacher, eds., *Latent Utopias. Experiments Within Contemporary Architecture* (Vienna, 2002), pp. 182–183.

Autumn Again

Multicasa Duisburg

05.4

LAND USE FOR HORSE RACING
HAMBURG TROT RACETRACK

SPECTATORS' STAND/CATERING
HAMBURG
GROSS FLOOR AREA 52,940 SQ M
PLANNING AUG 2000

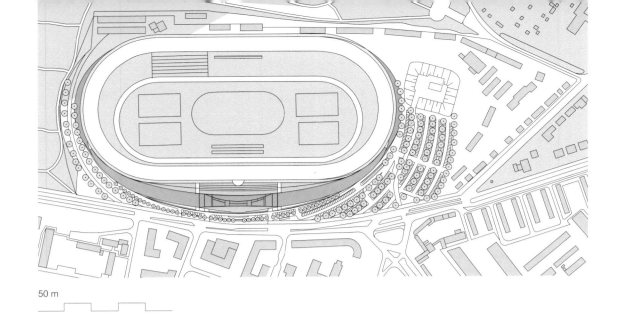

50 m

LAND USE FOR HORSE RACING

The first official trot race in Germany took place in Hamburg on May 31, 1874; the pioneering work for the professionalization of this sport was performed by the Altona Racing Club. In 1880, a 1,320-meter-long grass track was opened in Altona-Bahrenfeld; in 1901, the trot track was founded at its current location. The sport had to live with the Kaiser's ban of totalizator betting machines in 1881, the prohibition of Sunday races in 1894, and the fact that the wooden stands in the Bahrenfeld grounds were burned for heating in the cold winter of 1947. But in Bavaria, and especially in western Germany, betting proceeds and attendance at racetracks continued to grow during the postwar period. Despite their popularity, both of the Hamburg trot race clubs found themselves facing economic difficulties, including the eventual bankruptcy of the trot race club in Hamburg-Farmsen. The objective of the new commitment to the traditional trot racetrack in Bahrenfeld—which is located south of the Altona Volkspark and close to the Desy particle accelerator—is primarily to ensure the continued economic security of trot racing in Hamburg. The land use for this new, traffic-quieted, mixed-utility spectator building calls for the actual spectator stands to be placed in the center, complete with a betting room, restaurant, and casino, as well as additional building sections for use by other parties. In stating that, "stadiums are hyper-commercial projects," Jacques Herzog seemed to be describing his new functional hybrid for the FC Basle, which is a stadium, shopping center, café and home for seniors in Basle's St. Jakob Park. Thanks to the conservatories carved into the overall usage plan, and to the tailored developments which have nothing to do with the sports events, no problems have arisen within the construction alliance in Hamburg. In fact, the trot racetrack profits from its dynamic spatial framework, while the hotel and office tract use the landscape and infrastructure synergistically.

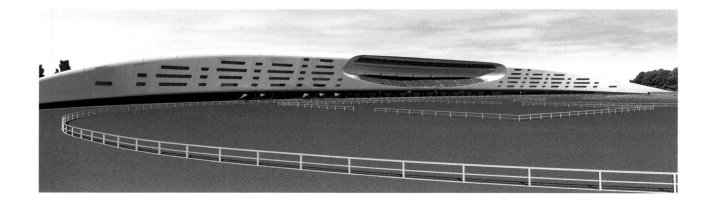

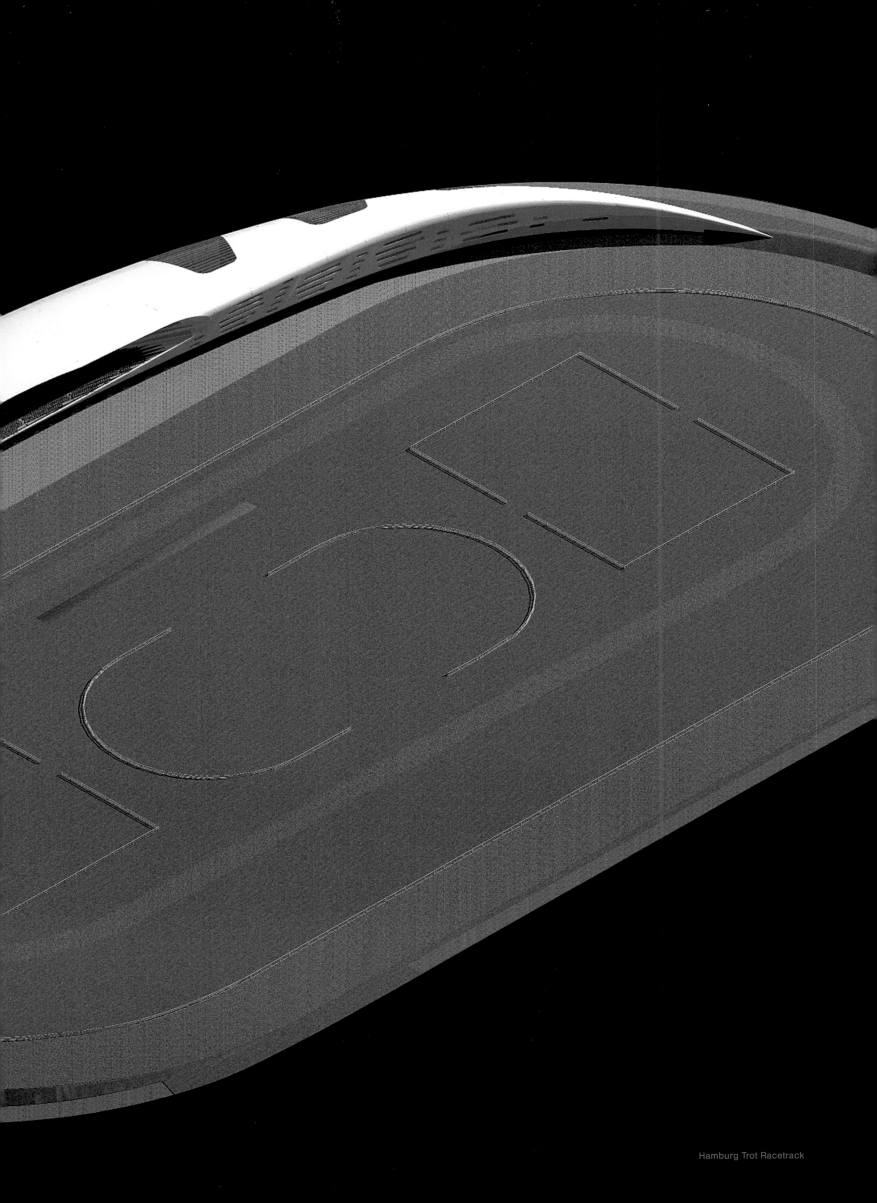

Hamburg Trot Racetrack

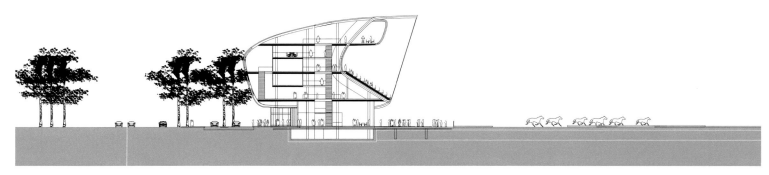

Cross section

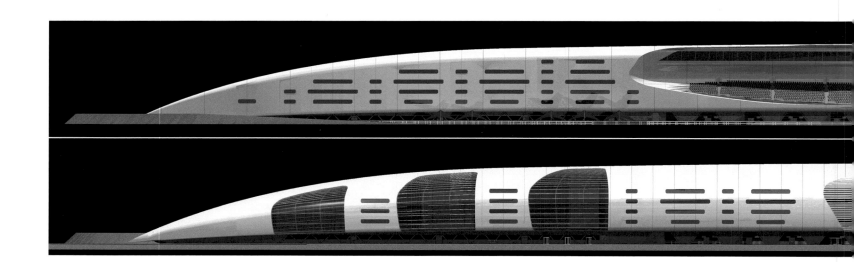

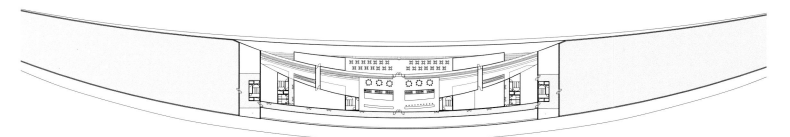

Plan of level 4/VIP area, media, press

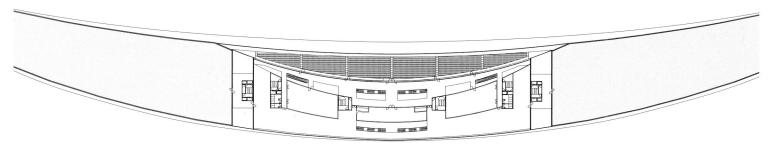

Plan of level 3/stands, casino, refreshments

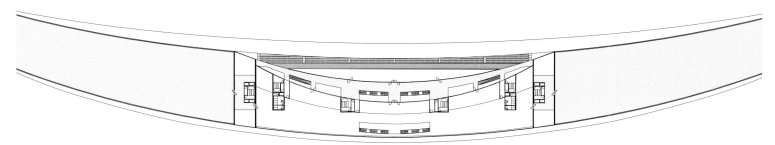

Plan of level 2/casino

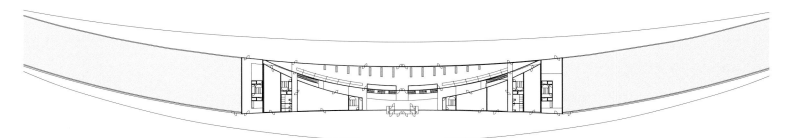

Plan of level 1/lobby, betting counters, shops

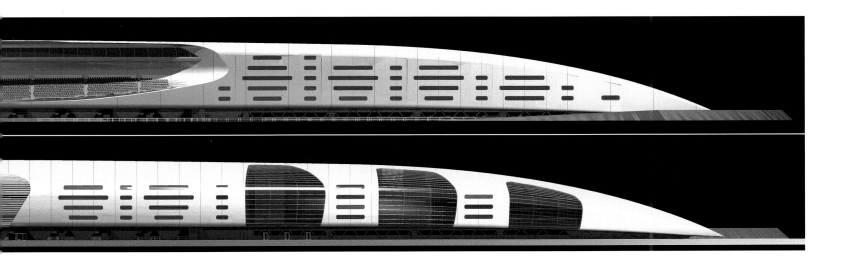

Hamburg Trot Racetrack

Hamburg Trot Racetrack

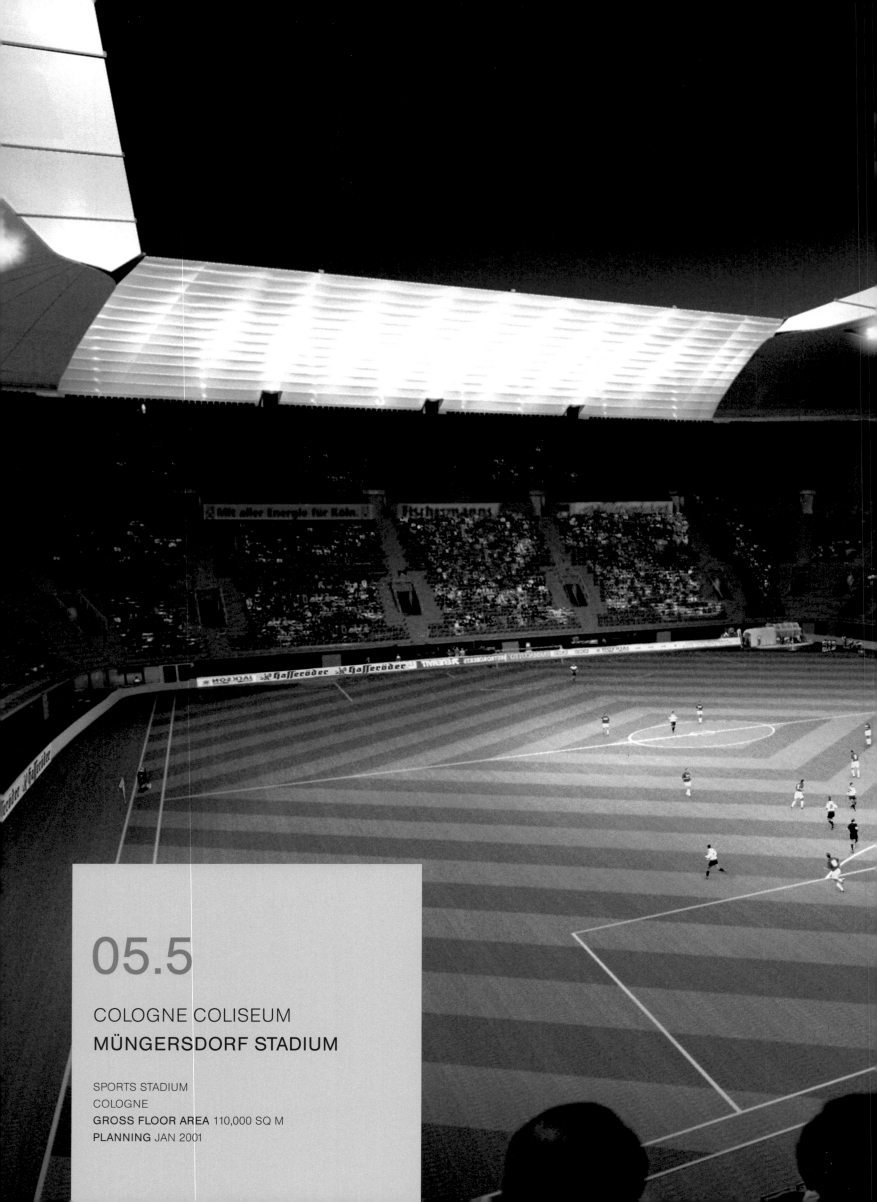

05.5

COLOGNE COLISEUM
MÜNGERSDORF STADIUM

SPORTS STADIUM
COLOGNE
GROSS FLOOR AREA 110,000 SQ M
PLANNING JAN 2001

Site plan

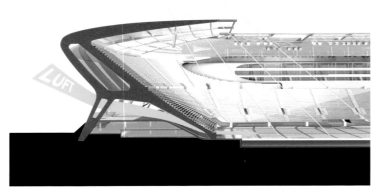

Schematic section

COLOGNE COLISEUM

Apart from rare exceptions, football stadiums—like hospitals and highway bridges—seem to have abandoned architecture in favor of economic efficiency. In the face of grandstands truncated at right angles down to the last seat, one is hard pressed to speak even of functionality. As they awarded first prize for the "RheinEnergieStadion," which has since been realized, the competition jury bemoaned the lack of spirit in the design, commenting that the tensile structure of the roof appeared excessively orchestrated and no longer up-to-date. The attribute of modernity is nevertheless uppermost in the organizers' criteria and not only for the World Soccer Championship in 2006. The competition called for a conversion during day-to-day operations, creating a "modern football arena" with at least 45,000 covered seats. The high-profile building from 1923, which the future chancellor Konrad Adenauer enlisted to promote "a spirit of community and voluntary integration" after the war defeat, became "the mother of German stadiums." Set within the largest European sports complex—55 ha, complete with playgrounds, pools, woodland trails and day spas—the building's equipment and features were outstanding enough that the city of Cologne competed for a while as host for the Olympic Games in 1936. Even the successor structure from 1972 was praised in the press as "unique in Germany" (DIE ZEIT); it served as a venue for "headliners" as diverse as the Rolling Stones and the pope. Thus the goal of the competition design was to establish a link, both in sensibility and in form, to the two successful original structures. Mobile roofs above the south side and stands ventilated from below ensure that the turf is easy to maintain, while the distinctive shell form with views of the sports park and colourful, luminous roof membranes provide the necessary image.

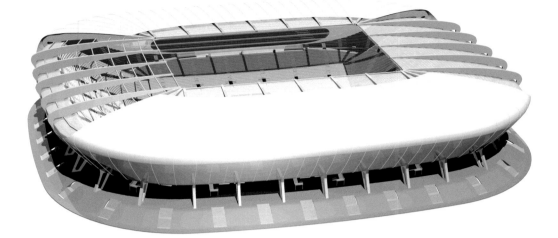

Müngersdorf Stadium

Müngersdorf Stadium

RED HAMBURG
HAMBURG PLANETARIUM

PLANETARIUM
HAMBURG
GROSS FLOOR AREA 2,696 SQ M
BUILT OCT 2002–AUG 2003

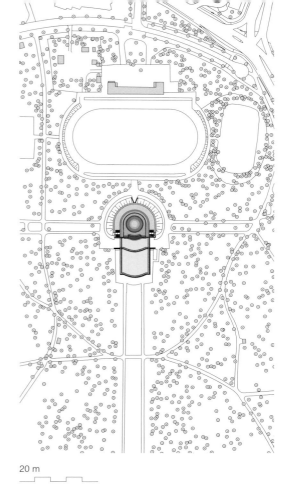

20 m

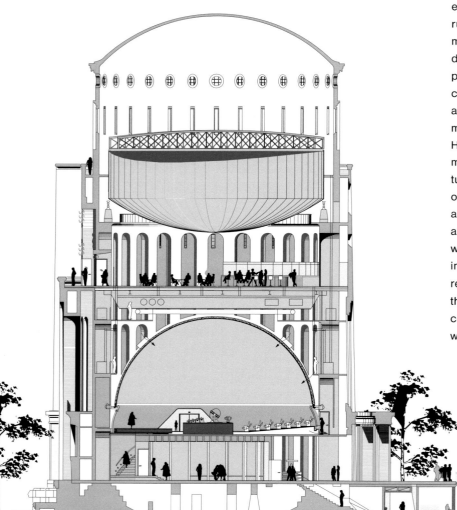

Longitudinal section

RED HAMBURG

Fritz Schumacher, who took on the post of city architect in 1909, began work on the design for Hamburg's city park—at 180 hectares the largest public green space in the city—while he was still in Dresden. In addition to new architectural concepts in this landscape park complete with playing fields, theme gardens, riding arena, outdoor pool, dance platform, and outdoor theatre, above all for the densely populated districts of Barmbek and Winterhude, the axial arrangement of baroque models in this people's park was also evident in numerous buildings: main restaurant (Stadthalle), Café, rural pub, dairy pub (in the style of a Lower Saxony farm), refreshment kiosk, and a water tower (Oscar Menzel, 1913/15) as a "point de vue" of the large axis through the park and a western counterpart to the Stadthalle in the east. In 1929/30, the water tower was converted into a planetarium housing a collection on the history of astrology and astronomy. Prior to assuming his new post, Schumacher had sketched his plans with ashlar masonry. It was only in Hamburg that he transformed them into brick buildings. Schumacher's city park thus marked the beginning of a new architectural physiognomy for the city. "If one looks upon the Stadtpark not only as a recreation area, but considers the variety of the spatial and functional divisions within the park and its buildings quasi as an ideal city, then brick—in concert with green space and water—was used as the definitive urban building material for the first time in this location." (Hermann Hipp) The listed building is being restored to its original condition and provides a new structure for the streams of visitors on three different design dimensions. The conversion plans include both the plinth structure and the historic water container (exhibition, refreshments).

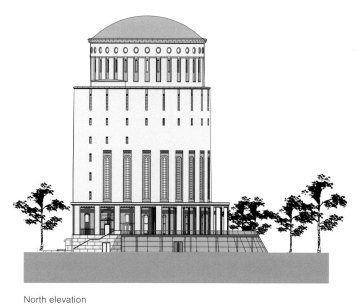

North elevation

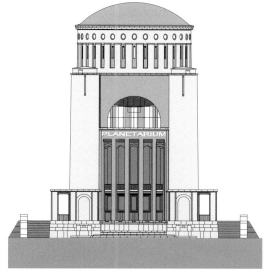

East elevation

Hamburg Planetarium

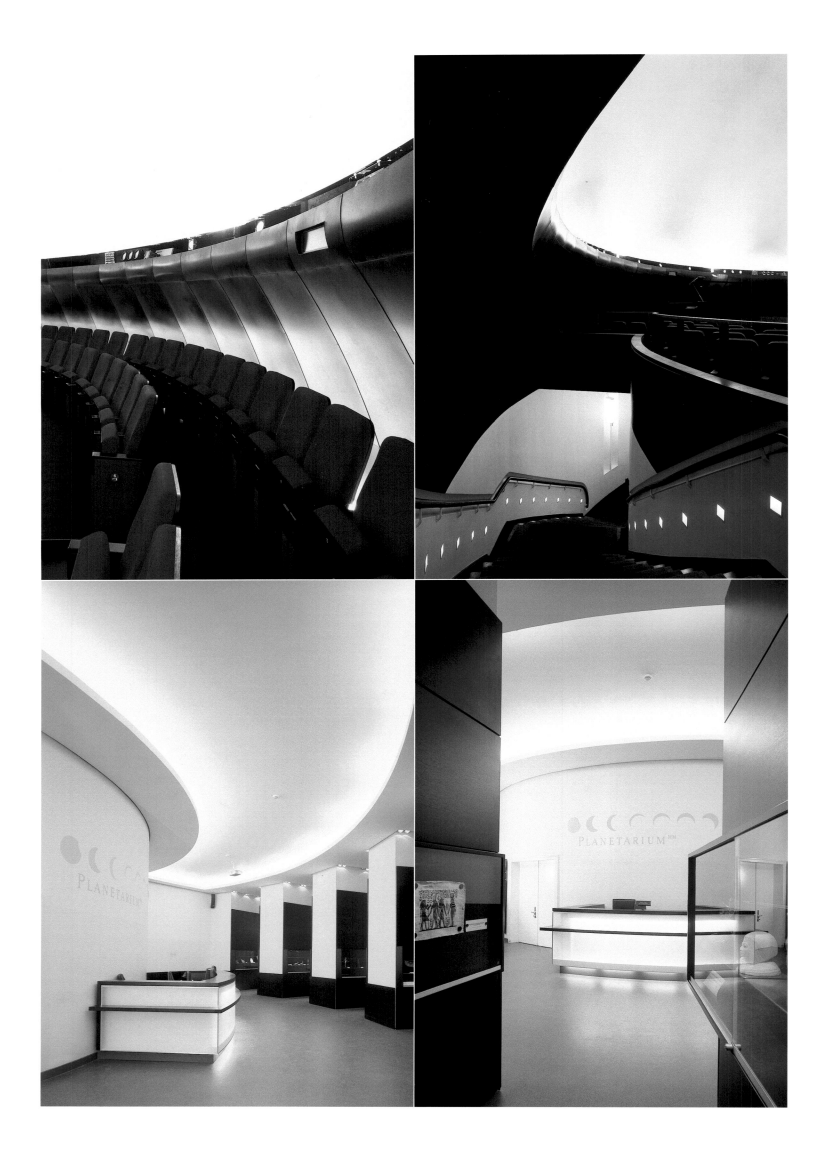

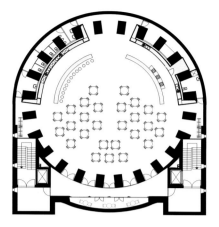

Plan of 3rd floor, restaurant

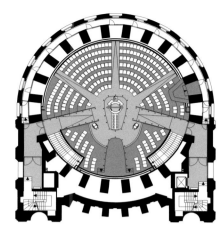

Plan of 2nd floor, auditorium

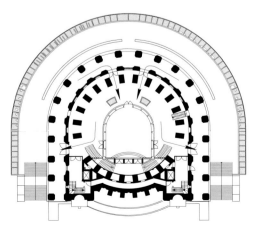

Plan of first floor, lobby

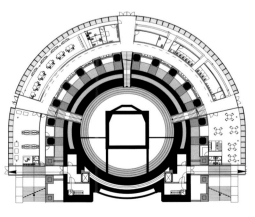

Plan of suspended floor, lower level, offices

Hamburg Planetarium

05.7

KNOWLEDGE-BASED FORM
KLIMA-HAUS BREMERHAVEN

MUSEUM
BREMERHAVEN
GROSS FLOOR AREA 15,000 SQ M
PLANNING MARCH 2003
COMPETITION 2003, 3RD PLACE

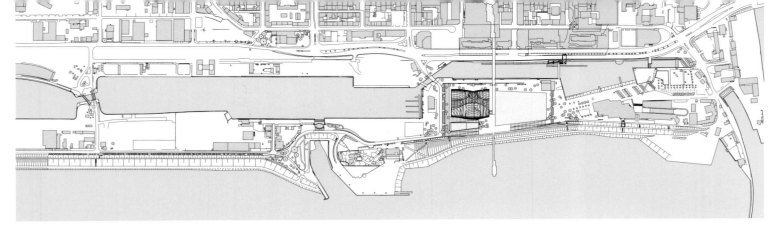

100 m

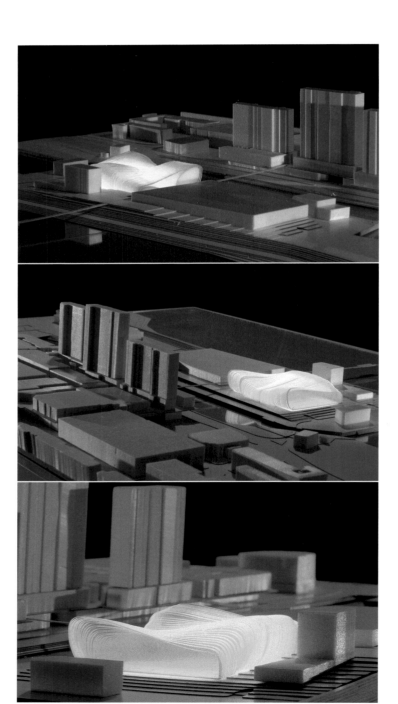

KNOWLEDGE-BASED FORM

The blob embodies progress in architecture: thus the unmistakable message of "Blobmeister" at the German Museum of Architecture in Frankfurt (2001) and of "Latente Utopien" at the Landesmuseum in Graz (2002). All too fervently, the protagonists praise their revolutionary morphing of form that showcases the entire gamut of digital computer art. In 1960, the project was still called "Phantastic Architecture" named after a book by Ulrich Conrads and Hans G. Sperlich; by 1988 it had become "Visionary Architecture" under the pen of Günther Feuerstein. As far back as half a century earlier, the Futurists' manifesto of 1914 called for "plastic dynamism, music without rhythm and the art of noise, expressions we employ without mercy in our struggle against cowards enthralled to tradition." The avant-garde of the time rarely went beyond declarations of intent. Builders of automobiles, airplanes, and locomotives had a better grip of streamlined form than architects, who, like Hermann Finsterlin in the 1920s, created colourful erotic paper dreams as alternatives to "housing crates" and "objective coffins," but were unable to realize most of their dreams, the notable exception being Frank Lloyd Wright's organic mature work. Similarly, the "incunabula" of the IT-Baroque have also failed to go beyond the stage of experimentation thus far; the number of unknowns is still too great. In this experiential museum, however, the idea of founding the formal vocabulary of architecture in science and not only in the imagination has been distilled into an exhibition theme: the Earth's climate. A new building is emerging, shaped, it would seem, by the climate and by the sea winds broken by the existing development: fitting into the urban fabric and nevertheless making a mark, it has attracted much attention. The topography of the building invites an association with the choppy waves and windswept dunes of the nearby coastal landscape.

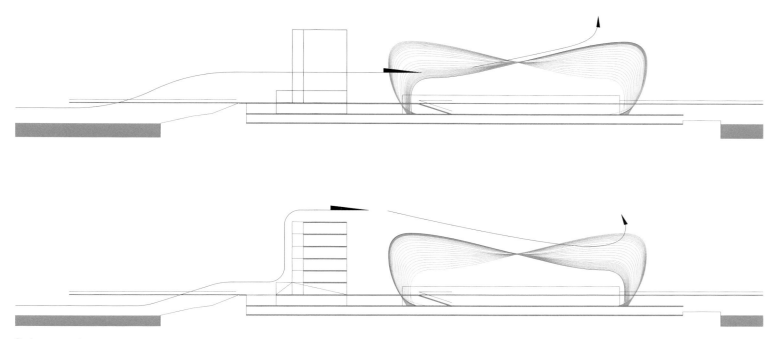

Design concept

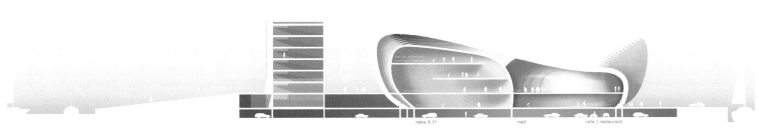

Cross section

Klima-Haus Bremerhaven

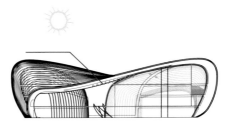

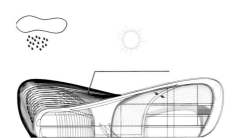

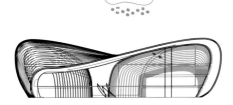

Air-conditioning concept summer

Air-conditioning concept transitional period

Air-conditioning concept winter

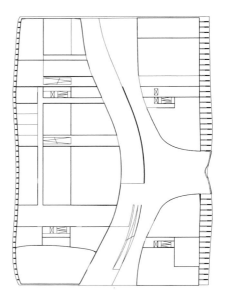

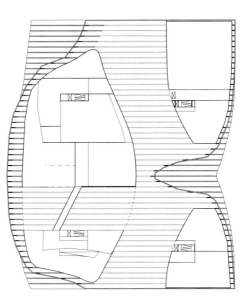

Plan of level 1, mall

Plan of level 4, exhibition

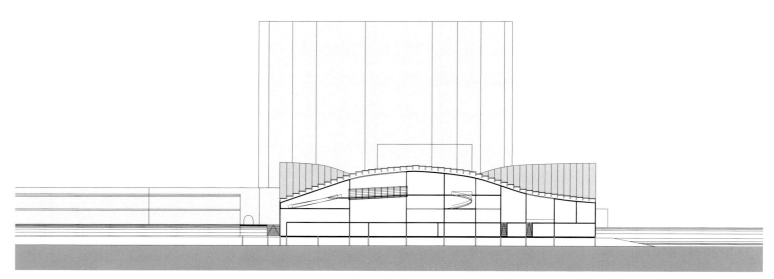

Schematic section

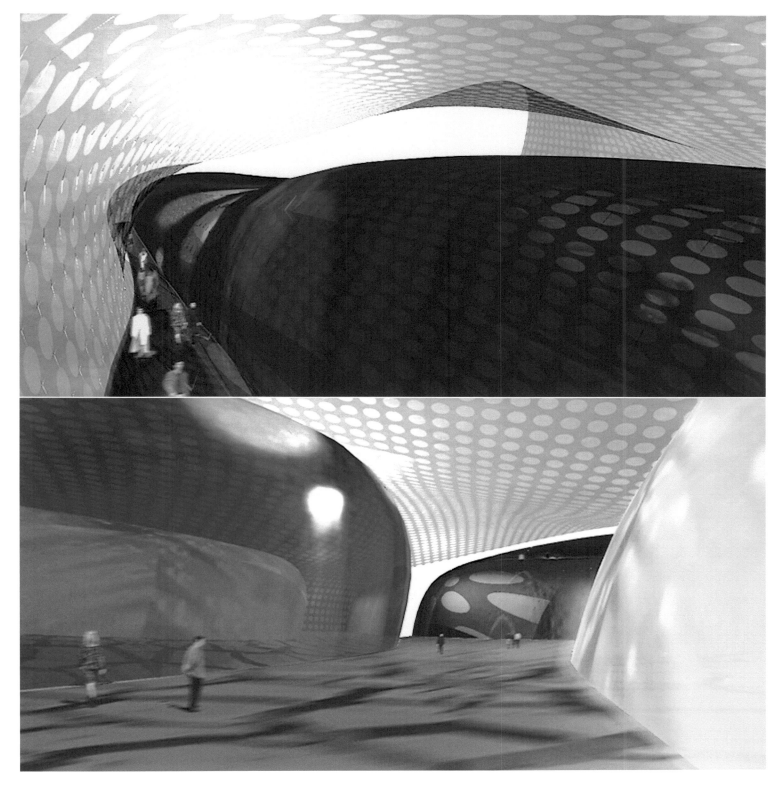

Klima-Haus Bremerhaven

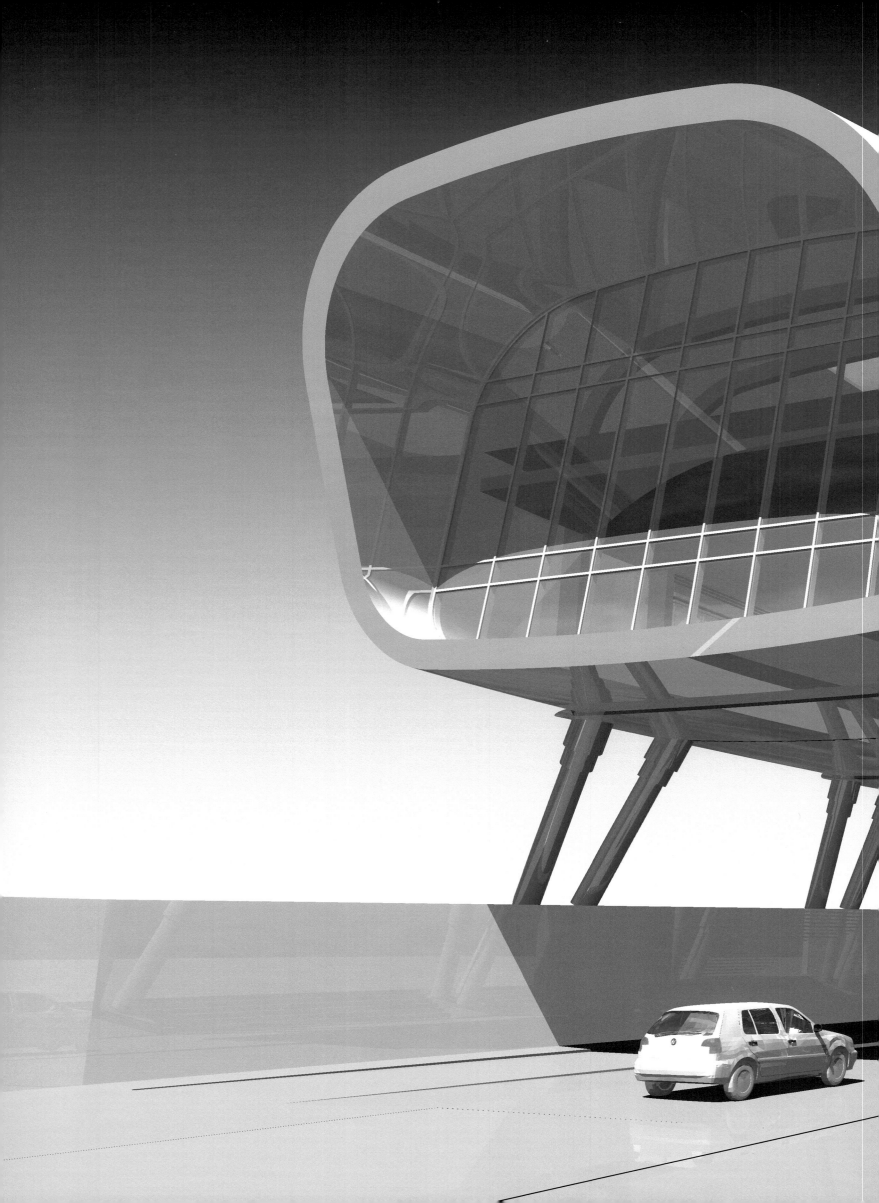

05.8

FLEXIBLE SPATIAL CONTINUUM
CASINO HAMBURG

CASINO
HAMBURG
GROSS FLOOR AREA 3,100 SQ M
PLANNING FEB 2003

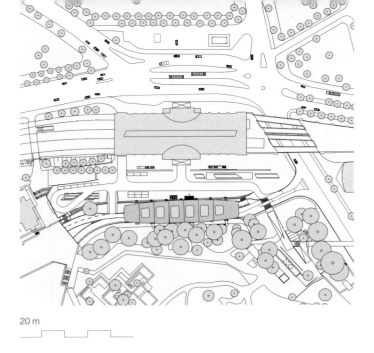

20 m

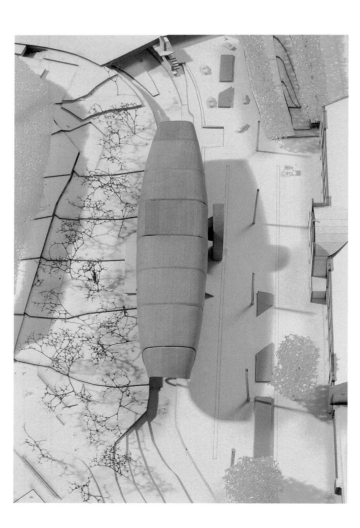

FLEXIBLE SPATIAL CONTINUUM

Marlene Dietrich knew them all and judged Friedrich Weinbrenner's casino at Baden-Baden to be the most beautiful casino in the world. Today, Berlin's happy-go-lucky crowd comes together on Marlene-Dietrich Square in the Daimler City in front of the Germany's largest casino designed by Renzo Piano. This site was originally reserved for Mercedes Benz showrooms. With tips alone amounting to millions every year, one might expect a spectacular extravagance and yet there is hardly any architectural glamour in this field in Germany. Gambling, having outgrown the opulent spa casino, is now targeted to capture the ready cash of the masses. "American-style casino" is the slogan for the symbiosis with a supermarket that has been created in Hamburg-Schenefeld. The target here is the public at large, the average punter in shirt-sleeves, whose thoughts even at noon are already obsessed by playing the barrels decorated with fruit symbols, invented a century ago by a citizen in Württemberg and originally intended as toy cashiers. What counts is the strategically chosen site, not the structure itself: fabric by the yard, instead of finely woven yarn. What could be more logical than setting up a casino at an airport, railway station, or highway interchange? Only three percent of the population frequent classic casinos. Therefore, the target consumers that count are not habitual gamblers, but people, who have no idea that they may have a passion for gambling. Established formalities of the casinos of old are unsuited to capturing a wider audience. The new Hamburg casino at the Dammtor railway station offers an architectural answer to the universal lack of direction and form, due in no small measure to the success of virtual casinos. Here the solution does not rely upon technological discretion; it triggers and allows for emotions.

Planten un Blomen   Casino   Dag Hammarskjöld-Square   Dammtor railway station

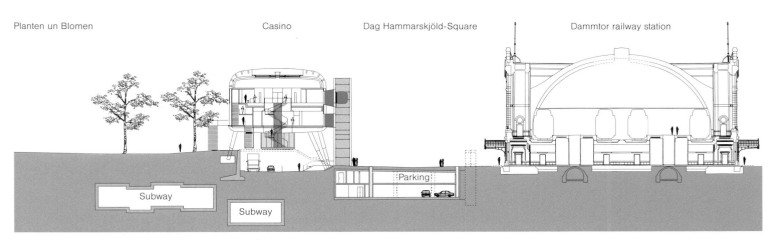

Subway

Subway

Parking

Cross section Casino, Dammtor railway station

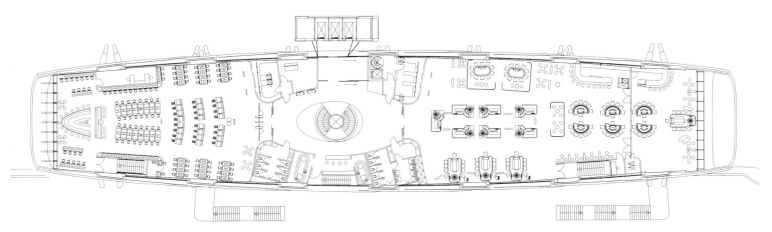

Plan of 3rd floor

Casino Hamburg

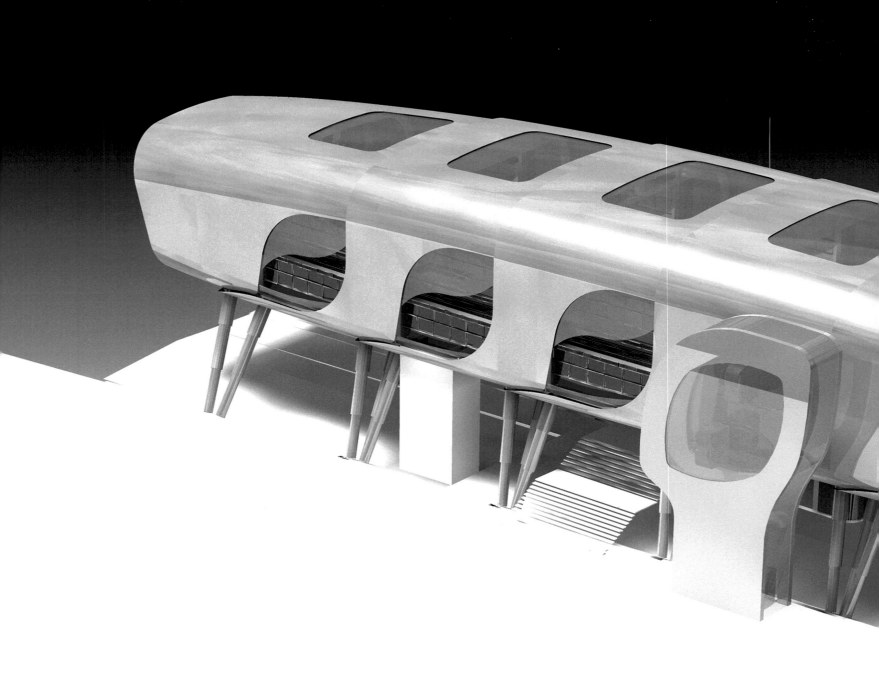

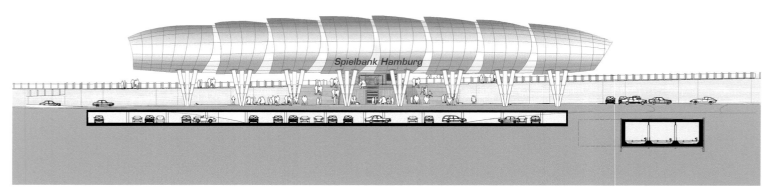

Preliminary design

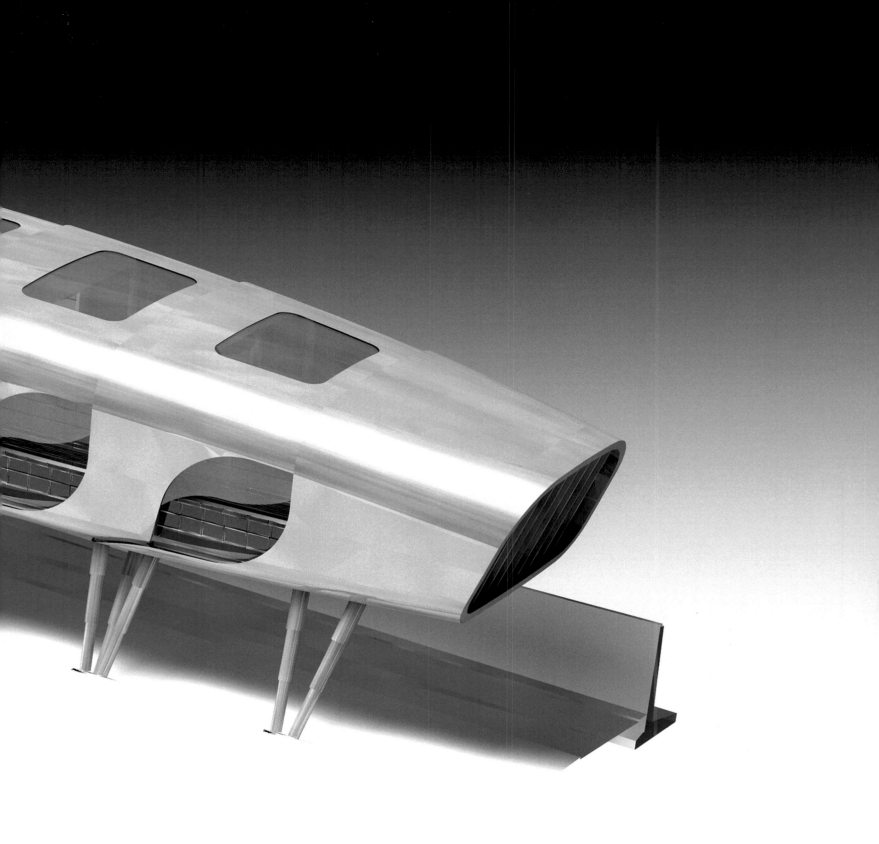

Casino Hamburg

05.9

LEISURE PARADISE IN THE DESERT
DUBAI WATER EXPERIENCE

WATER PARK WITH AQUARIUM AND HOTEL
DUBAILAND
GROSS FLOOR AREA 42 HA, DEVT. APPROX. 80,000 SQ M
PLANNING DEC 2004

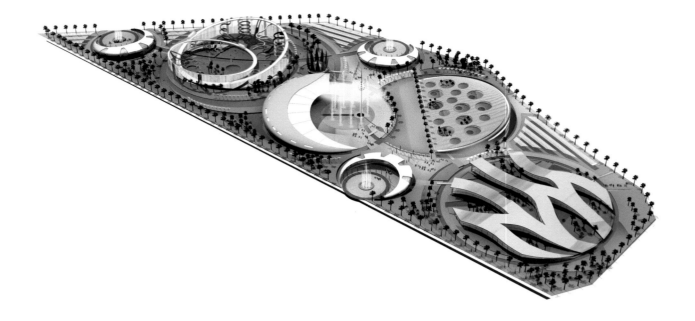

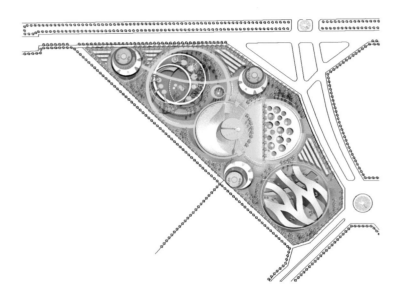

LEISURE PARADISE IN THE DESERT

Within a few decades, the small Bedouin town of Dubai in the second largest emirate on the Persian Gulf has grown into a desert boomtown. The wealth generated from oil deposits discovered in the 1960s has in the meantime shifted to tourism: projections for the free trade zone predict 15 million tourists for the year 2010. In view of the dwindling resources of the liquid gold, promoting tourism equals planning for the future. Nowhere is this idea being translated more rapidly and glamorously into urban development and architecture than in the United Arab Emirates. Next to the utopian "Bubble City"—a city literally suspended at 200 meter height in the air, powered by two enormous helium balloons and an antigravity engine—the 300 artificial islands of the future project "The World" (2008), where the rich will be housed on a map of the world reproduced in coarse pixels, seems almost mundane by comparison to the "The Palm," a project currently under construction where land is being reclaimed in palm-leaf pattern. Even the construction of the tallest skyscraper in the world, Burj Dubai, with a planned height of 705 meters and the largest shopping mall in the world is assured. In addition, the desert metropolis hopes to increase its leisure appeal with a 70-kilometer-long subway (2012), a Formula 1 racecourse, the ongoing beach extension, and, finally, the Dubailand amusement park. "Aqua Dubai," at 25 ha the largest waterpark in the Middle East, is designed to transport the appeal of water into the 2-kilometer distant hinterland, Dubai's desert land-scape. An artificial cloud serves as a symbol visible from afar: "punctured" by a needle-shaped observation tower, it will disperse its precious content in individual "drops," attractions arranged in a circle across the planted desert. The program includes a waterpark with slides and roller coaster, hotels, an aquarium, a dolphinarium, a museum, water shows, an entertainment complex, and restaurants.

Dubai Water Experience

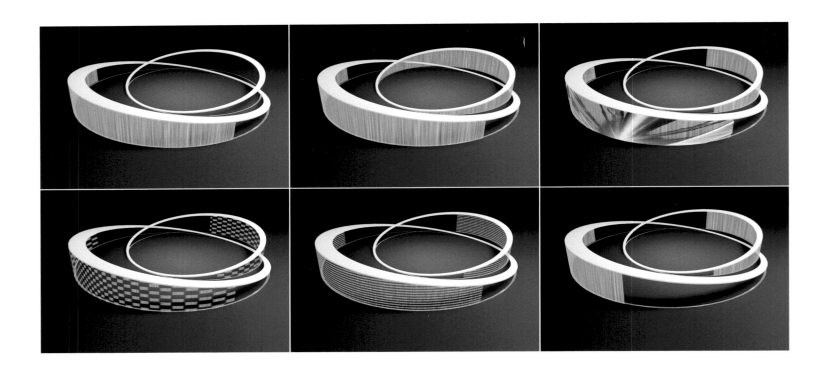

Dubai Water Experience

The spatial experience of public life, the idea of the city as a place of congregation, of social exchange as a rite and right, has been almost completely erased from our cities. In the new millennium, the pendulum of perplexity in urban design has swung from the petty public design in the form of park bench and bollard in the 1980s to a revival of the high-rise in Germany. Both markers continue to be embellished with historical curlicues without a clear direction. Like the street lamps in the old town, the modern, previously blazing high-rises are now being cloaked in historic dress. Munich is beginning to wonder whether this is a wise strategy, since the external image of the "Fünf Höfe" arcades, to which Herzog & de Meuron dedicated ten years of work, is almost completely subsumed by the "historic" image of postwar facades. Is the preservation of historic monuments truly served by Hamburg's decision to base the urban silhouette around the Binnenalster on a Merian engraving dating back to the seventeenth century? Even though most of the buildings gathered there have long since lost their historic glamour through the effects of war and the stringent rationalization of reconstruction? Hans Kollhoff, who had already steered Berlin in the direction of Manhattan, chose an adaptation of the neo-gothic Chicago Tribune Tower from 1925 for Frankfurt's future vertical "scale leap" for want of original reference points in the city. Unlike the pioneering futurists at the beginning of the last century, Kollhoff makes escape the central motif of trade. As if post-modern architecture still had to be invented.

NOSTALGIA

Even a century ago when the United States was still an emerging power, it was deemed fashionable to resort to eclecticism in order to shake off sentiments of cultural inferiority. Nouveau-riche barons of commerce and industry played Renaissance prince and demanded stage sets in the Beaux-Arts style instead of ahistoric modernism in an entourage of greenhouses and exhibition halls. Today, a new kind of obsession with the past has taken hold; anything that appears binding and impervious to change is highly popular, past happiness in what has been is constantly beckoning. Hans Kollhoff is fanning the flames of this passion with gothic church towers, gilded battlements, borrowing from Schinkel, Ledoux, and Manhattan, all the while gloating over the lack of theory among his colleagues without ever having to bring a theory of his own into play. Populism is a facile approach to waging battle. However, proponents of the architectural flight into the past fail because the complexity and density of the original cannot be reproduced with today's

means and abilities. A few happy exceptions aside, such as Quinlan Terry's country homes, the result is backdrops against more backdrops, and copies of copies. Regardless of how tempting the dream of disused architecture may be, the fate of this short-term popularity has more in common with Walt Disney. Retro has nowhere to go without being anchored in a clear time reference. Building bridges to the past or rather from it to the present can only succeed if there is a solid foundation in ideas and not merely pure nostalgia. Exchanging blind faith in the new for an even blinder faith in the old remains but a pious hope, the realization is as flat as it is flimsy. Genuine past is damaged.

URBANITY

Even though the new architectural benchmarks operate without historical references and although the most recent modern wraps itself in a void of structural grid and glass, the city is not enriched with "focal points of experience" through this unbridled megalomania, as the investors for the Millennium Tower in Vienna would have us believe. In ancient Rome, the public life of the city was undoubtedly more organized: in the streets, on the squares, in the amphitheater, circus, and stadium. Simply because electronic voyeurism via Internet and monitor had not been invented? Over the course of two millennia, the massive scale of urban spaces and buildings created for public service at ground level evolved into an expression of the urban dynamic, into reference and identification points for urban dwellers. The city has no similar focal points today. If retro-culture is the order of the day, then at least let it not be narrow-minded facades at the center of interest and of the city, but a splendid site of public life.

The Hamburg architects Jens Bothe, Kai Richter and Hadi Teherani are on the tracks of these urban stages by designing massive sculptural forms, the significance of which is reflected in their unique scale, but also in their fundamental form. Spherical or elliptical UFOs, elongated, mysteriously lit zeppelins, agile multi-functional halls or glass cubes with a mysterious inner life seem to glide into the amorphous image of the city like space shuttles, identifying new meeting places for the departure into the twenty-first century. Vividness is called for in the scale of the urban plan alone. These are often surprising sites, whose usefulness as building lots had gone undiscovered. In the local vernacular, people speak of futuristic architecture, of a scaly creature, an alligator back, a spine or an elongated fish.

As symbols of being different, and especially dedicated to societal exchange for this reason, these projects attract much attention. A clear majority voices their approval because for once architecture is not insisting on asceticism in a Protestant ethic of space, or on fear of joy and pleasure, on a denial of the visual. On the contrary, emotional references are expressly allowed. This is true for the "Berliner Bogen" office building and the striking "Dockland" in Hamburg, as well as for the Airrail-Center in Frankfurt, the Dortmund railway station project, the Multi Casa project on the site of the freight railway station in Duisburg, the glass cube for the ruin of the Nikolaichurch, the new Alster arcades and the Europe-Passage in Hamburg. Even the sophistication in organisation and space that characterizes the "Deichtor," its predecessor, the 12-story "Doppel XX" office building with its double cross in the plan, an ancient, Egyptian hieroglyph for the city, and the Kieler Sparkasse, completed years ago, achieve surprising degrees of expansion and approximation of public space. A section of the teller hall at the savings bank in Kiel, with a discrete glass screen, is accessible to the public day and night. These architects have no time for antisocial buildings. Like choreographers, they are interested in the human movements in the city.

COMMUNITY

Setting the stage for community—beyond traffic jams and museum queues—is an important source for the collective identity, especially in a society, which isolates the individual more than ever today. Robert Venturi, the great ideological forefather of post-modern architecture, was never more wrong than on the last page of his famous book *Complexity and Contradiction in Architecture*. There, some thirty years ago, he declared that Americans no longer need a piazza and the passegiata—the traditional stroll around market square and church in Italy. Americans, Venturi insisted, were better off at home in front of the television (or, today, the computer monitor): "There is a general belief that open space is something precious for our cities. It isn't."[1] Modern cyborgs, citizens of cybercities crouched in front of their computer keyboards are repeating the same thesis today. Urban space and public buildings have become superfluous, they state. With the usual envious glance toward the United States, urban models from Chicago to Prague are slated to land on the junk heap of history. Yet the installation of data highways has in no way lessened traffic chaos; the idea of the metropolis is as alluring as ever.

Does anyone truly wish to experience the live-events of the city in front of the tube at home? Can the real experience be replaced in the much-praised "City of Bits," when virtual audience members register their applause as an encoded reaction via buttons and levers or have limited interactive input into camera angles? This approach failed to function even in the less complex competition between television and cinema, which has long since been decided and not to the disadvantage of the cinema. Urbanity, the most complex relationship between humans and space, characterized by openness and an explosive mix, will not lose its appeal through the tube. It is significant that the Cybercity cannot operate without the city metaphor. Paul Virilio was wrong when he wrote that the city would "soon be superseded by a telescopic conurbation in which the public image in real time will replace the urban public space of the res publica."[2] The private tele-terminal will not become the reference point; instead, the city remains the reference point. On the contrary, the media euphoria does not provoke a "raging standstill" (Paul Virilio), but a raging mobility, whose increasing acceleration threatens to diminish every experience, relationship and condition into banality. The traveller in both high-speed train or airplane cannot tap into the experience of space, landscape, stillness, and body. The world is spread out before him ready-made: for walking, driving, consuming on effortless and dispassionate flying visits. As the spread of computerization increases, so does the yearning for the immediacy of concrete, original events. One does not have to, but one wants to be on location. There is no other explanation for the obsession with travel. Architecture and city cannot even be fully captured and preserved as a photographic still life, never mind the public and cultural life pulsating within it. The Dutch poet Cees Nooteboom experienced his happiest moment with regard to a location in the circle of buildings around the Plaza Mayor in the Spanish town of Salamanca, not while watching a travel show on television.

PUBLIC LIFE

Perhaps the large public in the world's major museums is less in search of art than of public life through art. The Getty Center in Los Angeles, a blend of Tuscan rock-cut town and colossal bricolage in the Imperial Roman pattern, combines urbanity and art in the vein of urban ensembles designed with a total command of composition. In a city, which like a one-road village squared is nothing more than an agglomeration without boundaries or contours, the museum—fortress and treasury amidst the raging storm of the information revolution—becomes the intensive care unit for public life and urban culture. Art alone cannot restore this wasteland, which is referred to as public "space" for lack of an alternative, to fertile life. Artists encounter only desolateness, "stock piles, interstices of the non-designed and the non-articulated" (Bazon Brock), but no concrete reference points.

Yet the citizens of the city are driven by a yearning for greatness that reflects their own position and significance. The dream of Berlin's Stadtschloss is a clear symptom, albeit a socially irrelevant example, of this yearning. Alexis de Tocqueville, the great prophet of age of mass culture, interpreted the public need for space, the stark contrast between many small and a few large buildings, as a central phenomenon of democracy. Wide squares and large public buildings, indicated on the city map by area only without indication of height, provided an immediate image and experience of urbanity in ancient Rome. West of the Umbrian town of Orvieto, imperial Rome was to be recreated as a leisure and education park called "Roma vetus"—the history of horizontal urban space to original scale on an area of 360 hectares.

SECONDARY WORLDS

Evidently, people are no longer satisfied with the reality of the city alone. We need virtual secondary worlds such as Walt Disney's small town model Celebration, imperial Rome, or at the very least a "CentrO-" shopping town as in Oberhausen in addition to the old city center and the resurrection of historic backdrops. Even narrow floors on high-rises reaching for the sky are no more than places of refuge that are further and further removed from the stage of the city with an emphatic insistence on technology. All they have to offer are isolated, private box seats with a view of the city, which is incapable of fulfilling the promise of its skyscraper-studded skyline because of a lack of communication grids. Frank Lloyd Wright was quite right in laughing at the "extended telescopes, raised elephant trunks, Bedford stone rockets, gothic toothpicks, modern fountain pens, which sell verticality to the earth worms in the village street down below." This did not, however, stop him and his ambition as an architect from wanting to break all records with his "One Mile High" tower, a 1.7 kilometers and 528-story high building.

Wenzel Hablik, the visionary Expressionist architect carried the vertical city to the extreme at the beginning of the last century by designing colonies in the air and flying settlements that were equipped with propellers and finally surrendered all attachment to the ground. For the city and its urbanity, such a farewell could only have been advantageous over time, because its horizontal dimension would have remained untouched. After a century of high-rise history, Frankfurt is nevertheless seeking salvation in taking a vertical leap in scale. A horizontal leap with the help of monumental public buildings would be more attractive in terms of social space, but it would require more than a chess game between the city and investors after the motto: rook puts king in checkmate.

INTEGRATION

It is no accident that there were visionary illustrations of creating horizontal links in the tower- and elevator-dominated city of New York through daring bridge constructions at a time when high-rises were still in their infancy and the term "skyscraper," coined some 115 years ago, did not even exist. This motif that was also adopted by the Futurist Sant'Elia. By comparison, the 58-meter-long glass sky bridge between the 41st and 42nd floor of Cesar Pelli's twin towers in Kuala Lumpur is no more than a sketch and a makeshift measure: just another exclusive vantage point, purely symbolic glitter for the boomtown. The 185,000 square meters of floor area across 88 stories of the currently tallest structure in the world could have been utilized far more usefully if they had been integrated into the city for public use. Even Radio City in New York's Rockefeller Center, which Rem Koolhaas praised early on for its multifunctionality, can serve as a positive model. High-rises do not offer an escalation in urbanity, but a refuge for voyeurs. There is no more pitiful scene than to experience Los Angeles on a Sunday from a rotating restaurant atop the kind of high-rise built by John Portman: a film without sound and action. In thirteenth-century Italy, the extravagant towers of the magnates were simply capped to the benefit of the beauty and space of the city. Today, on the other hand, cities indulge in banal city crowns in the form of anonymous stacked office towers for lease that serve no other purpose than the personal enrichment of investors operating on a global scale. Given these conditions, the final meaning of the high-rise, namely that of enriching the city at a few select locations with a specific, unique landmark, is hard to achieve. The "cloud hangers" planned by BRT at Cologne's Rhein-auhafen are a rare highlight with horizontal booms in a sea of banality between "Cologne Tower" and "Main Tower."

Germany is quickly catching up with the United States in terms of high-rise development, if only thanks to Chicago couturier Helmut Jahn.

Oddly enough, serious attempts at developing large public space in a new manner, which is BRT's goal, are nevertheless suspect as autistic Americanisms. And yet this is the only way to breathe new life into the ailing city. Johann Wolfgang von Goethe had already noticed in the arena of Verona "that the people, when they feel and see themselves together, are startled to perceive themselves as a *gestalt*, a form, 'animated by a common spirit'" and noted as much in his diary, *the Italian Journey*. Thomas Wolfe and Truman Capote created literary monuments to this collective illusion of happiness in unforgettable paragraphs on New York."[3] The principle, as described by Goethe, is simple: as soon as "something worth seeing happens on the ground and everyone runs together, those at the edge of the crowd seek to rise above those at the front by any means available: people climb onto benches, roll out barrels, drive up in cars, lay down boards this way and that, occupy a neighboring hilltop, and soon a crater is formed." In Berlin, this phenomenon was once referred to as "Tempodrom" and newly installed under the title "Stage for Urban Culture," unfortunately with strong religious overtones.

The task that is decisive and formative for the city is not to break private records of soaring heights, but to create spaces for the social events and focal points of identity in the European city. The Hamburg BRT-team is following this path in their small and large projects. A street does not simple become public space because it does not belong to a private individual; a building need not be lost to the public because it was built by a private individual. The site of congregation in the Amsterdam of the nineteenth century, for example, was a citizens' palace, which was erected in 1864 thanks to the initiative of physician, chemist, and bread manufacturer Samuel Sarphati. It was a colossal structure, far surpassing the scale of the rest of the city. For four decades, the privately owned public spaces in New York have demonstrated that private and public need not be mutually exclusive; on the contrary, they can be complementary attributes. Modelled after Mies van der Rohe's Seagram Building on Park Avenue, 320 buildings benefit from offering an urban expansion to the public space. "As soon as the client receives permission to create additional floor area, he agrees to design, build, and maintain a space that is accessible to the public and to offer it for public use without limitations. Although the space remains in the possession of the client, he must cede the rights that are associated with private ownership. The space is thus added to the 'free world' of public spaces and the client is not allowed to be selective or otherwise regulatory with regard to its users, or to change the space according to his individual ideas or hand it over for private use."[4] In the twenty-first century, there will be a need for new social capacitors, Rem Koolhaas calls them "built superconductors." What these new locales of public life will ultimately look like and how they will function as social capacitors are questions to which the Hamburg architects are seeking to provide a preliminary answer.

Klaus-Dieter Weiss

Notes

1   Robert Venturi, Complexity and Contradiction in Architecture, New York 1977

2   Paul Virilio: *Revolutionen der Geschwindigkeit*, Berlin 1993, p. 65

3   Vittorio Magnago Lampugnani: Die Ästhetik der Dichte, in:
    Hongkong Architektur. Die Ästhetik der Dichte, Munich 1993, p. 9

4   Juliane Pegels: …and it does work! New York Citys Erfahrung mit privately owned
    public space, *Polis. Zeitschrift für Stadt und Baukultur* 1/2003, p. 25

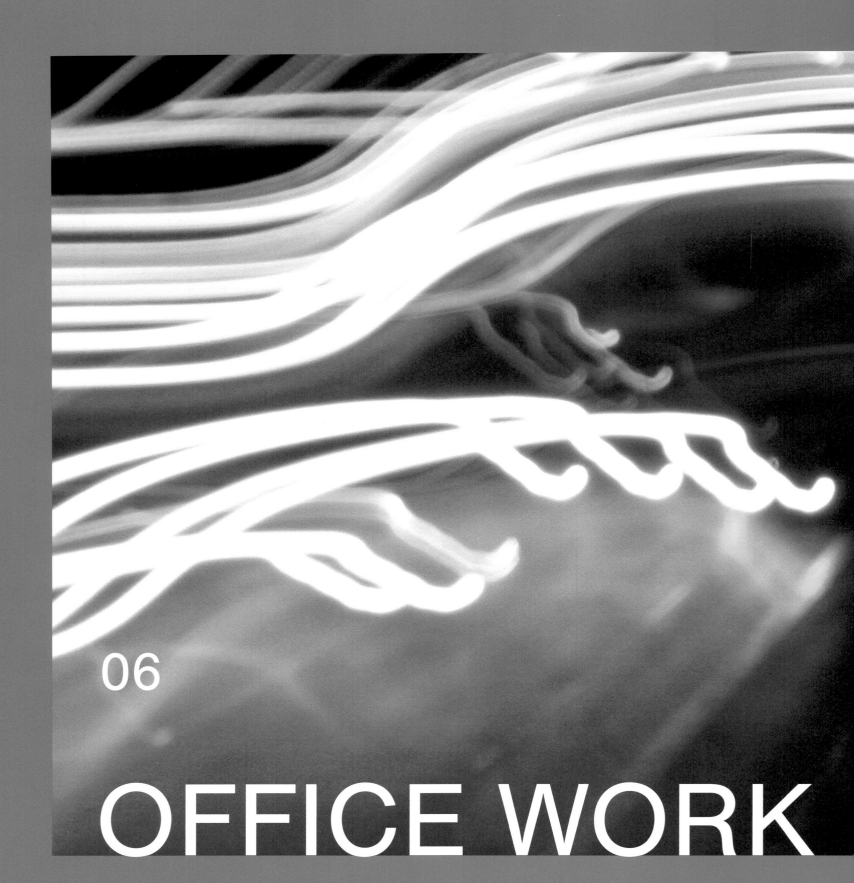

06

OFFICE WORK

Independent of its changing organizational forms—and despite its vitreous curtain facades—the office still functions as a simple black box. For centuries, human beings have attempted to master "informal" life by creating closed spaces in which the variety of existence and its accompanying manifestations are "formally" recorded—once in files, now in date records. Offices have thus become machines that not only define society but also transform social and natural processes. In other words: the modern world is, provided the office is. The invisible world inside naturally fuels distrust; however, frustrations also arise within the data regime itself, and these only worsen as bureaucracy continues its move into cyberspace. The decisive factor is the flow of data, not the person processing it.

Given the hypercomplex dynamics of such controlled processes, narration and symbolism no longer have a regulating effect on life. Workers in the office spend more time communicating with machines than with other human beings. The office itself has become a machine, and the work in it can be compared to industrial production on the conveyor belt. The computer is the final stage in the transferal of Taylorism from production to administrative processes. On the one hand, the office must not forego form with all its difficulties. On the other hand, communication, complexity, and dynamism cannot be restricted to separate areas, no matter how large or flexible these are. Communicational openness—not necessarily defined as a lack of borders—is the decisive factor within the building and beyond its boundaries. Nowhere has this urban principle of layered functions been articulated more boldly than in the Swiss Re headquarters in Munich, designed by BRT. The continuously expandable, dense interconnection of exterior and interior space manifests itself in a play of stairs, foot-bridges and halls as a symbol of modern nomadic society. With the three-dimensionality of a hypertext, it links project teams and the business system in a labyrinthine and yet systematic manner. The levels include a project team, business system, and knowledge base. On the lower level, knowledge is generated, classified, integrated into context and made available. This layer is not represented by institutionalized unity, but by corporate vision, culture, and technology.

Whereas the office has always been the driving force behind developing new communication technologies, mankind seems to have reached the ultimate codification and formalization of life with the computer. The content and rhythm of office work is, for the most part, determined by the computer, and often the amount of money invested in data processing is now equivalent to the construction costs of the entire office complex. It is with great urgency then, that data architecture must be reconciled with the image and work atmosphere of the office building in order to overcome anxieties and to enhance motivation. The question of office quality does not have only an architectural dimension, but an urban planning dimension as well. Or did the collapse of the twin towers of the World Trade Center mark the start of a bureaucracy that is utterly devoid of images and symbols? It is noteworthy that in the many stages leading up to the attack, architecture was not sacrificed for security.

A city is a dynamic, creative, cosmopolitan, and historical blend. Urbanism is not necessarily a question of population size, but rather a disposition which itself results from a certain way of dealing with space as a factor of social interaction. In spite of all the euphoria for new communication forms and technologies—and given the homelessness of a "cold," high-tech communication society—we have, quite obviously, not moved beyond the human or "warm" communication community to be found in urban networks. What is at stake here is the inhabitability of a social space whose future is highly dependent on the communicational quality of conurbations.

06.1

A STEADY FLOW OF TRANSACTIONS
KIEL SAVINGS BANK

BANK
KIEL
GROSS FLOOR AREA 7,000 SQ M
BUILT APRIL 1994–MARCH 1996
BDA-PREIS 1999 ARCHITEKTUR IN SCHLESWIG-HOLSTEIN,
2ND PRIZE

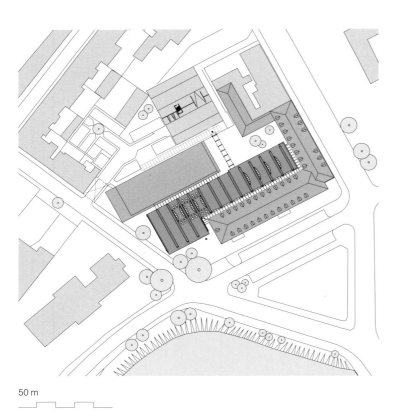

50 m

A STEADY FLOW OF TRANSACTIONS

The second project that BRT realized also targets a mass phenomenon relating to architectural denial. In terms of their buildings, a large number of savings banks and financial institutions communicate with customers on the supposedly solid basis of middle-class banality and creditworthy convention. And yet this practice stands in glaring opposition to the technical equipment now used in banking. With the introduction of automatic tellers that are usable around the clock and the attendant reorganization of customer service and financial transactions, the functional structure of the bank changed so radically that, despite long-held reservations, spatial and design innovations became realistic. In the Kiel Savings Bank, the different uses of the counter room by day and by night seem an especially consistent extension of this development. The architects achieved the double usage through the aid of a movable glass building set within the building. Their inspiration came from the glass chamber music hall that in 1990 was set as a modern element into Berlage's stock exchange in Amsterdam. Whereas the conversion of the stock exchange necessitated the creation of an acoustic partition between the small hall and the adjacent larger one (to be installed without any change to the historical structure), the glass elements in the savings bank divide space for security reasons. The main entrance, lobby, and counter area remain open around the clock. The only difference: outside normal opening hours, customers can only gain access with a valid bankcard. Glass walls restrict movement to the area of the computer terminals, but customers have an unchanged view of the spacious room, which is also used for cultural and other events.

South elevation

"Building good architecture always means departing from the beaten tracks." Kai Richter

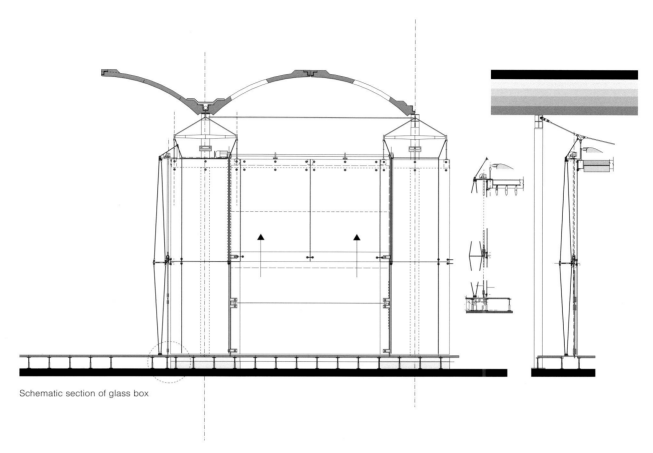

Schematic section of glass box

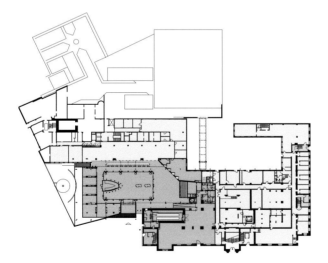

Plan of first floor, customer reception hall

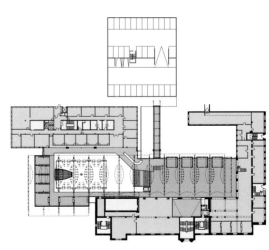

Plan of second floor, customer reception hall

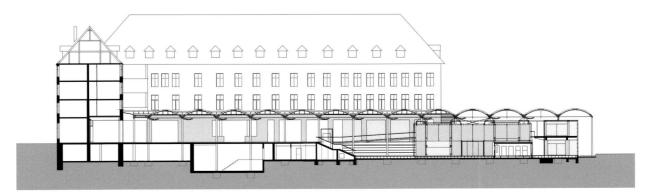

Longitudinal section

Kiel Savings Bank

Kiel Savings Bank

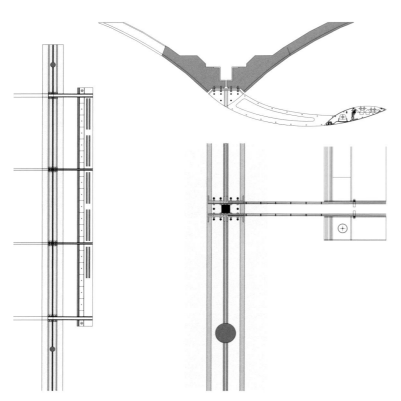

Multi-functional light, communications, and monitoring system

06.2

STACKED GARDEN CITY
DOUBLE X OFFICE HIGH-RISE

OFFICE BUILDING
HAMBURG
GROSS FLOOR AREA 20,000 SQ M
BUILT JULY 1997–AUG 1999
COMPETITION 1995, 1ST PLACE; ARCHITEKTURPREIS 2000
WESTHYP-STIFTUNG; FIABCI PRIX D'EXCELLENCE 2001

STACKED GARDEN CITY

The hieroglyph for "city" in classical Greek, propelled twelve stories into the air (and into the third dimension), formed the basis of this new type of office building. With great spatial extravagance, the architects widened the normally narrow ventilation space within the double glass facade (only a superficial sign of environmental thinking) and created hanging gardens with lemon trees. The building's glass shell is designed to keep out noise and weather. The office structure, set as a double "X" into the square glass block, only meets this shell on its outer end points and is accompanied on its rise to the skies by six building-high triangular atriums. At the center of the building, between both office "letters," this web of space opens to form a seventh square atrium that, like the others, can be regulated climatically via retractable glass roofs. Open-plan, combination and individual offices are grouped around this airy core, and from their inner position they are linked to the exterior via two-story gaps in the Xs. Seven-meter-high gardens and luxurious relaxation areas, interacting with the twelve-story entrance hall, were created as a kind of greenhouse window in accordance with construction regulations. Long before the Dutch Pavilion at the Expo in Hanover transformed stacked landscapes into the boldest metaphor for the future, BRT combined interior, intermediary and exterior spaces in this practical, highly flexible city structure. It is situated less than ten minutes from the central station in the direct vicinity of BRT's follow-up "Berliner Bogen" project. An airy, light and green labyrinth has evolved—one that has often been dreamed of, but has never been realized quite so impressively.

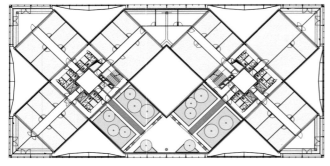

Plan of 3rd/7th floor

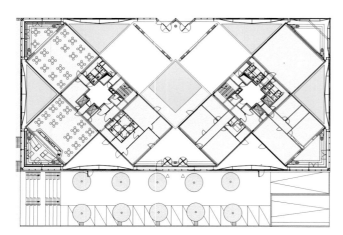

4 m

Plan of first floor

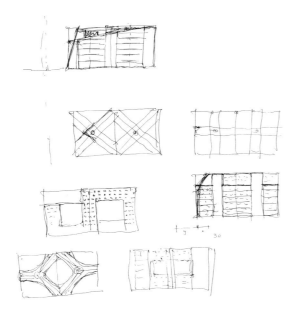

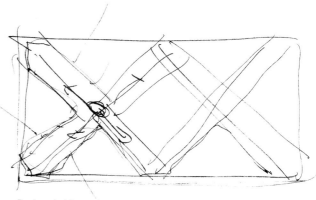

Design sketches

Double X Office High-Rise

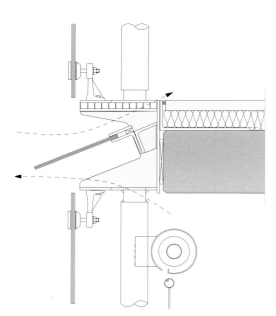

Detail of ventilation bulkhead

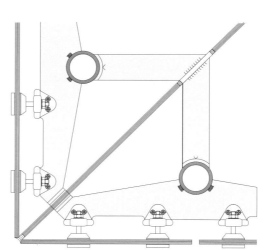

Detail of facade

"With high-tech there is always the danger of wanting to substitute complex technology for simple physical processes. Just for aesthetics' sake." Hadi Teherani

Double X Office High-Rise

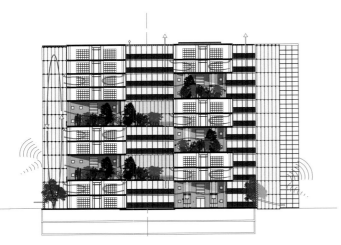

Sections of air-conditioning system

WINDOW ON THE CITY

This building is a "sensation," a "cathedral," a "city of the future," a "building emblematic of our time," the "sum of economic pressure and emotional dream-world," and "probably the best example of office construction in years," claimed the *Süddeutsche Zeitung* euphorically on April 19, 2000. "In a single form it combines cutting-edge technology with contemporary trends and anxieties. It reconciles the yearning for a radical departure with the desire for radical isolation … At first glance this is not obvious, since from the outside the new office building looks like a beautiful glass box that has crash-landed in rather ugly surroundings—in an area where Hamburg stops being the Hamburg of blue water, white villas, and green Barbour jackets and slowly becomes Dortmund."

Between Heidenkampsweg, the southern Hamburg highway feeder, and the Mittelkanal waterway, the architects have linked two crosses to form a spatial web that is punctuated by the glowing red of its glass and enamel balustrades. Rising twelve stories and covering 9,000 square meters of surface area, the suspended glazing is currently the tallest in Europe. The resulting pure cube of glass flies in the face of usual sculptural office design, which insists on establishing a distinctive symbol within the amorphous structure of the city. And yet within this cube—sheltered from noise and weather behind its protective glass cover—one encounters a super symbol. The multi-story building with its unique floor plan is of a modest height in keeping with the Hamburg skyline. It was made possible by the client's willingness to modernize and keep rents low in the adjacent factory building, which was once used to produce artificial sausage skins and now provides studio space for artists, sculptors, and designers.

One of the oldest symbols of the city is the cross or "X." The Egyptian hieroglyph with which the historian Joseph Rykwert demonstrated this claim consists of a cross within a circle—two elemental and enduring elements of the city. In his central study "The Conscience of the Eye: The Design and Social Life of Cities," Richard Sennett refers to the fundamental significance of this symbolism. "The circle is a single, unbroken, closed line: it suggests enclosure, a wall or a space like a town square; within this enclosure, life unfolds. The cross is the simplest form of distinct compound lines: it is perhaps the most ancient object of environmental process, as opposed to the circle, which represents the boundary defining environmental size. Crossed lines represent an elemental way of making streets within the boundary, through making grids."

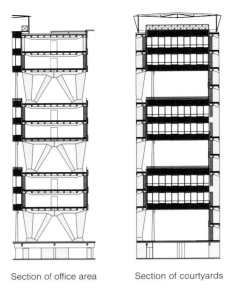

Section of office area   Section of courtyards

"They demand a rent of less than 12 euro per square meter of office space. With only two cores and a very effective building depth of 13.50 meters that left enough money to build a really high point-fixed hanging facade." Hadi Teherani

The Hamburg office block thus becomes the dual symbol of city and urbanism in an immediately intelligible and plausible way—in particular since the building is an open one.

The point of intersection in the "X" structure contains the minimized entrance cores, the service and sanitary facilities, kitchenettes, photocopying rooms, and the building's technical installations. Around these cores, office areas of 140 or 220 square meters radiate out on ribbed slabs resting on visible consoles. The office areas conform to the shape of the cross and are free of internal supports. The sliding windows on the inner facade allow for a partition wall connection every 1.25 meters. The outer points of the ground plan offer prestigious, city-oriented discussion areas bounded by what was originally planned as a red concrete segment. Apart from a few office zones on the longitudinal sides of the cube, only these "windows on the city" push forward to the external facade. As a precaution, a supporting ventilation system was installed at this point due to the increased exposure to sun. The entire shell consists of 560 prefabricated elements and is supported by the substructure on 384 piles. Only the four wall panels in the ground-floor corners were constructed on the site. This prefabricated construction method allowed each floor to be assembled in only fourteen days.

HANGING GARDENS

The spandrels of the two "X" forms create space for six building-high winter gardens and a central atrium. The loads of the external glazing, which extends 42 meters in front of the winter gardens, are transferred to the construction via a story-high structure and concrete cantilever arms. Adjustable glass roofs and ventilation slats 5 meters above street level automatically regulate ventilation without use of air-conditioning. A test procedure was developed beforehand to collect the required climatic data. The computer-supported system takes into account temperature, wind conditions, working hours in the offices, as well as rain and smoke reports. The design allows for unrestricted technical communication between the thermal-insulated and the cold facade surfaces within the structure. Ribbed concrete slabs, prefabricated on a just-in-time basis for the entire project, create the necessary climatic reservoirs. Positioned in a constantly alternating pattern, floor gardens almost 7 meters high allow for a view from the inner office areas out into the surroundings—beyond two projecting, 13.2-meter-deep office landings that are free of supports. The plants and water surfaces in the

gardens influence the internal climate, which, within limits, follows the rhythm of the seasons and is decisive for maintaining the thematically designed magnolia, bamboo, azalea and citrus gardens. The reservoir capacities of the unclad reinforced concrete construction and the Brazilian slate floor regulate the atmosphere both in summer and winter. The building-within-a-building concept reduces the heating costs for the office areas by almost 50 percent.

The surprised visitor may well have the impression that a great deal of usable space is lost in this labyrinthine structure, which interweaves a large amount of open space with relatively few office landings. Compared to the standard solution of a ring-like structure with a central air well, every square meter of office space seems to bring with it a large amount of "unused" open space. The views through the simply constructed sliding windows, which are not exposed to rain or weather and therefore are not thermally insulated, lead to a luxurious emptiness, since every office is situated off a winter garden. However, in mathematical terms, the opposite is the case, as indicated by the high proportion of window area and the construction of the inner facades. The minimization of the access surfaces and the maximization of structural depth result in 16 square meters of utilizable space per 18 square meters of total surface. Costs for fire protection were considerably reduced through model simulations on a scale of 1:20 that made it possible to do without a sprinkler system. In case of fire, escape routes are provided by two winter gardens, which are pressure-ventilated via metal gratings. The internal connecting halls and the internally located security stairwells are illuminated naturally via surfaces of glass brick. These have been classified as F90 fire resistant according to German regulations. With net construction costs of 1,140 euro per square meter—including a 172-car underground garage—rental costs on completion amounted to less than 12 euro per square meter plus 2.50 euro for overhead. The floor gardens, covering a total area of 2,000 square meters, are not rental space but used free of charge. With only two stairwells and the simplest facade and sunshield technology behind the external climate and sound barriers, the Double X office building is not only an economic and environmental masterpiece, but marks the pinnacle of architectural symbolism as an urban super sign under glass. Offering an unusual degree of value for money, the building was fully rented one year prior to completion. For the time being, a single company is using the building's entire 20,000 square meters of space, thus optimally exploiting the symbolic power of the architecture for corporate identity. However, it is possible for separate parties to rent the 72 office units, each with roughly 200 square meters of

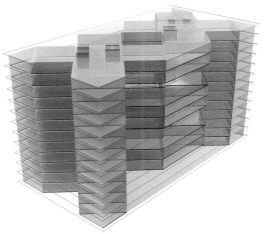

Office areas

floor space. These can be divided into single, combination or open-plan offices, and if desired, connected via naturally lit hallways in the building cores.

Once again we find that a provocative spatial idea, which is enormously effective in economical terms, outdoes rival firms that merely glorify technology and form. The succinct lesson that one learns here is that architectural "wonders" are always achieved in spatial terms. Ornate facade projects, whether by Jean Novel or Theo Hotz, cannot replace the emotionalism of the third dimension. The building also fits in perfectly with the row pattern of the surrounding neighborhood. Of all the ideas this building communicates, the central one is that innovative architects will always find eager clients, despite the problems their profession may have realizing concepts. On the other hand, office space designed as mass product, devoid of spatial inspiration and environmental intelligence, will be difficult to rent out, whatever the state of the economy. People are becoming more aware that architecture can soar when competing for clients and staff.

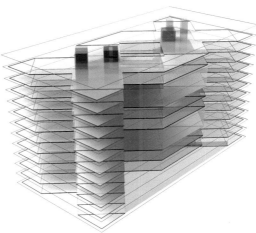

Gardens

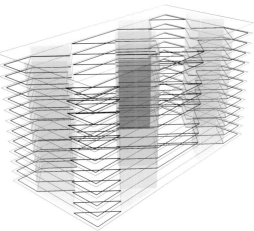

Voids

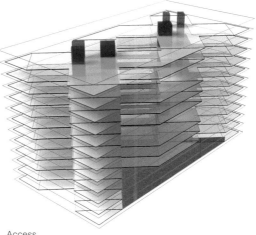

Access

Double X Office High-Rise

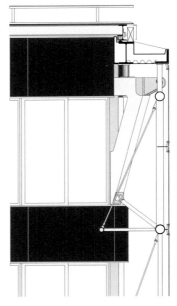

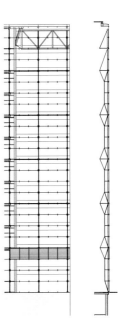

Detail of facade suspension, 12th floor

Schematic section of courtyard facade

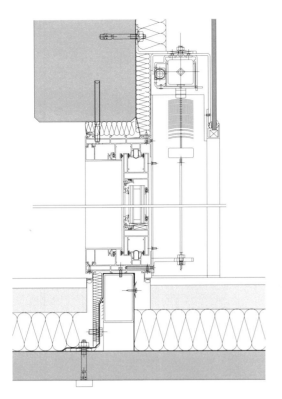

Detail of doors to atrium, first floor

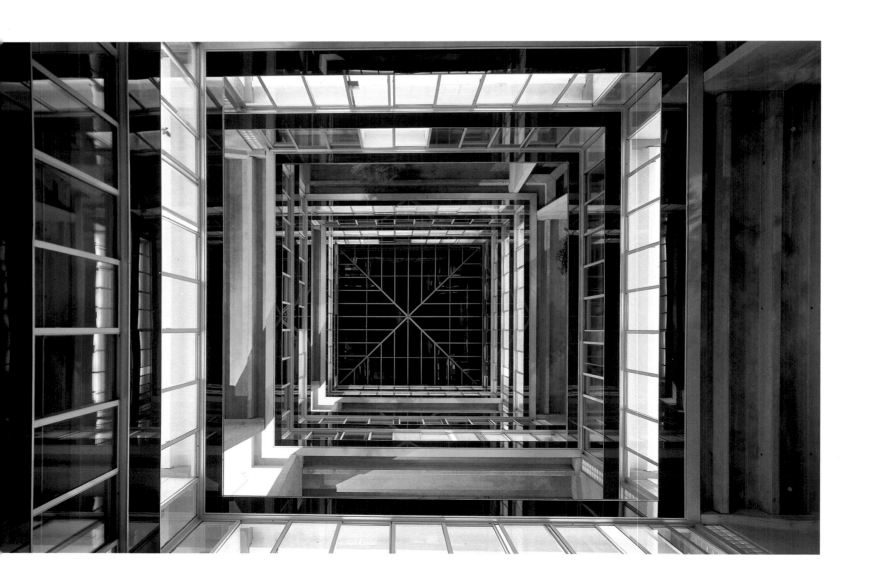

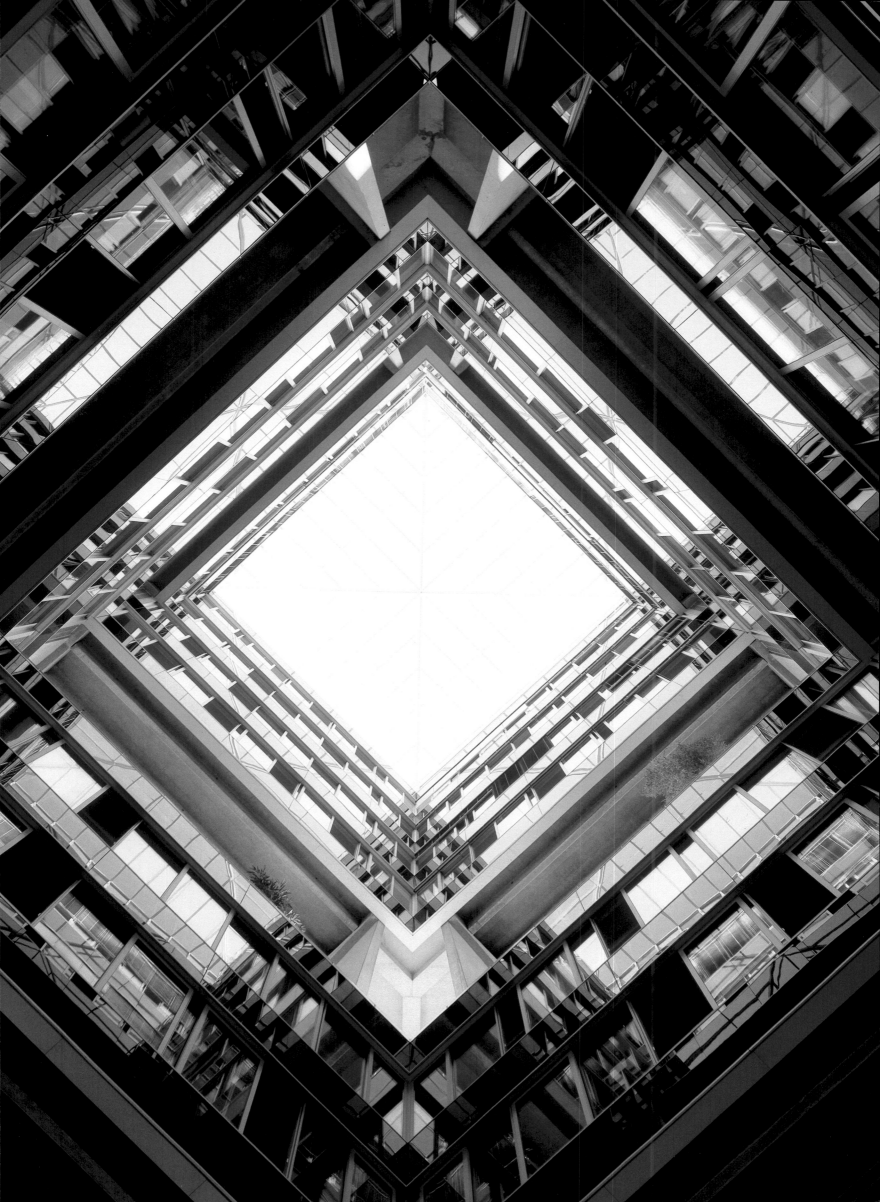

"The conservatories were originally designed to optimize the lighting in the depths of the building. More than anything else, though, they ensured that the building's hourly air-change ran at seven-times the natural rate." Kai Richter

Double X Office High-Rise

Elevator car

06.3

HIGH-RISE IN THE REAR
ABC-BOGEN OFFICE BUILDING

OFFICE BUILDING
HAMBURG
GROSS FLOOR AREA 16,200 SQ M
BUILT MARCH 1998–AUG 2000
COMPETITION 1995, 1ST PLACE

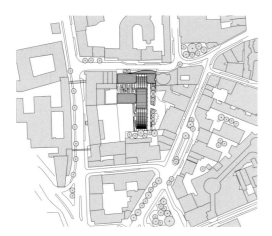

HIGH-RISE IN THE REAR

In 1958, Ernst Bloch addressed the transparency and openness of modern architecture, stating: "The broad window that captures the exterior world requires an exterior world full of appealing structures. The door fitted with glass right down to the floor needs sunshine to come streaming in." Bloch feared that, when used to reconcile both realms, total transparency would place interior space at the mercy of the exterior world. This politically motivated fear was shared by many of the first modern designers. These days glass is used almost exclusively for aesthetic purposes, and such a symbolic interpretation of the material—which Sigfried Giedion described in 1941 as the "reconciliation and penetration of the individual and societal sphere"—may seem outmoded to many. And yet there is some validity to the core statement, since new threats have replaced the Nazis and the Gestapo to which Bloch alludes. In a horrifying parallel to September 11, 2001, Bloch's thoughts even ran to "earthscrapers," which were "holes in the roofs of a cellar city." The eleven-story ABC-Bogen high-rise is only 100 meters from the Gänsemarkt and has been integrated into Hamburg's inner city with great skill. The building has a barrel-shaped glass roof, but its uniqueness does not lie in the technical computations of the glass shell or the energy technology necessary for it. Rather, it arises from its spatial dynamics on a highly problematic site. The high-rise is a "protected" rear building that submits to its narrow city location, and along with the front building, it terminates the block while adapting to the adjacent building's curved facade. It qualifies its presence in a public space through a restrained architectural vocabulary.

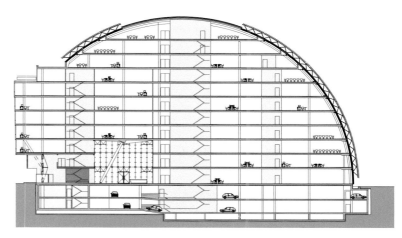

Longitudinal section

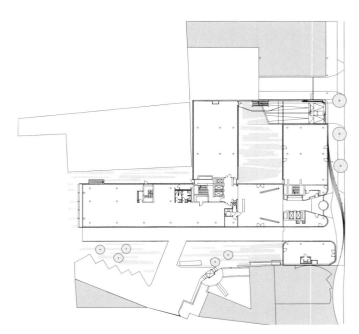

Plan of first floor

Plan of 4th floor

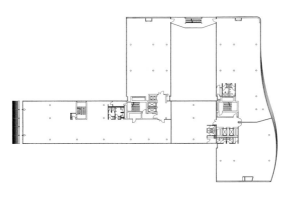

ABC-Bogen Office Building

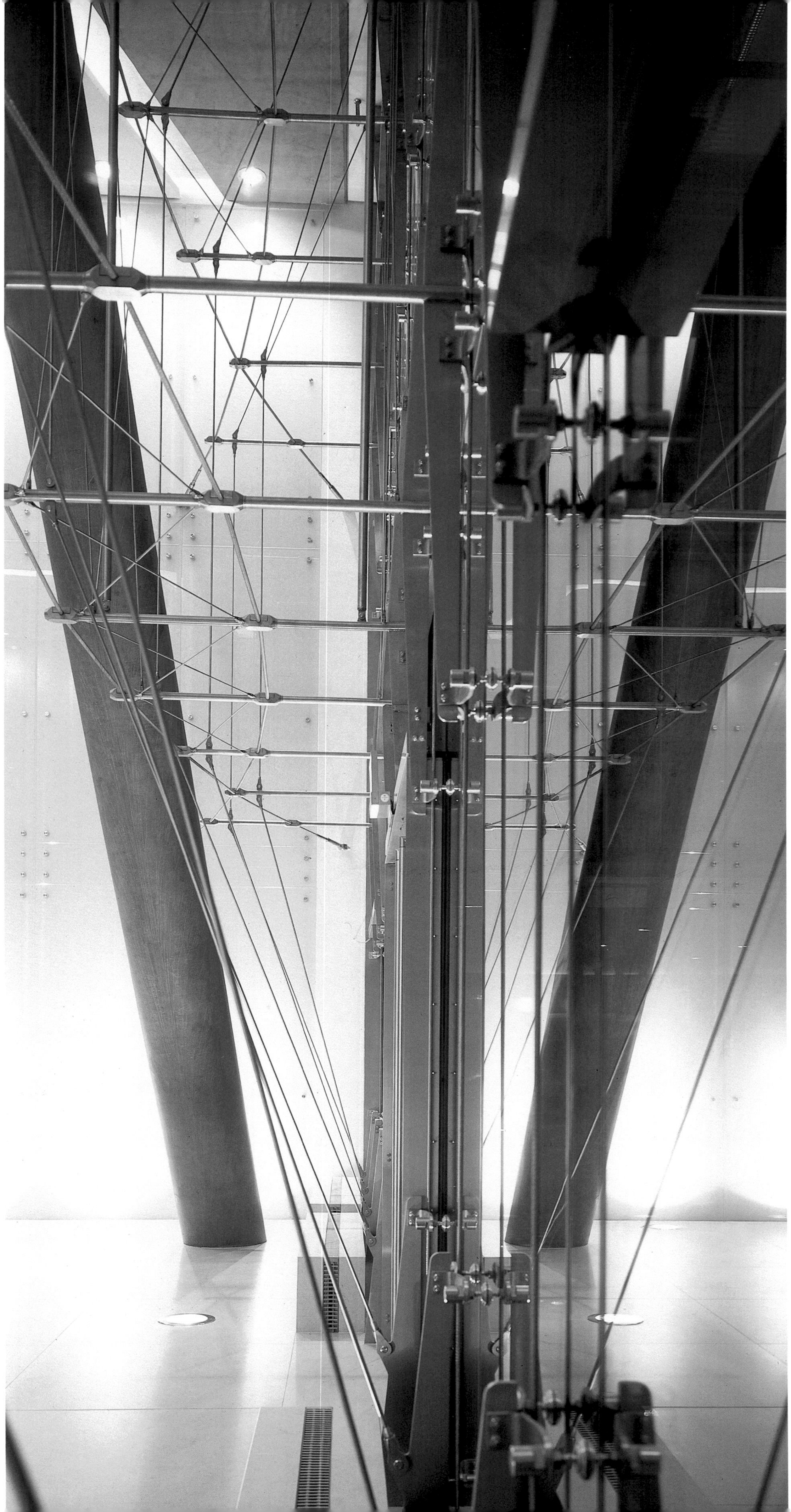

06.4

ARCADIA FOR EMPLOYEES
**BERLINER BOGEN OFFICE
BUILDING**

OFFICE BUILDING
HAMBURG
GROSS FLOOR AREA 43,000 SQ M
BUILT AUG 1998–DEC 2001
DEUTSCHER STAHLBAUPREIS 2002, NEPIX BUILDING
AWARD 2002, MIPIM AWARD 2003

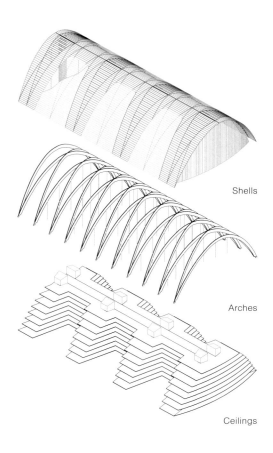

Shells

Arches

Ceilings

ARCADIA FOR EMPLOYEES

With attractive cultural and commercial locations lacking, the task of bringing culture back to the city has surprisingly fallen to the commonplace office building. In the "modern, Darwinian working world," (Ulrich Beck) grand spaces that promote staff motivation and company loyalty are required for today's "knowledge workers," and are seen as decisive production factors transcending location. The 140-meter-long "airship hangar," which has a glass skin and integrated winter gardens, is situated alongside a six-lane highway and forms the border between the city and a faceless industrial area. The only historical point of reference is Fritz Höger's office building across the way, built in 1928. Eugène Freyssinet's airplane hangar in Orly (1925) goes a long way toward explaining the kinship between Höger's brick and pilaster structure and the modern steel parabola spanning the canal (for which the site first had to be invented). Both buildings break with convention, living from their structural frame. The eight floors of the Berliner Bogen are suspended on crossing, glass-roofed arches and, for the most part, do without supporting columns. The offices inside differ in layout and orientation. Environmental building does not remain a mathematical puzzle here, but takes on human contours in the overlapping exterior, intermediary, and interior spaces. Social commitment is a function of exposure, of integration into the surroundings, as well as the urban quality of places in the community. In 1967, the first Hamburg office building was torn down because it was regarded as "plush in the age of the machine" (Ernst Bloch). Now the modern office building is once again developing into a synonym for the city.

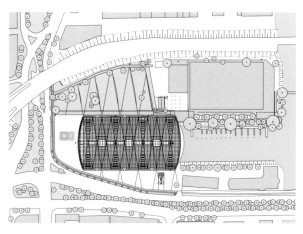

20 m

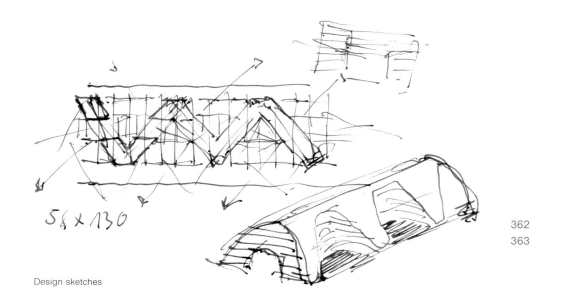

Design sketches

5 d x 130

Berliner Bogen Office Building

"The glass skin is based on the igloo principle: the smallest envelope area for the maximum content."

Jens Bothe

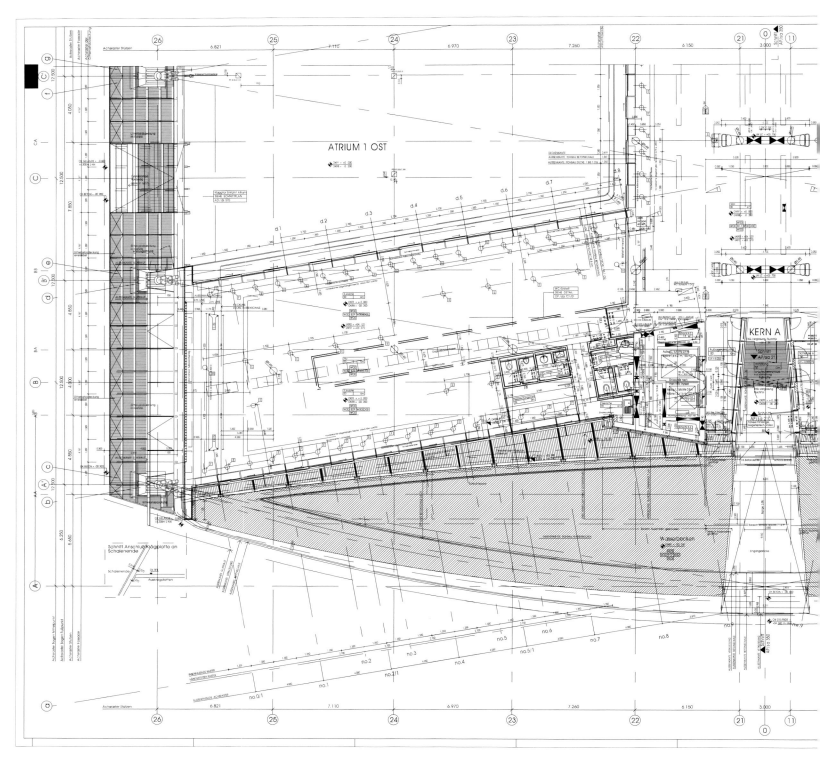

Working drawing of first floor/main entrance

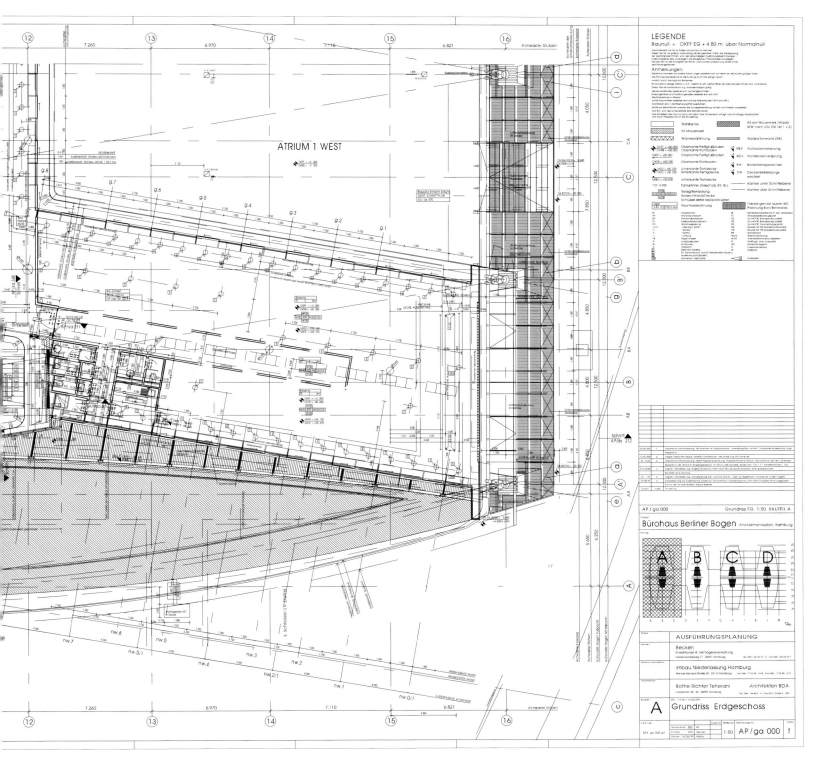

ATRIUM 1 WEST

LEGENDE

Baunull = OKFF EG + 4.80 m über Normalnull

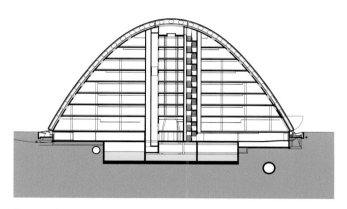

Cross section

A "BRIDGE" TEEMING WITH LIFE

At first glance, this building at the northern end of the City-Süd industrial area is confusing. Is it a train station? An airplane hangar? A gate to the city of Hamburg? The dimly lit airplane hangars that Eugène Freyssinet designed in Orly in the early 1920s appear to be related typologically. Freyssinet, the most important pioneer in the field of prestressed concrete, created his halls with 9-centimeter-thick reinforced concrete arches that brace the structure on its longitudinal sides. In contrast, the "airplane hangar" in Hamburg, which is 140 meters long, 10 meters wide and 36 meters high, is encased in glass from its lowest to its highest point, with three trapezoid winter gardens integrated into each side. In 2002, the structure not only won the steel industry's architecture award, but was also named the most original office building in northern Europe at the North European Property and Investment Exhibition. Delicate-looking white concrete arches shimmer under steel and anti-sun glazing, familiar to us from airplane and automobile construction. With the diverse play of light, the catchword "double facade" gains a special aesthetic value here, and yet it is not the material, but the space in between that shows the architects' skill. With today's unlimited technical possibilities, the right material is only an aid in defining the right spatial proportions. The northern concrete arch shows this. Especially bold in design, it appears to intercept the glass roof over the concave arched entrance facade. However, there is a steel beam above it, between the glass skin and the concrete.

The answer to the riddle is the site, which technically does not exist and was thus not the subject of any development plan. A glass pump station and the water near the entrance (which can only be crossed via a bridge) are oblique allusions to the curious situation. Lying beneath the complex is a 7-meter-deep pool that holds 22,500 cubic meters of water. It is a spooky catacomb, reminiscent of the spaces in Munich that are currently being used for concerts. The storm water storage pool is part of the city's drainage system and balances out unequal rainfall in the canals. In the event of heavy rainfall, water from the entire eastern area of Hamburg converges here and can rise to a point that is just 60 centimeters below the foundation slab of the underground garage, which was integrated into the old canal bed without any excavation. Surely it is understandable why nobody hit upon the idea of building "on the water" at the end of the canal. On the other hand, if spaces with different functions are stacked on top of each other like this, the dense

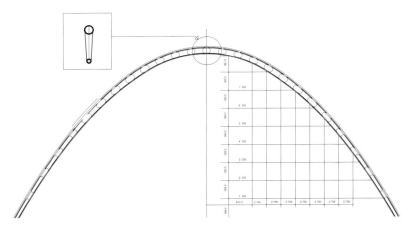

Structural principle of steel arch

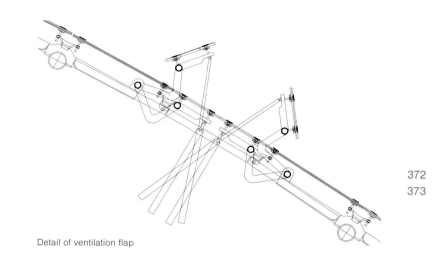

Detail of ventilation flap

"The people of Hamburg immediately found a name for all our buildings. Every taxi driver knows them." Jens Bothe

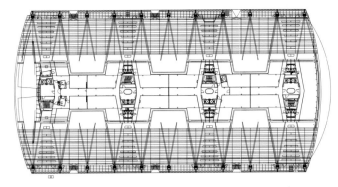

Plan of 8th floor

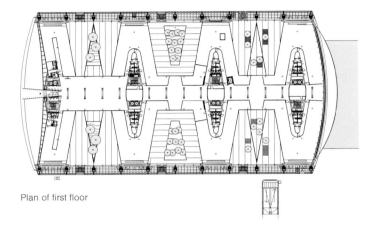

Plan of first floor

experience of city life will not be encroached upon by civil engineering measures such as banal car parks and transformer plants.

The offices in the steel parabola have sliding, story-high glass elements, and the individual floors hang on the frame as if from a bridge. Within a short period of time, this bold mammoth form made a non-place into an "address"—no small feat in Hamburg. The building shares its structural aesthetic with Fritz Höger's 1928 clinker brick and pilaster building across the way. As represented by both of these buildings, 1920s modernism and contemporary glass constructivism have more in common than is demonstrated by many recent office buildings and their reputed historical counterparts. The oversize machine shapes, sheltering arches, dynamic floor plans and flexible office arrangements have led to surprisingly diverse spatial situations that can be quite willful despite their transparency. They are not the architecturally underdeveloped platforms of a morphing office, which strands the individual worker in the middle of nowhere. The chance dispersal of rooms—with exhibition walls partitioning a space optically without giving it support or a sense of composure—are not based on any profound spatial concept, but rather on a superficial organizational idea. Concepts of office space viable over the long-term cannot be developed without architectural goals and structures. Flexible modern offices often resemble camping sites at which noise-dampening tent tarps and windscreens are creatively rearranged at least three times a week. But is this necessary? Why do we need total spatial flexibility if electronic networks know no borders? One fundamental error lies in the assumption that space will more effectively promote creativity and innovation if the spatial structures can be easily changed. And yet occupants cannot achieve high spatial quality by refusing to

Office areas

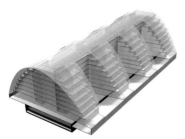

Gardens

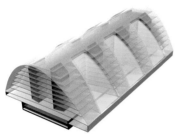

Access

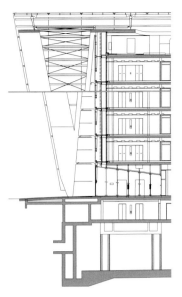

Facade section north, main entrance

define space. Only within set limitations can an environment be created and empty space avoided.

As cities grow, there are greater cost benefits in moving out of them. However, the European city is not in a state of crisis, in spite of what many claimed in the past. Nor is the business community bidding farewell to urban architecture. On the contrary, sophisticated, knowledge-based companies continue to look for urban locations in order to present themselves to the public in impressive buildings. Until recently, it was thought that information technology would have a more devastating effect on the city than the train or the automobile. Now the unsentimental, computer-generated face of de-urbanization has laid the foundation for a revitalization of city centers that have allegedly only been kept alive by tourism. The glass office "bridge" shows this trend. Originally designed for exclusive use by an insurance company, it provides 32,000 square meters of floor space for up to 79 tenants or 1200 employees. Almost 90 percent of the space was rented out before completion—in contrast to the economic disaster of the Düsseldorf Media Harbor, in which William Alsop's Colorium is 95 percent empty. The rents (20 euro per square meter) are considerably higher than those in the modern office buildings in the adjacent City-Süd industrial area. Such rents are usually only to be had at prime locations in the city or on the coveted banks of the Elbe. An architecture that is both utopian and realistic has even lured tenants away from first-class districts such as these. This has proved once again that BRT's emotionally charged spatial experiments—which, though futuristic-looking, are grounded in everyday life and economics—act as veritable magnets. The glass "wave" is one of the few (and most recently selected) office buildings at "New German Architecture," a five-year traveling exhibition presided over by an international jury.

DRAMATIZING STRUCTURE

The structure consists of crossing, cantenary-shaped, two-hinge arches that rest on pile foundations at the edge of the former street. Massive cast-steel joints dramatize the flow of forces at the visible footings. The arches are made of two circular tubes, 16 and 25 centimeters in diameter, and sheet steel with holes. Tubular purlins, up to 12 meters long, rest on top, and cast-steel cantilever arms are mounted on these in 1.3-meter intervals to hold the skin of laminated safety glass. The structure looks like a huge machine part with trapezoids shaved out. The floor plans grow smaller toward the top of the arches, which appear to shoot wildly

through space under the atriums' glass skin. The design dramatizes structure in way reminiscent of the transfer of load in Gaudí's work. The four cores correspond to the diamond-shape of the building. One hundred and twenty tons are suspended on the steel arches, and yet, inside and out, it is "only" the ceiling edges of the diagonal wings that are held (in addition to the glass facade). In order to counteract the upward force of the storage pond, the middle area loads are transferred downward via concrete pillars. In the middle axis of the first floor—the spine of the building—slanted pillars with centering beams compensate for the different column patterns on the underlying and overlying floors. In the critical phase of construction in which the temporarily supported concrete ceilings were connected to the steel structure, the delicate-looking arches sank—as calculated—by 25 millimeters.

The environmental advantages of the Berliner Bogen come not only from the utilization of the previously "non-existent" site above the storage pond, but also from the building's double shell and the use of a building-within-a-building concept. The glass shell was tailor-made for the solid building structure within. The winter gardens function as climatic buffer zones, reducing the cost of the facades and sunscreens, which are controlled from each room. The gardens, which are connected to the central entrance axis on the ground floor, dampen street noise and serve as prestigious halls for rests and exhibitions. The atriums open to the street space via large, motorized tilt doors. To get outside, occupants cross a footbridge of wooden planks running above a grate-covered drainage ditch. Only on its southern canal side does the building have a single-layer thermal-insulating facade. The glass balustrades here are partially printed, and electrically controlled horizontal ribs offer protection from the sun. In line with a "low-tech" approach, rooms are ventilated naturally, and the structure makes passive use of solar energy and warm air flows between the facade levels. In this "glassy" way, heating costs can be cut in half.

After this building made such a splash, all of Hamburg was curious about the next piece of property that BRT would take on. The architectural office took the city by surprise with a 288-meter-high glass lighthouse set down in the harbor. Derived from the shape of a water drop, the streamlined form serves as a signpost for the city's spectacular waterfront. Like the "wave" that BRT integrated into the urban landscape, the lighthouse has been inspired by Hamburg's amphibious character and stands for the transition from water to city. Certainly one should commend Hamburg for its willingness to implement such innovative

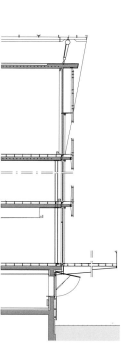

Facade section south

Berliner Bogen Office Building

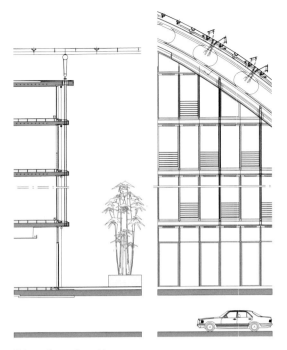

Schematic section atrium

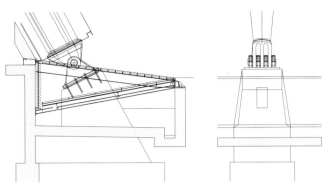

Detail of steel arch, hinged joint

solutions. Berlin is the counter-example, showing the extent to which city government can get in the way. Nicholas Grimshaw's "Armadillo," which houses the communication center of the chamber of industry and commerce, was tormented for years by the construction administration until it finally perished in captivity. In Berlin, modernism—as an antithesis to the revered Schinkel—can only be admired in museums. The Berliner Bogen demonstrates that monumental architecture can respect the dignity of those upon whom it leaves its lasting impression, since here the brute force of the large form dissolves into a powerful, transparent, multilayered and subtle play of opposing forces. In their explanation of architecture's poetic power, Dorothea and Georg Frank write that creative architects distinguish themselves by reconciling an obsessive love of detail with a bold openness for large perspectives. This statement explains BRT's building exactly.

Urbanism is not an aspect of real, material space, but rather describes the relationship between the people collected therein and "their" space—whether in the city or at the workplace. An architecture based on communication-oriented spatial ideas and urban involvement offers us the chance to bring architectural form and social practice into synch. It makes it possible to rediscover the social sense of the urban. Like other disciplines, architecture must repeatedly elaborate its link to society. In organization theory, "collective intelligence"—which is no longer imaginable without the computer and Internet—corresponds to "organizational knowledge and learning." Above and beyond individual contributions, this only evolves in the complex communications network of an organization. However, this communication network is not pure electronic cyberspace, but rather always functions within a space. It is dependent on distances, layerings, gradations, cross-links, and an orienting spatial articulation.

We can only avoid an architectural and urban-planning rut if we reflect upon communication processes, if planning and strategy teams work not only *in*, but *on* communication patterns. In order to promote communication cultures, a spatial substrate is required that derives the necessary flexibility from formal profusion rather than neutrality and emptiness. Only spaces that are redundantly structured and latently overstructured can encompass both separation and connection. In the ongoing quest for alliances, symbioses, and docking opportunities, this means that we must—in terms of urban planning—abandon the self-sufficient large complex on the periphery and shift to the re-urbanization of city centers with densely networked clusters. If intelligence and urbanism are made congruent in this way, consumer terms such as "entertainment value" and "tourist attraction" will become superfluous, even at the recreation level.

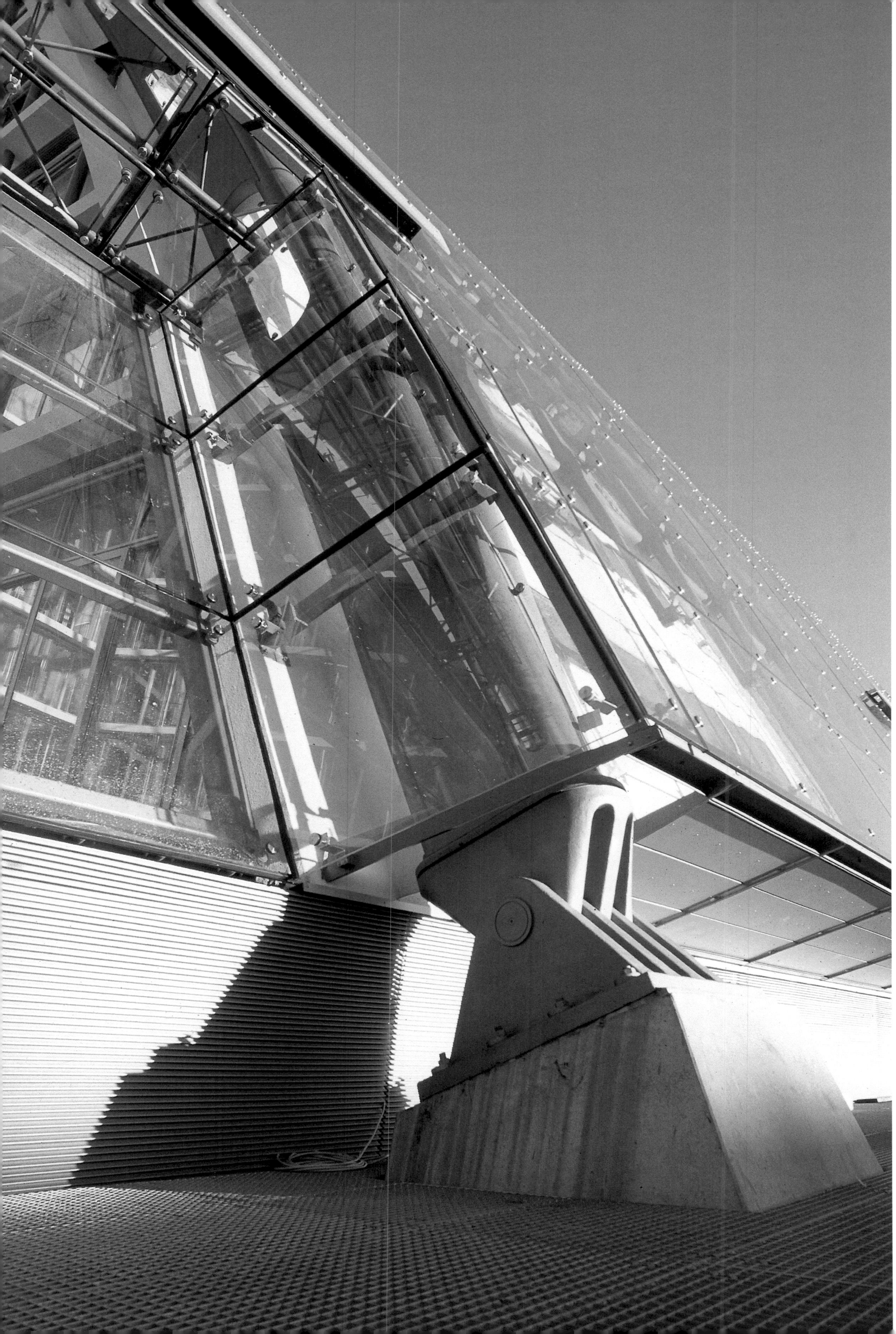

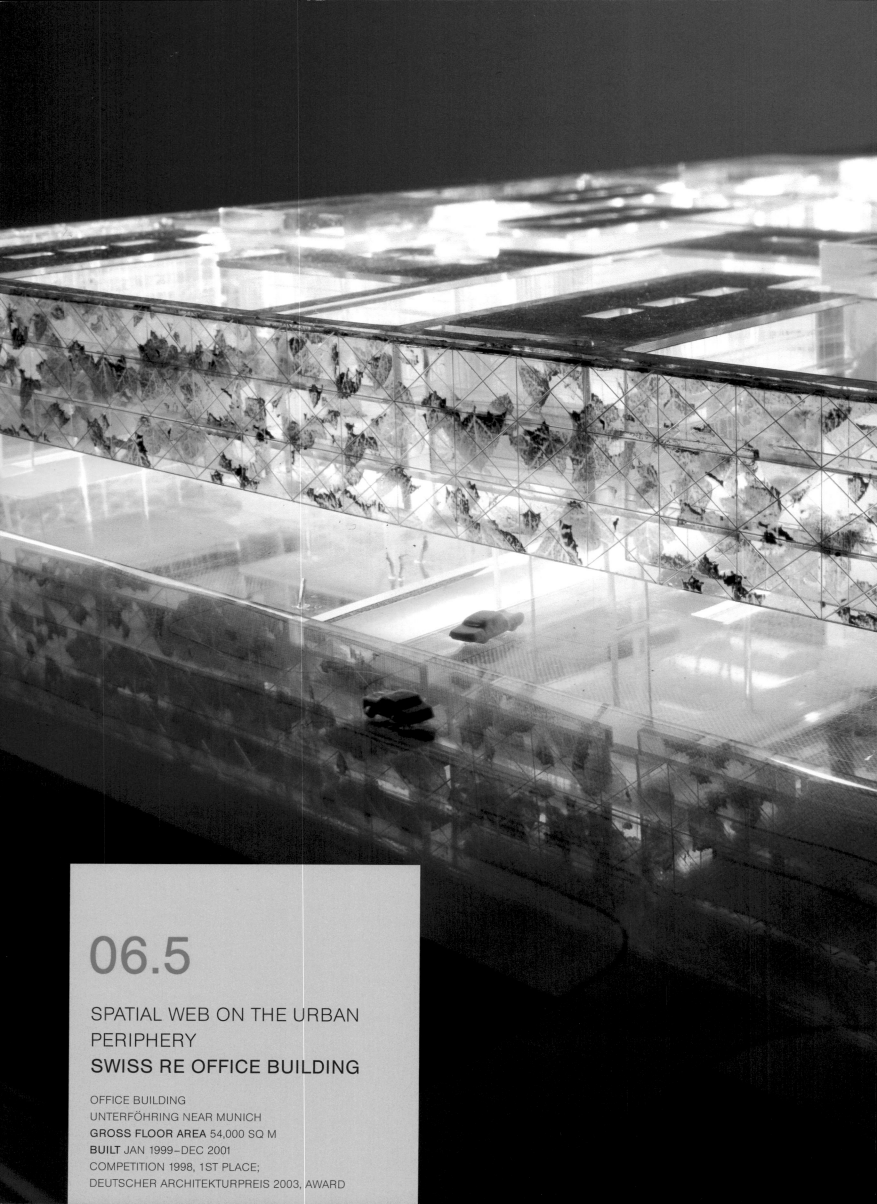

06.5

SPATIAL WEB ON THE URBAN PERIPHERY
SWISS RE OFFICE BUILDING

OFFICE BUILDING
UNTERFÖHRING NEAR MUNICH
GROSS FLOOR AREA 54,000 SQ M
BUILT JAN 1999–DEC 2001
COMPETITION 1998, 1ST PLACE;
DEUTSCHER ARCHITEKTURPREIS 2003, AWARD

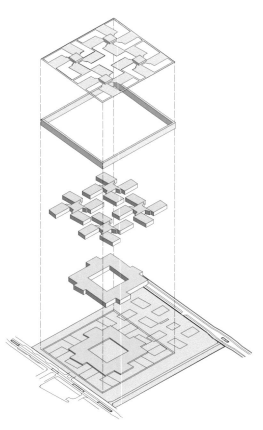

Structural principle

SPATIAL WEB ON THE URBAN PERIPHERY

We have now passed those two well-worn milestones of 1984 and 2001, and who would have thought that architecture, as the engine of public aesthetic debate, could be responsible for grand spaces and intoxicating urbanism instead of cold glass functionalism and the mathematical exercise of ecology. Even if environmental criteria are justified, an overly scientific "ecologization" of architecture that only offers a new justification for modernism's old functionalism and utility cannot respond to the dynamics of a societal development that even in its bureaucracy aims to create subjectivity as the individual link between concentration and communication. Thus, the "opulent retro-architecture of our time," which constantly seeks the "reconstitution of an architectural convention" (Heinrich Wefing), is caught in a never-ending vortex. By contrast, this web of space, concealed behind a bold hovering hedge, has its origins in the unrealized space-station utopias of Eckhard Schulze-Fielitz, Yona Friedman and Constant Nieuwenhuys. The continually expandable, dense interconnection of inner and outer space manifests itself in a play of stairs, footbridges and halls as a symbol for modern nomadic society. As a branding strategy for a company group, this urbanistic architectural principle is both labyrinthine and systematic. Individuality within this structure does not emerge from form but from spatial reference. In reconnecting the shards of 1960s tradition, the architectural concept of infinite space offers new contents and strategies that amount to much more than a backwards recounting of history à la Berlin and do not attempt to silence committed clients by means of aesthetic categories.

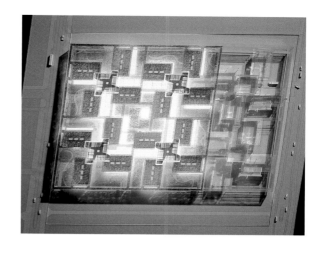

Swiss Re Office Building

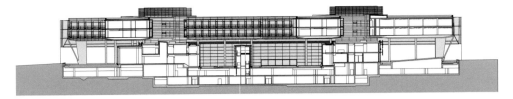

Longitudinal section

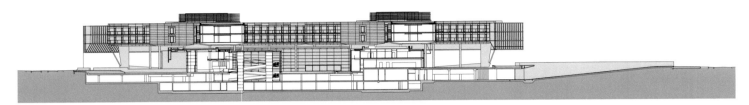

Cross section

PERIOD OF EXPANSION

In 1998, real estate sales in the city limits of Munich rose by 50 percent to 5.3 billion euro. This was topped only by Berlin, a city three times larger. In the year 2000, the metropolis so loved by corporate headquarters registered over one million square meters of new office space for rent, the fifth record year in a row, and once again the highest total renting performance ever achieved in a German location. The vacancy rate of just 0.2 percent was presumably the lowest for commercial real estate anywhere in the world. There is no talk of "the company community, that location which until recently gave life-long orientation primarily to the lowest third of all earners, that place where one of the most beautiful sentences of the world is spoken every day: 'Well, then, see you tomorrow…'" becoming more fleeting and virtual, as Mathias Greffrath predicts.[1] Only the classical, concrete, and in the words of Oskar Negt, "dead work" has emigrated to the southern hemisphere; however, this world of mines and assembly lines appears to be more than replaced by the world of computers in the executive offices of the globe. What is missing in Germany, the largest labor market in central Europe, is the socially intelligent distribution of work. The encouragement of education and knowledge, on the one hand, is at the same time confronted with a strange deprecation of their contents on the part of pure business on the other. Here, the political will is missing, just as in the objectives set for city construction. In Amsterdam, on the eastern docklands near the main train station, a large-scale project was launched to build compact townhouses and sky-charging social housing projects. Rotterdam is also reinventing itself in the former harbor area. With the battle cry "High-rise is a must!" the city is pinning its hopes even more vehemently on a compact, pedestrian-friendly central city and the skyscrapers required for this—including those for housing. While 5,719 apartments were generated in Munich in the year 2000, another 7,000 were built in the convention city of Riem. With a realistic demand of an average of 620,000 square meters of office space annually, office construction still regularly finishes laps ahead of housing. The construction material and investment engine of the city is thus the office building. Increasingly, employed knowledge workers only experience the city at work, unless their employers choose to realize their corporate philosophies in the industrial parks in such locations as Unterföhring, Hallbermoos, or Oberpfaffenhofen.

For years now, Munich has invested twice as much per capita in its infrastructure than the average of the ten largest German cities. While cultural institutions elsewhere are being starved, in Munich, renovation, expansion, and new construction are the order of the day. Not even swimming pools, new subway lines, and a program to restore the Isar River to a more natural form are considered too extravagant. Not to mention the abundance of attractive mountain peaks, beer gardens, and boating areas. Does Munich, for lack of residential space, lure more perhaps with its bucolic environs than with an urban focal point, which ultimately can only serve as a temporary, luxurious stage for leisure? With the "new Munich addresses," large-scale islands and ribbons of city development and, for instance, in the main train station, even the dream of a high-speed Paris–Munich–Budapest route are becoming more likely. But here, too, office buildings dominate, not housing. The best that can be said about the flexible development concept, according to the city planning officer, is that its provision of luxury apartments in the city can ensure the supply of affordable family housing on the margins. Once work supposedly disappears, will the cities thus develop into a paradox office labyrinth with accumulated leisure operations, linked to the postmodern return of the courier jobs of late antiquity and the feudal period? Today over than seven million people in Germany have less than 460 euro per month at their disposal.[2] Otto Steidle sought symbolic redress in the office idea "Everything is Housing." According to this concept, in 1995 the T-Mobil headquarters in Bonn created residential courtyards in the 1950s style— housing for 2,100 employees. A communications technology corporation in a Trojan horse of bright, idyllic housing is hardly a fundamental solution to the problem.

In the network of global cities, Munich, unlike Frankfurt, is neither an Alpha city nor a Beta city. A recent sociological model calculating the office networks of the one hundred largest corporate-oriented service enterprises worldwide (banks, financial services, advertising, accounting) rated Munich as a third-class Gamma city—in the shadow of Düsseldorf, and on the same level as Berlin and Hamburg. However, in individual disciplines such as the legal or the banking system, or in the sphere of media, Munich does have Alpha qualities: In the legal sphere, on the same level as Düsseldorf; in banking, right behind Frankfurt; as a media location, ahead of Berlin, Hamburg, Frankfurt, Düsseldorf, and Cologne.[3] The prerequisites for a well considered, condensed, and intermixed city architecture could hardly be better in all of Germany. But does Munich's "new period of expansion" actually correspond to a new expansion-period mixture of functions? And is the city thus the antithesis of functionalism, which sorted everything into niches, and is still sorting? Why is it that, even today, the mixture of housing, trades, and businesses in neighborhoods built during the era of expansion at the turn of the last century

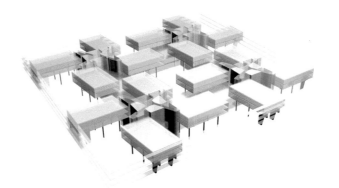

Office units

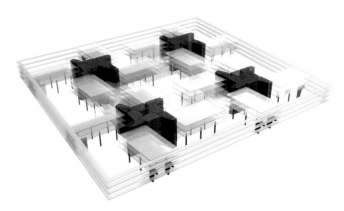

Access cores/hedge

works, and works better than in areas that were explicitly planned for mixed usage today?

Even the quantities in the recipe, the ingredients in their relationship to each other, have shifted. If primarily office space is built, it is a waste of time to hope that it will be mixed with housing and shops. Not to mention that there is no demand for so much "nostalgia" unless someone's image can benefit. Nobody thinks about spatial forms of organization on the higher level any more, is the resigned conclusion. But is the New Arbitrariness of an industrial park actually a workplace worth striving for? Or, is it even reasonable and practical? Disregarding the savings in planning cost and effort? The way to reach the headquarters of Swiss Re, one of the largest reinsurers in the world, is to sneak in from the commuter train as if escaping through back courtyards after a holdup. Granted, these back courtyards are the product of city expansion, not city revitalization. Nevertheless, in this location, where the industrial park could not be circumvented for lack of space, the construction of the Swiss Re building in Unterföhring succeeded in creating an innovative office city behind a suspended hedgerow. The huge property's original, unfettered freedom from any adjacent buildings was used to redefine the spatial requirements of a knowledge-based corporation.

ART PARK

For the moon-landing corporation of Swiss Re, originally located in the *Englischer Garten*, the architects designed not a body of shining aluminum shaped parts, but a lively, walk-in mantle consisting of a suspended hedgerow. This stages the outlook onto the property itself. While the fairy tale Snow White hedge is not yet distinct as a characteristic image, the explosive power of the pioneering spatial configuration behind it can hardly be imagined. The architects declared their experiment—contracted by Swiss Re for its "House of 100 Professions"—a "spatial staging of the linkage of individuality and group cohesion to a creative unity." In fact, the dense linkage between landscape, art park, and two completely different double-story office layers piled on top of each other has succeeded in creating a new exchange between large spaces, communication and community, and concentrated work in secluded rooms surrounded by green space, for individuals or groups of up to 800, or currently 580 employees (27,360 square meters effective area). The parallelogram-shaped property allows the building to be expanded by 50 percent. The insignificant furnishing variations of the office planners—who are

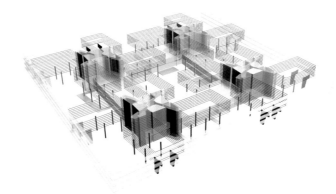

Special areas

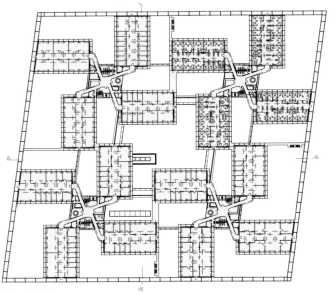

Plan of 4th floor

"It bothered me not being able to satisfy the people working on the commercial estate. That is why not only the workforce had to move, but also the English Garden they were all so fond of." Hadi Teherani

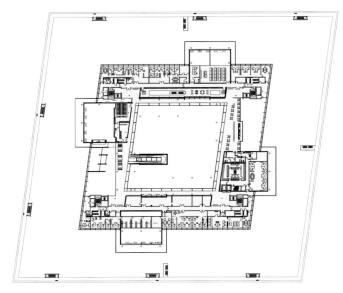

Plan of 2nd floor

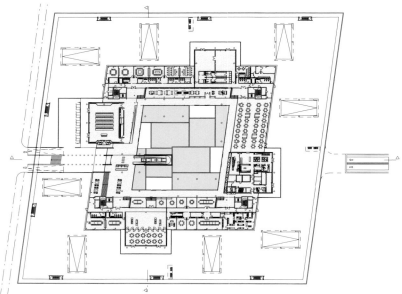

Plan of first floor

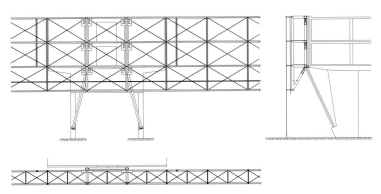

Structural principle for vine frame/hedge/escape route

better at reveling in fashionable concepts than in three-dimensional visions of space—thus face an architectural alternative, which, in a smoothly networked, layered configuration of space, makes it superfluous to latch on to any quickly outdated office fashion. The building is structured like a city, with streets, squares, and meeting spaces, which are recessed far behind the hedge and building boundary. This area is surrounded by the main building and by the two sets of four office groups, which are suspended and arranged in the shape of a windmill. The office groups have four units for twenty-four employees each, and are accessed via four kernels at the corners of the parallelogram. All socially and spatially relevant transitions between the plenum and the private sphere are represented here, imparting both to employees and to customers the feeling that they are of the utmost importance. Among these are the luxury of a jogging track along the hedge; the artificial garden by Martha Schwartz inside the hedge path, which, along with the roof, is color-coded red, yellow, blue, and green for the purposes of orientation; and, not least, the penetration of a non-hierarchical atmosphere in both the interior and exterior, on all levels of communication and concentration, all the way to the subterranean garage.

THE NATURE OF CULTURE

Even without its Sleeping Beauty hedge, the building structure of Swiss Re in Unterföhring, which lacks a facade and appears impenetrable—opens up a new relationship between landscape and architecture, between outside and inside, between technology, art, and nature. Its classical modern style presents landscape and nature most powerfully behind floor-to-ceiling windows, where it is distanced and incidental, as on a cinema screen in sunlight. In contrast, biomorphism, with its gushing and swelling natural vocabulary, appears to be so narcissistically occupied with its changing forms that it generally can do without the exterior as a point of reference. The decisive flaw in the reasoning of its champions lies either in the assumption that natural shapes can manage without regularities, or in the fact that a spatial field of conflict could emerge without a contrast between "natural" architecture and "natural" surroundings. A house shaped like a drop of water hence no longer needs a lakefront. It is easy to see through to the technical lack of perspective by the masters of the blob. Not even the blob can create transparent, heat-resistant, and soundproof glass. The artificial, autistic euphoria of the shapes of the exhibition pavilions, recycling facilities, churches, ventilation towers and subway stations either avert themselves from their surroundings in an

introverted manner, or vary holes in the facades of prefabricated buildings in file-to-factory technology—as in the "key building of the current architecture revolution"[4] (Andreas Ruby), the Düsseldorf Neuer Zollhof office complex by Frank O. Gehry.

More decisive than the exercises in shaping a digital *Jugendstil*, or "process-controlled design according to poetic considerations," (Bernhard Franken) are architectural operations on the complexity of spatial relationships—interior as exterior, and the space between both spheres. An architecture not according to nature, but rather in unison with nature. If that was ever the objective of the "blob" and the "bubble," even the selection of the heading was wrong. At first glance, in its permeation of garden and office space, the labyrinthine spatial weave of the Swiss Re succeeds in spatially and structurally optimizing the office building. Perhaps this topological advance will not be recognized in its entire magnitude until the plants have integrated themselves more strongly into the medial value of the architectural image—especially the 600-meter-long and more than 10-meter-high suspended green facade of 160 wisteria and 40 Virginia creepers. The hedge is to achieve its full cover by 2005, only then will the building appear completed in its entirety. But even then the image of this topological architecture will not be safe from seasonal and architectural changes.

TOPOLOGY

In topology, the "science of place," or the geometry of pure relations between positions, the concept of surroundings is used to abstract from all ratios of dimensions and magnitudes. Topological characteristics of a settlement structure, for instance, are independent of formal changes in details. Even additions and vertical extensions leave the structure untouched. Trees, branches, and flow systems are examples of open systems. In closed systems, the connections form network-like meshes. The structure of this office building was triggered by the search for the best spatial organization for a knowledge-based corporation. Reinsurers collect, store, and link knowledge in order to explain, justify, and predict insurance risks. The spatial city differentiates vertically between closely connected representation, communication, and knowledge storage in the two-story base around the meditative inner courtyard, and the four working groups recessed over this courtyard, operating autonomously in four—or, at some later date, six—"trees." The unusually luxurious embedding of this specific office landscape in a three-dimen-

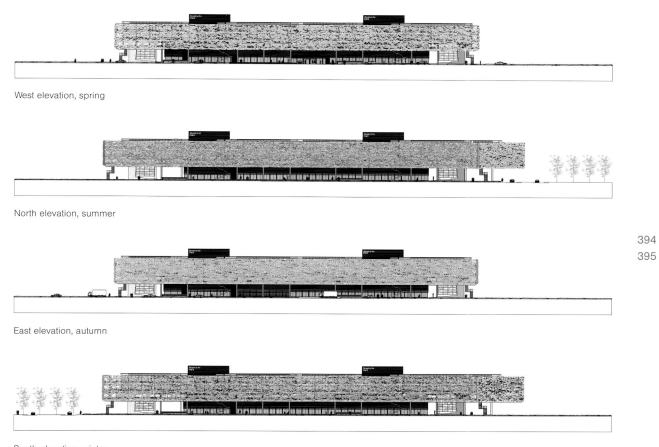

West elevation, spring

North elevation, summer

East elevation, autumn

South elevation, winter

Swiss Re Office Building

"The building is rather like an autonomous city with its own emotions and high-lights, with districts, squares, parks, leisure and cultural facilities." Hadi Teherani

sional garden landscape—which streams through the entire building, from the subterranean garage to the roof—is a logical and inevitable conclusion. The structure of the building consistently complies with the economy of knowledge, shifting as needed between communication and concentration. The supposedly "open" system of the sixteen "office units" in the four development cores are thus connected closely through the paths arranged on two levels through the "crowns" of the suspended hedges. This was conceived not only for the pleasure of a fresh air "clois-ter," or as a substitute for the *Englischer Garten*, but also for reasons of security.

          Despite all of the facility's urbanistic complexity, which theoreti-cally could be described infinitely, its success is in realizing individuality not only in the form of its appearance, but in its reference to space. Reviews by the media have made comparisons to other architectural images: Habitat 67 in Montreal, Unité d'Habitation in Marseille, the Nether-lands' Expo pavilion in Hanover, and others. However, in this case espe-cially, it is imperative to understand landscape planning and garden architecture as an integrated component of a process-oriented, multidi-mensional contextuality, compliant with the procedure of the transfer and expansion of knowledge. The hurdles for the American, architecturally oriented garden artist Martha Schwartz (inner courtyard, interior gardens, roof gardens) and Peter Kluska, the landscape architect from Munich whose work focuses on structuring ecological life communities (sus-pended hedge, exterior park, extensive roof planting, planning of execu-tion and foreman of construction) were thus all the higher. On the one hand, garden areas were to be created, so to speak, within the architec-ture, on the parallelogram-shaped property enclosed by the hedge facade, between the subterranean garage below and the "office units" above. On the other hand, the cluster-shaped structure of the three-dimensional projection of the field property required an orientation guide—realized in the form of four different garden sections sorted by color—which is occasionally separated in the inner courtyard by illumi-nated walls of atomized spray. Fantasy and an integrated artistic experi-ment have thus impressively taken over from the surrounding parks of

the old school. The specifications of the building plan, which dictated a thick screen of trees against the feared heterogeneity of the industrial park, could thus be evaded. However, the archaic picture of the tree is deeply intertwined with this architecture. The welcome gesture of the tree house, graduated far into the depths, forgoes any visible barrier to access.

1   Mathias Greffrath: Ein Brief über Arbeit, Liebe, Glück, Geschichte – An die junge Frau mit Rucksack und Fahrradsattel vor dem Deutschen Theater, in: Stefanie Carp, Daniel Libeskind, Jan Philipp Reemtsma: *Alles Kunst? Wie arbeitet der Mensch im neuen Jahrtausend, und was tut er in der übrigen Zeit?* Reinbek 2001, p. 94

2   Thomas Eckardt: Arbeitnehmer sind auch nur Menschen, *Süddeutsche Zeitung*, March 4, 2002

3   cf. Florian Rötzer: Im Netzwerk der globalen Städte, *Telepolis*, April 19, 2002, and the original studies listed there

4   Andreas Ruby: Beyond Form. Architektur im Zeitalter ihrer digitalen Produzierbar-keit, in: Peter Cachola Schmal: *digital/real. Blobmeister. Erste gebaute Projekte*, Basel/Boston/Berlin 2001, p. 208

Swiss Re Office Building

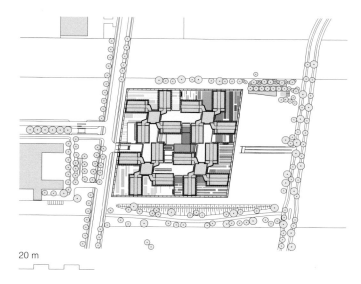

20 m

Swiss Re Office Building

Swiss Re Office Building

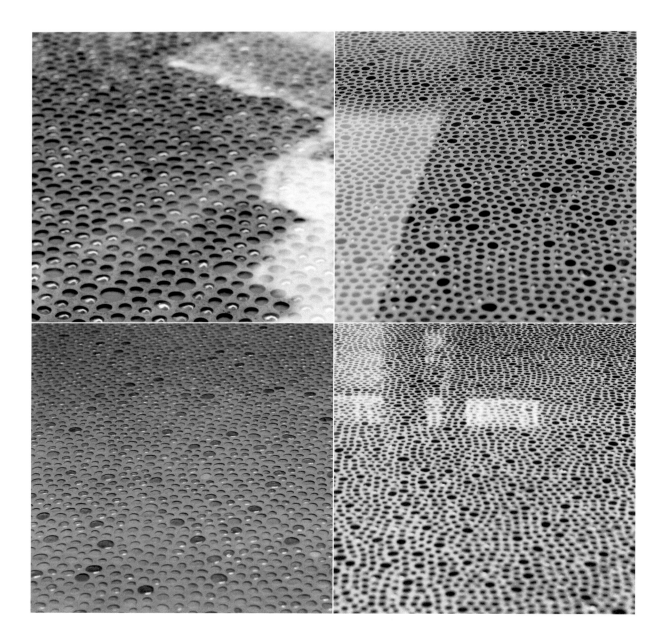

"Good architecture is
like good music:
it takes shape between
the notes." Kai Richter

06.6

PERISCOPE IN A SEA OF HOUSES
GRIMM 6 OFFICE BUILDING

OFFICE BUILDING
HAMBURG
GROSS FLOOR AREA 2,500 SQ M
BUILT AUG 2000–SEP 2001

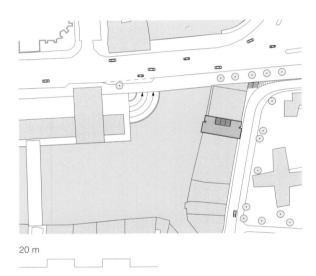

20 m

Rear front, Nikolaifleet, 1939

PERISCOPE IN A SEA OF HOUSES

The 1920s-style office building is experiencing a renaissance in Hamburg, helping to define the image of the commercial district. Now, though, it is characterized by a vitreous interaction with urban space. By creating a specifically modern contrast and not superficially copying old materials, the new buildings allow the city's historical background to be seen in a new light. Investor architecture has once again become synonymous with city image, even if the term itself remains controversial. Located on a tiny plot of land, BRT's glass tower is an ingenious aesthetic composition. Unlike the adjacent office buildings, which are much too broad, it manages to pay homage to the picturesque variety of merchant buildings that make up the historical harbor of the old city. Until the city's warehouses were built, these historical hybrids—three or four windows wide—were used for residential, office, and storage purposes. Verticality, differing building heights, many small parts, and a gable motif were important elements in the design of BRT's new building on Nikolaifleet, which fills the last gap in the old city torn open in the war. However, its architectural vocabulary is entirely new. The two-story lobby, the spacious, protruding penthouse (open on three sides), and the third-dimensional effect of the inward-bent facade are conceptual assets for which the architects had to fight with economic (i.e., investment-related) arguments. The upper floor has been set back from the facade in order to create a more dramatic view of the ruins of St. Nicholas (with the third tallest spire in Germany) and the Lever-Haus, designed by Cäsar Pinnau for the Hamburg-Süd Shipping Line, one of the first office high-rises with a curtain facade of glass. The result is a Manhattan-like skyline enhanced by the historical neighbors and the amphibious character of Hamburg. Only the inward gaze guarantees concentration.

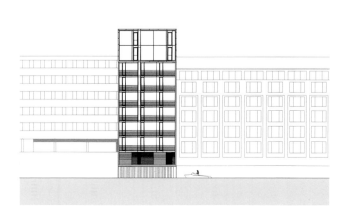

West elevation, Fleet

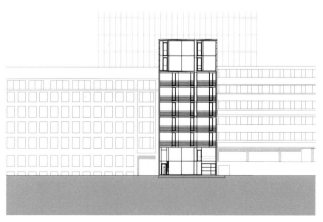

East elevation, street front

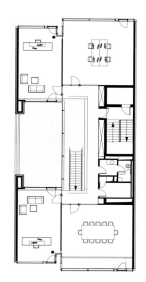

Plan of 7th and 8th floor

Grimm 6 Office Building

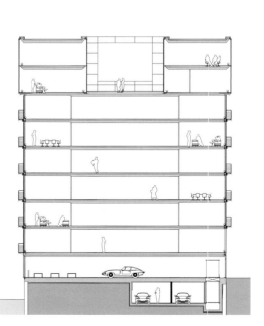

Longitudinal section

Grimm 6 Office Building

06.7

CONFIGURATION OF EDGES
KAY DEGENHARD HOUSE

OFFICES/RETAIL
BERLIN
GROSS FLOOR AREA 786 SQ M
BUILT JAN 2003–JUNE 2004

CONFIGURATION OF EDGES

The building, which closes a gap in the Berlin cityscape, does not submit to the authority of adjacent roof edges or the monosyllabic linearity of the row. Within a mature design framework that has been defined but not narrowly interpreted, it incorporates deviations from the regular block structure that in fact do not yet exist in great detail. The different uses of the commercial building, which functions as an inner-city "display" for a fashion and design center in Treptow, have given rise to a kind of magic glass cube with a flat roof that nimbly responds to the minor infractions committed by the neighboring buildings. The concrete-framed "houses within the house," each of which has its own stairway and colored glass facade, appear to be made up of many small pieces and do not try to curry favor with the neighboring *Gründerzeit* architecture, but nonetheless take it seriously. The architects were able to adopt the different heights and window proportions of the adjacent buildings without superficially copying the traditional facades. The protruding concrete "cornice" enhances the three-dimensionality of the facade even in places where it could not be realized due to urban-planning restrictions. To be sure, the variation of building sections—with shop, office and customer-service space—is not in the end an absolute success in functional terms, since the upper two-level office runs over the border of the facade on the inside. And yet this is a reformed modernism that does not autistically exclude neighboring buildings by means of glass joints, but helps these buildings to achieve their full effect—and such a modernism is not dependent on functional successes.

20 m

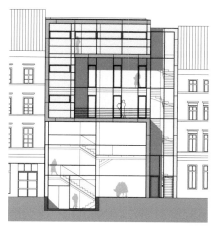

South elevation, garden

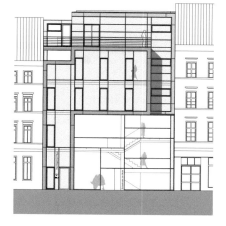

North elevation, street

Kay Degenhard House

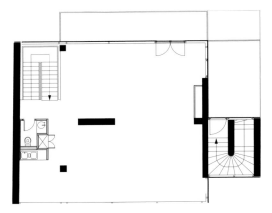

Plan of 5th floor

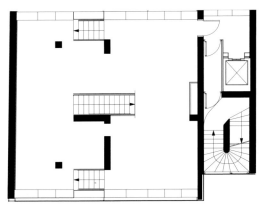

Plan of 2nd floor

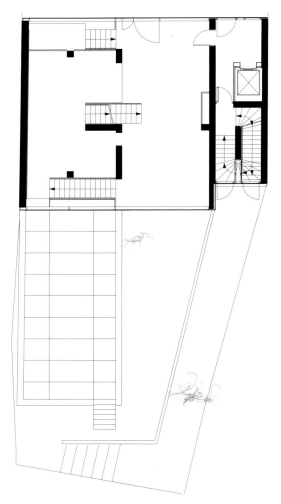

Plan of first floor

"The goal of a good design is clarity and simplicity within complexity." Hadi Teherani

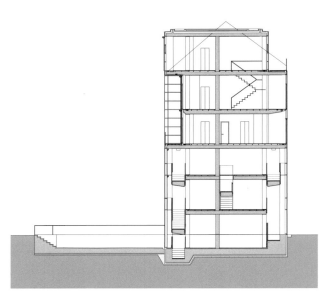

Longitudinal section

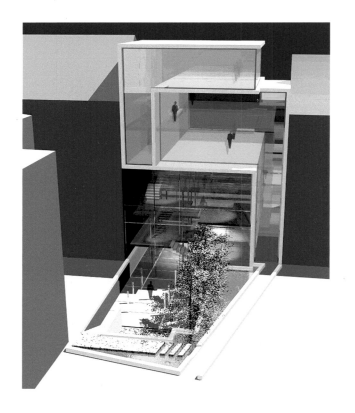

Kay Degenhard House

06.8

STRUCTURALISM IN GLASS
CARRÉ MAINZER LANDSTRASSE

OFFICES
FRANKFURT/MAIN
GROSS FLOOR AREA 26,700 SQ M
BUILT JUNE 2001–FEB 2003

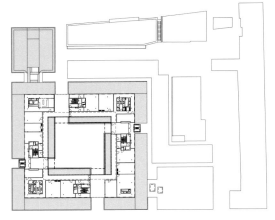

Plan of 7th floor

Plan of 5th floor

Plan of 3rd floor

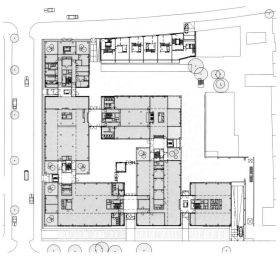

Plan of first floor   10 m

STRUCTURALISM IN GLASS

Located in the Gallus district to the east of the A5, between the expanded fair grounds on the former freight station site and the tracks of Frankfurt's central railway station on the far side of the Westhafen, the compact block for residential, business, and commercial uses, lies close to the city and to transportation routes. The six- to eight-story structure is comprised of individual building blocks around a central atrium and numerous integrated greenhouses that seem labyrinthine in the interior, while completing the block on the exterior. It comes alive in the office and housing section through sculpturally documenting the individual compartments of each apartment or office group in the facade as an individual point of reference, and alluding to it in two-story compositions in the office tower. Although changing organisational forms and group structures of highly flexible office areas (open-plan, combination, tri-plan) are no longer clearly traceable on the exterior today, each employee has the benefit of an individual point of reference on the outside and the inside—not least of all due to changing forms and arrangements of two-story greenhouses at the corners lit from both sides. What was a neutral glass envelope is thus transformed into an eloquent facade and a plastic building fabric with urban divisions—sufficiently flexible to meet the needs of the surroundings despite urban density and to overcome the constraints of the site. The intense integration of greenery contributes greatly to the agreeable atmosphere, which this building exudes. In this manner the office building takes on the character of a directionless urban pattern with individual qualities, symbiotically incorporating non-office functions, while nevertheless ensuring the legibility of the labyrinth that is the city.

"I don't want to design just any old anonymous architecture. In my opinion, individuality and personality play a decisive role." Hadi Teherani

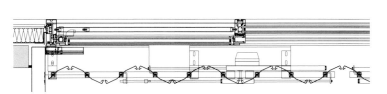

Section of solar shading, horizontal

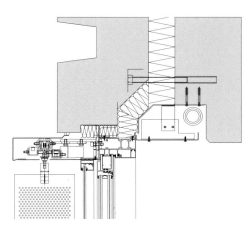

Section of solar shading, vertical

Carré Mainzer Landstrasse

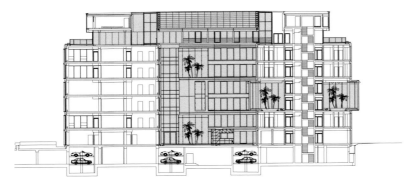

Cross section

06.9

WORKING AND LIVING
LOFT BUILDING AT ELBBERG

OFFICE BUILDING
HAMBURG
GROSS FLOOR AREA 3,340 SQ M
BUILT APRIL 1996–JULY 1997
COMPETITION 1994, 1ST PLACE; BUILDING OF THE YEAR
1997; BDA HAMBURG ARCHITEKTURPREIS 1999

WORKING AND LIVING

This small assemblage of lofts, reminiscent of the Chilehaus and the Flatiron Building, is located on a problematic site in the flood area near Hamburg's fish market. It adroitly navigates the difficult waters between the desire for traditional beauty and the widespread aversion to modernism's gridded mediocrity, to which the Prussian-motivated package design of Berlin succumbs with all its mathematical schematism. The building presents us with two faces: the wavy glass facade overlooking the water and the finely detailed copper shingles facing the slope. The duality expresses a sense of doubt rather than eternal truth, disquietude rather than ritual and rules. It never goes to the extremes seen in the extravagant deconstructive creations of fun-loving sheet-metal artists. The architects have succeeded in bringing together hidden and transparent spheres as well as symbolic and abstract architecture to create a modernism that resolves its own contradictions. This visionary, doubly defined interpretation of the theme "flagship of stone" wrestles like David against Goliath in a city where there is an ongoing love affair with brick architecture, where one hapless imitation of Höger's Chilehaus goes up one after the other. At the heart of the struggle is the biased belief—taken up once again by the *Frankfurter Allgemeine Zeitung* in its coverage of the Berlin Palace debate—that there is no single place in the world where Bauhaus successors, in the broadest sense of the word, co-exist successfully with the architecture from 1900. Precisely this kind of criticism could be leveled at the bordering areas of the warehouse district, which make rigid use of brick, and the Kehrwiederspitze across the way—despite its diplomatic red outfit.

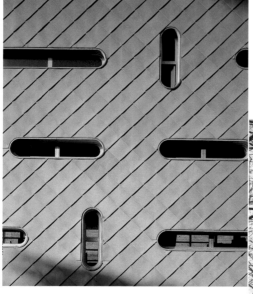

"We built a gross floor area of 2,800 square meters over a 400-square-meter traffic island." Kai Richter

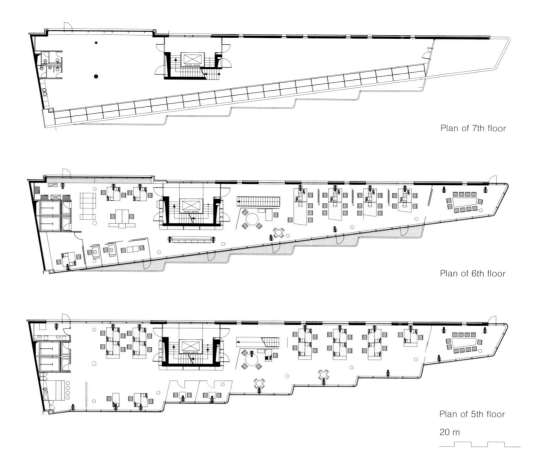

Plan of 7th floor

Plan of 6th floor

Plan of 5th floor

20 m

A CITY ON THE WATER

The city of Hamburg derives its distinct international flair from the urban power of water. This harbor town—the "grand synthesis of Atlantic and Alster" (Helmut Schmidt)—is situated "not on a narrow, stingy body of water like the Spree, but rather on a magnificently broad emerald current that flows into the horizon" (Alfred Kerr). With the return of architecture to the Elbe, to the pungent sites of the fish trade, to the harsh beauty of warehouses and cranes, the white city, the garden city, the brick city, and the business city are looking south—and embracing the new millennium. In contrast to contemporary Berlin, so enamored of the past, Hamburg has always known that urban visions cannot be based on nostalgia and the reconstruction of old buildings. In 1885 more than 20,000 people had to sacrifice their residential neighborhood (nearly 1000 buildings) for the city's much-admired, sleepy warehouse district, which is still used today as a kind of treasure island for carpets, coffee, and spices. The city's awe for Fritz Schumacher cramped its architectural style. After the 1962 flood, the edge of the harbor between St.-Pauli-Landungsbrücke and the Deichtor market halls became a front row seat with an unobstructed view of the busy harbor stage. Now renewed competition is coming from Altona, its onetime Prussian opponent. West of the old fish auction house, the landscape becomes unruly and authentic: it is Hamburg's best location for busy waterfront life this side of the planned "Hafen-City" urban expansion project.

If even the legendary Berlin chronicler Alfred Kerr preferred the "city on the water" to the "up-and-coming imperial city" of Berlin, water cannot be an unimportant criterion for urban beauty. There are now plans to revitalize and create a denser pattern of life in Hamburg using approaches tested in London, Barcelona, and Sydney—ones observable at the Westhafen in Berlin. They center on redeveloping abandoned quay facilities with complex utilization concepts. The focal point of this back-to-the-Elbe strategy is the projected "Hafen-City" surrounding Magdeburg Port: the project, which in the next 25 years will expand the inner-city area by more than a third of its current size, is much bolder and larger in

scope than Berlin's new neighborhood at Potsdamer Platz. Encompassing 155 hectares, it has been hailed as a "waterside Latin quarter," a "Hanseatic Amsterdam" and the "Manhattan of the North." Unfortunately, the conventional buildings that went up on the Kehrwiederspitze are a poor warm-up act for this grand show, only diluting and not accentuating the famous warehouse district. More innovative solutions are to be found on the Altona waterfront. The main stage is the oldest man-made harbor facility in Hamburg. Built in 1724, two decades after the Sunday fish market opened, it was named after an old fortress. In contrast to Hamburg, this is not a commercial harbor, but rather a fish and grain market. Fish-processing plants, a malthouse, and a grain storehouse (now home to the Stilwerk design store) now line the edge of the harbor, which once attracted the largest fishing fleet in Germany but today only draws refrigerated trucks.

Revitalization does not mean imitating the megalomaniacal city administration of Florence, which sought to surpass the works of both the Old and New Worlds when constructing its cathedral. On the other hand, the architectural history of a dynamic city must rise above uniformity and mediocrity. The identity-promoting brick provinciality favored in Hamburg is a two-edged sword. For over two decades the city has been doubly "red"—with its brick architecture and the alliance between the working and merchant classes (Helmut Schmidt). The song lyrics written for Vienna are also applicable to Hamburg: "Kleiner roter Ziegelstein, baust die neue Welt" ("Small red brick, you build the new world"). In fact, in political and architectural terms, Hamburg seems more obstinate in implementing this color principle than its socialist Austrian counterpart. With the construction of the city's warehouses in 1890, the emergence of the office building district, and Fritz Schumacher's brick development houses in the 1920s, red became the traditional color of progress. It has remained so ever since, though the progressive nature of the city's architecture is surely contestable. Despite the glass implants by BRT, Hamburg has served as a role model for stony Berlin. With his architectural color theory, Egbert Kossak—Hamburg's chief building director up to 1998—deserves some credit for creating a consistent city image, and yet

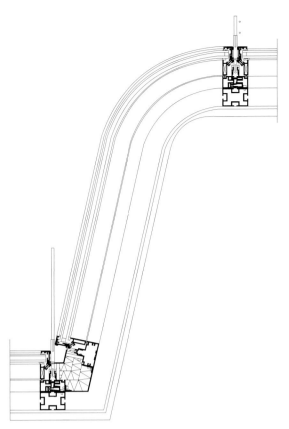

Facade section, horizontal

he also paved the way for a great deal of mediocrity and heightened fears that the city's common theme would go down in architectural extravagance. It is no surprise that pressure built up that was not vented in five architectural forums with international participation. With the Loft Building and its dual architectural significance, BRT resists tradition and yet it woos it at the same time—with glass and copper.

TIME-BOUND

Although it is a lot smaller and does not make use of a single brick, the Loft Building on the edge of the wholesale fish market in Hamburg—with a superb view of the Elbe and the harbor—is the legitimate successor to Hamburg's architectural trademark, the Chilehaus by Fritz Höger (1924). The waves of glass and the pre-patinated copper shingles put on a brilliant show, not attempting to be "post-everything" like Gehry's Guggenheim Museum in Bilbao, but rather seeking the topicality and the expressive, integrative force of a visionary modernism specific to Hamburg. In this modernism, the copper shingles—as the counterpart of the glass skin – are given surprising significance. Covering the building from the highest to the lowest point, they express the young architects' rebellion against Hamburg's "urban visions," so wrongheaded and in need of explaining. The story goes back to the new buildings on the Kehrwiederspitze near the historical warehouse district. According to Egbert Kossak, these were realized after too much back-and-forth, which prevented "a much more interesting ensemble, one with a more lively architecture" from emerging—let alone a "world-class architectural event." Fritz Schumacher, the Chilehaus, and the beauty of the city as a whole were used to justify their mediocre design. The choice of brick in Hamburg is often more important than the message of the architecture, and this selection is often made with a reference to the city's glorious past. As a matter of fact, Oldenburg clinker brick was bought long before Fritz Höger was commissioned to design the Chilehaus, and it was not his first choice. Through this tactical move, the developers merely wanted to save

money. "What am I supposed to do with this junk?" a despairing Höger reputedly said upon seeing the bricks.

Fritz Schumacher may have insisted on "a restraint that engenders uniformity," but he also wanted to give architecture, as its "highest goal," the opportunity "to surpass the lifestyle of an era in the service of an idea." He wanted it "to anticipate the way of life that an era is in truth striving for." This pioneering spirit is manifest in the time-bound quality of the warehouse district, the Chilehaus, and the Jarresstadt housing development; in the buildings by Gustav Oelsner, Fritz Schumacher, and Karl Schneider; in the Philipsturm and the tropical greenhouse at the 1953 International Horticultural Exhibition (both torn down); in the large market hall and botanical gardens designed by Bernhard Hermkes in the early 1960s; in the Gruner und Jahr building by Otto Steidle and Uwe Kiessler; and in the ferry terminal by William Alsop near the Loft Building (which unfortunately lost much of the dynamic force of the original design). On the other hand, it is not present in the timeless superficiality of brick "investor architecture" that has kept the warehouse city from becoming a "world event." In 1998, even one of the city's cultural magazines considered the time ripe for Hamburg, despite its aesthetic sleepiness, to participate in the "creativity of an alert era" and overcome the resistance of the "brick barons" and their longtime mentor, Egbert Kossak, a trained mason and architect himself.

Seen against this backdrop, the Loft Building by BRT, which emerged from a competition, is a signal of the necessary resistance. It is not meant as provocation, but rather explores counter-arguments and counter-materials under a dynamic saddle roof (with dormer!) whose true character can only be seen from the air. There is even a large amount of red in the design, in a narrow metal strip that conceals the sun sails. The adjacent multifamily brick building from Germany's *Gründerzeit* has been smoothly integrated into the aesthetic. From an architectural and technical point of view, the wedge-shaped structure, which offers 2,800 square meters of building space, handles the extremely pointed, sloping property

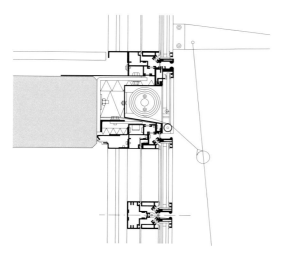

Facade detail 2nd–6th floors

Facade section

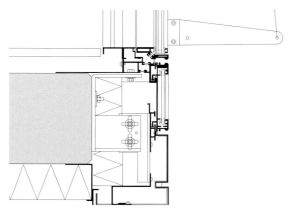

Facade detail 2nd floor

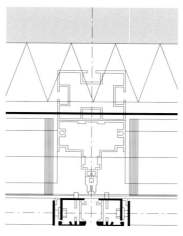

Facade detail, horizontal section above post

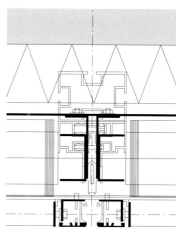

Facade detail, horizontal section above expansion joint

so well (right down to the specially designed ceiling flood lights) that a new chapter has been opened in Hamburg's architectural history.

Nearly two decades after the first brainstorming session, the sweeping structural transition of the Altona waterfront is gradually making progress, and soon crumbling quay walls, bumpy streets, and decaying, partially abandoned warehouses will become a thing of the past. Situated above this waterfront is the "Altonaer Balkon" (Altona Balcony), an elevated green area that extends the axis formed by the train station, Platz der Republik and town hall. When the locals go on their Sunday walks, this is the traditional highpoint and an ideal place to instruct youngsters on the economy of the port city of Hamburg and the activities in the Altona fishing harbor. Originally there were plans to connect the stairway of the Loft Building to the back slope via a small footbridge fitted out with prepatinated copper that matched the building's northern face. This plan explains one detail of the facade design that otherwise seems puzzling.

As a point of orientation and piece of city sculpture, the Loft Building has given rise to further development initiatives. Before the building was constructed, the large, barren, and yet prominent site was not optimally used. By day heavy trucks serving the struggling fish industry rumbled by; by night it was a red-light district. Thus it came as no surprise that the proposed plans to build residential and office lofts met with the immediate approval of the city, although the existing harbor development plan did not provide for residential use. In spite of the oversupply of office space, this elegant office building, willful in its functional division, was overrun with requests from creative companies looking for space. For the time being, then, plans to accommodate apartments in the lower, western part of the building have temporarily been abandoned, though there is no disputing how charming it would be to live here, even with the unfortunate Kehrwiederspitze in view.

SHIP MOTIF

Above the street, the building's wave-shaped oriel windows push forward into public space in seven-meter intervals. The technically sophisticated, finely detailed facade has integrated sun screens and hardly recognizable window casements. The heating and cooling system for the roof, which is in places two-stories high, is concealed in facade's hollow sections. The spaces behind the facade are generally five-meters deep, excluding the hallway. Occupants can create large rooms that extend over half or the entire floor, or set up individual offices, oriented to

the spacing of the oriel windows, screened only acoustically so as not to impede views. The stairway, with a vista of the adjacent green space, has been conceived as a vertical space for communication and rests. Since the building stands on slanted round columns, there is additional space underneath for parking. This is also the location of a side entrance for the doorman. The main entrance lies two stories above this on the northern side, where it is safe from floods. The end of the building, corresponding in design to the oriel windows, does not entirely fill out the knife-sharp tip of the property, but leaves this function to a sculptural strip of steel. The building has many maritime details—the railing above the oriels, the as yet incomplete "jetty," the bull's-eye windows, the glittering fish-scale facade in the rear, the waves and reflections of light on the water side of the building, the sun sails, and the hull-shaped roof (behind which—viewed from the Altona Balcony—ships unexpectedly come into view on the way to the harbor). These create a strikingly real ship motif (or better yet "windjammer motif" once the sun sails are in place). Though often evoked by architecture, this motif is rarely treated as seriously as it is here. The viewer almost yearns for the next flood to see whether this hovering, lightweight vessel is firmly anchored to the ground. And yet it must remain where it is since it plays such an important role in the architectural debate in the brick city of Hamburg, fighting as David once did against Goliath.

The perfection of the structure lends it an invulnerability at the center of the opposing movements described above. An especially striking feature is that right up to the roof the design has been doubly defined in two entirely different moods. One reason for this lies in the expressive power of the building, which could not have been achieved homogeneously with just any material. The scaly skin is made up of small copper sheets that have been mounted on the curved concrete discs of the structural frame. They change appearance with every passing cloud and ray of sunshine. The individual facade elements continually age—and do so with dignity. In other words: the range of materials that Fritz Höger considered to be "architectural gems" is expandable; brick does not have a monopoly on surface sensuousness and variety. Experimenting with the antithetical principles of tradition and modernism, the architects came up with an ingenious combination of copper and glass; materials that create a seamless transition from wall to roof and thus broaden the expressionistic capabilities of architecture.

A second reason is that, with their choice of materials, the architects illustrate the contrast between nature and technology, between the land and water sides of the building, between a facade with window openings and a curtain facade, between the stability of urban planning/structural anchoring and the intoxication of a world high on communication. BRT eschewed the arbitrary nature of trendy developments. Instead they fill old roles with a new cast and hire an innovative director. With a sure hand, they succeed in capturing a dynamic that for purely technical reasons Emil Fahrenkamp, a contemporary of Mies van der Rohe, was not able to achieve at the pinnacle of his career, when he designed his Shellhaus in Berlin. Though made of steel, this looks like stone.

06.10

DOCKLAND CHARM

ELBBERG CAMPUS ALTONA

OFFICES/APARTMENTS
HAMBURG
GROSS FLOOR AREA 7,600 SQ M
BUILT APRIL 2001–MAY 2003
BUILDING OF THE YEAR 2003, AIV

DOCKLAND CHARM

Situated on the historically most important business and residential street in Altona, this courageous example of Hamburg urban development offered a unique opportunity to explore urban integration models without poking holes in the fabric of the city. After the war, all of Altona (in 1800, Denmark's second largest city after Copenhagen) was extinguished by "New Altona." The only exception was the flood area on the edge of the harbor. And yet New Altona's car-friendly progressiveness failed, leaving behind a wasteland. The architectural highlights among the new buildings on the waterfront include the cruise ship terminal with its office and restaurant, and the Loft Building with its ingenious ambiguity and complex utilization concept. Following in the footsteps of the Loft Building, with its urban, Manhattan-like design, the Elbberg Campus bridges the gap between city center and the Elbe. The tiered ensemble takes as its central theme the charming topography of the "Altonaer Balkon," a green area with a broad vista of the harbor and river, situated at the same height as the center of town. Above a hidden, two-story garage, the architects created a lively neighborhood of stairways and paths reminiscent of the more finely detailed Elbe suburb of Blankensee with its tiny captains' houses. Linked to the existing network of paths, the project explores Charles Moore's principle of exterior space grasped as interior space. The office and loft buildings have been integrated into the green slope as three distinct building sections and are the architects' response to the landscape motif. The project offers a complex usage package and creates an urban quality with its large public terrace and the offices in the crowning structure on Grosse Elbstrasse.

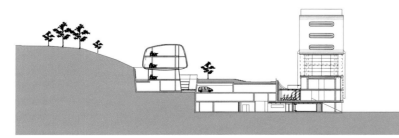

Section

South elevation

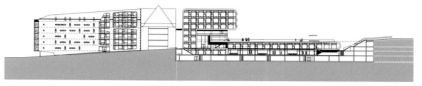

North elevation

450
451

Elbberg Campus Altona

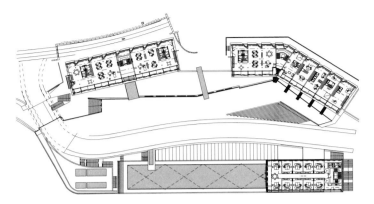

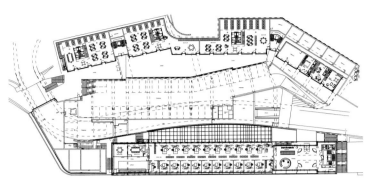

Plan of 7th floor

Plan of 4th floor

10 m

Elbberg Campus Altona

Elbberg Campus Altona

"The building resembles a container ship in homage to the industrial charm of the harbor." Jens Bohe

Elbberg Campus Altona

"Although our task is to respond to the history of the site, this should not translate into currying favor in a sentimental or historicizing manner." Hadi Teherani

06.11

A SHIP'S BOW FOR ONLINE
CAPTAINS
DOCKLAND OFFICE BUILDING

OFFICE BUILDING
HAMBURG
GROSS FLOOR AREA 13,544 SQ M
BUILT APRIL 2004–SEP 2005

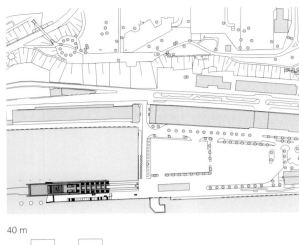

40 m

Adalberto Libera, Casa Malaparte, Capri 1938–1940

Office areas

Facade

Access

A SHIP'S BOW FOR ONLINE CAPTAINS

The cosmopolitan city of Hamburg, Germany's leading multimedia center, derives its distinct international flair from the urban power of water. The harbor town—as a "grand synthesis of Atlantic and Alster" (Helmut Schmidt)—is situated "not on a narrow, stingy body of water like the Spree, but rather on a magnificently broad emerald current that flows into the horizon" (Alfred Kerr). With the return of architecture to the Elbe, to the pungent sites of the fish trade, to the harsh beauty of warehouses and cranes, the white city, the garden city, the brick city, and the business city are looking south—and welcoming the new millennium. In contrast to contemporary Berlin, so enamored of the past, Hamburg has always known that urban visions cannot be based on nostalgia and the reconstruction of old buildings. After the 1962 flood, the edge of the harbor between St. Pauli-Landungsbrücke and the Deichtor market halls became a front row seat with an unobstructed view of the busy harbor stage. Now renewed competition is coming from Altona, its onetime Prussian opponent. West of the old fish auction house, the landscape becomes unruly and authentic: this is Hamburg's best location for busy waterfront life this side of the planned "Hafen-City" urban expansion project. The Dockland building has its own jetty and a 40-meter bow. The cleverness of the building is that it makes the distant ferry terminal by William Alsop (1991) part of its steamer motif (it is only a pity the completed terminal lost the dynamic force of the original design). For those approaching Hamburg by water, the building is a striking city gate, and with its accessible lookout platform, bar, and restaurant, it is an ideal place for landlubbers to observe ships and ferries in the harbor.

"(In a project like this) you learn what it means to create a superstructure above a federal waterway." Jens Bothe

Dockland Office Building

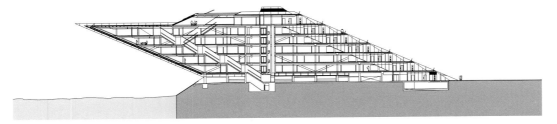

Longitudinal section

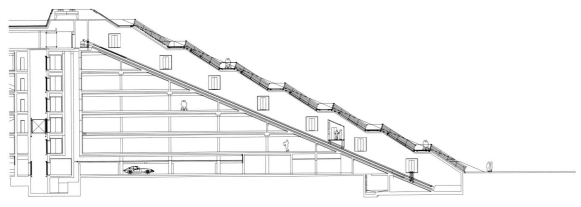

Schematic section of sloping elevator

Plan of 7th floor

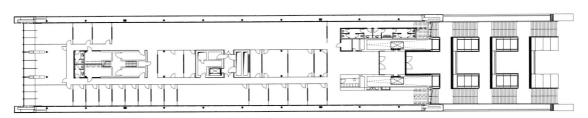

Plan of 4th floor

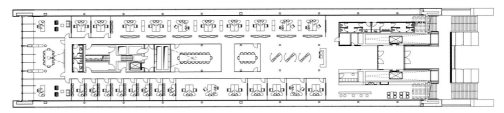

Plan of 2nd floor

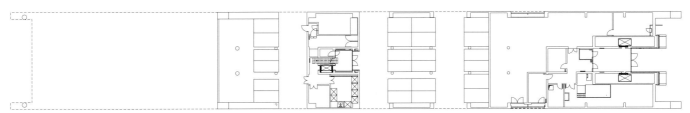

Plan of first floor

Dockland Office Building

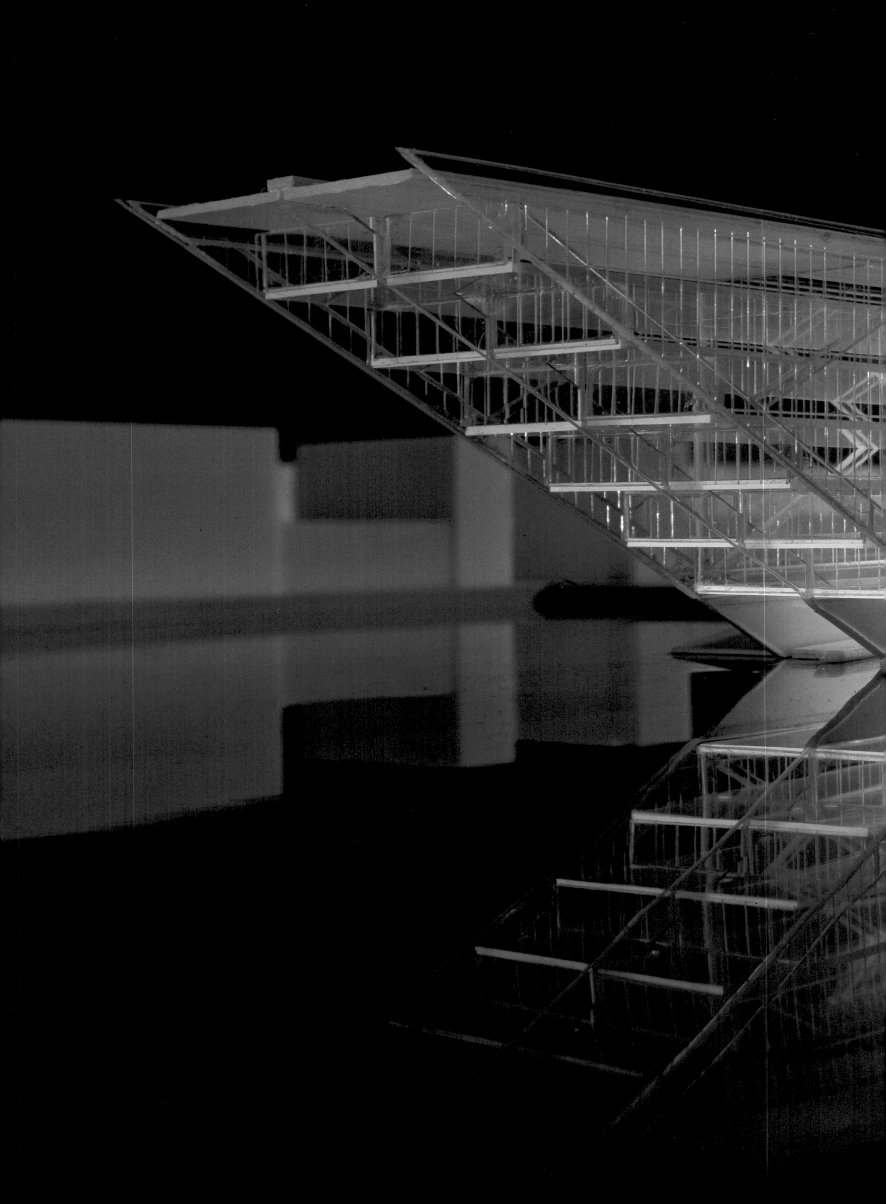

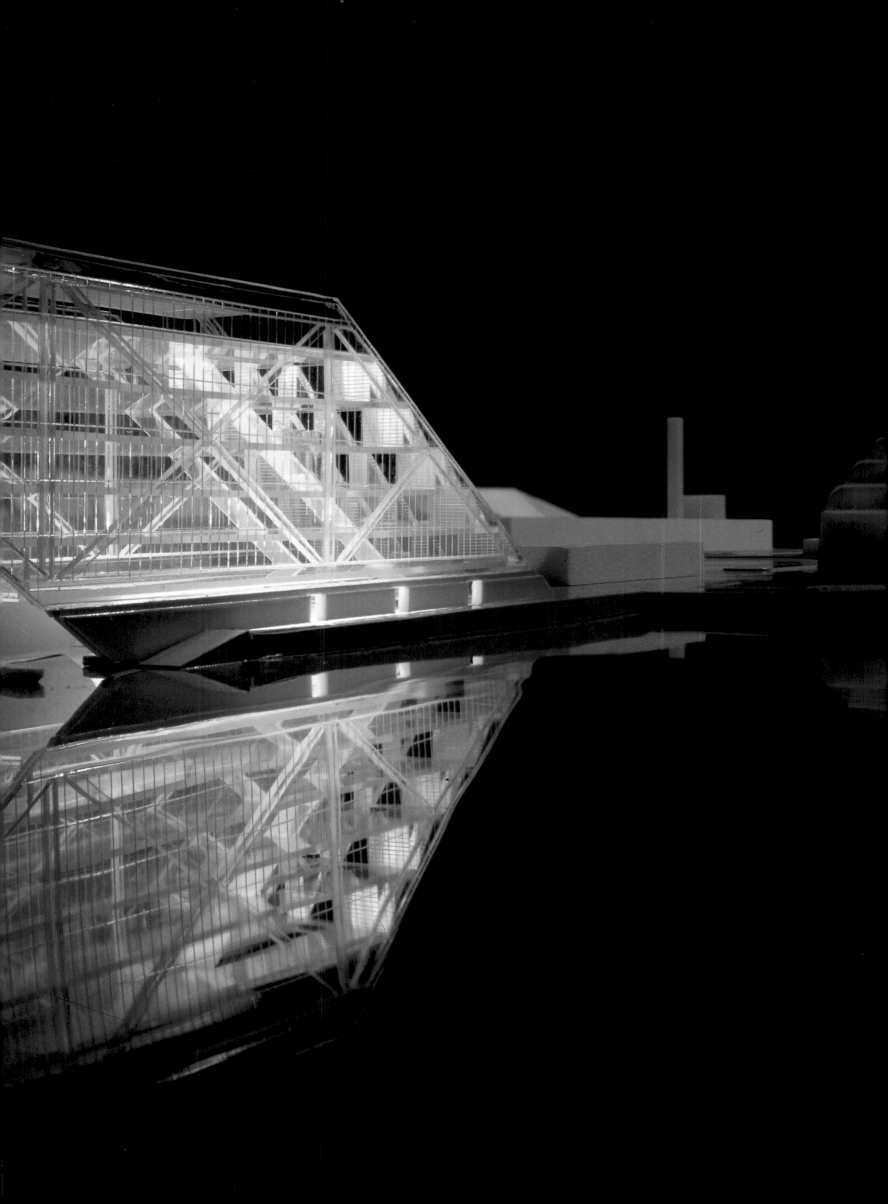

URBAN PERMEABILITY
DEICHTOR OFFICE BUILDING

OFFICE BUILDING
HAMBURG
GROSS FLOOR AREA 24,000 SQ M
BUILT AUG 2000–MAY 2002
COMPETITION 2000, 2ND PLACE; FEMB AWARD 2003
»OFFICE OF THE YEAR«
BDA HAMBURG ARCHITEKTURPREIS 2005

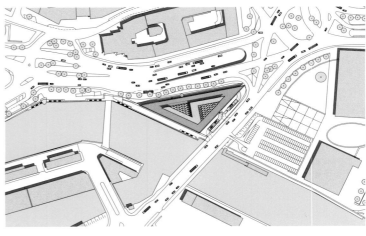

20 m

Fritz Höger, Chilehaus, Hamburg, 1921–1924

URBAN PERMEABILITY

In the east end of the warehouse district, there are a few lone buildings in the dense concentration of office structures that surround the Chilehaus and Messberghof, signposts of the onetime industrial redevelopment area. Situated on the border between the existent city and the largest urban expansion project in Europe—Hamburg's new "Hafen-City"—the triangular Deichtor building (home to BRT's new offices) lies at the interface between the historical and future metropolis, between streetside development and a more open architectural style. In the same place where *Spiegel* magazine planned to build its own glass high-rise, the ten-story prism, coming to a point like the Chilehaus, conveys the image of a modern Hamburg to train passengers and car drivers arriving in town. In terms of typology, the office building—as a compressed glass-encased block—reveals some similarity to its historical neighbors, and yet it is far more complex. The rigid old "atrium" motif has been rearranged—not least for energy, climatic, and acoustic reasons. Daylight, city space, atriums, loggias, and hanging gardens inter-weave with meandering rows of offices to form a seemingly labyrinthine web of space. Given the myriad views through and out of the glass shell, it is often difficult to distinguish between inner and outer worlds. Two building-high spaces, illuminated from the roof above, have been integrated into this play of geometry and entrance axes. They permeate the two four-story entrance halls (themselves connected on the ground floor) and the four three-story gardens or "city windows." The material and colors of the city across the way project themselves into the adjacent halls, with the result that the building's boundaries are once again blurred, with different effects by night and by day. This building sounds a retreat from the concept of the "asocial building." It signals the dissolution of a "Protestant ethics of space" and its "compulsive neutralization of the environment" (Richard Sennett).

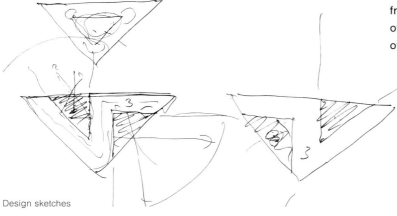

Design sketches

"The structure is mirrored on every fourth floor within the tri-angular contour of the building. This results in fabulous interior spaces, allows light to penetrate deep into the building and opens a window overlooking the city on every side." Jens Bothe

Deichtor Office Building

Deichtor Office Building

FOCAL POINT

"When I observe a tree through three panes of glass, I never know whether I see a tree, or the mirror image of the tree showing through, and if two trees happen to appear next to each other on a glazed surface, I never know whether there is a second tree, or whether there is a real tree at all. This form of illusion is intentional: through the destabilization of perception, it allows the creation of a mental space and the introduction of scenery, a scenic space, without which, as we know, buildings would be mere constructions and the city a mere agglomeration. And it is from this very loss of scenery, this way of seeing, this entire dramaturgy of illusion and seduction, that all of our cities suffer, damned to fill up the space with functional architecture—be it useful or useless." Jean Baudrillard, 1999

The Deichtor, one of the main gates within the rampart fortifications, has always been a distinctive focal point of development for Hamburg. When the Hafen-City plans are realized, enlarging the inner city on the Elbe side by 100 hectares of land and 50 hectares of water, the Deichtor will be revitalized even without the traditional narrowness of a city gate. The new sector of the city can only be reached by bridge; the traffic—expected to travel over the five land crossings on the city side, the Niederbaumbrücke, the Brooksbrücke, the Kornhausbrücke, the Oberbaumbrücke (at the Deichtor), and the Oberhafenbrücke—is correspondingly high: an estimated 36,000 vehicles per hour. This contrasts with the historical role of the Deichtor: the city's first public playground was constructed there in 1814; the first rail link was realized in 1842 in the form of the Berliner Bahnhof, at approximately the current location of the railway bridge across Amsinckstrasse, south of the recently abandoned Transrapid station for the same route. In 1911, the Deichtor market was opened: 3 hectares of sales space for 2,266 market stands. Up to 15,000 people a day haggled over the prices of fruit, vegetables, potatoes, and flowers. In 1962, the "belly of Hamburg" moved east from the Deichtor market halls, completed in 1914, to the neighboring Hammerbrook district. The market halls served as the location of the wholesale flower market until 1984. In 1989—on the occasion of the harbor's 800th birthday—the artistic achievements of the "Deichtor Halls," with their exhibition area of 6,000 square meters, were already on a par with those of the largest art spaces in northern Europe. After what the monument preserver and art historian Hermann Hipp called a "somewhat too elegant renovation," the reference to their typological origin as a market was expunged from their name.

Conceived of as a steel skeleton around 1910, there was still hope that the engineering structures would provide a catalyst for the revitalization of architecture, unlike the "romantic castle of uprightness" (Manfred Sack) of the Speicherstadt (warehouse district) or the neo-Renaissance style of the first Kontorhaus (counting house), erected in 1886. In rivalry with Fritz Schumacher, appointed in 1909, this engineering performance remained restricted to such structures as the market halls. On several occasions in the 1920s, highly modern and much bolder market halls were planned at the Deichtor, but their execution was frustrated by the global economic crisis. The Schumacher era during the period of the Weimar Republic thus left a more enduring mark on the city than any globally respected technical achievements. In 1932, the rail-bound "Flying Hamburger," which helped establish the "streamlining style" in the U.S., linked Hamburg to the world as the first regular express diesel train in the world, with a travel time of just 2 hours and 18 minutes to Berlin (160 kilometers per hour): an achievement that was not reproduced until the modern ICE trains began running in 1998.

KONTORHAUS

Until the construction of the Speicherstadt, the largest amphibian brick ensemble in the world—begun in 1885, and declared a historical monument in 1991—this historical functional hybrid traders' building, only three or four windows wide, was a residence, office, and warehouse all at the same time. With the restriction of the free-trade area to the harbor area of the Speicherstadt, the canals and traders' houses of the old city lost their function serving long-distance trade and providing housing and workplaces in the middle of the operating warehouses. The first investor, Heinrich von Ohlendorff, recognized the opportunities offered by the counting house as a new type of building, and in 1886, along with his personal architect Martin Haller (1835–1925), established the Dovenhof: a new kind of multifunctional rental office and service building with a post office and pneumatic post, steam heating, a steam-driven paternoster, its own electricity supply, and supplementary gas lighting for two restaurants. To increase the light yield of the conventional genre architecture, the window frames were made of iron. The objective even back then was "to put at the disposal of every branch of commerce the required, practically furnished localities on a rental basis." An increasingly flexible skeleton structure, the Kontorhaus with its courtyard (derived from the money counting tables, unlike the office building, which is derived from the desk) developed into the leading form of big city architecture. Despite all of its

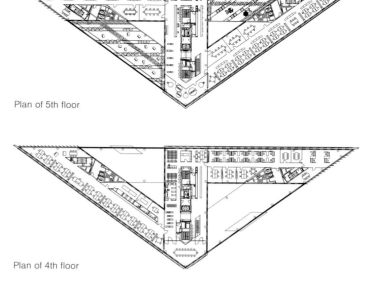

Plan of 5th floor

480
481

Plan of 4th floor

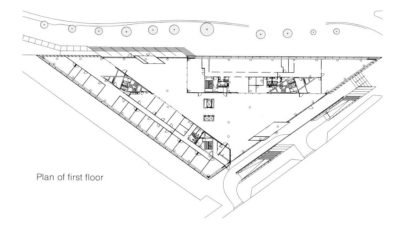

Plan of first floor

functional and technical advances, however, the Dovenhof was an aesthetic failure. It offered only conventional neo-Renaissance, in the words of Ernst Bloch, "plush in the machine age," and thus was torn down in 1967—for the *Spiegel* magazine building by Werner Kallmorgen. What a historical irony that the glass skyscraper disk planned for *Spiegel* magazine at the Deichtor location in 1993, on the exact location of the Deichtor office house, was not realized. Considering the height limit of the Kontorhaus quarter, based on the height of the Speicherstadt, skyscrapers appear questionable from today's perspective; this is certainly true for the existing post-war buildings at the Klosterwall as well. Most importantly, and imperative for the location today, the office building constructed at Deichtor—unlike the planned skyscraper—succeeds because it has no rear facade, but rather three equally representative sides.

Designed as part of a city plan by Fritz Schumacher, construction of the Kontorhaus quarter, so characteristic for Hamburg, was begun in 1921. Triggered by the cholera epidemic of the year 1892, the half-timbered houses in the alley district south of Steinstrasse were torn down in 1912. Located directly north of the Deichtor office house is the former Ballinhaus by the architects Hans and Oskar Gerson, its original designation a reminder of Albert Ballin (1857–1918), who invented ocean cruises, launched the largest and fastest steamers of his age and expanded the shipping company Hapag to a global power: 175 ocean steamers calling at 400 ports on four continents on scheduled cruises. Today Hamburg is also considered the European city of the music boom. Hip hop is just as much at home here as rock, pop, and techno. According to calculations by the Hamburg economic authorities, music media companies in Hamburg have a yearly turnover of 1.5 billion euro. That is more than 50 percent of the entire German music media market. Seventy percent of all music media sold in Germany comes from Hamburg. The city's cosmopolitan atmosphere has attracted around 800 music companies so far: music publishing houses, music media manufacturers, sound studios, concert promoters, and so on. The location's advantage in the music business is based not least on the city's highly developed media and communication business. Establishing the headquarters of Warner Music Germany in the Deichtor Office Building was thus of significant political importance for the location. The surprisingly economical rent prices at this prominent location, for a low-tech building that makes due without air-conditioning and floor heating, played a considerable role in the success of the project.

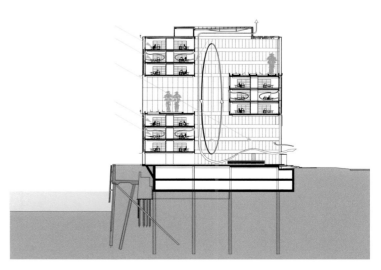

Air-conditioning concept

"The needs of the people living and working in a building form the basis of its architecture." Kai Richter

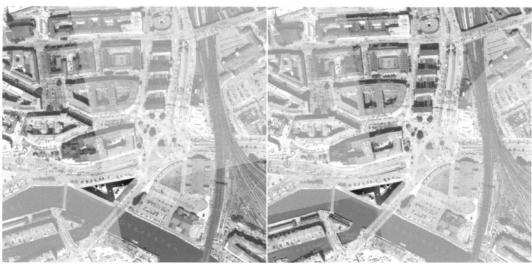

Orientation concept: harbor/transport/city/
Speicherstadt

Deichtor Office Building

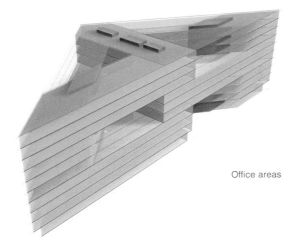

Office areas

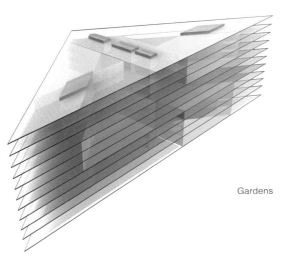

Gardens

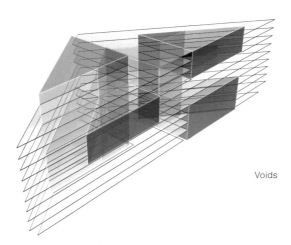

Voids

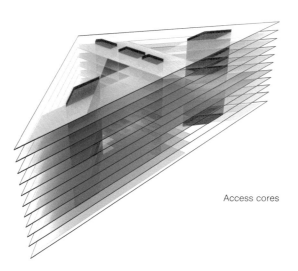

Access cores

SECTOR BOUNDARY

In the knot of streets, railroad, and harbor, at the boundary between the city and the future Hafen-City, the largest city expansion in Europe, the Deichtor triangle, provokes a decision between the past and the future. Hamburg holds itself to be self-confident and conservative. Unlike Frankfurt or Hanover, the city has maintained its silhouette for the most part, except for business at the port. The view from the Lombards-brücke to the buildings on the edge of the Alster interior still corresponds to a Merian engraving from the seventeenth century. Along with tradition, however, the modern must remain visible as well. The greater danger lies in retreating into a supposedly intact world of the past. The motive for such a retreat is insecurity in view of the uncertainties and challenges of the future. This insecurity is understandable, but the aesthetic corsets of the past do not help us either. City and society mean more than the sum of individuals and the satisfaction of quantifiable needs. The differen-tiated social mesh of interaction and exchange needs a spatial context, but also special, prominent locations. Collage City does not mean building in the context without changing it. Continuing to build in the context of the existing city plan, disturbing the architectural and/or city-planning context, renovating and changing—all of these actions belong to the spectrum of possible and thinkable interventions. Urbanity is more than an aesthetic phenomenon.

OFFICE WORLDS

Hollywood has shown a different kind of office: "overfilled desk, mountains of documents with bookmarks sticking out of them, overflow-ing ashtray, files, telephone, pens and pencils, pages, books, dust, the cone of light of the black lamp on a tiny, free writing space, while every-thing around it gets lost in chaos."[2] The chaos has yielded to emptiness: huge, empty tables; big screens; light, boundless spaces that appear to soar upon invisible wings all the way to the historical facades of the build-ings outside the window. In the data lines of the computer, according to Hartmut Böhme, flows the "blood" of our society, mathematicized infor-mation for the control of technical peripheries, which "no art can ever make 'physiognomic' in this sphere of the algorithm."[3] Seen, but not to be recognized, are: automobile manufacturing and slaughterhouse, cold rolling factory and foreign exchange department, facility construction and Aids research, intensive care unit and bomb factory, and so on. Spatial, architectural, artistic, and social compensations are required in order to keep office work from degrading into an organic prosthesis of the artificial intelligence of humans. In opposition to the elimination of everything organic in this "brave new world"—including the organs closest to the brain, the eyes and the hands—the office must offer resistance as an urban thinking space and location of communication.

Phases of intensive work in the office require phases of inten-sive relaxation. The "nine to five" workday is losing importance, thus also the classic daily timetables and office architectures. The more strongly the working world is dominated by office spaces, the more alienated the

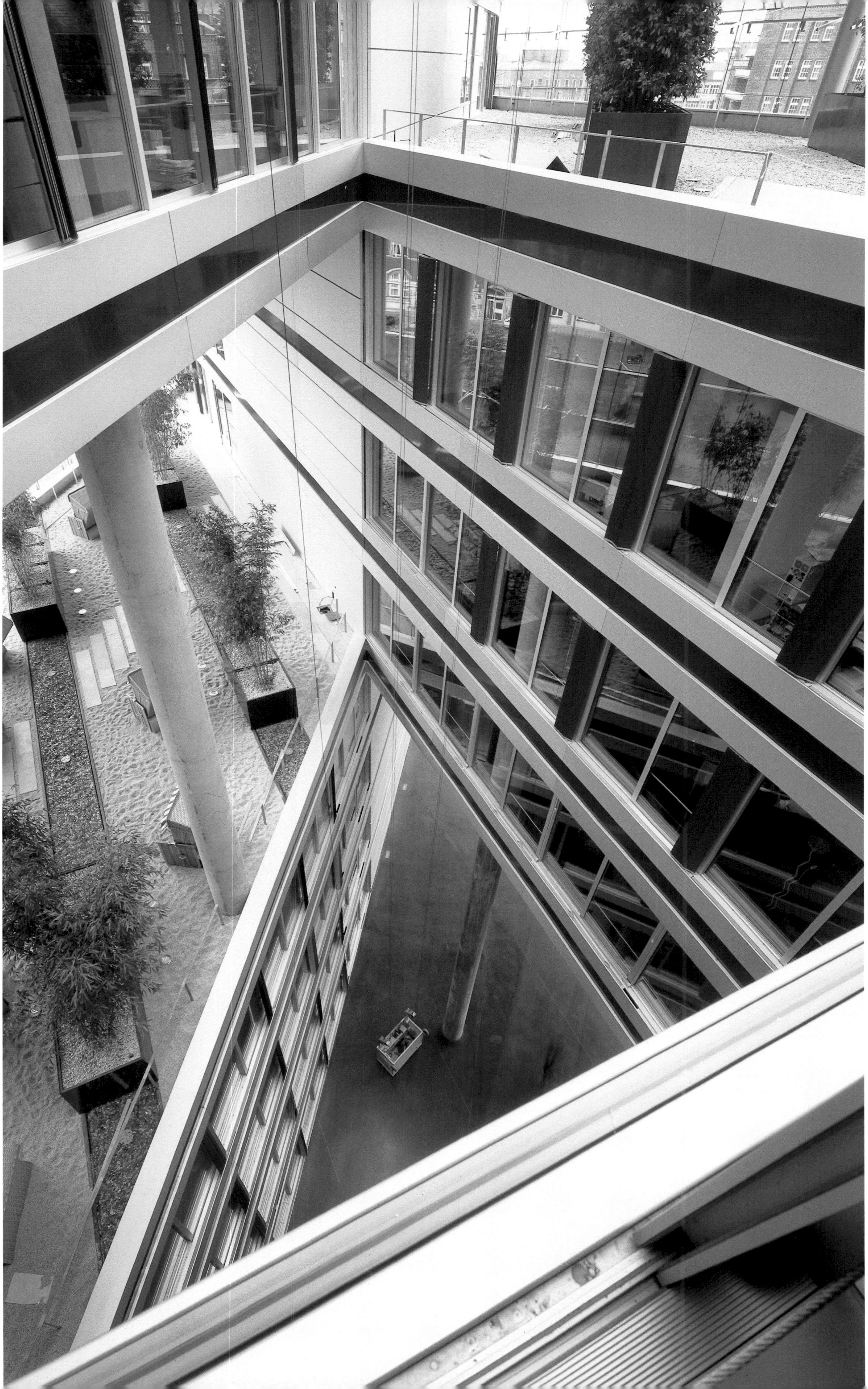

workers located there feel. Contact with nature in the city becomes more important. After the hedonistic ego culture of the 1980s, characterized by the "e factors" (extroverted, extreme, eclectic, exotic), sociologists today speak of an integration culture, characterized by intimacy, introversion, intensity and integration. Thus, the Hamburg agency Kreativphase has declared the trend "Nature, Inc." to "one of the greatest megatrends of this century: Nature Incorporated describes a new kind of respect, dealing with and implementation of nature in our society, which, along with wellness, constitutes an inseparable unity."[4] The overlapping of leisure and work time, along with the necessity for medial communication, is changing what previously was fixed as the "everyday office work schedule" and thus all necessities of its arrangements. Wellness and fitness are being integrated into the direct vicinity of residence and workplace. Thus, the service society is generating other forms of relaxation than did the production and industrial society. The line is blurring between exteriors and interiors. After the courtyard of the 1920s and the garden atrium of the 1970s, today we have the indoor garden. The technical equipment of the office workplace may allow new spatial flexibility, but at the same time, being bound to the information and communications apparatus provide grounds for a new immobility—with working hours on the rise. With the time spent at the workplace increasing, the interest in directly experiencing authentic surroundings increases.

AMBIVALENCE

Lewis Mumford expected from architecture, beyond the constructive art of engineering, a sphere of expression with the goal of overcoming anyone who entered a palace, making devout anyone who moves in a cathedral, but making "self-confident, bourgeois, responsible, and critical" anyone "who walks through a city and experiences ambiguity." As more and more people all over the world communicate on the Internet, a kind of separated intimacy is created—an absent presence. According to the sociologist Ulrich Beck, these virtual neighborhoods can also create new social movements that produce a new kind of locally bound urban dynamic. The Deichtor Office Building provides a model for this "productivity of the 'and'"[5]—an experimental arrangement for further experiences in practice, for instance, with respect to the use of the entry halls and gardens on each story. In this sense, office buildings are community institutions as well, a kind of social-ecological architecture according to the concept of "open-minded space" or "hospitable spaces," which contribute to the new formulation of public space—"against the homoge-

nization of the electronic media, against the loss of place, against the triumph of fragmentation" (Rem Koolhaas)—above all, against the "re-traditionalization"(Ulrich Beck) predominant in Germany, against the "back to the future" with the help of the costume boxes of the past. Even before the inferno of post-9/11 New York, Ulrich Beck spoke out against the hysteria of security: "Not migration and opposition, not even conflicts, not even when they are violent, destroy the productive chaos of the large city. Its enemy is the hysteria of security, the militant grip of order, which wants to exterminate the ambivalences with the roots… If it is correct that the city symbolizes the laboratory of civilization, then here is where the decision is made whether and how the either-or of urbanity and ecology can be dissolved by a 'both-and.'"[6] Not until more modernity and greater urbanity are demanded is the ecological balance secured. "Open-minded spaces" ask about the chances of the public, and expand the history of the place into the public. This is, according to Beck, the most difficult architectural objective of all, but without the art of the "and," there will be no progress. If architecture cannot change society, then a reflexive modernity can at least influence the way people move through their spaces, and in these spaces perceive their connection, their coherence—including all of their contradictions.

DESIGN

With the objective of a holistic pervasion of the building's task, or at least with the claim to unify architecture and design through innovative products, the architects faced the necessity of occupying themselves with the design of the furnishings. The design company founded for this purpose is represented in the Deichtor Office Building through four products. The all-in-one work mobile "ST@NDBY-Office" complies with the economic idea of desk sharing, but avoids its disadvantages: the loss of one's own workplace, the loss of the private sphere, the loss of status. The worker keeps his own workplace, which can be collapsed and parked in a space otherwise only big enough for rolling cabinets. The economy of space refers not to the workplace, but only to its required space. Variations of this principle are implemented in the forms of a kitchen box and a media station. In addition to the dimmable workplace lamps integrated in the "ST@NDBY-Office," the "Balance" ceiling and floor lamps—a movable module in both variants—cover lighting needs without being perceived as foreign objects in the context of the architecture. "Transparency" and "TecWave," plastic and fabric floorings, respectively, offer floors a completely new kind of grace. TecWave unifies the sensual qual-

ities of a woven carpet with the formal minimalism of a hard surface. The flat weave maintains its color in the stabile range of warp and woof. The metallic yarn invokes an impression of technology and has a reflective surface that refracts the light. The multilayered "Transparency" plastic flooring, transparent on the surface, was laid for the first time in the Deichtor Office Building. The varying prints on its backing merely perfect the sterile character of a concrete surface.

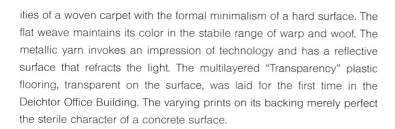

1 Jean Baudrillard: *Architektur: Wahrheit oder Radikalität?* Graz/Vienna 1999, p. 12

2 Hartmut Böhme: Gehäuse des Unsichtbaren: Timm Rauters Fotografien der dritten Industriellen Revolution, in: Timm Rautert: *Gehäuse des Unsichtbaren* (catalog of the Ruhrland-Museum Essen), Essen 1992, p. 88

3 Hartmut Böhme ibid.

4 quoted in: Thies Schröder: Relax – Wie Büromenschen entspannen. Zwischen Bürostuhl und Nature Inc., a-matter (www.a-matter.de), *related 43*, 09/04/2002, p. 3

5 Ulrich Beck: Risiko Stadt – Architektur in der reflexiven Moderne, in: Ulrich Schwarz (ed.): *Risiko Stadt? Perspektiven der Urbanität,* Hamburg 1995, p. 44

6 Ulrich Beck: ibid., p. 52-53

"We should feel comfortable where we work, because, after all, it is the place where we spend the greater part of our lives." Hadi Teherani

Deichtor Office Building

Deichtor Office Building

Design sketch "St@nd-by Office"

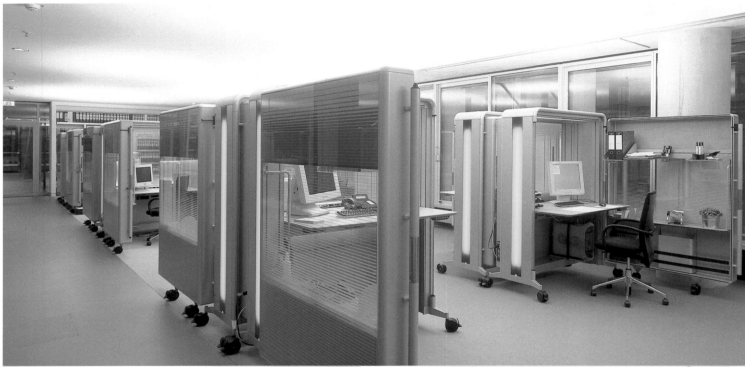

Typology: "Silver" office chair

"The Arbeitsmobil "St@ndby-Office" can be folded up and fitted into any elevator, making it possible for employees to move office in no time at all."

Hadi Teherani

"Buildings that create identity need a clearly defined, graphic architecture that offers functional advantages and also radiates emotions." Hadi Teherani

Deichtor Office Building

APPENDIX

COMPLETE WORKS

Neue Alsterarkaden	ABC-Bogen Office Building	Asian Games, Qatar	Airporthotel, Hamburg	Arnulfpark, Munich
Roofing over shop window fronts	Office building	Master planning for Asians Games	Hotel	Offices/hotel/apartments
Alsterfleet/Neuer Wall, Hamburg	ABC-Straße 19, Hamburg	Qatar, Asia	Airport, Hamburg	Arnulfstraße, Munich
Gross floor area 400 sq m	Gross floor area 16,200 sq m		Gross floor area 18,000 sq m	Gross floor area 80,000 sq m
Nov 1995, Jan 1998–Dec 1998	07/1995, 03/1998–08/2000	Jan 2003	July 1992	April 2004
Report	Competition, 1st place	Competition	Report	Competition, 1st place

Airbus Restaurant R06, Toulouse		Airbus A3XX Halls	Am Zirkus, Berlin	Office Building at the Harbor
Company cantine		Factory halls	Offices/apartments	Office building
Toulouse, France		Hamburg-Finkenwerder	Am Zirkus 1, Berlin	Bei den Mühren 5, Hamburg
Gross floor area 2,200 sq m		Gross floor area 315,275 sq m	Gross floor area 30,000 sq m	Gross floor area 6,500 sq m
June 2004		Oct 2000	July 2000	June 2003
Report/competition		Competition, 3rd place	Competition, 1st place	Study

Ballindamm Office Building	Swiss Re Office Building	Bei den Mühren Office Building	Berliner Bogen Office Building	
Offices/retail	Office building	Office building	Office building	
Ballindamm 38, Hamburg	Dieselstraße 11, Unterföhring near Munich	Bei den Mühren 1, Hamburg	Anckelmannsplatz 1, Hamburg	
Gross floor area 165 sq m	Gross floor area 54,000 sq m	Gross floor area 3,000 sq m	Gross floor area 43,000 sq m	
May 2003	09/1997, 01/1999–12/2001	10/1998, 02/2000–10/2002	08/1998, 08/1998–12/2001	
Direct commission process	Competition, 1st place	Direct commission process	Report	

Billwerder Deich	Train Station, Lattakia Syria	Lycos Office Building	Medienhafen, Düsseldorf	Melatengürtel Office Building, Cologne	Name
Offices/apartments	Train station/retail/apartments/hotel	Office building	Office building	Office building	Use
Entenwerder, Hamburg	Lattakia, Syria	Gütersloh	Franziusstraße, Düsseldorf	Melatengürtel, Cologne	Location
Gross floor area 20,000 sq m	Gross floor area 40,000 sq m	Gross floor area 88,806 sq m	Gross floor area 28,200 sq m	Gross floor area 12,430 sq m	Area
July 1996	Oct 2001	Sep 2000	07/2001, 02/2004–02/2006	June 2000	Date
Report	Competition, 1st place	Competition, 2nd place	Competition, 1st place	Competition	Type

	BMW Werk, Leipzig	Böhringer		Porsche, Bietigheim
	Office building	Offices/training center/exhibitions		Office building
	BMW Main building, Leipzig	Ingelheimer Straße, Ingelheim		Porschestraße 1, Bietigheim-Bissingen
	Gross floor area 40,000 sq m	Gross floor area 49,000 sq m		Gross floor area 19,000 sq m
	Oct 2001	July 1996		Jan 2000
	Competition	Competition, 4th place		Competition, 3rd place

Reichpietschufer Office Building	Doppel-Z Office Building	Brachmühle Süd, Vienna	Berliner Tor Center	Train Station Forecourt, Bremen
Office building	Office building	Offices/retail	Office building	Offices/retail
Reichpietschufer 92/Hiroshi-mastr. 28, Berlin	Spaldingstraße, Hamburg	Brachmühle Süd, Vienna	Beim Strohhause 31, Hamburg	Bremen
Gross floor area 16,168 sq m	Gross floor area 15,700 sq m	Gross floor area 145,000 sq m	Gross floor area 22,000 sq m	Gross floor area 40,000 sq m
June 2001	Nov 1997	April 2000	04/1998, 04/2000–10/2001	Dec 2001
Competition, 1st place	Report	Competition, 3rd place	Competition	Study

C&A Glass Bridge

Corridor

Bugenhagenstraße 32, Hamburg

Gross floor area 32 sq m

10/1994, 11/1996–03/1997

Direct commission process

Citta di Bologna, Cologne

Store development

Flandrische Straße 4, Cologne

01/1994, 02/1994–06/1994

Direct commission process

Campus, Kelsterbach

Offices/apartments

Conversion of Enka-Werke, Kelsterbach

Gross floor area 150,000 sq m

Feb 2002

Report

Multi-purpose hall, Flensburg

Multi-purpose hall/university campus
Kanzleistraße, Flensburg

Gross floor area 11,000 sq m

March 2000

Competition

Crystal Tower, Dubai

Residential/retail building

Sheikh Zayed Road, Dubai, United Arab Emirates

Gross floor area 47,000 sq m

May 2004

Study

Main Station, Dortmund

Train station/retail/leisure center

Main station, Dortmund

Gross floor area 255,265 sq m

July 1997

Competition, 1st place

Deelböge Office Building

Office building

Salomon-Heine-Weg 70-74/ Deelböge 19, Hamburg

Gross floor area 33,565 sq m

July 2001

Direct commission process

Debitel, Stuttgart

Office building

Conversion of airport grounds Böblingen-Sindelfingen

Gross floor area 52,000 sq m

Jan 2000

Study

Villa, Ahrensburg

Residential building

Ahrensburg

Gross floor area 969 sq m

02/1995, 05/1996–07/1998

Direct commission process

Dorint Hotel, Hamburg

Hotel

Schröderstiftstraße 3/ Rentzelstraße 58, Hamburg

Gross floor area 10,420 qm

07/2000, 11/2000–07/2002

Study

Facade of Dibbern

Office building of a porcelain manufacturer
Heinrich-Hertz-Straße, Bargteheide

03/1995, 03/1996–08/1998

Direct commission process

H2Office, Duisburg Innenhafen

Office building

Schifferstraße 174, Duisburg

Gross floor area 22,500 sq m

6/2001, 6/2002–11/2004

Competition, 1st place

Tango Tower

Offices/hotel

Kennedydamm, Düsseldorf

Gross floor area 42,310 sq m

May 2000

Study

Lufthansa, Frankfurt

Office building

Frankfurt/Main

Gross floor area 20,000 sq m

Aug 1999

Competition

Dubai Marina Tower

Residential building

Dubai, United Arab Emirates

Gross floor area 24,000 sq m

May 2004

Study

Dockland

Office building

Van-der-Smissen-Straße, Hamburg

Gross floor area 13,544 sq m

01/1998, 04/2004–09/2005

Direct commisssion process

Docks 8, Prague

Office building

Liben, Prague, Czech Republic

Gross floor area 27,500 sq m

Jan 2002

Competition, 1st place

Domstraße, Hamburg

Office building

Domstraße 18, Hamburg

Gross floor area 9,000 sq m

May 2001

Study

Deichtor Office Building

Office building

Ost-West-Str. 1/Oberbaumbrücke 1, Hamburg

Gross floor area 24,000 sq m

02/2000, 08/2000–05/2002

Competition, 2nd place

DeTe Immobilien Television Tower

Office building

Rentzelstraße/Lagerstraße, Hamburg

Gross floor area 22,566 sq m

Oct 1999

Report

Training Center Deutsche Vermögensberatung AG

Offices/training center

Braaker Grund 10, Stapelfeld

Gross floor area 2,385 sq m

09/1997, 08/1998–01/1999

Direct commission process

Dubai Water Experience

Waterpark with aquarium and hotel

Dubailand, United Arab Emirates

Gross floor area 42 ha, ca. 80,000 sq m

Dec 2004

Feasibility study

Name
Use
Location
Area
Date
Type

European Central Bank

Administration

Kaiserstraße 29, Frankfurt/Main

Gross floor area 1,000,000 sq m

Sept 2003

Competition

Expressgut-Gelände, Freiburg

Offices/retail/hotel

Expressgutgelände Schnewlinstraße, Freiburg

Gross floor area 17,000 sq m

Feb 2004

Competition

Emirates Industrial Bank, Dubai

Bank/office building

Al Garhoud Road, Dubai, United Arab Emirates

Gross floor area 10,000 sq m

July 2004

Competition

Loft Building at Elbberg

Office building

Elbberg 1, Hamburg

Gross floor area 3,340 sq m

06/1994, 04/1996–07/1997

Competition, 1st place

Train Station, Frankfurt Airport

Long distance train station

Airport, Frankfurt/Main

Gross floor area 38,155 sq m

02/1996, 11/1996–05/1999

Competition, 2nd place

Edilquadrifoglio, Rom

Office building

Via Sofia 8, Rom, Italy

Gross floor area 12,000 sq m

April 2004

Study

Lofthouse, Elbchaussee

Residential building

Elbchaussee 372, Hamburg

Gross floor area 8,103 sq m

June 1999

Direct commission process

Office World at Elbschlosspark

Office building

Elbchaussee 372, Hamburg

Gross floor area 18,166 sq m

07/2002, 09/2003–09/2005

Direct commission process

Car & Driver Showroom

Car dealer's/repair shop/garage

Friedrich-Ebert-Damm 110, Hamburg

Gross floor area 9,160 sq m

10/1989, 11/1990–05/1991

Direct commission process

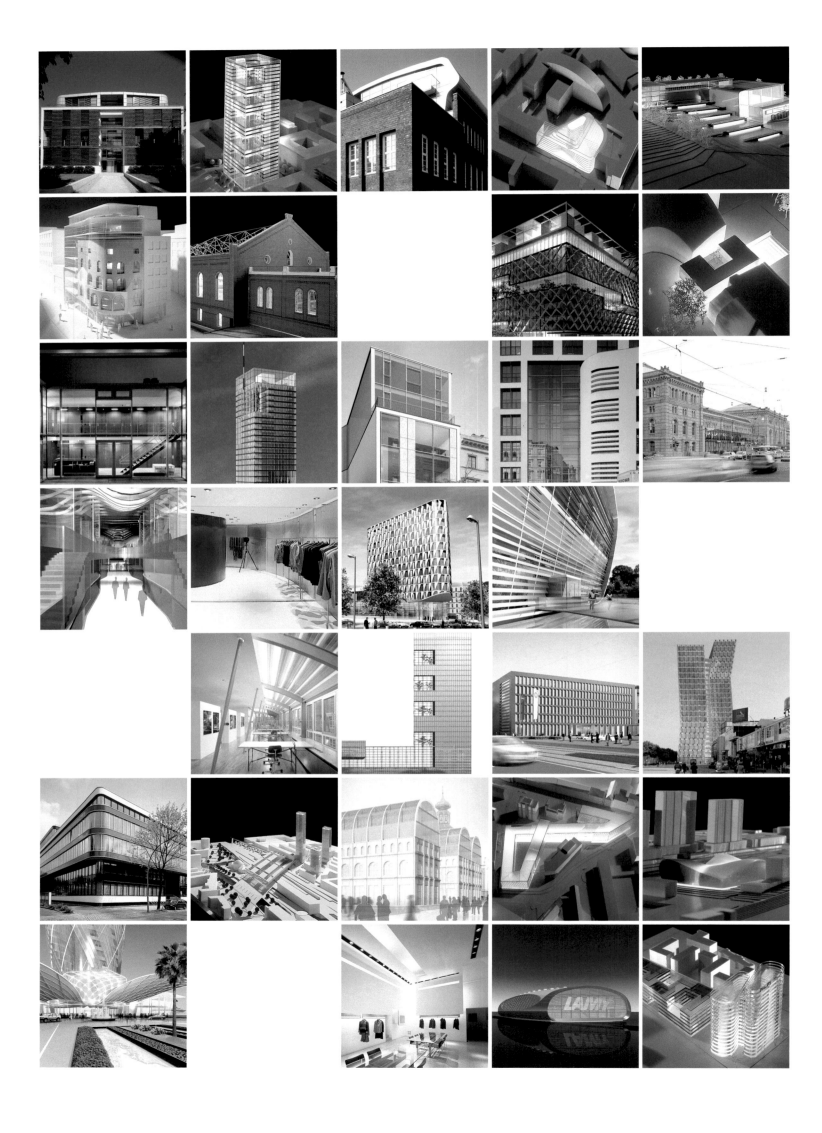

Apartment Building Fährhausstraße Residential building Fährhausstraße 11, Hamburg Gross floor area 2,349 sq m 03/1996, 07/1997–06/1998 Direct commission process	**Forum Oberkassel** Office building Oberkassel, Düsseldorf Gross floor area 41,756 sq m June 2000 Competition, 1st place	**Falkenried** Offices/apartments Falkenried 13, Hamburg Gross floor area 7,284 sq m 05/2000, 12/2001–03/2003 Competition, 1st place	**Fuhlentwiete, Hamburg** Office building Fuhlentwiete 12, Hamburg Gross floor area 15,733 sq m Jan 2000 Direct commission process	**Firmengebäude Wöhner, Coburg** Office building Mönchrödener Straße 10, Rödental Gross floor area 5,415 sq m Aug 2001 Study
Office Building at Gänsemarkt Offices/retail Gänsemarkt 13/Jungfernstieg 46, Hamburg Gross floor area 1,745 sq m May 1996 Study	**Halle K, Gasstraße Hamburg** Offices/retail/catering Gasstraße, Hamburg Gross floor area 5,603 sq m Dec 1995 Competition		**German House, Dubai** Offices/retail/hotel Al Mina Road, Dubai, United Arab Emirates Gross floor area 17,000 sq m July 2003 Competition	**St. Nikolai Parish Hall** Congregational room Harvestehuder Weg 116, Hamburg Gross floor area 650 sq m June 2000 Competition, 3rd place
Grimm 6 Office Building Office building Grimm 6, Hamburg Gross floor area 2,500 sq m 08/1999, 08/2000–09/2001 Direct commission process	**Garden Tower, Dubai** Apartments/retail Sheikh Zayed Road, Dubai, United Arab Emirates Gross floor area 45,000 sq m May 2004 Study	**Hohe Bleichen** Offices/apartments Hohe Bleichen 13, Hamburg Gross floor area 1,858 sq m 02/2003, 12/2003–07/2005 Direct commission process	**Pacific House** Office building Holzdamm 28–32, Hamburg Gross floor area 9,200 sq m 02/1994, 05/1995–05/1997 Report	**Hanover Main Station** Train station/retail Hanover Gross floor area 42,300 sq m 07/1996, 02/1998–02/2000 Competition, 1st place
Passage Hamburger Hof Shopping mall Jungfernstieg/Poststraße, Hamburg Jan 1999 Report	**Herrenhaus, Cologne** Store development St.-Apern-Straße, Cologne HNF 100 sq m 01/1989, 02/1989–04/1989 Direct commission process	**Hotel at Ostseehalle, Kiel** Hotel Ziegelteich/Kleiner Kuhberg, Kiel Gross floor area 9,135 sq m Sep 2002 Competition, 1st place	**Home Order TV, Munich** Office building Munich Gross floor area 25,000 sq m June 2001 Competition	
	Hopfensack BRT Office Office floor Hopfensack, Hamburg HNF 300 sq m March 1992 Direct commission process	**High-rise in Parkstadt, Schwabing** Office building Parkstadt Schwabing, Munich Gross floor area 6,500 sq m July 2002 Competition, 1st place	**Central Administration Office of British Petrol (BP), Bochum** Office building Wittener Straße 45, Bochum Gross floor area 20,200 sq m 07/2003, 06/2004–12/2005 Report	**High-rise Reeperbahn 1** Offices/hotel Reeperbahn 1/Zirkusweg 20, Hamburg Gross floor area 35,000 sq m June 2003 Competition, 1st place
Humboldt Campus Offices/bank Humboldtstraße 58–62, Hamburg Gross floor area 9,600 sq m 08/2001, 01/2002–03/2004 Direct commission process	**ICE Train Station, Cologne Exhibition Grounds** Train station Cologne-Deutz Gross floor area 132,330 sq m Dec 1999 Competition	**Iljinka Street, Moscow** Hotel Iljinka Straße 3/8, Moscow, Russia Gross floor area approx. 20,000 sq m April 2004 Study	**Jahreszeitenverlag, Hamburg** Office building Poßmoorweg/Dorotheenstr./ Moorfurthweg, Hamburg Gross floor area 33,375 sq m 01/1999, 09/2003–09/2005 Competition, 1st place	**Museum Klima-Haus** Museum Bremerhaven Gross floor area 15,000 sqm March 2003 Competition 3rd place
Kish Island, Iran Hotel Kish Island, Iran Gross floor area 87,000 sq m May 2003 Competition		**Kiton Showroom, Milan** Fashionrooms for presentation for wholesalers Via S. Andrea 19, Milan, Italy Gross floor area 333 sq m 05/1999, 08/1999–08/2000 Direct commission process	**Lamy Distribution Center** Warehouse, assembly workshop of typewriter manufacturer Grenzhöfer Weg 32, Heidelberg Gross floor area 2,600 sq m July 2000 Direct commission process	**Lübeckertordamm, Hamburg** Office building Lübeckertordamm/Sechslings- pforte, Hamburg Gross floor area 30,000 sq m Nov 2002 Competition, 2nd place

Name
Use
Location
Area
Date
Type

Train Station, Madrid Train station/retail/leisure center Train station grounds Chamartin, Madrid Gross floor area 275.000 sq m May 1998 Report	**Nuova Sede della Regione Lombardia** Seat of government, Lombardy Milan, Italy Gross floor area 105,000 sq m April 2004 Competition, 5th place	**Mainpark** Specialised discount store Lengfeld, Würzburg Gross floor area 6,860 sq m July 1995 Study	**Multicasa, Duisburg** Specialised discount store/ leisure facilities Conversion of freight depot site, Duisburg Gross floor area 401,567 sq m May 1998 Report	**Multimedia Center, Rotherbaum** Office building Rothenbaumchaussee, Hamburg Gross floor area 11,127 sq m May 2000 Competition, 4th place
Fair Hafencity, Hamburg Fair hall Kirchenpauerstraße, Hamburg Gross floor area 330,700 sq m July 1998 Report		**Extension of Exhibition Site, Hamburg** Exhibition halls Karolinenstraße, Hamburg Gross floor area 113,000 sq m April 2003 Competition, 2nd place	**Carré Mainzer Landstraße** Offices/apartments Mainzer Landstraße 178–190, Frankfurt/Main Gross floor area 30,200 sq m office space, 3,800 sq m residential space 07/2000, 06/2001–03/2003 Direct commission process	**Malaja Nikiskaja, Moscow** Office building Malaja Nikiskaja 31, Moscow, Russia Gross floor area approx. 5,500 sq m April 2004 Study
Transrapid railroad, Berlin–Hamburg Train station, station planning Hamburg main station and Moorfleet, Schwerin March 1998 Report	**Müngersdorf Stadium, Cologne** Sports stadium Aachener Straße 999, Cologne Gross floor area incl. stand 110,000 sq m Jan 2001 Competition	**Business Park, Moscow** Offices with conference center Moscow, Russia Gross floor area 200,000 sq m Aug 2004 Direct commission process	**Museum of World Architecture** Museum Göteborg, Sweden Oct 1998 Competition	**Elbberg Campus, Altona** Offices/apartments Elbberg 8–10, Hamburg Gross floor area 7,600 sq m 02/1999, 04/2001–05/2003 Direct commission process
Glass Pavilion Nikolai Church, Hamburg Prayer, concert and exhibition room Ost-West-Str./Hopfenmarkt/ Neue Burg, Hamburg Gross floor area 360 sq m Oct 1997 Competition, 1st place	**Neumühlen Office Building** Office building Neumühlen 19, Hamburg Gross floor area 7,100 sq m 10/1996, 04/2001–09/2002 Direct commission process	**Neuer Wall Office Building** Offices/retail Neuer Wall 37, Hamburg Gross floor area 4,132 sq m 12/2000, 01/2002–06/2003 Direct commission process	**Office Center, Moscow** Office building Sadownitscheskaja 3/7, Moscow, Russia Gross floor area approx. 40,000 sq m April 2004 Study	**Olympia Halle, Leipzig** Exhibition building Conversion of swimming stadium Leipziger Olympiapark, Leipzig Gross floor area 5,000 sq m Aug 2003 Competition
Kay Degenhard House Offices/retail Oranienburgerstraße 86a, Berlin Gross floor area 786 sq m 03/1999, 01/2003–06/2004 Study	**Othmarschen Park** Offices/retail/catering Othmarschen, Hamburg Gross floor area 129,000 sq m July 1998 Report	**Papestraße Train Station, Berlin** Train station Papestraße, Berlin April 1996 Study		**Corner Building, Prague** Office building Krizikova Str./Saldova Str. Prague, Czech Republic Gross floor area 18,000 sq m Feb 2002 Direct commission process
	Palm Island, Dubai Hotel Dubai, United Arab Emirates Gross floor area 43,000 sq m Oct 2002 Competition	**Hamburg City Waterworks** Offices/workshop Pinkertweg 3, Hamburg Gross floor area 5,125 sq m 07/1997, 07/1998–03/1999 Direct commission process	**Ponte Kiton, Naples** Corridor Viale della Industria, Arzano (Naples), Italy Gross floor area 445 sq m 04/1999, 11/1999–10/2001 Direct commission process	**Planetarium, Hamburg** Planetarium Hindenburgstraße 1b, Hamburg Gross floor area 2,696 sq m 04/2001, 10/2002–08/2003 Study
Prague Old Cornloft Residential Karlin, Prague, Czech Republic Gross floor area 12,945 sq m Sep 2002 Competition	**Police Headquarters, Hamburg** Administration Hindenburgstraße 47, Hamburg Gross floor area 63,892 sq m 01/1996, 12/1997–01/2000 Competition, 1st place	**Europa-Passage** Shopping mall/offices Paulstr./Hermannstr./ Ballindamm, Hamburg Gross floor area 140,000 sq m 04/1997, 2002–2007 Direct commission process	**Living Bridge** Bridge/apartments/retail Versmannstr, Hafencity to Veddel, Hamburg Gross floor area 200,300 sq m 01/2004 Study	**Praterstern, Vienna** Train station/office building Roofing for Nordbahnhof, Vienna Gross floor area 20,000 sq m Sep 1998 Study

Name
Use
Location
Area
Date
Type

Rhodarium, Bremen Hothouses Bremen Gross floor area 12,345 sq m June 1998 Competition, 4th place		**Rieselfeld Office Building** Offices/retail Rieselfeldallee, Freiburg Gross floor area 26,161 sq m May 2001 Direct commission process	**Rheinauhafen, Cologne** Residential/offices/culture Rheinauhafen, Cologne Gross floor area 52,950 sq m 05/1992, 03/2004 Competition, 1st place	**Casino, Hamburg** Casino Dag-Hammarskjöld-Platz, Hamburg Gross floor area 3,100 sq m Feb 2003 Study
Spreedreieck, Berlin Office building Friedrichstraße, Berlin Gross floor area 15,000 sq m Sep 2001 Study	**Schlosshotel, Heidelberg** Hotel Heidelberger Schloss, Heidelberg Gross floor area 12,000 sq m Aug 2001 Report	**sh:z Printing Center** Printing center/office building Fehmarnstraße, Rendsburg-Büdelsdorf Gross floor area 12,500 sq m 09/1999, 12/1999–08/2001 Report	**Sandtorkai Office Building** Office building Am Sandtorkai 60, Hamburg Gross floor area 6,300 sq m 11/2001, 03/2003–03/2005 Competition, 1st place	**Savings Bank, Kiel** Bank Lorentzendamm 28–32, Kiel Gross floor area 7,000 sq m 11/1992, 04/1994–03/1996 Direct commission process
Porsche Center, Stuttgart Office building Stuttgart Gross floor area 24,000 sq m Jan 1998 Competition	**Stadtparkturm** Office building Hindenburgstr. 49, Hamburg Gross floor area 8,870 sq m 02/1999, 10/1999–01/2001 Direct commission process	**Spitze Speditionsstraße, Düsseldorf** Offices/hotel/leisure center Speditionsstraße, Düsseldorf Gross floor area 36,801 sq m Sep 2000 Competition		**Scholz & Friends** Office floor Kehrwiederspitze, Hamburg Gross floor area 5,000 sq m 06/1999, 08/1999–12/1999 Direct commission process
Tobias Grau Building Offices/warehouse/factory of lamp design Siemensstraße 35b, Rellingen Gross floor area 4,160 sq m 11/1995, 04/1997–04/1998 07/2000–07/2001 Direct commission process	**Lighthouse** Offices/retail/hotel Baakenhöft, Hamburg Gross floor area 104,000 sq m Feb 2002 Study	**Airbus Toulouse after-sales-service center** Office building Toulouse, France Gross floor area 24,700 sq m June 2003 Competition, 2nd–4th places	**Bahrenfeld Trot Racetrack** Spectator's stand/catering Luruper Chaussee, Hamburg Gross floor area 52,940 sq m Aug 2000 Report	**Upgrading of the Waterfront, Triest** Town-planning competition Triest, Italy May 2002 Competition, 1st place
Transrapid Station, Schwerin Train station Schwerin Gross floor area 8,200 sq m May 1998 Competition, 2nd place		**Multifunctional Theme Park (prototype)** Shopping center/leisure facilities Gross floor area 175,000 sq m 1996 Study	**Untersachsenhausen, Cologne** Office building Komödienstr./Tunisstr. Cologne Gross floor area 30,000 sq m Oct 2003 Report	Name Use Location Area Date Type
Palm Paper-Mill Administration/office building Aalen-Neukochen Gross floor area 1,883 sq m 08/2000, 03/2001–07/2002 Competition, 1st place	**Hohenfelde Office Building** Office building Landwehr/Lübecker Straße, Hamburg Gross floor area 20,293 sq m 02/2001, 04/2002–07/2004 Direct commission process	**Double X Office High-rise** Office building Heidenkampsweg 58, Hamburg Gross floor area 20,000 sq m 05/1995, 07/1997–08/1999 Competition, 1st place	**Wexstraße Office Building** Office building Wexstraße 16, Hamburg Gross floor area 3,046 sq m 10/2000, 10/2001–07/2002 Study	**Hotel Weber, Helgoland** Hotel Nordosthafen, Helgoland Gross floor area 13,600 sq m Sep 2001 Study
Westhafen, Frankfurt Residential building Westhafen, Frankfurt/Main Gross floor area 4,700 sq m Jan 2001 Study	**Villa, Moscow** Residential building Nikolino/Moscow, Russia Gross floor area 1,400 sq m Feb 2002 Study		**Municipal Services, Wolfsburg** Customer service center Hesslinger Straße 1–5, Wolfsburg Gross floor area 2,500 sq m Sep 2001 Report	**Zentrum Zukunftsenergien, Berlin** International solar center/offices/catering Stralauer Platz 33–34, Berlin Gross floor area 16,944 sq m 03/1999, 01/2001–08/2002 Report

OFFICE HISTORY

1988–1991 Car & Driver, Rheinauhafen Cologne …

BRT's history begins in the old town of Cologne, among historic city gates and churches, surrounded by antique dealers, art galleries and high-end retailers for interior decoration. In the hustle and bustle of the city, St. Apern street is a quiet, verdant oasis. Restaurants and interesting service providers, a made-to-measure tailor, a language school, jewellers and, last but not least, a bookshop specializing in art and architecture, the most renowned of its kind in the city, combine to create the fertile urban environment in which the idea of BRT begins to blossom. Working at his first Apple computer paid for with earnings from a commission and an enthusiast when it comes to the new technologies, Jens Bothe soon realizes to which degree CAD will revolutionize his profession. The first color scanner in Germany is thus delivered to St. Apern Street. Long before Hadi Teherani has secured the first major project, Car & Driver in Hamburg, and the first competition award with the Rheinauhafen project in Cologne, and even Kai Richter has become a full member of the team, Jens Bothe is already working with competition modalities, architects' contracts and their impact on the final architectural outcome. During the start-up phase of the collaboration, Hadi Teherani, who had worked in his parents' fashion boutique in Hamburg in his final year at high school, drew clients into the ground-floor studio not only with architecture but also with his own label of tailored men's suits. This retail sideline proved to be a successful means of overcoming the threshold barrier, opening the door onto the architecture studio and serving as a strategic stage for establishing contacts. Even then, weekends were often reserved for a more dramatic harbor city. Cologne presented itself as an attractive choice primarily as a result of the shared apprenticeship at the office of Joachim and Margot Schürmann, which Hadi Teherani had been the first among the trio to select after completing his studies. It was an experience that translated into striving for perfection and the realization that, ultimately, the only thing that matters is the built result.

1991–1996 Kiel Savings Bank, High-rise Double X, Loft Building …

"I have struck Hamburg, that good-for-nothing Sodom, from my geography. I avoid everything that reminds me that it exists." Unlike Gottfried Semper, who was at odds with his fate and had to celebrate his successes elsewhere, Hamburg acted like a magnet for the young trio from Kirchen/Sieg, Cuxhaven and Teheran, who met during their first semester at the Polytechnic University in Braunschweig. The partnership is founded in 1991 in Hamburg's old town in the "Hopfensack," where Gottfried Semper had once lived with his parents, on historic ground surrounded by legendary trading companies with international connections. Once they were established in Hamburg, the first sailing excursion took them to the Cape Verde Islands. Everything is re-invented during these first years of rapid growth, nothing and no one was to serve as a model. The mission is to subsume all structures and all decisions to the single goal of realizing groundbreaking architecture. Gradually, each of the three partners would assume different spheres of responsibility: financial and legal, implementing the design on a 1:1 scale and developing ideas for design and projects—if necessary, even without a given task or an available building lot. From the very beginning, the compelling force of the studio lies in the surprising designs created by Hadi Teherani, who has no need for a commission to develop ideas. The architectural parallel with Semper, who was never able to realize his grandiose design for the reconstruction of St. Nikolai Church after the great fire of 1842, is expressed in the architect's rebuttal to his successful competitor from Cologne, unlike whom Semper desisted from basing his design on Cologne Cathedral: "One ends up stealing from the past and lying to the future. But the greatest betrayal of all is to the present, because it is a denial of its existence and a failure to create monumental testaments for the present day."

1996–2002 Tobias Grau, Train Station Frankfurt Airport, Berliner Bogen, Swiss Re, Deichtor, Elbberg Campus ...

The architects move into the first self-designed studio—the Pacific-Haus located between the main train station and the Außenalster, the Kunsthalle and the Hotel Atlantic. Hadi Teherani insists again and again that the partnership's leaps in development should also be translated in the firm's spatial environment, thus making use of it for further success. The projects Car & Driver, Lofthaus and Alster arcades, as well as the competition awards for the ABC-Bogen building, the police headquarters, the Double X high-rise, the main train station in Dortmund, the Multi Casa project in Duisburg, the Oraneum in Berlin and the Swiss Re building in Munich have made a trademark of the acronym BRT—not only to the joy of professional colleagues. Whereas the rapid rise of the team leads to mounting scepticism among professional circles and in professional journals, finally sparking an open conflict about the train station project in Dortmund, initiated by other competitors and based in an ideological debate on the issue of privatization versus public sphere—a conflict that has a lasting negative impact above all on the city—surprisingly the most positive response to their work comes from the public and the dailies. The experiment of animating architecture with an emotional sensibility, of giving it not only proportion and transparency, elegance and lightness, but above all expression and aura, in the old spirit of the Bauhaus, creates seductive spatial contrasts in an environment that is entirely defined by technology and electronics, and does so without attempting to emulate styles of the past. BRT's internationally renowned office buildings are always leased at a faster rate than the general contractors led by Kai Richter can build them. The architects' passion of continuing to build in their city, of helping the metropolis to make its mark in the worldwide competition of cities, has also captivated investors. A new axis of evil, investors are generally regarded as hostile to architecture and disinterested, in the long-term, on being linked with architectural success stories of their own. Still—even in comparison to Berlin—Hamburg is attracting a lot of attention by forging powerful alliances between architects and investors, who often dream up spectacular building projects on their own initiative. The new Hamburg Philharmonics in a historic warehouse or the urgently needed bridge across the Elbe, incorporating a park and thousand residential units as if they were mere afterthoughts, are but the most spectacular projects.

2002–today Lofts Falkenried, home[4], Dockland, Lighthouse, Living Bridge ...

In 1991, at the time of the first major project Car & Driver, the team consisted of ten architects. By 2003, the firm had grown to 140 employees. The various teams are comprised of architects, engineers, product designers and graphic designers, Experience in CAD, graphic design, and model building expands the spectrum of services to such a degree that all areas of project management from rendering to animation to access systems can be handled internally. BRT Engineering GmbH is also active as a general contractor for national and international projects. Additional offices are already in operation in Moscow and Dubai. BRT has a customized network, which is regularly expanded and upgraded, to facilitate internal communication. This technological tool is expertly maintained and constantly perfected to the latest standards. In addition to these multi-layered approaches to architectural integration, the partnership has further solidified its competencies through the product design offered by Hadi Teherani AG. Hadi Teherani quickly gained recognition as a designer, from the iF and reddot design award to the Design Award of the Federal Republic of Germany. Today, the tasks range from small architectural urban building components to large solitary structures to internationally recognized furnishings, sanitation appliances, lighting fixtures, doorknobs and floor coverings. The synthesis of architectural, emotional symbol and economic as well as ecological function that characterizes the architects and designers, now emphasizes the image of numerous international enterprises. At the same time, the complexity of the office headquarters on the Deichtor—the principal gateway to the Hanseatic city's waterfront development—has been enhanced once again. It is now the center where both utopian and realistic metropolitan projects are being developed, all with a view to accentuating and updating the image and significance of the city in the spirit of Semper.

BIOGRAPHIES

Jens Bothe
Dipl.-Ing. Architect BDA

Jens Bothe (*1959), whose initial wish to become a journalist, if possible a photojournalist, is in charge of designing the service profile, the implementation strategies and BRT's corporate culture, for every aspect related to the temperamental and scintillating instrument that is the computer, and moreover for the external and internal controlling and the coordination required for these areas. The son of merchants with a strong maritime family history could also have embraced the profession of being a patent attorney, dividing his time between research and the negotiating table: understanding and presenting complicated contexts in an accessible fashion, employing language as a tool, going to bat for inventors and innovators ... It is the musician, autodidact, lateral thinker, and aesthete in Bothe who opens the window onto architecture and makes him into an architect. His first fee as an architect was used to purchase an Apple Macintosh. After the years of studying and traveling, with Hamburg always beckoning, the sailor, software developer and automobile enthusiast had already begun to focus on CAD even prior to the official founding of the partnership, which had in effect already existed since the first semester at the Polytechnic University in Braunschweig in 1978. This created the internal structure for implementing the shared vision and the management of the expertise present in the firm, in addition to family, three children, sailing and skiing, music and design.

Kai Richter
Dipl.-Ing. Architect BDA

Kai Richter (*1958), whose original desire was to become a recording engineer after having spent fifteen years playing the violin (double major in music/physics), but who had already set his sights on architecture as a small boy and completed his studies at the Polytechnic University in Braunschweig with the highest distinction, looks after the team, the distribution of tasks and roles for each stage of planning, the coordination and interface management with clients, experts, and authorities. His passion for music, an important financial basis during the years at university, is very much present in the architectural domain through the use of terms such as mood, tempo, line-up, coordination, and melody. The would-be pianist, to whom the piano has remained the most fascinating instrument of all, is a master of team play be it at the office or in sports, or as No. 10 when playing hockey. Richter is fascinated by people with passion; he is inspired by the power and energy they radiate. Ultimately, the focus is on the joy of being a good architect as one of three partners, of being able to participate in the others' fields of expertise at any time in addition to his own areas of responsibility. Of necessity, there is little enough time for the family, five children from toddler to adult, for sports, music, and participation in the church community, while the dream of teaching architecture must be remain just a dream for now.

Hadi Teherani
Dipl.-Ing. Architect BDA

Hadi Teherani (*1954), a native of Teheran and Hamburg resident by choice, creative "trouble-maker," painter, draftsman, designer, architect, member of the Academy of Fine Arts, Hamburg, and above all tireless innovative spirit with an unfailing sense for opportunities, trends, people, and realistic visions, arrived in Hamburg at age six, to become a soccer champion in the SV Eidelstedt, to abandon drawing as an act of pure reproduction and to discover his own path without any inhibitions. The creative head of the architecture team BRT and the design firm Hadi Teherani AG, who practices in life what he thinks, studied architecture in Braunschweig more by chance than by intent, taught at the Polytechnic University in Aachen and began his career as an architect and fashion designer in Cologne. In charge of the firm's in- and output in terms of acquisitions, concepts, and design, all the way to the quality assurance of the completed building or project, the media-savvy visionary has conceived his own home on the Außenalster as a practical model for a return to city living. The strategy of expanding the sphere of influence in the comprehensive spirit of the Bauhaus all the way to product design was almost inevitable, given the background and a passion for perfection. Ceaselessly engaged in a quest for answers to questions that no one has even posed, the determined trailblazer believes that the principal motive for architecture and design is emotionality. Object and goal of each aesthetic task are thus liberated from all stylistic prejudice and not only devoted to the objective scale of the spatial atmosphere of a complex situation. The creative workaholic's greatest passion is to give his imagination free reign in a harmonious environment without interferences. Ever since his years at university, this environment has been shared with his life partner, architect Linda Strüngmann. Interests and passions include the proximity to water, music, classic British cars, Moritz the Labrador, the Kois named Le Corbusier, Mies van der Rohe, and Giorgio Armani, and, last but not least, interesting people.

STAFF

Tarek Abd Rabbo, Martina Albers, Ulrike Alex, Kasimir Altzweig, Kai Arin, Reto Jacques Aus der Au, Daniel Bauschatz, Melanie Baustel, Katrin Becker, Alex Berk, Rogerio Bexiga, Andreas Bieber, Jürgen Bischof, Artur Bomerski, Wibke Braeunlich, Birgit Brakhahn, Sven Breuer, Luca Canali, Florian Canzler, Frank Chec, Gil Coste, Tanja Croll, Richard Czardybon, Kevin Darroch, Frederike de Vivie, Carla Doberas, Kirsten Drees, Rüdiger Ebel, Mathias Eichler, Tanja El Witwity, Katja Erdmann, Arne Erichson, Robert Erlac, Christiane Ernst, Christian Feck, Kim Fenck, Heidi Fletcher, Anja Forstreuter, Mike Friedrichsen, Francis Ganet, Andreas Gatzow-von der Heide, Marco Gauer-Nachbaur, Petra Gebhart, Andreas Gerhardt, Lutz Gnosa, Roland Göppel, Frank Görge, Jörg Grabfelder, Anja Grannemann, Ralf Grigoleit, Paul Gronemeyer, Beatrice Grünzig, Anja Hahnke, Volker Halbach, Tobias Hamm, Rainer Hammer, Ingo Hartfil, Renate Hartmann, Simone Hartmann, Michaela Hauser, Andrea Hawlitzki, Martin Hecht, Markus Heller, Helmut Henke, Falco Herrmann, Heike Hillebrand, Stefanie Hillenkamp, Nadine Hinrichsen, Stefan Hofmann, Eike Holst, Benjamin Holsten, Michael Holzberger, Nicole Holzer, Michael Horn, Ulrike Horn, Dirk Hünerbein, Jörg Jahnke, Christian Jansen, Andreas Jochum, Theresa Jonetzki, Bernd Jungclaus, Martin Jürgenliemk, Björn Kantereit, Gabi Karsten, Uwe Kawohl, Andreas Keidel, Markus Kienappel, Alexander Kirchmann, Jessica Klatten, Anja Kleinschmidt, Gunther Klinger, Ute Knippenberger, Thilo Knöchel, Anja Koch, Tanja Koch, Tobias Kogelnig, Katrin Koulouri, Detlef Kozian, Ferdinand Kramer, Johannes Kramer, Heiko Krampe, Ina Kranz, Janina Krause, Fabienne Kübel, Wolfgang Labsch, Joachim Landwehr, Michael Langwald, Jens Launer, Oliver Lax, Amelie Lerch, Hansjörg Leuner, Oren Liebermann, Christiane Linnekogel, Astrid Lipka, Christian Löwnau, Tanja Lucas, Irene Manhart, Boris Manzewski, Peter Marquardt, Dennis Clayton Matthiesen, Alexander Maul, Stefan Mäusli, Göran Meyer, Kay Miksch, Danielle Mischitz, Semra Moritz, Ulrike Mühl, Bernd Muley, Dirk Nachtsheim, Hayo Nadler, Ilga Nelles, Corinna Neumann, Monika Niggemeyer, Dagmar Nill, Kim Nordsgard, Heike Ochs, Peter Olbert, Katja Pahl, Ali Pakrooh, Claudia Pannhausen, Marcus Pape, Susanne Paulisch, Maurice Paulussen, Sylvia Perk, Carolin Petersen, Katrin Petersen, Monika Pfretzschner, Alexandra Pier, Tatjana Pietsch, Kerstin Pietzsch, Jörg Purwin, Brigitte Queck, Erik Recke, Melanie Reichel, Amir Rezaii, Nicoletta Rhode, Christina Richter, Klaus Richter, Anja Richter, Guido Roth, Markus Röttger, Jörg Rügemer, Timo Saß, Jens Schetter, Stefanie Schleich, Nina Schmid, Stephan Schmid, Christina-Beatriz Schmidt, Miriam Schnell, Stephanie Schoel, Claus Schöffel, Laetitia Scholz, Jan Peter Schrick, Odalys del Carmen Schumacher Lopez, Marie-Louise Seifert, Elke Seipp, Barbara Sellwig, Sören Senkfeil, Joachim Sgodda, Ondrej Sklabinski, Sabine Söchtig, Marcus Sporer, Claudia Springmeier, Berthold Staber, Sylke Stahmann, Holger Stallbohm, Gabriele Steffens, Bettina Stölting, Simone Straub, Anke Stüper, Charlotte Szöts, Monica Tackenberg, Tatjana Tatzel, Ralf Thieme, Christina Tibi, Grischa Todt, Ulrich Treppesch, Yvonne van Tienhoven, Carsten Venus, Galina Viebke, Thomas Völlmar, Boris von der Lippe, Fariba Vossoughinia, Birgit Wagenknecht, Bashaar Wahab, Silke Walter, Angelika Wantulla, Rebekka Weber, Peer Weiss, Christel Wellhausen, Claus Wendel, Dominik Wenzel, Christopher Wilford, Jürgen Wilhelm, Stephen Williams, Arnd Woelcke, Caroline Wolff, Christoph Woop, Anja Zillgitt

BIBLIOGRAPHY (SELECTION)

ABC-Bogen Office Building, Hamburg

Dirk U. Hindrichs, Winfried Heusler (eds.): Facades. Building envelopes for the 21st Century, Basel 2004, pp. 112–113

Jürgen Knirsch: Büroräume, Bürohäuser, Leinfelden-Echterdingen 2002, pp. 138–141

Michael Wutzke: Skyline Guide Deutschland 2001/2002, Darmstadt 2001, p. 145

Hamburgische Architektenkammer (ed.): Architektur in Hamburg. Jahrbuch 2001, Hamburg 2001, pp. 26–31

Büro + Architektur, special edition DBZ Deutsche Bau-Zeitschrift 2000, pp. 3, 8

Engineering News Record, February 22, 1999, p. 19

Mathias Hein-Auty, Architekten und Ingenieurverein Hamburg (ed.): Hamburg und seine Bauten 1985–2000, Hamburg 1999, p. 146

Intelligente Architektur 19/1999, pp. 56–63

Petra Diemer (ed.): Bauten und Projekte. Architekten in Hamburg, Schleswig-Holstein, Niedernhausen 1999, pp. 28–33

A&B – Architektura & Biznes 10/1998, pp. 24–27

AIT 10/1998, p. 25

Hamburgische Architektenkammer (ed.): Architektur in Hamburg. Yearbook 1998, Hamburg 1998, pp. 164–175

ARCHITEKTUR + WETTBEWERBE 6/1996, p. 47

wallpaper, December 1st, 1995

AD Architectural Digest, ADAC Reisemagazin Hamburg, architektur & wirtschaft, Architektur & Wohnen, art, Atrium – Hamburg Lebensart und Design, BauNetz, Baumeister, Bild, DAB – Deutsches Architektenblatt, Das Architektur-Journal, DBZ Deutsche BauZeitschrift, Der Spiegel, Der Tagesspiegel, Die Welt, Elle, Hamburger Abendblatt, Hamburger Morgenpost, Handelsblatt, Managermagazin, P.M., taz hamburg, Welt am Sonntag

Swiss Re Office Building, Unterföhring near Munich

Martin Nicholas Kunz, Christian Schönwetter: Outdoor Living, Ludwigsburg 2005, pp. 52–57

DETAIL, Sonderausgabe Bauten und Projekte. Auswahl 2004, 2004, pp. 26–29

Phaidon Press, The Phaidon Atlas of Contemporary World Architecture, London 2004, p. 504

Werner Durth, EON Ruhrgas AG (ed.): Architektur in Deutschland '03. Deutscher Architekturpreis 2003, Zurich 2004, pp. 96–99

Tim Richardson (ed.): Martha Schwartz. Grafische Landschaften, Basel 2004, pp. 198–205

db deutsche bauzeitung 4/2003, pp. 38–42

Klaus-Martin Bayer: Büro International. Handbuch Moderne Bürogestaltung, Leinfelden-Echterdingen 2003, pp. 100–10

The Plan – Architecture & Technologies in Detail 2/2003, pp. 72–83

Fundacio Mies van der Rohe, ACTAR: Mie van der Rohe Award 2003, Barcelona 2003

art 3/2002, p. 131

DBZ – Deutsche BauZeitschrift 3/2002, p. 18

architektur.aktuell 4/2002, pp. 154–156

DAB – Deutsches Architektenblatt 4/2002, p. 18

AD Architectural Digest 4/2002, pp. 54–56

industrieBAU 4/2002, pp. 44–45

Baumeister Exkursion – Neue Architektur in München, 68/2002

Baumeister, Architektur und Landschaft 8/2002, pp. 38–45

AAA – Art, Architecture, Atmosphere 2002

AIT 10/2002, pp. 184–186

de Architect 10/2002, pp. 84–87

amc – Le Moniteur Architecture 10/2002, pp. 110–111

DAM Jahrbuch für Architektur in Deutschland, Munich 2002, pp. 94–99

Intelligente Architektur, September 1st, 2002

Michael Wutzke: Skyline Guide Deutschland 2001/2002, Darmstadt 2001, p. 222

archis 7/1999, pp. 60–71

Petra Diemer (ed.): Bauten und Projekte. Architekten in Hamburg, Schleswig-Holstein, Niedernhausen 1999, pp. 28–33

Hamburgische Architektenkammer (ed.): Architektur in Hamburg. Yearbook 1998, Hamburg 1998, pp. 164–175

Baumeister 5/1998

Bauwelt, April 17, 1998, p. 799

wettbewerbe aktuell 4/1998, p. 19

Bauwelt 1/1998

A & W Architektur & Wohnen, a dato architecture, Abend-zeitung, amc, Architektur + Wettbewerbe, Bauen mit Stahl – Dokumentation 613, BauNetz, Bauzaun (Swiss Re), bba, BDB-Nachrichten Journal, Bunte, Construire, Der Tagesspiegel, DETAIL, Die Gartenschau, Die Welt, ENLACE, Facility Management, Fertig Haus, Financial Times, Frankfurter Allgemeine Zeitung, Gebäudemanage-ment, glas, Glas – Österreichische Glaser-Zeitung, Hamburger Morgenpost, Hannoversche Allgemeine, Kieler Nachrichten, Madame, Mensch & Büro, Münchner Merkur, Neue Zürcher Zeitung, Reuters News Service, STERN, Süddeutsche Zeitung, Umrisse – Zeitschrift für Baukultur, Welt am Sonntag, Zeitschrift für Versicherungswesen

Berliner Bogen Office Building, Hamburg

Peter Lorenz: Entwerfen. 25 Architekten – 25 Stand-punkte, Munich 2004, pp. 36–41

Constructiva Oficinas '04, Barcelona 2004, pp. 1, 44–47

Dirk U. Hindrichs, Winfried Heusler (ed.): Facades. Building envelopes for the 21st Century, Basel 2004, pp. 86–87

Friedrich Grimm: Energieeffizientes Bauen mit Glas, Munich 2004, pp. 188–193

Glas, Architektur und Technik 2-3/2003, pp. 26–34

CA - contemporary architecture, Victoria/Australia 2003, pp. 20–23

The Plan – Architecture & Technologies in Detail 3/2003, p. 16

The Plan – Architecture & Technologies in Detail 4/2003, p. 93

Cesare Blasi, Gabriella Padovano: La sfida della sosteni-bilità, Naples 2003, pp. 48–49

Walter Meyer-Bohe (ed.): Atlas Gebäudegrundrisse, Vol. 3: Bauten für Dienstleistungen, Gewerbe und Verkehr, Stutt-gart 2003, pp. 50–51

Freie und Hansestadt Hamburg (ed.): Architektur als stadtbildprägendes Element. Merkzeichen und Bereiche, Hamburg 2003, pp. 31–33, 35

The Architectural Review 6/2002, pp. 56–59

DBZ – Deutsche BauZeitschrift 2/2002, p. 12

Ullrich Schwarz (ed.): Neue Deutsche Architektur. Eine Reflexive Moderne, Ostfildern-Ruit 2002, pp. 66–73

HOME (Japan) 8/2002

arcade 5/2002, p. 20

md – moebel interior design 10/2002, pp. 128–131

Hamburgische Architektenkammer (ed.): Architektur in Hamburg. Jahrbuch 2002, Hamburg 2002, pp. 18–25

Hildegard Kösters, Volker Roscher (ed.): BDA Hamburg Architektur Preis 2002, Hamburg 2002, p. 78

AIT 12/2002, pp. 12, 22–32, 80–83

Michael Wutzke: Skyline Guide Deutschland 2001/2002, Darmstadt 2001, p. 141

Peter Zec: best selection. office design 2001, Essen 2001, pp. 136–137

Petra Diemer (ed.): Bauten und Projekte. Architekten in Hamburg, Schleswig-Holstein, Niedernhausen 1999, pp. 28–33

A & W Architektur & Wohnen, A&B Architektura & Biznes, Albingia Panorama, architektur, architektur & wirtschaft, art, Atrium – Hamburg Lebensart und Design, Bauen mit Stahl – Dokumentation 613, BAUIDEE, Baumeister, Bau-meister Exkursion – Neue Architektur in Hamburg, Bau-technik, bauzeitung, bba, Bild, Brandschutz transparent, Brigitte, Büro '99 – Sonderausgabe DBZ Deutsche Bau-Zeitschrift, Das Architektur–Journal, DAZ, db deutsche bauzeitung, DETAIL, Die Welt, DIE ZEIT, ENLACE, Frank-furter Allgemeine Sonntagszeitung, Frau im Spiegel, GEO, Hamburger Abendblatt, Hamburger Morgenpost, Hannoversche Allgemeine, HÄUSER, Horner Wochen-blatt, Hot & Cool, ibodi., immobilien business, Immobilien

Zeitung, Interzum magazin, Kieler Nachrichten, Le Figaro – Édition Spéciale MIPIM, Mensch & Büro, Merian, MIPIM Daily News, Oldenburger Nachrichten, Präsentation der Preise in der Baukultur – 1. Konvent, STERN, Stuttgarter Zeitung, Süddeutsche Zeitung, Tageslicht, The Architectural Review MIPIM Future Project Preview 2003, Umrisse – Zeitschrift für Baukultur, Vogue

Main Train Station, Dortmund

Design Report 2/2001, p. 26

Hans-Martin Nelte (ed.): New Buildings and Projects. Architecture in Germany, Wiesbaden 2001, pp. 36–39

Bauwelt 41/2001, p. 11

l´ARCA 2/2000, pp. 12–19

Gert Kähler: Ein Jahrhundert Bauten in Deutschland, Stuttgart 2000, p. 223

DAB – Deutsches Architektenblatt 3/2000, pp. 70–71

Petra Diemer (ed.): Bauten und Projekte. Architekten in Hamburg, Schleswig-Holstein, Niedernhausen 1999, pp. 28–33

Hamburgische Architektenkammer (ed.): Architektur in Hamburg. Jahrbuch 1998, Hamburg 1998, pp. 164–175

ARKITEKTEN magasin 3/1998, pp. 28–29

Baumeister 1/1998, p. 12

Bauwelt 7/1998, p. 301

DAB - Deutsches Architektenblatt 4/1998, pp. 428–429

Design Report 12/1997, pp. 20/21

Wallpaper 11–12/1997, pp. 38

AD Architectural Digest, AEC-REPORT, Allgemeiner Anzeiger, archis, architektur & wirtschaft, Architektur & Wohnen Special 9, ARCHITEKTUR UND GESTALTUNG, Architektur-Forum Dortmund, Architekturführer Dortmund 1983–2000, art, Berliner Zeitung, DB mobil, DBZ Deutsche BauZeitschrift, Die Welt, DIE WOCHE, Dortmunder Rundschau, ELLE DECORATION, ENLACE, Erlebnis Welten, FOCUS, Frankfurter Allgemeine Zeitung, GERMAN COUNCIL Report, Immobilien Zeitung, Kölner Stadt-Anzeiger, Neue Ruhrzeitung, petra, P.M., PROJECTOR, RAUM & mehr, Rheinische Post, Ruhr Nachrichten, Stadt-Bauwelt, stern, Süddeutsche Zeitung, Süddeutsche Zeitung MAGAZIN, Szene Hamburg, Welt am Sonntag, Westdeutsche Allgemeine Zeitung, Westdeutsche Zeitung, Westfälische Rundschau, Westfälischer Anzeiger, ZOO, Zug

Villa, Ahrensburg

Bettina Rühm: Der optimale Grundriss, Munich 2004, pp. 46–47

Architektur & Wohnen 3/2003, pp. 98–104

DBZ - Deutsche BauZeitschrift 4/1997, pp. 89–92

Art, ENLACE, HÄUSER

Dockland Office Building, Hamburg

Wallpaper 7–8/2004, p. 105

AD – Architectural Digest 10/2004, p. 140

AIT 3/1999, p. 10

Altonaer Wochenblatt, architektur & wirtschaft, art, BAU-KULTUR, BauNetz, Bauwelt, Bild, DBZ Deutsche BauZeitschrift, Die Welt, Hamburger Abendblatt, Hamburger

Morgenpost, HÄUSER, ibodi., Immobilien Zeitung, Kieler Nachrichten

Deichtor Office Building, Hamburg

Rita Bake: Verschiedene Welten, Hamburg 2005, pp. 74–75

Interior Design 6/2004, pp. 1, 170–177, 230

H.O.M.E. 7–8/2004, pp. 102–107

Dirk U. Hindrichs, Winfried Heusler (ed.): Facades. Building envelopes for the 21st Century, Basel 2004, pp. 44–45

The Plan – Architecture & Technologies in Detail 6/2004, pp. 1, 68–81

Friedrich Grimm: Energieeffizientes Bauen mit Glas, Munich 2004, pp. 158–161

wettbewerbe aktuell 3/2003, pp. 93–97

Architektur & Wohnen 4-5/2003, pp. 140–141

DETAIL, special edition Bauten und Projekte. Auswahl 2003, 2003, pp. 28–32

AIT 9/2003, p. 16

Jürgen Knirsch: Büroräume, Bürohäuser, Leinfelden-Echterdingen 2002, pp. 22–23

Michael Wutzke: Skyline Guide Deutschland 2001/2002, Darmstadt 2001, p. 138

Bauwelt 8/2000, p. 9

wettbewerbe aktuell 5/2000, pp. 58–59

Hamburgische Architektenkammer (ed.): Architektur in Hamburg. Jahrbuch 2000, Hamburg 2000, p. 114

Aachener Zeitung, ADAC Reisemagazin Hamburg, architektur & wirtschaft, Baumeister Exkursion – Neue Architektur in Hamburg, BauNetz, Bild, contractworld 2003, DBZ Deutsche BauZeitschrift, Der Spiegel, DETAIL, Die Welt, Financial Times, Hamburger Abendblatt, Hamburger Morgenpost, Hanse Art, HÄUSER, immobilien business, Immobilien Zeitung, made in Germany – calendar 2005 (Foreign Affairs), Mensch & Büro, Nordwest-Zeitung, Objekt, piazza, Süddeutsche Zeitung – Beilage zur MIPIM 2003, tec21, Vogue, Welt am Sonntag, Wirtschaftswoche

Loft Building at Elbberg, Hamburg

Freie Akademie der Künste Hamburg (ed.): 25 Jahre Planen und Bauen in der Demokratie 1976–2000, Hamburg 2003, p. 73

Jürgen Knirsch: Büroräume, Bürohäuser, Leinfelden-Echterdingen 2002, pp. 148–151

Peter Zec: best selection. office design 2001, Essen 2001, pp. 136–137

Hans-Martin Nelte (ed.): Innenarchitektur. Interior Design in Germany, Wiesbaden 2000, pp. 50–59

Mathias Hein-Auty, Architekten und Ingenieurverein Hamburg (ed.): Hamburg und seine Bauten 1979–1999, Hamburg 2000, p. 35

Bund Deutscher Architekten BDA (ed.): BDA Handbuch 2000/2001, Bonn 2000, p. 140

Gunda Dworschak, Alfred Wenke: Metamorphosen, Neuwied 2000, pp. 74–79

Hildegard Kösters, Volker Roscher (ed.): BDA Hamburg Architektur Preis 1999, Hamburg 1999, pp. 30–35

Frantisek D. Sedlacek (ed.): AWA – Architecture Optimal

1999/2000. Preisgekrönte Architektur. Internationales Jahrbuch, Orlando/USA 1999, pp. 52–53 [*]

architektur.aktuell 6/1998, pp. 50–61

Hamburgische Architektenkammer (ed.): Architektur in Hamburg. Yearbook 1998, Hamburg 1998, pp. 164–175

art 6/1998, p. 143

BAUKULTUR 6/1998, pp. 64–65

db deutsche bauzeitung 3/1998, pp. 55–61

DBZ – Deutsche Bauzeitschrift 9/1998, pp. 73–80

HÄUSER 6/1998, p. 6

wallpaper 11–12/1998, pp. 82

wettbewerbe aktuell 3/1998, pp. 103–106

Peter Neitzke, Carl Steckeweh, Reinhart Wustlich (ed.): CENTRUM – Jahrbuch Architektur und Stadt 1998–1999, Wiesbaden 1998, pp. 162, 193–195

Architektur & Wohnen 6/1997, p. 126

Design Report 11/1996, pp. 90/91

DAB – Deutsches Architektenblatt 7/1995, p. 1280ff

wettbewerbe aktuell 7/1994, pp. 84–85

AD Architectural Digest, AIT, Altonaer Anzeiger, Altonaer Wochenblatt, architektur & wirtschaft, Architektur & Wohnen Special 9, Atrium – Hamburg Lebensart und Design, BAUIDEE, Baumeister Exkursion – Neue Architektur in Hamburg, BDB Nachrichten, Bild, Die Welt, ELLE PLUS, ENLACE, GEO Special, Hamburger Abendblatt, Hamburger Morgenpost, Kieler Nachrichten, max, Mensch & Büro, Musikexpress, stadtdialog, Süddeutsche Zeitung, Szene Hamburg, Tages-Anzeiger, tain, taz hamburg, ZEIT Punkte

Car & Driver Showroom, Hamburg

Freie Akademie der Künste Hamburg (ed.): 25 Jahre Planen und Bauen in der Demokratie 1976–2000, Hamburg 2003, p. 81

Dirk Meyhöfer: motortecture, Ludwigsburg 2003, p. 27

DBZ – Deutsche BauZeitschrift 1/2000, pp. 104–111

Mathias Hein-Auty, Architekten und Ingenieurverein Hamburg (ed.): Hamburg und seine Bauten 1979–1999, Hamburg 2000, p. 12

archis 7/1999, pp. 60–71

Petra Diemer (ed.): Bauten und Projekte. Architekten in Hamburg, Schleswig-Holstein, Niedernhausen 1999, pp. 28–33

Jürgen Knirsch: Eingang, Weg und Raum, Leinfelden-Echterdingen 1998, pp. 98–99

Ralf Lange: Architekturführer Hamburg, Fellbach 1995, p. 198

Baumeister 10/1995

db deutsche bauzeitung 5/1995

PROJETO 12/1995, p. 67

l´architecture d´aujourd´hui 297/1995

db deutsche bauzeitung 3/1995, pp. 6–7

Baumeister 2/1994, p. 8

Gerhard Hirschfeld: Konstruktion zwischen Kunst und Konvention. Ingenieurbaukunst in Hamburg von 1950–2000, Hamburg 1994

S I A – Ingénieurs et Architectes Suisses 26–12/1993, p. 516

ZEIT magazin 19/1993, pp. 66–73

db deutsche bauzeitung 6/1992, p. 2

db deutsche bauzeitung 1/1992, p. 14

glasforum 1/1992, pp. 12–26
HÄUSER 4/1992, pp. 84–85
Süddeutsche Zeitung, February 18, 1992, p. 40
Bauwelt 10/1991, pp. 2052–2057
DBZ – Deutsche BauZeitschrift 10/1991, pp. 1421–1428
ADAC Special, Antonoff CI REPORT '94, Architektur &
Wohnen, Architektur & Wohnen Special 9, Arkitekten, art,
AutoBild, BAUKULTUR, DAB – Deutsches Architekten-
blatt, DIE ZEIT, ENLACE, Hamburger Abendblatt, Ham-
burger Morgenpost, SPIEGEL Extra

Apartment Building Fährhausstraße, Hamburg

H.O.M.E. 5/2004, pp. 1, 26–34
Homes 1/2002
Nauja Statyba 3/2002, pp. 18–20
Die Welt, GEO Special, Hamburger Abendblatt, HÄUSER,
max, Welt am Sonntag

Lofts Falkenried, Hamburg

architektur.aktuell 10/2004, pp. 1, 74–85
wallpaper 5/2003, p. 65
Bauwelt, May 12, 2000, p. 10
Baumeister 5/2000, p. 82
Bild, db deutsche bauzeitung, Denkmalwelten der Großstadt, Die Welt, Hamburger Abendblatt, Hamburger Morgenpost, Immobilien Zeitung, stadtdialog, Welt am Sonntag, werk, bauen + wohnen

Grimm 6 Office Building, Hamburg

architektur.aktuell 5/2002, pp. 76–85
Hamburgische Architektenkammer (ed.): Architektur in
Hamburg. Yearbook 2002, Hamburg 2002, pp. 62–63
Hildegard Kösters, Volker Roscher (ed.): BDA Hamburg
Architektur Preis 2002, Hamburg 2002, p. 77
4light – Lichtblicke aus Hamburg, Baumeister Exkursion
– Neue Architektur in Hamburg, db deutsche bauzeitung,
Hamburger Abendblatt

Main Train Station, Hanover

Bauwelt 45/2001, p. 4
Bauwelt 22/2000
Hermann Otto (ed.): Architektur der EXPO-Stadt.
Architecture of the EXPO-City. Epochen Bauwerke Rund-
gänge, Hanover 2000, pp. 58–59
Bauwelt, August 29, 1997, p. 1792
architektur & wirtschaft, BauNetz, Einkaufscenter News
2001, Hannoversche Allgemeine, Immobilien Zeitung

home⁴, Cologne

HÄUSER 3/2004, pp. 6–7
Christian Schittich (ed.): High-Density Housing. Concepts, Planning, Construction, Munich/Basel 2004,
pp. 12–25
Smart Homes 10–11/2004, pp. 1, 4–5, 32–35
Bild, Die Welt, Hafenblick, Hamburger Abendblatt, Hamburger Morgenpost, Immobilien Zeitung, Welt am Sonntag

Highrise Reeperbahn 1, Hamburg

Baumeister 6/2004, p. 16
Deutsche Immobilienzeitung, March 31, 2003
Bild, Die Welt, Fertig Haus, Hamburger Abendblatt, Hamburger Morgenpost, Kölner Express, taz hamburg, Welt
am Sonntag

Living Bridge, Hamburg

DER SPIEGEL, June13, 2005, p. 125
BauNetz, Bild, Die Welt, Hamburger Abendblatt, Hamburger Morgenpost, Immobilien Zeitung, Kölnische Rundschau, n24.de, ndr.de, Netzeitung.de, sat1.de, Segeberger
Zeitung, SOL.DE, taz

Multicasa, Duisburg

Architektur & Wohnen 5/2000, p. 268
Petra Diemer (ed.): Bauten und Projekte. Architekten in
Hamburg, Schleswig-Holstein, Niedernhausen 1999,
pp. 28–33
Baukultur, BauNetz, Bild, DBZ Deutsche BauZeitschrift,
Dialog, Frankfurter Allgemeine Zeitung, German Council
Report, Hamburger Abendblatt, Hamburger Architektur
Sommer 2000, Immobilien Zeitung, Iserlohner Kreisan-
zeiger, Merkzettel - Bemerkenswertes zum Standort Duis-
burg, Neue Ruhr Zeitung, Rheinische Post, Süddeutsche
Zeitung, WAZ, Welt am Sonntag, Wochen Anzeiger, ZOO

Carré Mainzer Landstraße, Frankfurt

Frankfurter Allgemeine Zeitung, May 22, 2003, p. 43
Volker Albus, Jo Franzke (ed.): Architektur in Frankfurt
am Main 1999-2003, Hamburg 2002, pp. 122–123
Ingeborg Flagge, BDA Hessen (ed.): Frankfurt am Main.
Stadtführer zeitgenössischer Architektur, Frankfurt 2002,
pp. 34–35
BauNetz, Financial Times, Frankfurter Neue Presse,
Frankfurter Rundschau, Immobilien Zeitung, Neue Presse,
Rhein-Main.Net

Elbberg Campus Altona, Hamburg

Hamburgische Architektenkammer (ed.): Architektur in
Hamburg. Jahrbuch 2004, Hamburg 2004,
pp. 10–17, 128–135
Architektur & Wohnen 5/2003, p. 150
Jürgen Knirsch: Büroräume, Bürohäuser, Leinfelden-
Echterdingen 2002, pp. 126–127
Hamburgische Architektenkammer (ed.): Architektur in
Hamburg. Yearbook 1999, Hamburg 1999, pp. 86–87
ADAC Reisemagazin Hamburg, Altonaer Wochenblatt,
architektur & wirtschaft, art, Bild Hamburg, build, Die Welt,
Elbblicke, Elbe Journal, Elbe Wochenblatt, Habitat II,
Hamburger Abendblatt, Hamburger Morgenpost, Immo-
bilien Zeitung

Glass Pavilion Nikolai Church, Hamburg

BauNetz, DBZ Deutsche BauZeitschrift, Die Welt, Hamburger Abendblatt, Hamburger Morgenpost

Kay Degenhard House, Berlin

Bauwelt 8/2003, pp. 10–17
Berliner Morgenpost, Focus, Frankfurter Allgemeine Zeitung,
Hamburger Abendblatt, Immobilien Zeitung

Planetarium, Hamburg

db deutsche bauzeitung 3/2004, pp. 6–7
Bild, DB mobil, Die Welt, Hamburger Abendblatt, Ham-
burger Morgenpost, Hanse Art, Lufthansa Magazin,
Planetarium Hamburg

Praterstern, Vienna

Wettbewerbe Architekturjournal 20/2005, p. 83

Rheinauhafen, Cologne

Sabine Renz: Bauen + Wirtschaft. Architektur der Region
im Spiegel, Worms 2004, pp. 20–25
Claudia Kroth: Der Rheinauhafen Köln, Cologne 2001,
pp. 124–127
Peter Zec: best selection. office design 2001, Essen 2001,
pp. 136–137Hans-Martin Nelte (ed.): New Buildings and
Projects. Architecture in Germany, Wiesbaden 2001,
pp. 44–47
Bauwelt, May 5, 2000, p. 3
HÄUSER 5/2000, p. 20
polis 11/2000, p. 8
Peter Neitzke, Carl Steckeweh, Reinhart Wustlich (eds.):
CENTRUM – Jahrbuch Architektur und Stadt 1999/2000,
Wiesbaden 1999, pp. 156–159
SPIEGEL Extra 9/1996
Architektur & Wohnen, art, BauNetz, Bild Hamburg, Börse
Online, Die Welt, Financial Times Deutschland, Frankfur-
ter Allgemeine Sonntagszeitung, Frankfurter Allgemeine
Zeitung, ftd.de, koelnarchitektur.de, Köln Magazin, Kölner
Express, Kölner Rundschau, Kölner Stadtanzeiger, Kölni-
sche Rundschau, Plan 99 – Forum aktueller Architektur
in Köln, StadtBauwelt, Süddeutsche Zeitung

Casino, Hamburg

industrieBAU 2/2003, p. 13
BauNetz, Bild, Die Welt, Hamburger Abendblatt, Hamburger Morgenpost, Immobilien Zeitung

Spreedreieck Berlin

Eva-Maria Amberger, Berlinische Galerie (ed.): Fifty:Fifty –
Gebaute und nicht gebaute Architektur in Berlin
1990–2000, Berlin 2002, pp. 88–89, 120
H.O.M.E. 7–8/2002, pp. 80–81
Museumsjournal Berlinische Galerie 4/2002
Skyline XXV 1/2001, pp. 20–21
Børsen, Der Tagesspiegel, Focus, Hamburger Abendblatt,
Kunsthistorische Arbeitsblätter – Zeitschrift für Studium
und Hochschulkontakt, Liberation, Märkische Oderzei-
tung, Prinz – Stadtmagazin Berlin, www.faz.net,
www.ing.dk

sh:z Printing Center, Rendsburg-Büdelsdorf

DAB – Deutsches Architektenblatt (Hamburg, Schleswig-Holstein) 3/2003, pp. 16–17

Burkhard Fröhlich, Sonja Schulenburg (ed.): Metal Architecture. Design and Construction, Basel 2003, pp. 56–59

DBZ – Deutsche BauZeitschrift 5/2002, pp. 34–35, 40–43

AW Architektur + Wettbewerbe (Industriebauten), 6/2002, pp. 46–49

N.N.: Architektur ist die Vision des Möglichen in Verbindung mit der Intelligenz des Machbaren, 2002

Brunsbütteler Rundschau, Der Insel Bote, Deutsche Werkstätten Hellerau – Werkstättenbericht 10, Die Welt, Dithmarscher Rundschau, Flensburger Tageblatt, Holsteinischer Courier, Husumer Nachrichten, Marner Zeitung, Neue Zürcher Zeitung, Norddeutsche Rundschau, Nordfriesland Tageblatt, NZZ Online, Ostholsteiner Anzeiger, Schlei-Bote, Schleswiger Nachrichten, Schleswig-Holsteinische Landeszeitung, Stormarner Tageblatt, Sylter Rundschau, Wege ins Land – Ein Kultur-Magazin der Kieler Nachrichten, Wilsternsche Zeitung, WNO – Wirtschaft zwischen Nord- und Ostsee

Savings Bank, Kiel

Peter Lorenz, Stephan Isphording: Banken und Geldinstitute, Leinfelden-Echterdingen 2003, pp. 72–77

Ingeborg Flagge (ed.): Jahrbuch Licht und Architektur 2001/2002. Annual of Light and Architecture, Cologne 2002, pp. 116–117

Rudolf Schricker, Bund Deutscher Innenarchitekten (ed.): Innenarchitektur in Deutschland, Leinfelden-Echterdingen 2002, p. 57

Hans-Martin Nelte (ed.): Innenarchitektur – Interior Design in Germany, Wiesbaden 2000, pp. 50–59

BDA Schleswig-Holstein (ed.): BDA-Preis 1999. Architektur in Schleswig-Holstein, Kiel 2000, pp. 26–27

Petra Diemer (ed.): Bauten und Projekte. Architekten in Hamburg, Schleswig-Holstein, Niedernhausen 1999, pp. 28–33

Der Architekt 7/1999, p. 61

Architektur + Wettbewerbe 12/1999, pp. 13–15

Jürgen Knirsch: Eingang, Weg und Raum, Leinfelden-Echterdingen 1998, pp. 94–95

ABITARE 5/1997, pp. 158–165

N.N.: Gebäudeerweiterungen von Verwaltungsgebäuden, 1997

glasforum 1/1997, pp. 13–18

HÄUSER 2/1997, p. 10

AIT 12/1996, pp. 41–49

Hamburgische Architektenkammer (ed.): Architektur in Hamburg. Yearbook 1996, Hamburg 1996, pp. 44–49

ARKITEKTEN magasin 29/1996

Bauwelt 16/1996, pp. 932–933

Design Report 6/1996, pp. 36–39

MÖBEL RAUM DESIGN June–July/1996, p. 80

Klaus Alberts, Ulrich Höhns (ed.): Architektur in Schleswig-Holstein 1990–1996, Hamburg 1996, pp. 80–83

Architektur & Wohnen, Baumeister Exkursion – Neue Architektur in Kiel, bba, Beirat für Stadtgestaltung, Betriebswirtschaftliche Blätter, DAB – Deutsches Architektenblatt, Das dritte Jahrhundert, Deutsche Sparkassenzeitung, GLAS, Husumer Nachrichten, Kieler Express, Kieler Nachrichten, SPIEGEL Extra, Welt am Sonntag

Tobias Grau Building, Rellingen

Freie Akademie der Künste Hamburg (ed.): 25 Jahre Planen und Bauen in der Demokratie 1976–2000, Hamburg 2003, p. 83

DETAIL 6/2003, p. 668

Jacobo Krauel, Jennifer Brown: Office Interiors, Barcelona 2003, pp. 54–65

Cesare Blasi, Gabriella Padovano: La sfida della sostenibilità, Naples 2003, pp. 165–166

Freie und Hansestadt Hamburg (ed.): Architektur als stadtbildprägendes Element. Merkzeichen und Bereiche, Hamburg 2003, pp. 30–31

Jürgen Knirsch: Büroräume, Bürohäuser, Leinfelden-Echterdingen 2002, pp. 174–175

INTERIOR DESIGN 5/2002, pp. 272–277

Ulrich Königs, Vladimir Nicolic: Architektonik – Vom Entwurf zur Konstruktion, Cologne 2002, pp. 26–33

build 7–8/2002, pp. 32–33

Hildegard Kösters, Volker Roscher (ed.): BDA Hamburg Architektur Preis 2002, Hamburg 2002, pp. 64–65

Peter Zec: best selection. office design 2001, Essen 2001, pp. 136–137

The Architectural Review 1/2000, pp. 52–55

Hans-Martin Nelte (ed.): Innenarchitektur. Interior Design in Germany, Wiesbaden 2000, pp. 50–59

Hildegard Kösters, Volker Roscher (ed.): Architekten und Architektinnen BDA in Hamburg. Handbuch 2000/2001, Hamburg 2000, pp. 50–51

N.N.: Bauobjekte, Architekten und Planer 2000, pp. 290–291

Presenza Tecnica 2000, pp. 83–84

BDA Schleswig-Holstein (ed.): BDA-Preis 1999. Architektur in Schleswig-Holstein, Kiel 2000, pp. 18–19

architektur 3/1999, pp. 52–55

architektur.aktuell 3/1999, pp. 64–75

HÄUSER 1/1999, pp. 10–11

industrieBau 2/1999, pp. 12–15

wallpaper January/February 1999, p. 30

Wohn!Design 2/1999, p. 225

db deutsche bauzeitung 2/1999, p. 14

Hamburgische Architektenkammer (ed.): Architektur in Hamburg. Jahrbuch 1999, Hamburg 1999, pp. 28–35

Klaus Alberts, Ulrich Höhns (ed.): Architektur in Schleswig-Holstein 1996–2000, Hamburg 1999, pp. 110–113

Ingeborg Flagge (ed.): Jahrbuch Licht und Architektur 2000. Annual of Light and Architecture, Cologne 1999, pp. 130–133

Petra Diemer (ed.): Bauten und Projekte. Architekten in Hamburg, Schleswig-Holstein, Niedernhausen 1999, pp. 28–33

amc – Le Moniteur Architecture 1999, pp. 40–42

l´ARCA 141/1999, pp. 56–59

DAB - Deutsches Architektenblatt 8/1999, p. 1046

Architektur & Wohnen 6/1998, pp. 142–143

Hamburgische Architektenkammer (ed.): Architektur in Hamburg. Jahrbuch 1998, Hamburg 1998, pp. 164–175

Atrium 5/1998, p. 137

domus 4/1998

ELLE DECORATION 6/1998, pp. 34–38

möbel kultur 10/1998, pp. 50–51

OFFICE DESIGN 6/1998, pp. 28–32

PACE – Interior Architecture 10/1998, pp. 44–51

Architektur & Technik 6/1998, p. 81 ff

Design Report 4/1997, p. 6

AD Architectural Digest, ADAC Reisemagazin Hamburg, AIT, archis, Architektur & Wohnen Special 9, art, B.Ü.R.O., BauNetz, Das Architektur-Journal, DBZ Deutsche Bau-Zeitschrift, Designmetropole Hamburg – Branchenporträts (Chamber of Commerce Hamburg), Die Welt, ECONY, ELLE PLUS, ENLACE, FLARE, Gestalten mit Solarzellen – Photovoltaik in der Gebäudehülle, Hamburger Abendblatt, Highlight, Holzleimbau, Immobilien Zeitung, impulse, Informationsdienst Holz, Intelligente Architektur, Kieler Nachrichten, Leonardo, LICHT, Licht & Architektur, Lübecker Nachrichten, max, max – City Guide Hamburg, md moebel interior design, Mensch & Büro, Merian, Pinneberger Nachrichten, Pinneberger Tagesblatt, Pinneberger Zeitung, SCHÖNER WOHNEN, Stern, Studien aus dem Architekturlabor, Sunny magazine, TAGESLICHT, Umrisse – Zeitschrift für Baukultur, VectorWorks

Lighthouse, Hamburg

H.O.M.E. 9/2002, pp. 50–51, 88–89

Hamburgische Architektenkammer (ed.): Architektur in Hamburg. Yearbook 2002, Hamburg 2002, pp. 118–129

Allgemeine Bauzeitung ABZ, architektur & wirtschaft, Baumeister, Bergedorfer Zeitung, Bild, DER SPIEGEL, Die Welt, Die Welt – Sonderveröffentlichung EXPO REAL, Die Welt am Sonntag, dpa, Elmshorner Nachrichten, Freie Presse, General-Anzeiger, Hamburger Abendblatt, Hamburger Morgenpost, Harburger Anzeigen und Nachrichten, Immobilien Zeitung, Kieler Nachrichten, Kölnische Rundschau, Landeszeitung für die Lüneburger Heide, MATADOR, Mindener Tageblatt, Mitteldeutsche Zeitung, Osnabrücker Zeitung, Pforzheimer Zeitung, Pinneberger Tageblatt, Ruhr Nachrichten, Saale-Zeitung, Segeberger Zeitung, Süddeutsche Zeitung, TOP Magazin, Welt am Sonntag – Sonderveröffentlichung EXPO REAL, Westfalen-Blatt, Westfälische Rundschau

Transrapid Station, Schwerin

Hans-Martin Nelte (ed.): New Buildings and Projects. Architecture in Germany, Wiesbaden 2001, pp. 48–51

Petra Diemer (ed.): Bauten und Projekte. Architekten in Hamburg, Schleswig-Holstein, Niedernhausen 1999, pp. 28–33

Bild Hamburg, DBZ Deutsche BauZeitschrift, ENLACE

Train Station, Frankfurt Airport

Renault Nissan Deutschland AG (ed.): Renault traffic design award 2003, Brühl 2004, p. 9

Der Architekt 2/2004, p. 9

Alessia Ferrarini: STAZIONI dalla gare de l´est alla penn station, Martellago 2004, pp. 128–141

Nemetschek North America: IMAGES of CAD 2004, pp. 72–73

Freie Akademie der Künste Hamburg (ed.): 25 Jahre Planen und Bauen in der Demokratie 1976–2000, Hamburg 2003, p. 95

Walter Meyer-Bohe (ed.): Atlas Gebäudegrundrisse, Vol. 3: Bauten für Dienstleistungen, Gewerbe und Verkehr, Stuttgart 2003, pp. 264–265

Architectural Record 1/2002, pp. 120–123

Manuel Cuadra, Ingeborg Flagge: World Airports, Dresden 2002

WORLD ARCHITECTURE 2/2001

Michael Wutzke: Skyline Guide Deutschland 2001/2002, Darmstadt 2001, p. 104

Hans-Martin Nelte (ed.): New Buildings and Projects. Architecture in Germany, Wiesbaden 2001, pp. 40–43

Martha Thorne: Modern Trains and Splendid Stations. Architecture and Design for the Twenty First Century, London 2001, pp. 86–89

Metropolis 12/2001

Hildegard Kösters, Volker Roscher (ed.): Architekten und Architektinnen BDA in Hamburg. Handbuch 2000/2001, Hamburg 2000, pp. 50–51

Hamburgische Architektenkammer (ed.): Architektur in Hamburg. Yearbook 2000, Hamburg 2000, pp. 94–97

Architektur & Wohnen 1/1999, p. 175

DBZ – Deutsche Bauzeitschrift 4/1999, pp. 79–82

The Architectural Review 5/1999, pp. 78–81

Baumeister 8/1999, p. 6

AIT 7–8/1999, p. 8

DBZ – Deutsche Bauzeitschrift 8/1999, p. 16

db deutsche bauzeitung 9/1999, p. 14

Manuel Cuadra, Jo Franzke (ed.): Architektur in Frankfurt, Hamburg 1999, pp. 140–142

Petra Diemer (ed.): Bauten und Projekte. Architekten in Hamburg, Schleswig-Holstein, Niedernhausen 1999, pp. 28–33

Stahlbau 68, 12/1999, pp. 1029–1036

Hamburgische Architektenkammer (ed.): Architektur in Hamburg. Yearbook 1998, Hamburg 1998, pp. 164–175

AIT 10/1997, p. 32

Bauwelt 39/1997

Design Report 5/1997, p. 96

Bauwelt 37/1996, pp. 2112–2113

BDA, Deutsche Bahn AG, DAZ (ed.): Renaissance der Bahnhöfe. Die Stadt im 21. Jahrhundert, Braunschweig/Wiesbaden 1996, pp. 94–95

db deutsche bauzeitung 9/1996, pp. 16–20

The Times, November 26, 1996, p. 34

100 Jahre Dr.-Ing. Dr. E.h. Max Mengeringhausen – Pionier des elementierten Bauens, AD Architectural Digest, art, BAHNZEIT, Bauen mit Stahl – Dokumentation 873, Baumeister, Bautechnik 77, Berliner Morgenpost, Berliner Zeitung, Bild, Business Traveller, DAB – Deutsches Architektenblatt, Das Architekturjournal, DB mobil, DB PROJEKT, dbz-online, DER SPIEGEL, Der Tagesspiegel, Die Welt, Die Woche, dpa, ENLACE, Focus, Frankfurter Allgemeine Sonntagszeitung, Frankfurter Allgemeine Zeitung, Frankfurter Neue Presse, Frankfurter Rundschau, Gateway, Hamburger Abendblatt, Hamburger Morgenpost, Hannoversche Allgemeine, HOME (Japan), Immobilien Zeitung, Kieler Nachrichten, Kölner Stadt Anzeiger, Leonardo, Lübecker Nachrichten, max, Nassauische Neue Presse, Neue Presse – Hannover, Neue Revue, Offenbach Post, petra, Rhein Main Presse, STERN, Süddeutsche Zeitung, Szene Hamburg, taz hamburg, TECHNIK & WIRTSCHAFT, The Architectural Review, VDI Nachrichten, wallpaper, Welt, Welt am Sonntag, Wereldstations – Treinreizen in de 21e eeuw, Wirtschaftswoche

Palm Paper-Mill, Aalen

Aalener Nachrichten, Schwäbische Post

Double X Office High-rise, Hamburg

Johann Eisele, Ellen Kloft: Hochhaus-Atlas, Munich 2004, p. 277

Peter Lorenz: Entwerfen. 25 Architekten – 25 Standpunkte, Munich 2004, pp. 36–41

Friedrich Grimm: Energieeffizientes Bauen mit Glas, Munich 2004, pp. 182–187

Freie Akademie der Künste Hamburg (ed.): 25 Jahre Planen und Bauen in der Demokratie 1976–2000, Hamburg 2003, p. 75

Cesare Blasi, Gabriella Padovano: La sfida della sostenibilità, Naples 2003, pp. 50–52

Jürgen Knirsch: Büroräume, Bürohäuser, Leinfelden-Echterdingen 2002, pp. 142–147

The Plan - Architecture & Technologies in Detail 0/2002, p. 37

Rainer Hascher, Simone Jeska, Birgit Klauck (ed.): Office Buildings. A Design Manual, Basel 2002, pp. 250–251

Werner Durth, EON Ruhrgas AG (ed.): Architektur in Deutschland '01. Deutscher Architekturpreis 2001, Zurich 2002, pp. 112–115

DBZ – Deutsche BauZeitschrift 3/2001, pp. 86–89

Michael Wutzke: Skyline Guide Deutschland 2001/2002, Darmstadt 2001, p. 146

Peter Zec: best selection. office design 2001, Essen 2001, pp. 136–137

bauzeitung 9/2001, pp. 15–25

Henry Beierlorzer, Ernst Hubeli, Hans-Heinrich Jagau: Haus der Architektur: HDAX 01, Graz 2001

Hans-Martin Nelte (ed.): New Buildings and Projects. Architecture in Germany, Wiesbaden 2001, pp. 30–35

Karana Marketing Village: Transparenz und Sinnlichkeit, Dedenhausen 2001 Werner Durth, EON Ruhrgas AG (ed.): Architektur in Deutschland '03. Deutscher Architekturpreis 2001, Zurich 2002, pp. 34–35

Süddeutsche Zeitung, April 19, 2000, p. 18

Das Architekten-Magazin 5/2000, pp. 24–26

industrieBau 2/2000, pp. 54–56

Hildegard Kösters, Volker Roscher (ed.): Architekten und Architektinnen BDA in Hamburg. Handbuch 2000/2001, Hamburg 2000, pp. 50–51

Hamburgische Architektenkammer (ed.): Architektur in Hamburg. Yearbook 2000, Hamburg 2000, pp. 16–25

DETAIL 5/2000, p. 884

DAB – Deutsches Architektenblatt 5/1999, p. 631

Peter Neitzke, Carl Steckeweh, Reinhart Wustlich (ed.): CENTRUM – Jahrbuch Architektur und Stadt 1998–1999, Wiesbaden 1999, pp. 194–197

Mathias Hein-Auty, Architekten und Ingenieurverein Hamburg (ed.): Hamburg und seine Bauten 1985–2000, Hamburg 1999, p. 145

DBZ – Deutsche BauZeitschrift 12/1999, p. 12

Petra Diemer (ed.): Bauten und Projekte. Architekten in Hamburg, Schleswig-Holstein, Niedernhausen 1999, pp. 28–33

A&B – Architektura & Biznes 10/1998, pp. 24–27

Hamburgische Architektenkammer (ed.): Architektur in Hamburg. Yearbook 1998, Hamburg 1998, pp. 164–175

AIT Spezial – Intelligente Architektur 6/1997, pp. 10, 44–47

glasforum 6/1997, pp. 23–28

AIT, AON – Skyline inklusive, Architektur & Wirtschaft, Architektur & Wohnen, Architekturpreis für vorbildliche Gewerbebauten 2000, art, Atrium – Hamburg Lebensart und Design, BAUIDEE, Baumeister Exkursion – Neue Architektur in Hamburg, BDB Nachrichten, Berliner Zeitung, Bild Hamburg, Büro '99 – Sondernummer der DBZ Deutsche BauZeitschrift, Das Architektur Journal, Die Welt, Die WestHyp Stiftung – Architekturpreis für vorbildliche Gewerbebauten, DIE ZEIT, ENLACE, Forum Intelligente Architektur, Frankfurter Allgemeine Zeitung, GLAS – Architektur und Technik, Hamburger Abendblatt, Hamburger Morgenpost, Hannoversche Allgemeine, HÄUSER, immobilien business, Immobilien Zeitung, impulse, Intelligente Architektur, Leonardo, max, Merian, Neue Zürcher Zeitung, petra, SPIEGEL Extra, STERN, Stuttgarter Zeitung, Szene Hamburg, taz hamburg, Umrisse – Zeitschrift für Baukultur, Welt am Sonntag

EXHIBITIONS, AWARDS

EXHIBITIONS

1994   Hamburger Architektursommer »Next Modern«

1999   »plan99« Forum aktueller Architektur in Cologne

2000   Hamburger Architektursommer
        »BRT by Kumrow«, photographs by Klaus Kumrow
        »Urban Escape« video installations by Christina
        Lissmann

2001   »Modern Trains and Splendid Stations«,
        The Art Institute of Chicago

2002   »Worldstations in Utrecht«,
        Centraal Museum Utrecht

2002–   »Neue Deutsche Architektur«,
2007   Berlin, Milan, Hamburg, Copenhagen, Turin,
        Madrid, La Coruña, Sevilla, Valladolid, Porto, …

2003   Hamburger Architektursommer,
        »Atelier HafenCity«
        Mies van der Rohe Award,
        Fundació Mies van der Rohe Barcelona

2003–   »arcHH - Architektur Made in Hamburg«
2004   Hamburg, Vejle, Copenhagen, Tallin, Berlin

AWARDS

Building of the year 1991, Car & Driver Showroom, Hamburg
Building of the year 1996, Pacific House, Hamburg
Building of the year 1997, Loft Building at Elbberg, Hamburg
Building of the year 2002, Bei den Mühren Office Building, Hamburg
Building of the year 2003, Elbberg Campus Altona, Hamburg
AIV Architekten- und Ingenieurverein Hamburg e.V.

BDA Hamburg Architekturpreis 1999
Loft Building at Elbberg, Hamburg, 1st prize
Alsterarkaden, Hamburg, 2nd prize

BDA-Preis 1999 Architektur in Schleswig-Holstein
Tobias Grau Building, Rellingen, 1st prize
Savings Bank, Kiel, 2nd prize
Training Center DV AG, Stapelfeld, 2nd prize
Villa, Ahrensburg, 3rd prize

Deutscher Kritikerpreis 1999

Architekturpreis 2000 of the WestHyp-Stiftung for exemplary industrial
buildings, Double X Office High-rise, Hamburg,
award

FIABCI Prix d'Excellence 2001, Double X Office High-rise, Hamburg

Deutscher Stahlbaupreis 2002, Berliner Bogen Office Building, Hamburg

NEPIX Building Award 2002, Berliner Bogen Office Building, Hamburg

MIPIM Award 2003, Berliner Bogen Office Building, Hamburg

Office of the Year 2003, Deichtor Office Building, Hamburg
femb fédération européenne du mobilier de bureau

Deutscher Architekturpreis 2003, award, Swiss Re Office Building,
Unterföhring

RENAULT traffic design award 2003, Long Distance Train Station,
Frankfurt/Main

BDA Hamburg Architekturpreis 2005, Deichtor Office Building, 1st prize

PHOTO CREDITS

W. Beutler/Denkmalschutzamt Hamburg, Bildarchiv   414 center

Felix Borkenau, Hamburg   510 1/1

Markus Braun, Würzburg   11, 14, 66, 114, 178, 242, 314, 501

Marcus Bredt, Berlin   422/423, 425, 427, 508 5/1

BMW, Mini Prospekt   224 bottom

Martin Claßen, Cologne   28, 504 1/3, 506 4/2, 512 top

© Consortium Transrapid Nederland   160

Floyd Dean/getty images   96 center

H.G. Esch, Hennef–Stadt Blankenberg   495 top right

© European Space Imaging   7

Klaus Frahm, Hamburg   18/19, 23–27, 35 bottom, 36/37, 40–43, 45,
191top, 195, 210/211, 212 bottom, 216, 217, 224 top, 286/287, 289–291,
322 top, 324 top, 326, 327, 343, 354, 439, 440, 442–444, 446–449,
451–454, 455 bottom, 456–459, 462/463, 494 bottom, 495 top left,
bottom, 502 1/2, 504 1/1, 3/1, 3/2, 4/1, 5/4, 6/4, 7/5, 506 1/1, 1/3, 3/4,
5/2, 6/1, 508 3/5, 4/2, 6/5, 510 3/2, 3/5, 6/4, 512 bottom, 513 top

Hinrich Franck, Hamburg   467

Matthias Friedel, Hamburg   20 left, 34, 48 top, 104 top, 120, 184, 188–
190, 198 top, 212 top, 254, 320, 330, 348/349, 350 top, 362, 363 top
right, 388 top, 436/437, 438 top, 450 left, 466 top, 474 top

Andreas Garrelt, Hamburg   213 bottom

Gärtner + Christ, Hamburg   238, 239

Christoph Gebler, Hamburg   78, 155, 166, 169, 182/183, 186, 187,
252/253, 255–257, 370 top left, 386/387, 389 top, 502 4/1, 5/3, 504
7/3, 506 2/2, 508 1/1, 2/1, 4/1, 5/3, 7/5

Wolfram Gothe, Hamburg   102/103, 105, 109, 502 5/2, 506 5/5

Bernadette Grimmenstein, Hamburg   412/413, 414 bottom, 415–421,
506 3/1

Carlo Grossi/Virtual Architecture, Borstel-Hohenraden   82–86, 91–93,
218–219, 221, 504 3/5, 506 4/4, 508 4/3, 5/5, 510 2/1, 2/4, 7/2

Jörg Hempel, Aachen   21, 29, 46/47, 49, 51, 58–65, 70/71, 73, 79
bottom, 87, 99, 118/119, 121-128, 130-132, 134, 135, 170–172, 174 bottom, 175–177, 196/197, 198 bottom, 199–205, 207–209, 213 top,
236/237, 241, 246/247, 249, 250, 251 bottom, 258/259, 261, 263, 264,
292–294, 300, 301, 318/319, 321, 322 bottom, 324 bottom, 325,
328/329, 331–335, 338–342, 344–347, 350 bottom, 351–353, 355–
361, 363 top left, bottom, 364, 365, 368/369, 370 top right, bottom, 371,
372, 374, 375 right, 376–384, 389 bottom, 395–401, 406/407, 408 center, bottom, 409–411, 431, 432, 434, 435, 438 bottom, 450 right, 460
top, 469–473, 474 bottom, 475–479, 482, 483, 485–493, 494 top, 496,
497 bottom, 498/499, 502 1/1, 1/4, 2/5, 3/2, 3/3, 3/4, 4/3, 5/5, 6/2,
6/3, 6/4, 504 1/4, 1/5, 2/4, 3/3, 3/4, 4/4, 5/1, 5/3, 7/1, 506 1/2, 1/4,
1/5, 2/1, 3/5, 6/2, 6/4, 6/5, 7/3, 7/5, 508 1/2, 1/3, 1/4, 1/5, 2/3, 2/4,
5/2, 6/3, 7/2, 7/3, 7/4, 510 1/3, 1/4, 2/2, 2/3, 2/5, 3/3, 4/2, 5/3, 6/1,
6/2, 6/3, 6/5, 7/1, 7/5, 513 bottom

Heike Hillebrand/BRT   96 top, 100/101

HHLA, Hamburg   480

Benjamin Holsten/BRT   52–55, 57, 298/299, 302/303, 504 7/4,
506 7/4, 510 1/5

Michael Horn/BRT   365 bottom right

Kalavaal Architects, Dubai   504 2/1, 4/2

Holger Knauff, Düsseldorf   502 4/4

Julia Knop, Hamburg   104 bottom

Tim Corvin Kraus/Breimann & Bruun Landscape Architects   428/429,
433

Joachim Landwehr/BRT   94/95, 297

Gerhard Linnekogel, Hamburg   514 top, center

Bill Losh/getty images   96 bottom

Louise McGilviray, Crossford, Fife, Schottland   466 center

Alex Maclean/photonica   232

Kay Miksch/BRT   497 top

Heiner Müller-Elsner/Agentur Focus   373

Ulrike Myrzik & Manfred Jarisch, Munich   388 bottom, 393, 394,
402–405, 408 top

Janne Peters, Hamburg   191 bottom, 192–194

Erik Recke/Datenland, Hamburg   56, 136/137, 139–141,
144–146, 150–153, 156–159, 161, 163–165, 174 top, center, 215,
222/223, 229, 233–235, 251 top, 260 bottom, 266, 270–281, 285,
464/465, 502 2/4, 6/1, 504 2/2, 2/5, 4/3, 508 3/2, 6/4, 510 4/4, 5/1

Mies van der Rohe/Bauwelt   90

August Sander/Rheinisches Bildarchiv   75

Malcolm Sanders/getty images   48 bottom

Senatsverwaltung für Stadtentwicklung, Berlin   88/89, 424

Ondrej Sklabinski, Hamburg   80/81, 304–309, 337, 375 left, 391, 466
bottom, 484, 502 1/3, 1/5, 2/1, 504 4/5, 5/5, 6/2, 6/3, 7/2, 506 3/2,
3/3, 4/3, 5/4, 6/3, 7/1, 508 2/5, 3/3, 4/4, 4/5, 6/2, 510 4/3, 4/5, 5/4

Dirk Stewen, Hamburg   4, 514 bottom

Hadi Teherani/BRT   385, 455 top, 460 bottom, 461

Michael Wurzbach, Hamburg/© Tobias Grau, Rellingen   30–33,
35 top, 44, 510 4/1

J. Christoph Bürkle: El Lissitzky. Der Traum vom Wolkenkratzer,
Zurich 1991, 69, 72 center

Arnulf Lüchinger: 2-Komponenten-Bauweise, Den Haag 2000, 19, 230

Patricia Phillips, James Wines: SITE. Highrise of Homes, New York
1982, 42, 231

For some illustrations we were unable to determine the copyrights.
Any copyright holders are requested to contact the office BRT.

522

523

Design concept, layout and setting: Christina Hackenschuh, Stuttgart
Assistants: Markus Braun, Ute Kleim, Natascha Saupe
www.hackenschuh.com

Plans and drawings: Bothe Richter Teherani Architects

Projekt coordination: Jessica Klatten, Anke Stüper (Bothe Richter Teherani
Architects)

English translation: Adam Blauhut, Susan Richter, Robin Benson, Berlin;
Elizabeth Schwaiger, Toronto

Book fabric: WATERBORN by Kvadrat A/S Ebeltoft, Danmark
Architects and Publisher want to thank Kvadrat for the friendly cooperation.

A CIP catalogue record for this book is available from the Library of
Congress, Washington D.C., USA

Bibliographic information published by Die Deutsche Bibliothek
Die Deutsche Bibliothek lists this publication in the Deutsche National-
bibliografie; Detailed bibliographic data is available in the Internet at
http://dnb.ddb.de.

This publication is also available in a German language edition
(ISBN 3-7643-6629-X).

© 2005 Birkhäuser – Publishers for Architecture, P.O.Box 133,
CH-4010 Basel, Switzerland. Part of Springer Science+Business Media
Printed on acid-free paper, Zanders ikono new silk 150 g/m^2,
produced from chlorine-free pulp. TCF ∞

Printing and Binding: Offsetdruckerei Grammlich, Pliezhausen
www.grammlich.de

ISBN-10: 3-7643-2172-5
ISBN-13: 978-3-7643-2172-7

9 8 7 6 5 4 3 2 1

www.birkhauser.ch

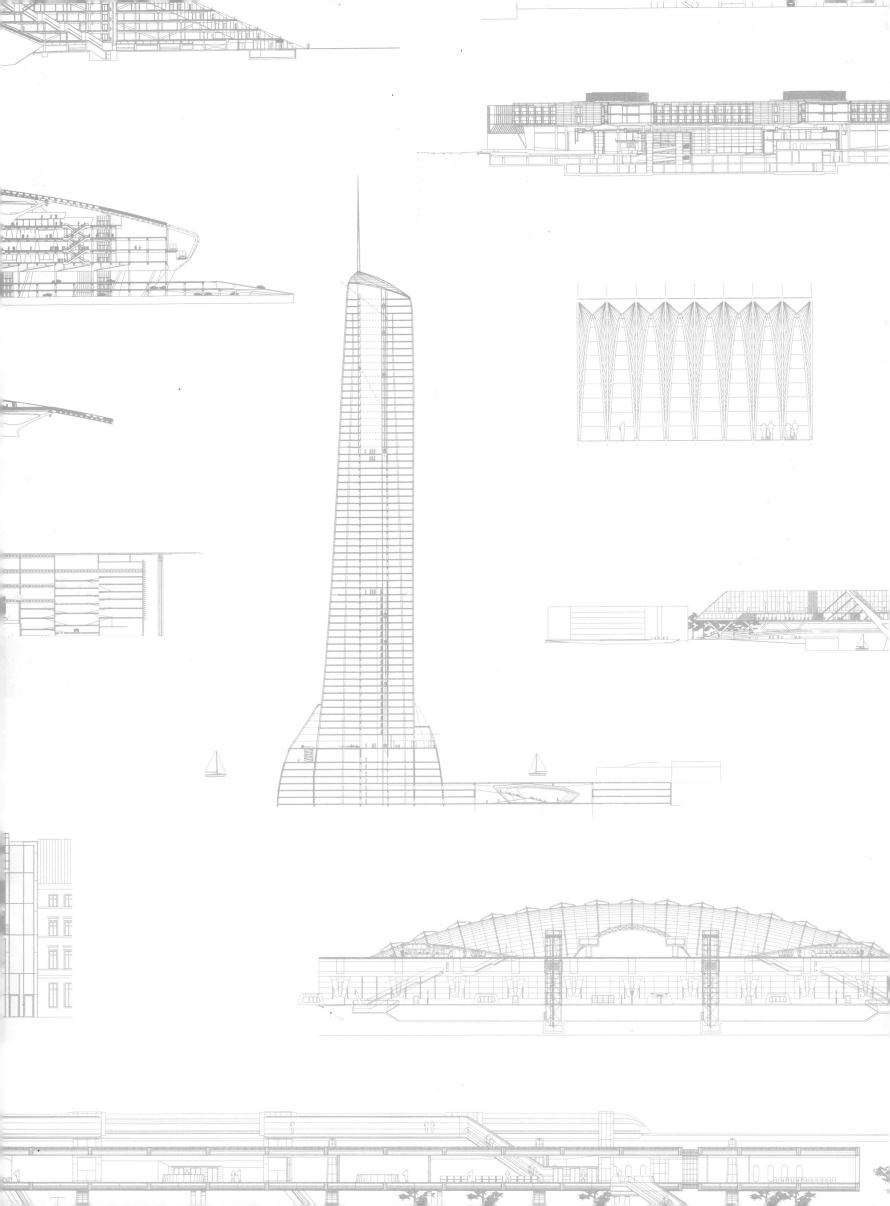